Trademark Protection and Territoriality Challenges in a Global Economy

ELGAR INTELLECTUAL PROPERTY AND GLOBAL DEVELOPMENT

Series Editor: Peter K. Yu, *Kern Family Chair in Intellectual Property Law and Director, Intellectual Property Law Center, Drake University, USA*

Rapid global economic integration and the increasing importance of technology and information goods have created the need for a broader, deeper and more critical understanding of intellectual property laws and policies. This uniquely-designed book series provides an interdisciplinary forum for advancing the debate on the global intellectual property system and related issues that intersect with transnational politics, international governance, and global economic, social, cultural and technological development. The series features the works of established experts and emerging voices in the academy as well as those practising on the frontlines. The series' high-quality, informed and accessible volumes include a wide range of materials such as historical narratives, theoretical explanations, substantive discussions, critical evaluations, empirical analyses, comparative studies, and formulations of practical solutions and best practices. The series will appeal to academics, policy makers, judges, practitioners, transnational lawyers and civil society groups as well as students of law, politics, culture, political economy, international relations and development studies.

Titles in the series include:

Copyright and the Public Interest in China
Guan Hong Tang

Genetic Resources and Traditional Knowledge
Case Studies and Conflicting Interests
Edited by Tania Bubela and E. Richard Gold

The Global Governance of HIV/AIDS
Intellectual Property and Access to Essential Medicines
Edited by Obijiofor Aginam, John Harrington and Peter K. Yu

Access to Information and Knowledge
21st Century Challenges in Intellectual Property and Knowledge Governance
Edited by Dana Beldiman

Trademark Protection and Territoriality Challenges in a Global Economy
Edited by Irene Calboli and Edward Lee

Trademark Protection and Territoriality Challenges in a Global Economy

Edited by

Irene Calboli

Professor of Law, Marquette University Law School, USA and Visiting Professor, Faculty of Law, National University of Singapore

Edward Lee

Professor of Law and Director of the Program in Intellectual Property Law, IIT Chicago-Kent College of Law, USA

ELGAR INTELLECTUAL PROPERTY AND GLOBAL DEVELOPMENT

Edward Elgar

Cheltenham, UK • Northampton, MA, USA

Published by
Edward Elgar Publishing Limited
The Lypiatts
15 Lansdown Road
Cheltenham
Glos GL50 2JA
UK

Edward Elgar Publishing, Inc.
William Pratt House
9 Dewey Court
Northampton
Massachusetts 01060
USA

A catalogue record for this book
is available from the British Library

Library of Congress Control Number: 2013947145

This book is available electronically in the ElgarOnline.com Law Subject Collection, E-ISBN 978 1 78195 391 4

ISBN 978 1 78195 390 7

Typeset by Columns Design XML Ltd, Reading
Printed and bound in Great Britain by T.J. International Ltd, Padstow

Contents

Editors and contributors

Graeme W. Austin is Chair in Private Law at Victoria University of Wellington (New Zealand) and Professor of Law at Melbourne University (Australia). With first degrees from Victoria University, Professor Austin graduated J.S.D. and LL.M. from Columbia University, where he held the Burton Fellowship in Intellectual Property Law. Before returning to Australasia in 2010, he was the J. Byron McCormick Professor of Law at the University of Arizona. He is an elected member of the American Law Institute. Professor Austin's most recent book (co-authored with Prof. Larry Helfer (Duke)) is *Human Rights and Intellectual Property Law: Mapping the Global Interface* (Cambridge University Press).

Irene Calboli is a Professor of Law at Marquette University Law School, a Visiting Professor at the Faculty of Law of the National University of Singapore, and a Transatlantic Technology Law Forum Fellow at Stanford Law School. She started her academic career at the Faculty of Law of the University of Bologna and held visiting positions at DePaul University College of Law, King's College London, the University of California Berkeley, the University Complutense, and the Max-Planck-Institute for Intellectual Property Law. Dr Calboli's research interests focus on trademark law and policy, overlapping intellectual property rights, and the protection of geographical indications of origin. She is an active member of the Academic Committee of the International Trademark Association (INTA), the International Association for the Advancement of Teaching and Research in Intellectual Property (ATRIP), the Association Littéraire et Artistique Internationale USA (ALAI-USA), and the Executive Committee of the Section on Law and Arts of the Association of American Law Schools.

Margaret Chon is the Donald & Lynda Horowitz Professor for the Pursuit of Justice, and formerly Associate Dean for Research at Seattle University School of Law. She is an active scholar and teacher of intellectual property and critical theory. Her current research explores the global governance dimensions of intellectual property, especially their distributional consequences and social justice implications. Professor Chon is the author of over 40 articles, book chapters and review essays on both intellectual property and on race. She has been affiliated with numerous institutions, including most recently New York University School of Law, where she was a 2011–12 Senior Global Emile Noël Research Fellow at the Jean Monnet Center for International and Regional Economic Law & Justice. In addition, she has been a Visiting Law Professor at George Washington University Law School, University of Hawaii School of Law, University of Michigan Law School, Notre Dame Law School, University of Washington School of Law and elsewhere. Throughout her professional career, she has been and continues to be active in various community and professional organizations, both nationally and internationally. She received her A.B. from Cornell University and her J.D. from University of Michigan.

Daniel C.K. Chow is the Associate Dean for International and Graduate Programs and the Joseph S. Platt-Porter, Wright, Morris & Arthur Professor of Law at the Ohio State University Michael E. Moritz College of Law. He writes and teaches in the areas of international business and trade, international intellectual property, and the law of China. He has written numerous books and articles in all of these areas. He is a frequent speaker at academic conferences and has testified before Congress several times and also before the International Trade Commission on intellectual property issues. He received his B.A. and J.D. from Yale University.

Graeme B. Dinwoodie is the Professor of Intellectual Property and Information Technology Law at the University of Oxford, Director of the Oxford Intellectual Property Research Centre, and a Professorial Fellow of St. Peter's College. Prior to his appointment to the IP Chair at Oxford in 2009, Professor Dinwoodie was a Professor of Law at the Chicago-Kent College of Law. He has also previously taught at the University of Cincinnati College of Law and the University of Pennsylvania School of Law, and from 2005–2009 held a Chair in Intellectual Property Law at Queen Mary College, University of London. He is the author of several casebooks and numerous articles on various aspects of intellectual property law. Professor Dinwoodie holds an LL.B. degree from the University of Glasgow, an LL.M. from Harvard Law School (where he was a Kennedy Scholar), and a J.S.D. from Columbia Law School (where he was a Burton Fellow). He was elected to membership in the American Law Institute in 2003, and is currently the President of the International Association for the Advancement of Teaching and Research in Intellectual Property (ATRIP). In 2008, the International Trademark Association awarded Professor Dinwoodie the Pattishall Medal for Teaching Excellence in Trademark Law.

Christine Haight Farley is a Professor of Law at American University Washington College of Law, where she teaches Intellectual Property Law, Trademark Law, International and Comparative Trademark Law, International Intellectual Property Law and Art Law. Professor Farley served as Associate Dean for Faculty and Academic Affairs from 2007 to 2011 and as Co-Director of the Program on Information Justice and Intellectual Property from 2005 to 2009. Professor Farley has taught at the University of Puerto Rico, the University of Paris Ouest, and at Monash University in Prato, Italy. In addition, she has lectured on intellectual property law in Australia, Canada, Columbia, Cuba, France, Italy, Jordan, Korea, Mongolia, Namibia, Panama, Peru, Portugal, Russia, Scotland, Switzerland and Turkey. Before teaching, Professor Farley was an associate specializing in intellectual property litigation with Rabinowitz, Boudin, Standard, Krinsky & Lieberman in New York. She received a B.A. from Binghamton University, a J.D. from University at Buffalo Law School, and an LL.M. and J.S.D. from Columbia Law School.

Leah Chan Grinvald is an Associate Professor of Law at Suffolk University Law School. She received her B.A. in East Asian Studies, *summa cum laude*, from the George Washington University. She later obtained a J.D. from the New York University School of Law, where she served as the Articles and Notes Editor for the *Journal of International Law & Politics*. She served as a law clerk for the Honorable Frank Sullivan, Jr. in the Indiana State Supreme Court. Before joining the faculty at Suffolk Law School, Professor Grinvald was an Assistant Professor at Saint Louis University School of Law. Professor Grinvald teaches courses in Contracts, Secured Transactions, Intellectual Property Survey, Trademark, and International Intellectual Property. Her research focuses on domestic and international enforcement of intellectual property laws. Prior to entering academia, Professor Grinvald served as global corporate counsel at Taylor Made Golf Company, Inc. She advised on a variety of legal issues including trademark, copyright, contract and employment law arising within Taylor Made and its affiliated entities located outside of the United States. Before Taylor Made, Professor Grinvald was a corporate associate with Latham & Watkins LLP and Clifford Chance US LLP.

Mary LaFrance is the IGT Professor of Intellectual Property Law at the William S. Boyd School of Law, University of Nevada, Las Vegas, where she has taught since 1999. She previously taught at Florida State University, in both the College of Law and the School of Motion Pictures, Television, and Recording Arts. Professor LaFrance is a *summa cum laude* graduate of Bryn Mawr College. She received her J.D. with

High Honors from the Duke University School of Law, where she served as Executive Editor of the *Duke Law Journal*. She simultaneously earned her M.A. in Philosophy from the Duke University School of Graduate Studies. Prior to teaching, she clerked for Judge Harry T. Edwards of the United States Court of Appeals for the D.C. Circuit, and practiced law for three years with the Washington, D.C. office of Fried, Frank, Harris, Shriver & Jacobson. Professor LaFrance has authored or co-authored five books, including *Intellectual Property Cases and Materials*, *Understanding Trademark Law*, *Understanding Intellectual Property Law*, *Global Issues in Copyright Law*, and *Copyright Law in a Nutshell*. Her articles have been published in numerous law reviews, including the *Southern California Law Review*, the *Vanderbilt Law Review*, and the *Emory Law Journal*.

Marshall A. Leaffer is Distinguished Scholar in Intellectual Property Law and University Fellow, Indiana University Maurer School of Law. He received his J.D. at the University of Texas and his LL.M. in Trade Regulation at New York University Law School. Leaffer teaches Copyright Law, Trademark Law, Intellectual Property Survey, and International Intellectual Property. He is the author of three books and numerous articles, including the best-selling treatise *Understanding Copyright Law*, now in its fifth edition. Leaffer is also the author of *Copyright Law: Cases and Materials*, 9th edition and *International Treaties on Intellectual Property*, 2nd edition. His current research focuses on the interplay of intellectual property law in a global marketplace. Before becoming a full-time teacher, he practiced trademark law with American Home Products Corp. and the firm of Haseltine Lake & Waters in New York. He also has served as attorney-advisor to the U.S. Patent and Trademark Office and the U.S. Copyright Office. He currently serves on the international executive committee of the Association Littéraire et Artistique Internationale, a non-governmental institution based in Paris that promotes the rights of authors worldwide.

Edward Lee is a Professor of Law and the Director of the Program in Intellectual Property Law at IIT Chicago-Kent College of Law. Professor Lee's research focuses on the ways in which the Internet, technological development, and globalization challenge existing legal paradigms. He also writes extensively about the intersection between free speech and intellectual property law, including the Framers' understanding of the Free Press Clause as a limit on using the Copyright Clause to restrict technologies. In addition to numerous articles, he co-authored a leading casebook with Daniel Chow titled *International Intellectual Property: Problems, Cases, and Materials* (West Group). Professor Lee is a *cum* *laude* graduate of Harvard Law School, where he was an editor and co-chair of the books and commentaries office of the *Harvard Law Review*. In 1992, he graduated Phi Beta Kappa and *summa cum laude* from Williams College with a bachelor's degree in philosophy (highest honors) and classics.

Jacqueline Lipton is the Baker Botts Professor of Law and Co-Director of the Institute for Intellectual Property and Information Law at the University of Houston Law Center. Prior to her academic work, she practiced as an attorney in the banking and finance area in several Australian commercial law firms as well as a brief stint as a member of the in-house counsel team at a major Australian bank. Her scholarship focuses on law and digital technology, as well as law and the creative arts, each with an international/comparative slant. She is the co-author of multiple editions of a leading cyberspace casebook *Cyberspace Law: Cases and Materials* (with Professor Raymond S.R. Ku) as well as sole author of *Internet Domain Names, Trademarks and Free Speech* (Edward Elgar, 2010) and *Security Over Intangible Property* (LBC Thompson, 2000). She has published in leading law reviews in the United States, Europe and Australia, including the *Northwestern University Law Review*, *Boston College Law Review*, *Washington University Law Review*, *Hastings Law Journal*, *UC Davis Law Review*, *Washington and Lee Law Review*, *Iowa Law Review*, *Harvard Journal of Law and Technology*, and *Berkeley Technology Law Journal*.

Lee Ann W. Lockridge teaches and writes in the area of intellectual property. Her courses include Introduction to Intellectual Property, International Intellectual Property, Advanced Trademark and Unfair Competition Law, Advanced Copyright Law, and Advertising Law. She is the co-author of a West casebook, *Intellectual Property: Cases and Materials* (4th edition 2012), and has authored law review articles on U.S. and international trademark and copyright law and on the intersection of both copyright and trademark rights with the First Amendment right of free speech. Professor Lockridge was elected to membership in the American Law Institute in 2012. Professor Lockridge graduated *summa cum laude* from Southwestern University, earning a B.A. in chemistry. She is a *magna cum laude* graduate of the Duke University School of Law, where she was a member of the Order of the Coif. She served as a judicial clerk to the Honorable Eugene E. Siler, Jr., of the United States Court of Appeals for the Sixth Circuit. Professor Lockridge is admitted to practice before the United States Patent and Trademark Office as well as in the state of Texas.

Doris Estelle Long is a Professor of Law and Director of the Center for Intellectual Property Law at the John Marshall Law School in Chicago, Illinois. She specializes in international intellectual property law, lecturing throughout the United States and in over 30 countries on five continents. She has taught in nine countries, including serving as a Fulbright Professor at Jiao Tung University in Shanghai, and as a Visiting Professor at Michigan State University School of Law. In 2000, she served as an attorney advisor in the Office of Legislative and International Affairs of the U.S. Patent and Trademark Office. She is the author of numerous books and articles and a monthly columnist on international intellectual property law for the *Chicago Daily Law Bulletin*. Before joining the John Marshall Law School, Professor Long was an attorney with the Washington, D.C. law firms of Arent Fox Kintner Plotkin & Kahn, and Howrey and Simon, specializing in the areas of intellectual property, unfair competition, and antitrust law. She is a graduate of Ithaca College, B.A. *summa cum laude*, Cornell Law School, J.D., *cum laude*, and holds an Executive Education Certificate from the Kennedy School of Government/Harvard University in Science, Technology and Innovation Policy.

Pierre-Emmanuel Moyse is an Intellectual Property Law Professor at the Faculty of Law at McGill University and the Director of the Center for Intellectual Property Policy. He is also responsible for the joint MBA-Law program in partnership with the Desautels Faculty of Management. Professor Moyse wrote his doctoral thesis on the law of distribution in copyright law (University of Montréal, published 2007) under the direction of Professor Ysolde Gendreau. Prior to joining McGill in 2007, he taught at both the University of Montréal and HEC Montréal. He is frequently called as an expert in litigation. He successfully argued the case of *Euro-Excellence v. Kraft Canada* in front of the Supreme Court of Canada in 2007, one of the most important recent intellectual property decisions. Professor Moyse currently directs research and conferences on the theme of "Competition Law and Innovation," an initiative which he launched in 2007. A prolific author, he is the director of publication of the Innovation and Competition series published by Les Éditions Thémis, and also the editorial consultant and one of the authors for the encyclopaedic work on Intellectual Property by JurisClasseur Québec/LexisNexis (2013).

Mary Wong joined the Internet Corporation for Assigned Names & Numbers (ICANN) in July 2013 as a Senior Policy Director. Up to June 2013 she was a Professor of Law and the Faculty Chair for Global

Intellectual Property (IP) Partnerships at the University of New Hampshire School of Law. She was also the founding Director of the law school's flagship applied research center, the Franklin Pierce Center for IP, and has been Special Counsel to a major international law firm in its New York and Brussels offices. As an academic, Mary was already involved in policy development work at ICANN, including on its new gTLD program, serving two terms as an elected member of ICANN's GNSO Council, which approved and manages the policies that apply to the new gTLD program. She was also appointed by ICANN's Nominating Committee to the ccNSO Council, which manages domain name policies in the country code namespace. Her research interests center on the international policy aspects of IP, in particular, the challenges posed by Internet and digital technology.

Peter K. Yu holds the Kern Family Chair in Intellectual Property Law and is the founding director of the Intellectual Property Law Center at Drake University Law School. He has served as Wenlan Scholar Chair Professor at Zhongnan University of Economics and Law in Wuhan, China and a visiting Professor of Law at the University of Haifa, the University of Hong Kong, the University of Strasbourg, and Washington and Lee University. Born and raised in Hong Kong, Professor Yu is a leading expert in international intellectual property and communications law. A prolific scholar and an award-winning teacher, he is the author or editor of five books and more than 100 law review articles and book chapters. He serves as the general editor of *The WIPO Journal* published by the World Intellectual Property Organization (WIPO). Professor Yu has spoken at events organized by WIPO, the International Telecommunication Union, the U.N. Conference on Trade and Development (UNCTAD), the U.N. Educational, Scientific and Cultural Organization (UNESCO), the Chinese, U.S. and EU governments and at leading research institutions from around the world. His lectures and presentations have spanned more than 25 countries on six continents, and his publications have appeared in Chinese and English and have been translated into Arabic, French, Japanese, Persian, Portuguese, Spanish, and Vietnamese.

Daphne Zografos Johnsson is a Legal Officer in the Traditional Knowledge Division at the World Intellectual Property Organization (WIPO). Prior to joining WIPO, she was a Lecturer and Course Director in Intellectual Property Law at the University of Reading, a Visiting Lecturer at Queen Mary, University of London, and a Visiting Research Fellow at King's College, University of London. Daphne holds a Ph.D. from Queen Mary, and an LL.M. in Intellectual Property Law from

University College London. Her research interests lie in the fields of intellectual property, traditional knowledge and genetic resources, as well as the use of intellectual property rights to support socio-economic development.

Foreword

When I teach courses in international intellectual property law, I often start by suggesting that much of the content that we will cover can be understood as an attempt to solve the problem of territoriality – both territoriality as a legal (political) concept, and territoriality as the dominant defining unit of social and commercial ordering. Understanding why *international* intellectual property law (apparently) paradoxically embraces a commitment to this foundational principle is crucial to an appreciation of the proper roles of international and local systems in regulating the creative and commercial environment. As the social power of territoriality comes under pressure from global trade and online activity, it might be tempting to jettison the legal principle entirely rather than to work out how to harness its enduring benefits in a contemporary context. But casting territoriality aside would be too simplistic a solution. Many of the contributions to the volume illustrate nicely the continuing importance of national autonomy, of difference and differentiation, of elevating local values in an increasingly global time. And others demonstrate the practical and political difficulties of substituting universal norms in place of what we now have. But that does not make this a conservative tome. It is very far from that. All the contributions recognise, and grapple with, the reality that intellectual property scholars must reconsider the normative and practical claims of territoriality in light of changing circumstances. But that reconsideration might sometimes lead us to reaffirm historical commitments and redouble efforts to preserve what powerful social and political forces might imperil. On other occasions, it results in acknowledgment that new institutions or new rules must be shaped to make it possible for intellectual property law to serve its core purposes. This is a subtlety that can be found throughout this volume; it is what makes international intellectual property law complex, and work like this vital.

The volume takes trademark law as its particular focus. The questions raised by territoriality pervade intellectual property law, but they are especially acute in the field of trademarks. Trademarks, as vessels for consumer understanding, have an inherently spatial dimension that reflects patterns of social and commercial exchange. Yet, the online world that renders borders porous and physical place less dominant is trademark-intensive. Thus, as the title to this book suggests, the global economy is a huge challenge to territoriality of marks. The magnitude of that challenge, however, may only inspire harder thought and greater readiness for innovation. The editors are to be commended for bringing together such a varied and thoughtful collection of contributions, all of which vigorously accept the challenge that this environment presents. The result is a thoroughly informative and thought-provoking read.

Graeme B. Dinwoodie
June 2013, Oxford

Acknowledgments

We would like to thank the many people who have participated in the realization of this volume with their academic prowess and in many other ways. In particular, we want to express our gratitude to our colleagues, all distinguished scholars, who contributed to the volume. We are honoured by their contributions and generosity in accepting our invitation to participate in this project despite their busy schedules and many competing commitments. Without exception, all contributors met the production deadlines promptly and ensured that the materials addressed in the chapters were both timely and followed the general theme of the volume. We have learned a tremendous amount from all our contributors, and we hope that this volume, now in print, makes them as proud as we are to have had the privilege of coordinating this project.

Special thanks are due to Graeme Austin for writing an introductory chapter and comprehensively setting the stage for the other distinguished contributions to this project. Likewise, we are sincerely indebted to Graeme Dinwoodie for writing the foreword and, more generally, for inspiring us in pursuing the idea of a collective volume on this topic. We also thank our publisher Edward Elgar, and Peter Yu, the editor of the *Intellectual Property and Global Development Series,* for believing in this project and agreeing to publish it. Chloe Mitchell, Tara Gorvine, Alison Hornbeck, and the editing team of Elgar worked hard and with unquestionable professionalism in order to make this volume a reality. Additional thanks go to Heather Stutz and Kevin Wleklinski, who provided excellent assistance during the editing process of the manuscript before the submission of the final draft to the publisher.

We dedicate this volume to our contributors and to all other colleagues in the intellectual property world who conduct research in the area of international intellectual property. Regardless of their "territoriality" – nationalities, languages, and academic affiliations – these scholars have long recognized the need to address transnational, comparative, and ultimately global issues in their works. Almost without exception, these scholars are open minded and very generous in sharing their ideas and insights with other academics, and in general. They have undoubtedly made this field very welcoming and exciting. We thank them for their generosity, and we refer to them as a guiding example for all academics researching and teaching in the area of intellectual property law.

Irene Calboli and Edward Lee
June 2013, Singapore and Chicago

1. Introduction: the inevitability of "territoriality challenges" in trademark law

Graeme W. Austin[*]

How territorially tethered are trademarks? Legally, the answer seems to be: "very." But if we move from legal doctrines and international treaties and consider trademarks in wider psychological, technological, and economic contexts, we might say: "not especially." This tension between formalistic legal principles and the realities of trademarks in the market-place is of enduring fascination. It is also of enormous practical relevance to firms wanting to roll out and protect brands on an international scale.

In large part, trademark law doctrines, international instruments, and procedural frameworks reinforce trademark's territoriality and the continued salience of the nation state to the creation and enforcement of trademark rights. Yet for many purposes, the strength and enforceability of trademark rights depend on what happens in people's minds, and the human mind is not a geographically confined thing. Because the sources that shape the human consciousness do not begin and end at a nation's borders, tensions will inevitably arise between trademark law's territoriality principle and the realities of consumer perceptions and behaviors. And when we focus on the supply side, on the firms that market trademarked products in the modern international economy, we see similar tensions. Multinational firms – many of which own "famous" trademarks, the very kinds of marks that most obviously challenge trademark territoriality – are not exactly renowned for their allegiance to the nation states in which they conduct business. Seemingly idiosyncratic domestic laws are irritants at best and, at worst, egregious sources of

*   Chair in Private Law, Victoria University of Wellington; Professor of Law, Melbourne University. Thanks to Thomas McKenzie, LL.B. (Hons.) student (graduating 2015), Victoria University, for excellent research assistance.

increased compliance and transaction costs, impediments to the inexorable rollout of the juggernaut "international" brand.

From a technological perspective, the territoriality principle can seem quaint or even retrograde. Consider the Apple® iPhone®, marketed under two of the world's most potent brands. Trademarks are meant to "mark" a "trade," in the sense that the mark symbolizes the underlying business source of the product – but what *trade* is being *marked*, and, indeed, *where* is it – when the component parts of the iPhone® come from at least seven different countries?[1] In the modern globalized economy in which many consumer goods are the product of long supply chains, are traditional concepts of the trademark, including the fundamental principle of territoriality, even relevant? Many brands are genuinely "*of* a place." Geographical indicators present a paradigm case. But modern marketing practices also create international brands that seem at once to be from everywhere and nowhere.

The enduring tensions between territoriality as a formal legal principle and the realities of trademarks in the consumer marketplace are part of what makes the issues explored in this volume so important and challenging. Each of the chapters in this volume advances our understanding of the issues that arise in this context, and provokes new thinking about future developments. In this introductory chapter, which Professors Calboli and Lee have kindly asked me to contribute, my principal aim is to explore in more detail why "territorial challenges," to use one of the phrases in this book's title, are inevitable in the global marketplace. To this end, this brief chapter will first provide some of the legal background to the broad theme of territoriality in trademark law. This background need be sketched only briefly here: some extraordinarily useful and enlightening analyses of trademark territoriality have been advanced by others.[2] Secondly, the chapter will explore a few of the reasons why the issues discussed in the chapters that follow are so important to our understanding of trademark rights in the modern global economy.

The notion of "trademark law's territoriality" reflects a cluster of different ideas. Most obviously, trademark rights have limited geographical scope, a point that was confirmed relatively early on by two United

---

[1] The iPhone® 4 component parts come from China, Germany, Japan, Korea, Switzerland, Taiwan, and the United States. *See* Ram Ganeshan, *The iPhone 4 Supply Chain*, OPERATIONS BUZZ (Nov. 28, 2010), http://www.operationsbuzz.com/2010/11/the-iphone-4-supply-chain.

[2] *See, e.g.*, Graeme B. Dinwoodie, *Trademarks and Territoriality: Detaching Trademark Law from the Nation-State*, 41 HOUS. L. REV. 885 (2004).

States Supreme Court cases, *Hanover Star Milling Co. v. Metcalf*[3] and *United Drug Co. v. Theodore Rectanus*.[4] Registration systems also underscore this sense of territoriality; whether understood as a confirmation of pre-existing rights acquired through use or a state grant of "new" rights created by the registration, the property in a trademark registration reflects the exercise of sovereign power. Of course, the exercise of that sovereignty can be delegated – as various initiatives reflect, including the Community Trademark System[5] and the Madrid Protocol[6] – but the link between the nation state and the grant and enforcement of trademark rights remains strong. As will be discussed later, there are exceptions to the idea that territoriality is, as the United States Federal Circuit has put the point, "basic to trademark law."[7] Even so, as a general matter, this "fundamental doctrine"[8] of trademark territoriality suggests that trademark law is a particularized instance of broad ideological, legal, and political commitments to the continued salience of the connection between the applicability of laws and the scope of the territory over which a sovereign exercises power.[9]

Strongly endorsing trademark territoriality, Justice Holmes once said (in a case involving the assertion of rights in the territory of Hong Kong), "A trade-mark started elsewhere would depend for its protection in Hong Kong upon the law prevailing in Hong Kong and would confer not rights except by the consent of that law,"[10] an idea that was also endorsed by the Privy Council in an appeal from Singapore, when it held that "[Goodwill] is local in character and divisible; if the business is carried

---

[3]   Hanover Star Milling Co. v. Metcalf, 240 U.S. 403 (1916).

[4]   United Drug Co. v. Theodore Rectanus, 248 U.S. 90 (1918).

[5]   Council Regulation 207/2009, art. 9(1)(b), 2009 O.J. (L 78/5) (EC). *See generally,* William Robinson, Giles Pratt and Ruth Kelly, *Trademark Law Harmonization in the European Union: Twenty Years Back and Forth*, 23 FORDHAM INTELL. PROP. MEDIA & ENT. L.J. 437 (2013).

[6]   Protocol Relating to the Madrid Agreement Concerning the International Registration of Marks, June 27, 1989, WIPO Pub. No. 204(E).

[7]   Person's Co. v. Christman, 900 F.2d 1565, 1568–69 (Fed Cir. 1990).

[8]   Barcelona.com, Inc. v. Excelentísimo Ayuntamiento de Barcelona, 330 F.3d 617, 628 (4th Cir. 2003); *see also* Vanity Fair Mills, Inc. v. T. Eaton Co., 234 F.2d 633, 639 (2d Cir. 1956) (referring to territoriality as a "fundamental principle").

[9]   *See generally* Kal Raustiala, *The Geography of Justice*, 73 FORDHAM L. REV. 2501 (2005).

[10]   Ingenohl v. Walter E. Olsen & Co., 273 U.S. 541, 544 (1927) (the spelling of "Hong Kong" in the quotation has been modernized).

on in several countries a separate goodwill attached to it in each."[11] These themes also underlie major international treaties in the trademark context. The Paris Convention, for example (compliance with the substantive articles of which is required by the Agreement on Trade-Related Aspects of Intellectual Property (TRIPS)), "recognizes the principle of the territoriality of trademarks."[12] Indeed, the very idea of national treatment seems to be premised on territoriality:[13] owners of intellectual property are concerned about how they will be treated under foreign nations' laws precisely because those laws are assumed to apply in the territories where the rights might be infringed. Procedural law touching on the enforcement of trademark law is also broadly in line with these ideas. In the European Union, the Brussels Regulation on Jurisdiction anticipates that many proceedings relating to the registered intellectual property rights will be litigated exclusively in the place of registration,[14] another endorsement, or, at least, tacit acknowledgement, of connections between disputes over trademarks and the nation states under whose laws the rights are secured.

These formalistic characteristics of trademark law perhaps look a little different in the light of the way some trademarks operate in the global marketplace. Even if, formalistically, trademark rights begin and end at a nation's borders,[15] consumer responses to brands are not necessarily so

---

[11]   Star Industrial Co. Ltd. v. Yap Kwee Kor [1976] F.S.R. 256 (P.C. Sing.).

[12]   4 J. THOMAS MCCARTHY, MCCARTHY ON TRADEMARKS AND UNFAIR COMPETITION § 29:25 (2013).

[13]   Curtis A. Bradley, *Territorial Intellectual Property Rights in an Age of Globalism*, 37 VA. J. INT'L L. 505, 543, 547 (1997) (reasoning that national treatment principle implies a territorial approach to choice of law).

[14]   Council Regulation EC 44/2001 art. 22(4), Dec. 22, 2000 (on jurisdiction and the recognition and enforcement of judgments in civil and commercial matters). The exclusive jurisdiction provision is facially limited to proceedings as to the registration or validity of the rights. However, it will often be the case that the validity of the plaintiff's rights will be put at issue in many cases involving the enforcement of the plaintiff's rights. *See generally* Graeme W. Austin, *The Concept of Justiciability in Foreign Copyright Infringement Cases*, 40 INT'L REV. INTELL. PROP & COMP. L. 393 (2009).

[15]   For present purposes, it is unnecessary to engage with issues arising from regional systems, the most obvious example of which is the European Union. These quasi-federalist approaches do not undermine the importance of territoriality: it is merely that the borders have shifted to the edge of the federal system. The regional exhaustion principle adopted within the European Union (*see* Joined Cases C-414/99 to C-416/99, Zino Davidoff S.A. v. A&G Imports Ltd., Levi Strauss & Co. v. Tesco Stores Ltd., Levi Strauss & Co. v. Costco Wholesale UK Ltd., 2001 E.C.R. I-8731). The concept of regional exhaustion is now

confined. As to doctrine, the relevance of consumer responses is most obvious in use-based systems: the *legal* strength of trademark rights can depend greatly on what occurs in people's minds. As the U.S. Supreme Court explained in the *Rectanus* decision, "[a] trade-mark ... is merely a convenient means for facilitating the protection of one's good-will in trade by placing a distinguishing mark or symbol – a commercial signature – upon the merchandise or the package in which it is sold."[16] Trademark rights are not rights in gross, at least not in the common law tradition. There is thus no "property" in the trademark except to the extent that the mark symbolizes, in the minds of consumers, a firm's goodwill.[17] Even in registration systems, the strength of the mark – the extent to which it has impacted consumers' minds – will be critical to its enforceability.[18]

The human imagination is not tethered within domestic borders; nor are the stimuli that shape it. For many, life is a constant shuffle across international borders. This is true not just of the (literally) high-flying executive; it also reflects the reality of life for many in "borderland" communities;[19] and, in the modern global city, with increasingly frayed commitments to the nation state, the stimuli that help shape the "consumer consciousness" derive from a multiplicity of sources, some local, many from elsewhere. Similarly, many consumer products are "internationalized," with seemingly little connection to specific geographical sources. Apple® is the source of the iPhone®; *where* it was manufactured has relatively little relevance. At the same time, the trademark laws of the place where it is marketed seem only tenuously connected with the consumer experience. To be sure, localized consumer protection laws,

---

embedded in EU Trademark Directive: Council Directive art. 7, 89/104, Approximate the Laws of Member States Relating to Trade Marks art. 7, 1989 O.J. (L 40) 1, 5 (EC).

[16] United Drug Co. v. Theodore Rectanus Co., 248 U.S. 90, 98 (1916).

[17] *See* William P. Kratzke, *Normative Economic Analysis of Trademark Law*, 21 MEMPHIS ST. U. L. REV. 199, 205 (1991): ("Until a word, name, symbol or device plays some informational or identificatory role with respect to a product it has no value.").

[18] As the Court of Justice of the European Union pointed out recently, "[i]n order to determine whether the use of a sign takes unfair advantage of the distinctive character or the repute of the mark, it is necessary to undertake a global assessment, taking into account all factors relevant to the circumstances of the case, which include the strength of the mark's reputation." Case C-487/07, L'Oreal v. Bellure, 2009 E.C.R. I-05185 at [44].

[19] *See generally* GLOBALIZATION ON THE LINE: CULTURE, CAPITAL, AND CITIZENSHIP AT U.S. BORDERS (Claudia Sadowski-Smith ed. 2002).

some of which are of imperative application, and cannot be avoided through contractual disclaimers and choice of law clauses,[20] are not entirely irrelevant to the value secured at the point of purchase. Yet the overall brand experience that accompanies the purchase of such products seems to have very little to do with the (territorially confined) domestic laws that create and protect the mark.

How trademark law should respond to the realities of consumers' experience in the global marketplace is a theme explored in a number of chapters in this volume. One obvious response to the realities of international marketing is the "famous" or "well-known" mark doctrine, which makes and facilitates the international expansion of brands.[21] As a number of chapters in this volume explain, the famous marks doctrine is not fully embraced in U.S. decisional law. The Ninth Circuit has held that a foreign trader could achieve priority in a mark in the United States even without "use in commerce" where "a substantial percentage in the relevant American market is familiar with the foreign mark."[22] The Second Circuit, however, has not been so accommodating, holding that this adaptation is for the U.S. Congress to make, not the courts.[23]

Another response is the willingness of some courts to apply domestic trademark laws in foreign territories. However much of an affront to the territoriality principle this might seem, under prevailing U.S. doctrine, this strategy remains possible.[24] In a leading case,[25] the Supreme Court countenanced the idea that U.S. trademark law could apply to the

---

[20]   In the U.S. context, Louisiana prohibits the enforcement of a choice of law clause in a contract where such a transaction has a connection to the state's territory. LA. REV. STAT. ANN. § 51:1418 (2001).

[21]   In particular, *see infra* Marshall A. Leaffer, *Protection of Well-Known Marks: A Transnational Perspective*; Leah Chan Grinvald, *Interactivity, Territoriality, and Well-Known Marks*; and Lee Ann Lockridge, *Territoriality (Mis)Understood: Enforcing Well-Known Marks in the United States*. An early initiative that facilitated international brand expansion was the Pan-American Convention of 1929, which is discussed in this volume by Professor Farley. *See infra* Christine Haight Farley, *The Pan-American Convention of 1929: A Bold Vision of Extraterritorial Meets Current Realities*.

[22]   Grupo Gigante v. Dallo, 391 F.3d 1088 (9th Cir. 2004). *See also* Karoun Dairies, Inc. v. Karoun Dairies, Inc., 2010 WL 3633109 (S.D.Cal. 2010).

[23]   ITC Ltd. v. Punchgini, Inc., 482 F.3d 135 (2d Cir. 2007).

[24]   *See generally* Graeme W. Austin, *The Story of Steele v. Bulova: Trademarks on the Line*, INTELLECTUAL PROPERTY STORIES 395 (Jane C. Ginsburg and Rochelle Cooper Dreyfuss eds., 2006) (examining the background to the leading U.S. case, Steele v. Bulova Watch Co. Ltd., 344 U.S. 280 (1952) and the subsequent case law it has generated).

[25]   Steele v. Bulova Watch Co. Ltd., 344 U.S. 280 (1952).

defendant's activities in Mexico. The significance of that case, and the scope of its holding, continue to occupy lower courts, as trademark owners seek to litigate issues relating to trademark infringement in U.S. forums,[26] and courts continue to explore the bases for allowing cases involving trademark rights arising under foreign laws to proceed.[27]

Yet another response has been a tendency toward the localization of trademark disputes, especially in the domain name context,[28] as is illustrated by case law that has emerged under the "reverse domain name hijacking" provisions of the U.S. Lanham Act (the Anti-Cybersquatting Consumer Protection Act (ACPA)).[29] The Fourth Circuit's decision in *Barcelona.com v. Excelentísimo Ayuntamiento de Barcelona*[30] concerned an application under ACPA by a Delaware corporation, Bcom, Inc., that had registered "www.barcelona.com," for a declaration that this registration was not unlawful under the U.S. Lanham Act. This followed proceedings under the Uniform Dispute Resolution Policy (UDRP)[31] that had been decided in favor of the Excelentísimo Ayuntamiento de Barcelona (the City Council of Barcelona). The City Council alleged that the defendant's domain name was confusingly similar to some 150 trademarks that it had registered in Spain, most of which included the name "Barcelona" in some form. Bcom invoked the "reverse domain name

---

[26] *See, e.g.*, Vanity Fair Mills v. T. Eaton Co., 234 F.2d 633 (2d Cir. 1956); Sterling Drug v. Bayer AG, 14 F.3d 733 (2d Cir. 1994); McBee v. Delica Co., 417 F.3d 107 (1st Cir. 2005); Les Ballets Trockadero de Monte Carlo, Inc. v. Trevino, 945 F.Supp. 563 (S.D.N.Y. 1996).

[27] For some courts, the citizenship of the defendant appears to be an especially salient issue. *See e.g.*, E.I. DuPont de Nemours & Co. v. Kolon Industries, Inc., 2012 WL 4490547 (E.D. Va. 2012).

[28] On the regulation of domain names generally, *see infra* Jacqueline Lipton and Mary Wong, *Trademarks, Free Speech, and ICANN's New gTLD Process*.

[29] 15 U.S.C. § 1114(2)(D)(v) (authorizes an aggrieved domain name registrant to "file a civil action to establish that the registration or use of the domain name by registrant is not unlawful under [the Lanham Act]"). This provision is designed to prevent what is sometimes called "reverse hijacking" or overreaching by mark owners. *See* Maruti.Com v. Maruti Udyog Ltd. 447 F.Supp.2d 494, 496 (Md. 2006).

[30] Barcelona.com v. Excelentísimo Ayuntamiento de Barcelona, 330 F.3d 617 (4th Cir. 2003).

[31] UNIFORM DOMAIN NAME DISPUTE RESOLUTION POLICY (UDRP), http://www.icann.org/en/help/dndr/udrp/policy. The UDRP specifically preserves the ability to litigate cases in national courts. *See ibid.* at § 4.k ("The mandatory administrative proceeding requirements … shall not prevent [the parties] from submitting the dispute to a court of competent jurisdiction for independent resolution …").

hijacking" provisions of the Lanham Act, which protect domain name registrants against trademark proprietors that "overreach" in their assertion of rights under the UDRP. ACPA enables a domain name registrant to establish that its registration or use is "not unlawful under this chapter," that is, under U.S. federal trademark law. The Fourth Circuit held that the district court had been wrong to apply Spanish trademark law to the dispute, and it remanded for consideration of the parties' rights under U.S. federal trademark law. The Court of Appeals invoked the *territoriality* of trademark law to justify application of U.S. trademark law to a dispute that involved a Spanish trademark owner whose trademarks are likely to have principal relevance to people within Spain. It might be objected that by localizing the case under U.S. law, the Fourth Circuit's approach is at odds with the "non-national" character of the UDRP.[32] At the same time, the approach can be understood to impinge upon the territoriality principle – to the extent that the Court insisted on the application of United States law to a dispute whose center of gravity seemed to be Spanish.

Yet another inroad to territoriality can be seen in the relaxation of rules relating to the exhaustion of trademark rights. Trademark owners' international licensing arrangements will often reinforce formalistic principles associated with territoriality, as different geographical regions are "carved up" through exclusive licensing arrangements. With many products marketed under internationally recognized brands, many consumers appear to be indifferent to the physical source of the products and respond positively to the efforts of entrepreneurs to source and import those products at the cheapest price point. "Gray marketing" thereby cuts across the "territoriality" represented by brand owners' attempts to silo national markets according to price points. A full-blooded gray market regime has the effect that sale of geographically confined rights in one country is in effect sale of those rights in every country in which there are sufficient similarities between goods such that consumers would not be confused.[33] Opportunities for gray marketing are enhanced when

---

[32]   *See generally* Graeme B. Dinwoodie and Larry Helfer, *Designing Non-National Systems: The Case of the Uniform Domain Name Dispute Resolution Policy*, 43 WM. & MARY L. REV. 141 (2001).

[33]   In the U.S. context, Justice Kagan appeared to make just this point in a recent case concerning gray market copyright-protected goods:

[A]s a matter of copyright theory, I had always understood copyright to – a copyright holder has a kind of a bundle of rights. It's not one right that applies everywhere in the world. It's you have your U.S. rights and you have your Chinese rights, you have your rights under each jurisdiction's law. And your

owners of any copyright in a product's packaging, trade dress and logos and, where relevant, the product configuration itself, are likewise precluded from enforcing their rights to prevent importation of legitimate products sourced from abroad.[34]

Do these developments, and others discussed in the chapters that follow, mean that territoriality should be jettisoned altogether? In the "global economy" do trademarks operate in a kind of state of nature – or, perhaps, "state of consumption" – in which the nation state no longer has any purchase? Literally, that is of course an overstatement: domestic laws, systems of registration, and so on continue to remain relevant to the existence and enforcement of trademark rights. But do all of these developments underscore the prescience of Sir Robin Jacob's observation that "the world will realize that at least for intellectual property the days of the nation state are over"?[35] Does the uncoupling of intellectual property from the nation state mean that this species of property is beginning to enjoy a kind of "pre-legal" existence?

These debates of course have a long pedigree. Jeremy Bentham, for example, took the opposite view (on property rights generally), and famously declared that "[t]here is no such thing as natural property ... it is entirely the work of the law,"[36] a theme that was vigorously elaborated

---

position is essentially to say that when I sell my Chinese rights to somebody, I'm also selling my U.S. rights to that same person, because the person who has the Chinese rights can just turn around and import the goods. I mean, that's the nature of your position, isn't it, that your U.S. rights are always attached when you sell more – your rights under the jurisdiction of another country?

Kirtsaeng v. John Wiley & Sons, Inc. 133 S.Ct. 1351 (2013) (Oral Argument), at 23.

[34] Kirtsaeng v. John Wiley & Sons, Inc. 133 S.Ct. 1351 (2013). *See also infra* Irene Calboli, *The (Avoidable) Effects of Territorially Different Approaches to Trademark and Copyright Exhaustion*; Mary LaFrance, *Avoiding Mutant Trademarks: A Statutory Exclusion for Copyrighted Accessories to Parallel Imports*; and Pierre-Emmanuel Moyse, *"La Confusion des Genres": Logos and Packaging as Copyrighted Works.*

[35] The Hon. Mr. Justice Jacob, *International Intellectual Property Litigation in the Next Millennium*, 32 CASE W. RES. J. INT'L L. 507, 516 (2000). Sir Robin's comments were specifically directed at the prospect of the creation of "truly international courts" to manage intellectual property disputes. *Ibid.*

[36] JEREMY BENTHAM, THEORY OF LEGISLATION vi, 111 (London, Paternoster Library, 1896).

upon by the Legal Realist movement.[37] And, as a descriptive matter, of course, not all trademarks *are* operating "beyond the local." If anything, we are seeing trends toward localized markets and localized use of marks.[38] Consumer responses to geographical indications and the use of trademarks by indigenous peoples as signals of authenticity are examples. Marketplace phenomena such as these indicate sites of consumer and producer resistance to the "globalizing" trends that present the most obvious challenges to territoriality.

Whether property of any kind, including property in trademarks, is "pre-legal" or an artificial legal construct probably distills a fairly sterile normative debate. The more important questions always relate to how the law responds to the variety of competing claims of accountability – or lack of accountability – to the nation state. The salience of that inquiry is reflected in the searching *contextual* analysis of the notion of territoriality that occurs in the following chapters in this book. This book is situated against a background of intense and increasing interest in the role of intellectual property and its societal and economic effects. Whereas intellectual property was once seen as a fusty and arcane branch of private law, it is difficult nowadays to get very far discussing intellectual property without also encountering very basic questions of justice and fairness.

As with all legal phenomena, it behooves us to consider carefully the kind of negative externalities that might be generated by the creation and enforcement of trademark rights.[39] Our sensitivity to those externalities

---

[37]   Joseph William Singer, *Review Essay: Legal Realism Now*, 76 CAL. L. REV. 465, 482 (1988) (discussing the legal realist perspective that "[a]ny definition of property and contract rights necessarily requires the state to determine the character of relations among citizens in the marketplace").

[38]   *See infra* Margaret Chon, *Marks and More(s): Certification in the Global Value Chains*; Doris Estelle Long, *Branding the Land: Creating Global Meanings for Local Characteristics*; and Daphne Zografos Johnsson, *Signs Beyond Borders: Moving from Commodity to Differentiated Exports in the Coffee Industry*.

[39]   *See generally* ROSEMARY J. COOMBE, THE CULTURAL LIFE OF INTELLECTUAL PROPERTIES: AUTHORSHIP, APPROPRIATION, AND THE LAW (1998). A number of chapters in this volume explore this theme. See, in particular, the chapter by Professor Chow, which explores the burdens imposed on developing countries by the creation and enforcement of luxury brands. *See* Daniel Chow, *Trademark Enforcement in Developing Countries: Counterfeiting as an Externality Imposed by Multinational Companies. See also infra*, for an example of national enforcement challenges, Peter K. Yu, *The Curious Case of Fake Beijing Olympics Merchandise.*

might also provoke us to think in more subtle ways about the best forums in which to ventilate those concerns. The creation and enforcement of rights also create duties on the rest of us.[40] As the title of this volume underscores, parts of the economy *are* increasingly "global." At the same time, *local* laws and *local* forums might provide some of the most powerful and appropriate sites for working through the myriad competing claims that are distilled by the expansion of intellectual property. The chapters that follow in this illuminating volume will offer a powerful lodestar as we navigate these difficult issues.

---

[40] Jeremy Waldron, *From Authors to Copiers: Individual Rights and Social Values in Intellectual Property*, 68 CHI-KENT L. REV. 841 (1993) (advancing a Hohfeldian analysis to the relationship between rights and duties in intellectual property).

PART I

Territorial norms and (global) well-known marks

2. Protection of well-known marks: a transnational perspective

Marshall A. Leaffer*

I INTRODUCTION

From its vigorous support of the Agreement on Trade-Related Aspects of Intellectual Property Rights (TRIPS Agreement)[1] to the current push in favor of the Anti-Counterfeiting Trade Agreement (ACTA),[2] the United States has been at the forefront in encouraging the effective protection of intellectual property rights worldwide. This is hardly surprising because the United States is the largest producer country of informational assets in the world and has reason to assure that those assets are protected abroad. In this chapter, I wish to discuss a departure in the general thrust of American policy in the international protection of what one might call "its first world assets."[3] I refer to the failure of United States law to create a coherent policy in the protection of well-known marks despite its treaty obligations under Article 6*bis* of the Paris Convention,[4] which

---

* Indiana University School of Law, Distinguished Scholar in Intellectual Property Law and University Fellow.

   [1] Agreement on Trade-Related Aspects of Intellectual Property Rights, Apr. 15, 1994, Marrakesh Agreement Establishing the World Trade Organization, Annex 1C, 1869 U.N.T.S. 229, 33 I.L.M. 1125 (1994), *available at* http://www.wto.org/english/tratop_e/trips_e/t_agm0_e.htm [hereinafter TRIPS Agreement].

   [2] *Anti-Counterfeiting Trade Agreement Final Draft*, OFF. OF THE U.S. TRADE REPRESENTATIVE (Dec. 3, 2010), *available at* http://www.ustr.gov/trade-topics/intellectual-property/anti-counterfeiting-trade-agreement-acta/previous-acta-texts.

   [3] Frederick M. Abbott, *Toward a New Era of Objective Assessment in the Field of TRIPS and Variable Geometry for the Preservation of Multilateralism*, 8 J. INT'L ECON. L. 77, 80 (2005).

   [4] Paris Convention for the Protection of Industrial Property, Mar. 20, 1883, last revised at Stockholm July 14, 1967, 21 U.S.T. 1583, 828 U.N.T.S. 305,

requires member countries to protect marks that are well known in a member country even though they are not registered or used in the protecting country.[5]

United States case law is in disarray on this issue and, for the moment, there seems to be no interest to remedy the problem legislatively. Some courts believe that the current provisions of the Lanham Act[6] are sufficient to accommodate the well-known marks doctrine, but most do not. Ultimately a modest amendment to the Lanham Act may be necessary to remedy a failure of American law in light of its treaty obligations and its stated policy in the effective protection of owners' rights across national borders. To place the problem in context, one could view the protection of well-known marks as an exception to the doctrine of territoriality, one that provides for the extraterritorial reach of well-known marks.[7]

Recognized as a worldwide norm, trademark law is "territorial."[8] The territoriality doctrine in trademark law is an international standard and is inscribed in the Paris Convention Article 6(3), which provides that "[a] mark duly registered in a country of the Union shall be regarded as independent of marks registered in other countries of the Union, including the country of origin."[9] Under this principle, "each country has its own trademark system governed by its own domestic statutory provisions."[10] To obtain trademark protection in a given country, a "company must satisfy the requirements as designated in that country's domestic laws."[11] For example, to establish trademark rights in U.S. law, a company must show priority of use in the United States, not priority of use anywhere in the world.[12] Conversely, a foreign mark holder who has not used his mark in the United States before someone else will not obtain priority under federal law.[13]

---

available at http://www.wipo.int/treaties/en/ip/paris/trtdocs_wo020.html [hereinafter Paris Convention].

   [5]   *See ibid.*
   [6]   15 U.S.C. § 1051 *et seq.* (2006).
   [7]   *See* Paris Convention, *supra* note 4, at art. 6(3).
   [8]   *Ibid.*
   [9]   *Ibid.*
   [10]   Rachel Brook, *The United States' Adoption of the Well-known Foreign Mark Exception*, 36 Fordham Urb. L.J. 889, 892 (2009).
   [11]   *See ibid.*
   [12]   *See ibid.*
   [13]   *See ibid.*

II THE TROUBLE WITH TERRITORIALITY: THE DILEMMA OF THE WELL-KNOWN MARKS

Despite its long-standing recognition, the territoriality doctrine has never existed in a pure state and continues to give way as commerce continues to expand across national boundaries in a world structured by air travel, satellites and the Internet.[14] Go anywhere in the world and you are likely to confront Coca-Cola, McDonald's, Microsoft, and Sony, to name only a few global brands. We live in a mobile society where immigrants bring into their adopted country knowledge of local brands from their country of origin. These developments have created a tension with the doctrine of territoriality, one that increases with time. Today, the goodwill of the trademark is hardly limited to the political confines of the nation state. Absent a uniform universal trademark system, a better system of trademark rights might be one that accommodates a territorially based trademark law with the reality that an owner's goodwill extends beyond the discrete borders of the nation state.

The shortcomings of strict territoriality are particularly acute for well-known marks. Put simply, these marks merit special protection because their very notoriety imposes heavy burdens. Owners of these marks are dogged by unauthorized uses and the oppressive, unremitting cost of policing their rights through private enforcement as well as civil and criminal litigation. They encounter repeated attempts to appropriate time-honored reputations, so that owners of well-known marks are obliged to spend continuously to reclaim their marks and to sustain their exclusivity. Owners of well-known marks face practical limitations. Even those who own the most famous and valuable marks are unable to use them everywhere and are unlikely to register them in all jurisdictions, in all the classifications, to cover all infringing activities. Worse, many owners of well-known marks, to defend their trademarks internationally, must spend wastefully on disputes even in countries where they do

---

[14] *See* Marshall A. Leaffer, *The New World of International Trademark Law*, 2 MARQ. INTELL. PROP. L. REV. 1, 28 (1998); *see also* Gary B. Born, *A Reappraisal of the Extraterritorial Reach of U.S. Law*, 24 LAW & POL'Y INT'L BUS.1, 29 (1992) (criticizing strict territoriality). For other views of territoriality, *see* Graeme B. Dinwoodie, *Trademarks and Territory: Detaching Trademark Law from the Nation-State*, 41 HOUS. L. REV. 885, 888 (2004); *see also* Graeme W. Austin, *The Territoriality of United States Trademark Law*, *in* 3 INTELLECTUAL PROPERTY AND INFORMATION WEALTH: ISSUES AND PRACTICES IN THE DIGITAL AGE 235, 236–39 (Peter K. Yu ed., 2007) (discussing the "domestic territoriality" of U.S. trademark law).

minimal business, and even then, their marks may remain at risk even after these unproductive policing expenditures. Fortunately, the Paris Convention in Article 6*bis* has incorporated an important exception to the doctrine of territoriality, a safety valve for the benefit of the owners of well-known marks.[15]

III   WELL-KNOWN MARKS AND THE PARIS CONVENTION

Article 6*bis* of the Paris Convention provides:

> The countries of the Union undertake, ex officio if their legislation so permits, or at the request of an interested party, to refuse or to cancel the registration, and to prohibit the use, of a trademark which constitutes a reproduction, an imitation, or a translation, liable to create confusion, of a mark considered by the competent authority of the country of registration or use to be well known in that country as being already the mark of a person entitled to the benefits of this Convention and used for identical or similar goods. These provisions shall also apply when the essential part of the mark constitutes a reproduction of any such well-known mark or an imitation liable to create confusion therewith.[16]

Introduced at The Hague Conference of 1925[17], Article 6*bis*[18] of the Paris Convention for the Protection of Industrial Property requires member countries to afford certain protections to well-known marks, regardless whether they are registered. Specifically, member countries must refuse or cancel the registration, and prohibit the use, of a well-known mark when applied for or used by an unauthorized party for identical or similar goods, when its use or registration would likely cause confusion.[19] Article 16.2 of the WTO Agreement on Trade-Related Aspects of Intellectual Property Rights (TRIPS)[20] extends Paris Convention Article 6*bis* to services and provides that members shall take into account that a mark is well known to a relevant sector of the public as well as

---

15   Paris Convention*, supra* note 4, art. 6*bis.*
16   *Ibid.*
17   *Ibid.* as revised at The Hague Conference on November 6, 1925.
18   *Ibid.* at art. 6*bis.*
19   *Ibid.*
20   The relationship between TRIPS and the Paris Convention is regulated in Article 2 of TRIPS, which incorporates all substantive provisions of the Paris Convention, and makes these binding on contracting parties who are not members of the Paris Convention. *See* TRIPS Agreement, *supra* note 1, at art. 2.

promotion of the mark.[21] Article 6*bis* provides for the protection of well-known marks, but is silent on two major issues. One open issue is whether use in the protecting country is required as a basis for protection. The second issue concerns the criteria to determine whether a mark is well known.

Whether use is required in the country where protection is being sought has been the subject of hot debate ever since the text of 6*bis* was first drafted. Article 6*bis* does not oblige member countries to protect well-known marks that have not been used in the jurisdiction, although it leaves them free to do so. In the 1958 Lisbon Conference, a proposal providing that use of well-known marks in the country where protection is sought is unnecessary to obtain such protection was rejected.[22] It is unfortunate that the proposal was not adopted because if a mark is well known, why should it be important whether it achieved notoriety through use or otherwise? That use should not be a requirement for the protection of a well-known mark was finally given quasi-formal recognition in WIPO's *Joint Recommendation on Protection of Well-Known Marks (1999)*, Article 2 (3)(a)(i) of which provides:

(3) [*Factors Which Shall Not Be Required*] (a) A Member State shall not require, as a condition for determining whether a mark is a well-known mark:
   (i)   that the mark has been used in, or that the mark has been registered or that an application for registration of the mark has been filed in or in respect of, the Member State;
   (ii)   that the mark is well known in, or that the mark has been registered or that an application for registration of the mark has been filed in or in respect of, any jurisdiction other than the Member State; or
   (iii) that the mark is well known by the public at large in the Member State.

(b) Notwithstanding subparagraph (a)(ii), a Member State may, for the purpose of applying paragraph (2)(d), require that the mark be well known in one or more jurisdictions other than the Member State.

---

[21]   Article 16.3 of TRIPS extends art. 6*bis* protection to well-known marks when used on unrelated goods or services in cases where the well-known mark is registered, if such use indicates a connection to the owner and the well-known mark owner would likely be damaged by such use. TRIPS Agreement, *supra* note 1, art. 16.3.
[22]   *See* 2 STEVEN P. LADAS, PATENTS, TRADEMARKS, AND RELATED RIGHTS: NATIONAL AND INTERNATIONAL PROTECTION 1253 (1975).

In addition to the question of use, the criteria for what constitutes a well-known mark is not specified in 6*bis*, and neither the Paris Convention nor the TRIPS Agreement provides a definition of a well-known mark. This has led to linguistic confusion and one can find such terms as "notorious," "highly renowned," "highly reputed" and "exceptionally well-known" "famous" marks. These terms have been used interchangeably in the literature – a linguistic muddle that can be avoided by making the distinction between well-known marks and famous marks. The latter would receive even greater protection to cover dissimilar goods and services; a distinction is recognized in 16(3) of the TRIPS Agreement.[23]

Again, WIPO's *Joint Recommendation on Protection of Well-Known Marks (1999)*, Article 2 (3)(a)(i), clarifies this terminology by establishing the factors that would determine whether a mark is well known:

> (1) [*Factors for Consideration*] (a) In determining whether a mark is a well-known mark, the competent authority shall take into account any circumstances from which it may be inferred that the mark is well known.
>
> (b) In particular, the competent authority shall consider information submitted to it with respect to factors from which it may be inferred that the mark is, or is not, well known, including, but not limited to, information concerning the following:
>   1. the degree of knowledge or recognition of the mark in the relevant sector of the public;
>   2. the duration, extent and geographical area of any use of the mark;
>   3. the duration, extent and geographical area of any promotion of the mark, including advertising or publicity and the presentation, at fairs or exhibitions, of the goods and/or services to which the mark applies;
>   4. the duration and geographical area of any registrations, and/or any applications for registration, of the mark, to the extent that they reflect use or recognition of the mark;
>   5. the record of successful enforcement of rights in the mark, in particular, the extent to which the mark was recognized as well known by competent authorities;
>   6. the value associated with the mark ...

Viewed historically, the well-known marks doctrine has had a long pedigree in international practice from its adoption in 1925 to its recognition in the TRIPs Agreement. As the following discussion will show, it has received less favorable treatment in the U.S.

---

23 TRIPS Agreement, *supra* note 1, art. 16(3).

IV TREATIES IN THE UNITED STATES

As a signatory of the major trademark conventions, it would appear that the United States has acknowledged the well-known marks doctrine in principle. No consistent policy on well-known marks, however, exists in the U.S even though the United States is a member of the Paris Convention and was a motivating factor in the shaping of the TRIPS Agreement. In fact, U.S. trademark law has never been applied in a coherent manner, consistent with Article 6*bis* of Paris. As the following discussion will show, there is little consensus on exactly what has been incorporated into U.S. trademark law in regard to the well-known marks doctrine.

One reason for this disorder is the way in which treaties are signed and ratified into U.S. law. Treaties enter into effect in the U.S. in two ways depending on whether the international agreement is self-executing or non-self-executing. Self-executing treaties become effective and enforceable immediately on ratification. By contrast, non-self-executing treaties require implementing legislation before they become a part of federal law. If a treaty is silent as to whether it is self-executing, the President must decide its status based on the intention of the United States upon signing the treaty, and whether existing law adequately permits the United States to fulfill its obligations under the treaty. U.S. courts are generally in agreement that the Paris Convention, which includes the well-known foreign mark exception, is not a self-executing treaty. Courts are divided, however, on to what extent the Lanham Act has incorporated the Paris Convention in U.S. law. This disarray is illustrated by the varying approaches taken by state courts, the Patent and Trademark Office, and Federal Courts.

V THE WELL-KNOWN MARKS IN THE UNITED STATES: A STUDY IN CONFUSION

A State Courts

Unlike the federal courts, the well-known marks doctrine has had some success on the state level and was recognized first by a New York trial court in 1936 in a common law action for unfair competition in the use of a trademark.[24] In a post-Lanham Act decision, a New York trial bolstered

---

[24] *See* Maison Prunier v. Prunier's Rest. & Café, 159 Misc. 551, 557–58, 288 N.Y.S. 529, 535–36 (N.Y. Sup. Ct. 1936).

the well-known marks doctrine in *Vaudable v. Montmartre, Inc.*,[25] in which a New York restaurant began operating under the name "Maxim's."[26] The defendant not only used the same name, it also used similar script for its sign and included other features designed to suggest a connection with the exclusive French restaurant.[27] The *Vaudable* court enjoined the New York company from the uses of its marks that would appropriate the goodwill of a restaurant recognized internationally.[28] It did so because the marks associated with the Paris Maxim's were well known, even though the Parisian restaurant owned no U.S. registration and had done no business in the U.S. The court noted that the scope of protection available against unfair competition had increased as a result of case law and legislation such as the Lanham Act.[29] Thus, the *Vaudable* court held that trademark holders who use their marks solely in foreign countries could under the proper circumstances protect their mark in the U.S. if the mark satisfies the standard of being well known.[30]

B   The United States Patent and Trademark Office (USPTO)

Similar to state law, the United States Patent and Trademark Office (USPTO) has applied the well-known mark doctrine to registration decisions. U.S. case law outlines a variety of non-exclusive and non-exhaustive factors that can be used in the analysis. These factors include, but are not limited to, the similarity of the marks, the relatedness or proximity of the goods and/or services, the strength of the plaintiff's mark including the level of commercial recognition, marketing channels used including the similarity or dissimilarity between the consumers of the parties' goods and/or services, the degree of care likely to be exercised by purchasers in selecting goods and/or services, the defendant's intent in selecting its mark, the evidence of actual confusion, the likelihood of expansion in product lines, and so on.[31] In this analysis, while no one factor is determinative, a strong or well-known mark will

---

[25]   Vaudable v. Montmartre, Inc., 193 N.Y.S.2d 332 (N.Y. Sup. Ct. 1959).
[26]   *Ibid.* at 334.
[27]   *Ibid.*
[28]   *Ibid.* at 336.
[29]   *Ibid.* at 335.
[30]   Brandon Barker, *The Power of the Well-Known Trademark: Courts Should Consider Article 6*bis *of the Paris Convention an Integrated Part of Section 44 of the Lanham Act*; 81 Wash. L. Rev. 363, 378 (2006).
[31]   *See, e.g.*, Polaroid Corp. v. Polarad Electronics Corp., 287 F.2d 492 (2d Cir. 1961), *cert. denied*, 368 U.S. 820 (U.S. 1961).

receive broader protection than a weaker mark. The Office essentially uses these same factors in deciding whether to protect a well-known mark. There is no separate analysis apart from likelihood of confusion or deceptiveness as to whether a mark is well known or not.

The USPTO will refuse registration of, or a third party may seek to oppose or cancel, a mark that conflicts with registered or unregistered well-known marks, foreign or domestic, that meet the test under Lanham Act section 2(a)[32] (d)[33]. Section 2(d) of the Lanham Act provides that a mark will be refused registration if it is likely to be confused with a prior registered mark or a prior mark in use in commerce and not abandoned. Section 2(a) of the Lanham Act provides that a mark will be refused registration if it is deceptive or falsely suggests a connection to persons, institutions, beliefs or national symbols. It is not necessary for a mark to be registered to obtain protection under section 2(a) or 2(d), but the mark must point uniquely to a source (known or unknown) such that consumers would be deceived if the goods or services of the applicant did not emanate from that source. Whereas the USPTO does not make a specific determination whether a mark is well known, it evaluates the strength of the mark in determining the scope of protection to afford a previously registered or unregistered mark against a pending application. For example, the Trademark Board in *The All England Lawn Tennis Club, Ltd. v. Creations Aromatiques*[34] granted plaintiff's request to block registration of a trademark for "Wimbledon Cologne" even though plaintiff was not itself using the Wimbledon mark on any product sold in the United States. More recently, the Trademark Board has "reiterated in dicta that owners of well-known foreign marks need not use those marks

---

[32]   15 U.S.C. § 1052(a) (2006).

[33]   15 U.S.C. § 1052(d) Trademark Trial and Appeal Board Manual of Procedure (TBMP) § 414(13) 3d ed. 2011. "Although information concerning a party's foreign use of its involved mark is usually irrelevant to the issues in a Board proceeding, and thus not discoverable, exceptions may arise where, for example, there is an issue as to whether a party's adoption and use of the mark in the United States was made in bad faith for the purpose of forestalling a foreign user's expansion into the United States, or where the foreign mark is 'famous,' albeit not used, in the United States." *Ibid; see, e.g.*, Polaroid Corp. v. Polarad Elecs. Corp., 287 F. 2d 492 (2d Cir. N.Y. 1961), *cert. denied*, 368 U.S. 820 (U.S. 1961).

[34]   All England Lawn Tennis Club v. Creations Aromatiques, 220 U.S.P.Q. 1069 (T.T.A.B. 1983).

in the United States to challenge the registration of marks likely to promote confusion on the part of consumers."[35]

C   The Federal Courts: the Ninth Circuit, Second Circuit Split

1   The Ninth Circuit: *Grupo Gigante v. Dallo*

Despite its recognition on the state level and by the Trademark Trial and Appeal Board, the well-known marks doctrine has not gained traction in the federal courts. In fact, there is a split in the circuits regarding the doctrine. In *Grupo Gigante v. Dallo*,[36] the Ninth Circuit adopted the well-known marks doctrine, as an application of section 43(a) of the Lanham Act.[37] Grupo Gigante, a Mexican Company, began operating a chain of supermarkets in Mexico under the name "Gigante" in 1962, and by 1991 had 100 stores in Mexico, six of them in Baja California (two in Tijuana).[38] In 1991, Dallo opened a grocery in San Diego under the name "Gigante Market" and in 1999 and 2000, Grupo Gigante opened three stores in Los Angeles.[39] Grupo Gigante brought an action for infringement of its common law rights in the U.S. under section 43(a).[40] The court faced the issue of whether a foreign trademark owner can sustain a cause of action in the United States as an exception to the territoriality principle?[41] And second, if so, what degree of renown must be shown to sustain a cause of action under section 43(a)?[42] The court declared that territoriality in trademark law is not absolute and when a mark reaches a certain exceptional level of notoriety overseas, the territorial principle can be overcome.[43] In order to qualify for an exception to the territoriality principle, the foreign user must demonstrate by a preponderance of the

---

[35]   ITC Ltd. v. Punchgini, Inc., 482 F.3d 135, 158–59 (2d Cir. 2007); *see also* British-Am. Tobacco Co. v. Philip Morris, Inc., 55 U.S.P.Q.2d (BNA) 1585 (T.T.A.B. 2000) (recognizing that there are exceptions in U.S. law to the doctrine of territoriality that are created by international treaties and conventions to which the United States is a party; Mastic, Inc. v. Mastic Corp., 230 U.S.P.Q. (BNA) 699 (T.T.A.B. 1986); Colt Indus. Operating Corp. v. Olivetti Controllo Numerico S.p.A., 221 U.S.P.Q. (BNA) 73 (T.T.A.B. 1983) .

[36]   Grupo Gigante S.A. de C.V. v. Dallo & Co., 391 F.3d 1088 (9th Cir. 2004).

[37]   *Ibid.* at 1094.

[38]   *Ibid.* at 1091.

[39]   *Ibid.*

[40]   *Ibid.* at 1094.

[41]   *Ibid.*

[42]   *Ibid.* at 1094–93.

[43]   *Ibid.* at 1094.

evidence that a substantial percentage of consumers in the relevant U.S. market are *familiar* with the foreign mark.[44] The court based its decision on an interpretation of the Lanham Act, and rejected Grupo Gigante's specific claims under the well-known marks doctrine of 6*bis* and unfair competition of 10*bis* of the Paris Convention.[45]

One weakness in the court's decision relates to its novel standard that it fashioned in determining whether a mark is well known.[46] It entered into new territory in adopting a "familiarity" standard that requires a higher level of awareness in the consuming public than secondary meaning but less than fame.[47] But what kind of evidentiary showing must be used to prove familiarity? The court mentions that one could look to "such factors as the intentional copying of the mark by the defendant and, whether customers of the American firm are likely to think they are patronizing the same firm that uses the mark in another country."[48] It is difficult to make the distinction between a familiarity standard and one for secondary meaning or fame. We already have the criteria for showing secondary meaning[49] or fame and both concepts have a pedigree in the Lanham Act[50] and in the case law.[51] Despite the holding in *Grupo Gigante* a majority of courts in the United States have ruled that the well-known marks doctrine does not exist as a matter of federal law.[52] These holdings are based on the fact that trademark law is essentially territorial and that treaties such as Paris and TRIPS are not self-executing in the United States.[53] The following Second Circuit case reaffirms these two principles articulated in Grupo Gigante, but, unlike that Ninth Circuit case, rejects any application of the well-known marks doctrine within the Lanham Act.

---

[44]   *Ibid.* at 1098.

[45]   *Ibid.* at 1099–1100.

[46]   *Ibid.* at 1098.

[47]   *Ibid.*

[48]   *Ibid.*

[49]   For the elements needed to prove secondary meaning *see* RESTATEMENT (THIRD) OF UNFAIR COMPETITION §13 Comment (e) (1995).

[50]   *See* 15 U.S.C §1125(c)(2) (2006) (stating a list of non-exclusive factors to determine whether a mark is famous under a dilution cause of action).

[51]   *See, e.g.*, Zatarain's, Inc. v. Oak Grove Smokehouse, Inc., 698 F.2d 786, 795 (5th Cir. 1983) (providing a list of relevant factors useful in determining secondary meaning).

[52]   *See, e.g.*, ITC Ltd. v. Punchgini, Inc., 482 F.3d 135 (2d Cir. 2007).

[53]   *Ibid.* at 161–65.

2   The Second Circuit: *ITC v. Punchgini*

ITC, a corporation that owned the international chain of restaurants, abandoned Bukhara for restaurant services in the U.S. in 1997 when the New York City and Chicago restaurants closed.[54] The mark was associated with an international chain of Indian restaurants that some magazines reviewed as the best Indian dining establishments in the world.[55] Two years later, Punchgini opened its restaurant, Bukhara Grill.[56] ITC argued that Bukhara was well known in India and Asia and in the U.S.[57] The court held that, absent use in the U.S., a foreign mark holder may not assert priority rights and that neither Paris nor TRIPS is self-executing.[58]

In rejecting the plaintiff's claims, the Second Circuit analyzed specific Lanham Act provisions dealing with registered marks and found that the Act never references the well-known marks doctrine. The court admitted that some American authorities in some contexts have treated famous marks as an exception to the territoriality principle.[59] It recognized that New York state courts and the Patent and Trademark Office have recognized the doctrine and have barred registration of marks that would be confused with the famous mark.[60] The court also acknowledged the decision in *Grupo Gigante* in the Ninth Circuit, holding that there is a famous mark exception to the territoriality principle.[61] The court admitted that there were strong policy arguments to applying the famous marks doctrine.[62] After all, "an absolute territoriality rule without a famous-mark exception would promote consumer confusion and fraud," and trademark aims, at its essence, to protect the consumer against confusion.[63] And it would appear that trademark law should be applied to prohibit companies from "fool[ing] immigrants into thinking that they are buying from the store back home."[64] But territoriality won the day and the court rejected the argument that 6*bis* of Paris and 16(2) of TRIPS are

---

[54]   *Ibid.* at 143.
[55]   *Ibid.*
[56]   *Ibid.* at 144.
[57]   *Ibid.*
[58]   *Ibid.* at 161–65.
[59]   *Ibid.* at 157–58.
[60]   *Ibid.* at 157–59.
[61]   *Ibid.* at 159.
[62]   *Ibid.* at 165.
[63]   Grupo Gigante S.A. de C.V. v. Dallo & Co., 391 F.3d 1088, 1094–95 (9th Cir. 2004).
[64]   *Ibid.* at 94.

self-executing treaties in U.S. law.[65] The court refused to depart from the principle of territoriality without congressional action amending the Lanham Act to accommodate a well-known marks doctrine.[66] The court pointed out that even "[i]n *Grupo Gigante*, the Ninth Circuit did not reference either the language of the Lanham Act nor Article 6*bis* of the Paris Convention to support recognition of the famous marks doctrine."[67] The court noted that "the absence of any statutory provision expressly incorporating the famous marks doctrine" is all the more significant because Congress has made its intent known through a multitude of amendments to the Lanham Act but never specifically addressed well-known marks.[68] The court did certify ITC's claims under New York law to New York courts, alluding to a possible cause of action in state court.[69] Punchgini represents the ambivalence with which the courts regard the well-known marks doctrine despite U.S. treaty obligations. Other countries, however, have treated the issue directly and in a reasonable manner in adopting a standard for determining the enforcement of the well-known mark in the protecting jurisdiction.

VI FAMOUS MARKS FROM A COMPARATIVE PERSPECTIVE

Unlike the United States, many foreign jurisdictions have applied 6*bis* of the Paris Convention, protecting well-known marks in their country without use of registration. In fact, the United States should follow the lead of most nations who have fully recognized the well-known marks doctrine, and should do so absent coherent recognition in the case law,

---

[65] ITC Ltd. v. Punchgini, Inc., 482 F.3d 135, 172 (2d Cir. 2007).

[66] *Ibid.*

[67] *Ibid.* at 160.

[68] *Ibid.* at 164.

[69] *Ibid.* at 165. Other courts within the Second Circuit also have rejected the view that the well-known marks doctrine was incorporated by the Lanham Act. *See* Almacenes Exito S.A. v. El Gallo Meat Mkt., Inc., 381 F. Supp. 2d 324, 328 (S.D.N.Y. 2005) (holding that only Congress, and not the courts, can incorporate the well-known marks doctrine into the Lanham Act); *see also* Buti v. Impressa Perosa S.R.L., 139 F.3d 98, 106 (2d Cir. 1998) (holding that no rights in the mark "Fashion Café" were created when an Italian company advertised its restaurant in the United States). *But see* Empresa Cubana del Tabaco v. Culbro Corp., 399 F.3d 462, 484–85 (2d Cir. 2005). The Second Circuit expressly left open the possibility that protection would be available for well-known foreign marks if they are "sufficiently famous." *See ibid.* at 480–81.

through an amendment to the Lanham Act. I have chosen three jurisdictions – Canada, Singapore, and South Africa – for their treatment of
the issue of well-known marks. I believe that these three jurisdictions are
representative of trends at work in the protection of well-known marks
and provide a template for an eventual amendment to the Lanham Act
accommodating 6*bis* of Paris.

A Canada

Canada, like the United States, "lacks explicit legislative provisions or
case law providing expanded protection for well-known marks."[70] Canadian trademark law, however, offers broad protection for well-known
marks.[71] It is not necessary to show use in Canada, to carry on business
in Canada, or prove the well-known status of the mark in Canada; it is
only necessary to prove that the mark has achieved at least a limited
reputation among the relevant public.[72] It is immaterial how the reputation is created through use in Canada or abroad as long as the reputation
exists in Canada.[73]

The leading decision is *Orkin Exterminating Co. v. Pestco Co. of
Canada.*[74] In *Orkin*, the American plaintiff operated an exterminating and
pest control service in the United States in association with the trademark

---

[70]   Ruby A. Zefo, Public Comment Report, United States Trade Representative's Special 301 Review Submission by Intel Corporation Regarding Canada,
(Feb. 15, 2011).

[71]   *See, e.g.*, Liz Somerstein, *Who Is Really Protecting Barbie: Goliath or the
Silver Knight? A Defense of Mattel's Aggressive International Attempts to
Protect its Barbie Copyright and Trademark*, 39 U. MIAMI INTER-AM. L. REV.
559, 581 (noting that Canadian jurisprudence has "enabl[ed] famous trademarks
to receive broad protection").

[72]   Ron Lehrman and Carlos Cucurella, *International Protection of Well-
Known Marks*, THE INTERNATIONAL WHO'S WHO OF BUSINESS LAWYERS 806,
available at http://www.frosszelnick.com/sites/default/files/20061017163104_1_
PUBLISHED_PDF_0.pdf.

[73]   *Ibid.*

[74]   Orkin Exterminating Co. v. Pestco Co. of Canada [1985] 50 O.R. (2d)
726 (Ont. C.A.); *see, e.g.*, Toho Co. v. Sears, Roebuck & Co., 645 F.2d 788, 792
(9th Cir. 1981) (holding that §44(h) gives foreign nationals referred to by §44(b)
a federal claim coextensive with the substantive provisions of the relevant
trademark treaty, which in that case was a bilateral agreement with Japan);
Vanity Fair Mills, Inc. v. T. Eaton Co., 234 F.2d 633, 644 (2d Cir. 1956) (holding
that the Lanham Act incorporates only limited protections against unfair competition, not a broad right as might be available if the Paris Convention were
self-executing); GMC v. Ignacio Lopez de Arriortua, 948 F. Supp. 684, 687 (E.D.

ORKIN & Design.[75] The defendant provided the same types of services, though not in the same geographic areas as the plaintiff.[76] In particular, the plaintiff did not conduct business to any significant amount in the Province of Ontario, where the defendant was located.[77] The action was initiated after the defendant began using the name "Orkin Exterminating Company" in addition to the mark ORKIN & Design, which was identical to the plaintiff's mark.[78] The plaintiff sued for passing off.

In reviewing the evidence on the evidentiary question, the court found that Canadians were exposed to the plaintiff's mark when vacationing in the United States and through advertising in American publications circulated in Canada.[79] Although the plaintiff had a handful of paying customers in Ontario, the Court specified that "the existence of customers in Ontario is one factor only in determining the extent of Orkin's goodwill in Ontario."[80] In awarding an injunction and damages, the Court decided that Orkin had proven appropriate reputation in Ontario to uphold an action for passing off.[81] The application of the doctrine of passing off to protect foreign-owned marks with a strong reputation in Canada as in *Orkin* also is consistent with Canada's obligations under

---

Mich. 1996) (agreeing that the Lanham Act incorporates the substantive provisions of the Paris Convention, including Article 10*bis*, by way of sections 44(b) and 44(h)); Maison Lazard et Compagnie v. Manfra, Tordella & Brooks, Inc., 585 F. Supp. 1286, 1289 (S.D.N.Y. 1984) (holding that a federal cause of action exists for unfair competition under the Paris Convention, §44(b), and §44(h)); *see also* J. Thomas McCarthy, *Lanham Act §43(a): The Sleeping Giant Is Now Wide Awake*, 59 LAW & CONTEMPORARY PROBLEMS 45, 48–50 (1996) (noting that the precise range of protection provided by §44 is unclear). In this chapter I do not address this open issue, nor do I rely on any arguments related to the self-executing or non-self-executing nature or effect of any portion of the Paris Convention under U.S. law.

[75]   Orkin Exterminating Co. v. Pestco Co. of Canada, [1985] 5 C.P.R. (3d), 433,438 (Ont. C.A.).

[76]   *Ibid.*

[77]   *Ibid.*

[78]   *Ibid.*

[79]   *Ibid.; see also* Stephanie Chong, *Protection of Famous Trademarks Against Use for Unrelated Goods and Services: A Comparative Analysis of the Law in the United States, the United Kingdom and Canada and Recommendations for Canadian Law Reform*, 95 TRADEMARK REPORTER 642, 677 (May–June 2005), *available at* http://www.inta.org/TMR/Documents/Volume%2095/vol95_no3_a4.pdf.

[80]   *Orkin*, 5 C.P.R. (3d) at 438.

[81]   *Ibid.*

Article 6*bis* of the Paris Convention and Article 16(2) of the TRIPS Agreement.[82]

B Singapore

Singapore is another jurisdiction that has implemented the Paris Convention 6*bis*. Foreign traders of unregistered well-known trademarks, who have not established goodwill in Singapore, can seek redress provided under section 55(2) of the Singapore Trademarks Act.[83] This section of the Trademarks Act was specifically enacted in 1998 for the benefit of traders from a Paris Convention or WTO country whose trademark is well known in Singapore. Section 55 expressly provides that the protection is available whether or not the trader conducts business or otherwise has a presence in Singapore.[84] Section 55(2) permits the trademark proprietor to seek an injunction for the unauthorized use of a trademark that is *identical or similar*, as a whole or an essential part, to the well-known trademark, made in relation to *identical or similar goods or services*, compared to those goods and services on which the well-known trademark are applied, where such use is *likely to cause confusion*.[85] Under section 55(3) well-known marks are given the same protection under a dilution rationale even where likelihood of confusion is not involved.[86] A trademark is deemed to be well known in Singapore if it is well known to a relevant sector of the public in Singapore. The proprietor of the well-known trademark is entitled to restrain by injunction un-authorized use in the course of trade of an identical or similar trademark or business identifier.[87]

---

[82]   *See* Paris Convention, *supra* note 3, at 6*bis*; TRIPS Agreement, *supra* note 1, at 16(2).

[83]   Singapore Trademarks Act, as amended by Act No. 3 of 2007, § 55(2), *available at* http://statutes.agc.gov.sg/aol/browse/titleResults.w3p;letter=T;type=actsAll. For an overview *see* Burton Org, *Protecting Well-Known Trade Marks: Perspectives from Singapore*, 95 Trademark Rep. 1221, 1226 (2005).

[84]   *See Chapter 12: Intellectual Property Law*, SINGAPORE LAW, http://www.singaporelaw.sg/content/iplaw2.html (last visited Apr. 9, 2012).

[85]   Singapore Trademarks Act § 55(2), *available at* http://statutes.agc.gov.sg/aol/browse/titleResults.w3p;letter=T;type=actsAll.

[86]   *Ibid.* at § 55(3).

[87]   *See Chapter 12: Intellectual Property Law*, *supra* note 84.

The landmark case in Singapore applying the doctrine of well-known marks is *Novelty Pte Ltd. v. Amanresorts.*[88] In this case, the Singapore Court of Appeal decided that a very exclusive luxury resort in Bali, Amanresorts, could restrain Novelty's use of Amanusa on a condominium development.[89] They could do so in their action for passing off and infringement under the well-known marks doctrine of section 55(3) of the Trade Marks Act.[90] The court clarified the difference between well-known marks that are known to a segment of the population and those marks which have received a much greater recognition to the public at large.[91] The court declared that marks which were "well known in Singapore" – recognized or known by *any* relevant sector of the public in Singapore – should not be protected against the use of similar or identical marks on *dissimilar* goods or services where such use did not give rise to confusion.[92] The only exception to the requirement of confusion was for marks which were "well known to the public at large in Singapore."[93] Thus, if a proprietor could show that his mark was "well known to the public at large in Singapore" by having a higher level of recognition as compared with merely being recognized or known by any relevant sector of the public in Singapore, the mark would be entitled to protection against the use of similar or identical marks on dissimilar goods or services where there was no likelihood of confusion.[94]

C South Africa

The issue of well-known marks protection arose in South Africa in the aftermath of the divestment movement and the trade embargo imposed by the United States. McDonald's was one such company that honored the embargo. Even though McDonald's was a registered proprietor of 52 marks in South Africa, it had not used them there for several years.[95] In 1993, Joburgers applied for registration for a number of McDonald's trademarks and simultaneously brought an action for expungement of the

---

[88] *Novelty Pte Ltd. v. Amanresorts Ltd.* [2009] 3 SLR(R) 216.
[89] *Ibid.*
[90] *Ibid.*
[91] *Ibid.*
[92] *Ibid.*
[93] *Ibid.*
[94] *Ibid.*
[95] McDonald's Corp. v. Joburgers Drive-Inn Restaurant (Pty.) Ltd. 1997 (1) SA 1 (A) at 13 (S. Afr.) *available at* http:// www.saflii.org/za/cases/ZASCA/ 1996/82.pdf.

trademarks owned by McDonald's for non-use.[96] To comply with the TRIPS Agreement, South Africa passed a new trademark law recognizing the well-known marks doctrine that became effective in 1995.[97] McDonald's brought suit under the new trademark provisions. In *McDonald's Corp. v. Joburgers Drive-Inn Restaurant*,[98] the Appellate Division reversed the district court's judgment even though there was no actual use in South Africa. The Appellate Division held that "sec [*sic*] 35(1)[99] pertinently extends protection to the owner of a foreign mark 'whether or not such person carries on business, or has any goodwill, in the Republic.'"[100]

The court raised two issues to determine whether a mark is well known in the republic. First, "must the mark be well-known to all sectors of the population?"[101] Second, "whatever the relevant sector of the population may be, what degree of awareness within that sector is required before a mark can properly be described as well-known?"[102] The court collapsed these two issues into a general standard based on the law of "passing off,"[103] concluding that "a mark is well-known in the Republic if it is well-known to persons interested in the goods or services to which the mark relates."[104] The court noted that "the concept of a substantial number of persons is well established"[105] in South Africa and that the standard "provides a practical and flexible criterion which is consistent with the terms of the statute."[106]

The court found that McDonald's had met its burden in establishing the requisite fame for the marks because: (1) it had spent over $900

---

[96]   *Ibid.* at 5.
[97]   Trade Marks Act No. 194 of 1993.
[98]   *Joburgers*, 1997 (1) SA 1 (A) at 35 (S. Afr.).
[99]   Trade Marks Act No. 194 of 1993, § 35. Section 35 gives effect to the provisions of the Paris Convention and TRIPS, a trademark which is protected by the Paris Convention as a well-known mark will be protected as a well-known mark in South Africa when the owner is "(a) a person who is a national of a convention country; or (b) a person who is domiciled in, or has a real and effective industrial or commercial establishment in, a convention country, whether or not such person carries on business, or has any goodwill, in the Republic." Section 35 is quite similar to the British Trademark Act of 1994 § 56.
[100] *Joburgers*, 1997 (1) SA 1 (A) at 33(S. Afr.).
[101] *Ibid.* at 35
[102] *Ibid.*
[103] *Ibid.* at 38.
[104] *Ibid.* at 37.
[105] *Ibid.* at 40.
[106] *Ibid.*

million in advertising per year worldwide,[107] (2) it had received 242 requests from South Africans who wished to enter into franchise agreements,[108] and (3) by the end of 1993, there were 13 993 McDonald's restaurants in over 70 countries.[109]

The *Joburgers* case presents another example of the coherent manner in which foreign jurisdictions have implemented the requirements of the Paris Convention and TRIPS as opposed to the incoherent treatment given by the United States. This raises the pertinent question of whether the Lanham Act itself is sufficiently broad to encompass the well-known marks doctrine, or whether Congress should amend the Lanham Act to comply with its treaty obligations. In my opinion, the Lanham Act provides, within its terms, an adequate basis for protection, but because of the lack of consensus on this issue, an amendment to the Lanham Act would be a more appropriate and practical resolution of the problem. What these three jurisdictions have expressed is a common standard: a mark is well known if it is well known to a substantial sector of the public. But does the Lanham Act allow for such a reading within its terms? The answer is unclear and case law is conflicting, thus necessitating legislative action.

VII THE NEED FOR AN AMENDMENT TO THE LANHAM ACT

That the Lanham Act already provides for the protection of well-known marks is an idea that has waxed and waned in case law and has provoked a lively debate in the academic literature.[110] The argument that the

---

[107] *Ibid.* at 44.

[108] *Ibid.* at 46.

[109] *Ibid.* at 44.

[110] *See, e.g.*, Barker, *supra* note 28, at 373–77 (claiming that sections 44(b), 44(h), and 44(i), read together, incorporate Paris Convention protection for well-known foreign marks without referring to §43(a)); *but see* Tashia A. Bunch, *Well-Known Marks Doctrine: Where Do We Go from Here?*, 90 J. Pat. & Trademark Off. Soc'y 227, 237 (2008) (concluding that protection for well-known foreign marks "has no basis in [current] federal trademark law and courts should not apply the doctrine until Congress adds it to the [Lanham] Act"); Alexis Weissberger, *Is Fame Alone Sufficient to Create Priority Rights: An International Perspective on the Viability of the Famous/Well-Known Marks Doctrine*, 24 Cardozo Arts & Ent. L.J. 739, 767–68, 770, 778 (2006) (arguing that well-known foreign marks are not protected by federal law and recommending amendment of the Lanham Act).

Lanham Act incorporates 6*bis* is based on the interpretation of sections 44(a), 44(b), and 44(h). Embodying the national treatment principle, section 44(h) provides that persons whose origin is a convention country are to be given protection against unfair competition. Section 44(b) extends the benefits of section 44 to persons from treaty countries the right to invoke section 44 to obtain protection under the treaty. One court[111] summarized: "In this way subsections (b) (h) work together to provide federal rights and remedies implementing federal unfair competition treaties." Professor McCarthy contends:

> that [The] Lanham Act §43 (a) enables a foreign national without a federal registration of its mark standing to sue in a federal court, to invoke the well-known marks doctrine of the Paris Convention Article 6*bis*, and prevail if its mark is so well known in the U.S. that confusion is likely.[112]

Thus, these three provisions read in conjunction would appear to allow claimants the power to invoke provisions of the Paris Convention, such as 6*bis* of the Paris Convention.

I find this to be a plausible reading of section 44, but there is hardly unanimity on this issue, which has been debated for over half a century. Unfortunately, the courts are still split on whether section 44 creates substantive rights derived from the Paris Convention.[113] In this situation of disaccord, an amendment to the Lanham Act section 43(a) specifically incorporating Article 6*bis* is overdue. Such an amendment should provide that an owner of a mark that has become well known in a substantial segment of the population could enforce his rights against a third party who uses the mark to violate section 43(a)(1)(A). It should also specify that the owner of a well-known mark need not have used the mark in U.S. commerce and that it need not be known nationally throughout the United States. To determine whether a mark is well known to a

---

[111]   Toho Co., Ltd. v. Sears, Roebuck & Co., 645 F.2d 788, 792 (9th Cir. 1981).

[112]   Thomas J. McCarthy, *McCarthy on Trademarks and Unfair Competition* §29:4 (4th ed. 2012).

[113]   See Anne Gilson LaLonde, *Don't I Know You From Somewhere? Protection in the United States of Foreign Trademarks that Are Well Known but Not Used There* 98 TRADEMARK REP. 1379, 1395–96 (2008) (collecting cases and offering a critique that section 44 substantively incorporates the Paris Convention) "[T]he well-known marks protection in the TRIPS Agreement has not been implemented in the Lanham Act ... Locating in the Lanham Act a well-known marks exception to the U.S. use requirement takes a combination of fancy footwork and wishful thinking." *Ibid.* at 1395–96.

substantial segment of the population, the evidence should adopt the standard reflected in the World Intellectual Property Organization's *Joint Recommendation Concerning Provisions on the Protection of Well-Known Marks.*[114] An amendment would remedy the problem in a transparent fashion and would lay to rest the tortured debate on whether the Lanham Act incorporates substantive provisions of the Paris Convention.

VIII CONCLUSION

In an ideal world, an owner of a well-known mark should register his mark for all classes of goods and services worldwide. The practical reality is something else. To register one's mark in approximately 200 jurisdictions and over 40 classes of goods and services is an expensive proposition indeed. Moreover, to maintain multi-class registrations in countries that have use requirements, it may be necessary to launch a sales program of ancillary goods to keep the extended registration coverage in force. This can mean setting up uneconomic limited sales operations where full-scale operations are not yet in place, something marketing people justifiably abhor. It may involve the creation by the trademark owner of unwanted additional businesses or other investment in activities designed not to make a profit but to maintain trademark rights. Sometimes these exercises may not even work. This is why the 6*bis* safety valve is so important in today's commercial environment. Most countries have recognized the practical plight of owners of well-known marks, adhering to the letter of 6*bis* of Paris. It is unfortunate that the United States has not followed in their footsteps, and it is ironic that there are certainly more American companies than in any other country that have attained the status of a well-known mark. As a global leader in intellectual property, the United States has traditionally been a strong supporter for robust intellectual property rights. For the United States to deny protection for a foreign well-known mark – in direct conflict with its international treaty commitments – diminishes its bargaining position

---

[114] *See generally* WORLD INTELLECTUAL PROPERTY ORGANIZATION, PUB. NO. 833(E), JOINT RECOMMENDATION CONCERNING PROVISIONS ON THE PROTECTION OF WELL-KNOWN MARKS (1999), *available at* http://www.wipo.int/about-ip/en/development_iplaw/pub833-toc.htm#TopOfPage.

in this vital domain of world commerce.[115] The time is ripe for an amendment to the Lanham Act to fulfill the requirements of Paris and the TRIPS Agreement.

---

[115]   Andrew Cook, *Do As We Say, Not As We Do: A Study of the Well-Known Marks Doctrine in the United* States, 8 J. MARSHALL REV. INTELL. PROP. L. 412, 418–19 (2009).

3. Interactivity, territoriality, and well-known marks

Leah Chan Grinvald[*]

I INTRODUCTION

The majority of articles discussing the well-known marks doctrine typically begin with an overview of how the "global marketplace" has created a space where foreign trademarks easily cross boundaries.[1] These articles cite the advances in technology and travel that allow consumers from different nations to view products and their corresponding trademarks through television, the Internet, and while traveling in foreign countries.[2] Due to this, trademarks that are well known in their home nation can become more easily well known in foreign nations.[3] Therefore, the argument continues, the test for whether a foreign mark has become well known in other nations should be based on the extent to which those foreign consumers had the ability to visually perceive the foreign trademarks (while at home or on foreign travel).[4] I call this theory of well-known marks the "passive perception" theory because it bases consumer recognition of foreign marks on the ability of consumers to passively perceive foreign trademarks.

---

[*] © 2014 Leah Chan Grinvald, Associate Professor of Law, Suffolk University Law School. This chapter is an updated adaptation of my article, Leah Chan Grinvald, *A Tale of Two Theories of Well-Known Marks*, 13 VAND. J. ENT. & TECH. L. 1 (2010).

[1] *See, e.g.*, Frederick W. Mostert, *Is Goodwill Territorial or International?*, 12 EUR. INTELL. PROP. REV. 400, 440 (1989); Amir H. Khoury, *Well-Known and Famous Trademarks in Israel: TRIPS from Manhattan to the Dawn of a New Millennium!*, 12 FORDHAM INTELL. PROP. MEDIA & ENT. L.J. 991, 993 (2002).

[2] *See* Frederick W. Mostert, *Well-Known and Famous Marks: Is Harmony Possible in the Global Village?*, 86 TRADEMARK REP. 103, 103 (1996) [hereafter Mostert, *Harmony*].

[3] *See, e.g.*, Mostert, *supra* note 1, at 447.

[4] *See infra* Part IV.A.

37

While these advances in technology and travel are undisputed, the underlying assumptions of the passive perception theory are faulty. The assumptions of the passive perception theory are twofold: that a passive perception theory is consistent with the norms of international trademark law, and that consumers can come to recognize foreign marks simply through visual cues. I seek to disprove these assumptions and, in addition, propose my own theory of well-known marks, one that is based on interaction with foreign marks. As I will discuss below in Part II, the norms of international trademark law are clearly in favor of territoriality and registration. Although the well-known marks doctrine was born from an international recognition that strict adherence to the territoriality principle can produce inequitable results, the doctrine was intended as a limited exception only. Not only does the passive perception theory expand the exception beyond its intended boundaries, but as I argue in Part IV below, it may also incentivize certain multinational corporations to bypass the international registration system.

In addition, recent studies in cognitive psychology provide evidence that undermines the second assumption of the passive perception theory, as I demonstrate in Part III below.[5] More and more, consumers are being inundated with advertising, which has led to an antipathy among consumers to commercials.[6] In order to come to recognize a mark as such, studies have shown that consumers need to interact with the product and its corresponding mark. My interactional theory of well-known marks takes into account these developments, as well as the norms of the international trademark system, and, as I argue below, provides a better theory of well-known marks recognition.

II NORMS OF THE INTERNATIONAL TRADEMARK SYSTEM

The international trademark system fosters two norms of trademark law, that of registration and territoriality. Each principle will be discussed in turn.

---

[5]   *See* Kenneth Chang, *Enlisting Science's Lessons to Entice More Shoppers to Spend More*, N.Y. TIMES, Sept. 19, 2006, at F3; Frank R. Kardes et al., *Construal-Level Effects on Preference Stability, Preference-Behavior Correspondence, and the Suppression of Competing Brands*, 16 J. CONSUMER PSYCHOL. 135, 136 (2006).

[6]   *See* Rebecca Tushnet, *Gone in Sixty Milliseconds: Trademark Law and Cognitive Science*, 86 TEX. L. REV. 507, 512 (2007).

A Registration

There are two distinct avenues for providing for trademark rights. The first avenue developed in England (and later spread to English colonies, such as the United States), which granted trademark rights to the first user of a trademark in commerce. This "common law" approach to trademark rights attempted to mirror the reality of the nature of trademarks at the time, namely that trademarks were used to identify and purchase goods. The second avenue developed in civil law jurisdictions, where all trademark rights were granted by the state to the first person to file and perfect a registration application.[7]

Of the two, it can be seen that the registration system was the winner internationally, as it was adopted as the preferred method for trademark rights in the first international treaty to deal with trademark protection, the Paris Convention for the Protection of Industrial Property ("Paris Convention").[8] Although one could argue that the preference for registration shown in the Paris Convention stemmed from the dominance of first-to-file nations at the early conferences of the Paris Union, later developments in the international trademark system show a clear intention of establishing rights through registration.[9] This is shown through the efforts of the international community to harmonize and simplify registration efforts across jurisdictions through the Madrid Agreement and later in the Madrid Protocol, as well as in the Agreement on the Trade-Related Aspects of Intellectual Property ("TRIPS").[10] While the

---

[7] *See* INTELLECTUAL PROPERTY LAW GUIDEBOOK: CHINA 58 (2007).

[8] Paris Convention for the Protection of Industrial Property art. 4(C)(1), July 14, 1967, 21 U.S.T. 1583, 828 U.N.T.S. 305 [hereinafter Paris Convention].

[9] *See* Arthur P. Greeley, FOREIGN PATENT AND TRADEMARK LAWS § 140 (1899) (listing and discussing the various countries with registration-only systems); 1 Stephen P. Ladas, PATENTS, TRADEMARKS AND RELATED RIGHTS §§ 46, 47 (1975) (listing the various countries present at the conferences in 1878, 1880 and 1883).

[10] Subsequent to the Paris Convention, the Madrid Agreement was adopted in 1891 and the Madrid Protocol in 1989. *See* Madrid Agreement Concerning the International Registration of Marks art. 4, Apr. 14, 1891, as amended Sept. 28, 1979, 828 U.N.T.S. 389 [hereinafter Madrid Agreement], *available at* http://www.wipo.int/madrid/en/legal_texts/trtdocs_wo015.html. Together, the two agreements comprise the "Madrid System," which eases the requirements of international registration. *See* Eugenia Baroncelli et al., *The Global Distribution of Trademarks: Some Stylized Facts* 6 (World Bank Policy Research, Working Paper No. 3270, 2004), *available at* http://ssrn.com/abstract=610311. The Agreement on Trade-Related Aspects of Intellectual Property ("TRIPS") also favors

international trademark system accommodates first-to-use jurisdictions, it does not allow first-to-use jurisdictions to require that applications for registration be based on actual use.[11]

Additional support for the norm of international trademark registration can be found in the policies underlying the international treaties that provide for international registration. One of the main motivators for convening the Paris Union in the late nineteenth century was a concern that lack of international protection for trademarks (and other industrial property, such as patents) was inhibiting the free movement of goods across national boundaries.[12] A robust international registration system lowers the barriers to the transnational movement of goods and services because it provides greater certainty in trademark protection, which allows entities to reap the benefits of investing in their marks.[13] This then increases the incentives for these entities to expand their sales to other nations, providing a benefit to both the exporting nation (boosting the gross domestic product) and the importing nation (providing necessary or a desired variety of products to consumers).

B   Territoriality

Another hallmark of the international trademark system is territoriality.[14] This means that acquisition and vindication of rights in a trademark are at the national level, not at the international level. While international treaties have set minimum standards for member nations to meet when providing protection to trademarks, each nation has the right to set its own particular procedures and standards within the international framework. This has meant that different entities may own the same trademark in different jurisdictions, and the corresponding consumer recognition may differ from nation to nation. A trademark holder will need to ensure

---

registration. *See* Agreement on Trade-Related Aspects of Intellectual Property Rights art. 15(3), Apr. 15, 1994, 33 I.L.M. 1125 [hereinafter TRIPS].

[11]   *See* TRIPS, *supra* note 10, at art. 15(3).

[12]   The specific event that spurred the first convention of the Paris Union was the World's Fair hosted in Vienna in 1873. The international participation was disappointing and due in part to concerns over theft of industrial property, which was not universally protected in all countries at the time. *See* WORLD INTELL. PROP. ORG., WIPO INTELLECTUAL PROPERTY HANDBOOK: POLICY, LAW AND USE 241 (2nd ed. 2004).

[13]   *See* Leah Chan Grinvald, *A Tale of Two Theories of Well-Known Marks*, 13 VAND. J. ENT. & TECH. L. 1, 10–14 (2010).

[14]   *See generally* Graeme B. Dinwoodie, *Trademarks and Territory: Detaching Trademark Law from the Nation-State*, 41 HOUS. L. REV. 885 (2004).

that it acquires rights to trademarks in each nation that it wishes to do business, and, if its marks are infringed, seek vindication of its rights in the particular nation where the infringement is occurring. This norm of territoriality can be seen in the Paris Convention, which contains various provisions acknowledging the territoriality of trademarks and their protection.[15] In addition, TRIPS explicitly continues this norm of territoriality in Article 1, along with incorporating the specific provisions from the Paris Convention that also recognizes the territoriality of trademarks.

However, the international trademark system can produce inequities where the adherence to the norms of registration and territoriality are strict. For example, where an entity has used a trademark in a first-to-file jurisdiction but has not registered it, a third party can later register that same mark and acquire superior rights to the same mark.[16] This concern of unscrupulous entrepreneurism is heightened in today's global economy, where ease of international travel may mean products cross borders before their corresponding marks have been registered. An unscrupulous entrepreneur can take advantage and register the mark before the original mark holder does, acquiring superior rights in the mark. The entrepreneur can then either prevent the original mark holder from entering the market by selling the same products itself, or attempt to sell the mark back to the foreign mark holder.[17]

C Well-Known Marks: A Limited Exception to International Trademark Norms

The international community addressed this problem by creating a limited exception to the territoriality and registration norms with the well-known marks doctrine. In 1925, the Revision Conference in The Hague adopted Article 6*bis* to the Paris Convention, which provided for the first time a well-known marks exception to the international trademark system.[18] The current version of Article 6*bis*(1) provides:

> The countries of the Union undertake, ex officio if their legislation so permits, or at the request of an interested party, to refuse or to cancel the registration, and to prohibit the use, of a trademark which constitutes a reproduction, an

---

[15] *See* Paris Convention, *supra* note 8, at arts. 4, 6.

[16] *See* Stephen P. Ladas, *International Protection of Well-Known Trademarks*, 41 TRADEMARK REP. 661, 662 (1951).

[17] *See, e.g.*, Person's Co. v. Christman, 900 F.2d 1565 (Fed. Cir. 1990).

[18] *See* G.H.C. Bodenhausen, GUIDE TO THE APPLICATION OF THE PARIS CONVENTION FOR THE PROTECTION OF INDUSTRIAL PROPERTY 89 (1968).

imitation, or a translation, liable to create confusion, of a mark considered by the competent authority of the country of registration or use to be well known in that country as being already the mark of a person entitled to the benefits of this Convention and used for identical or similar goods.[19]

In 1994, the exception was broadened with Article 16(2) and (3) of TRIPS, which applies the well-known marks exception to both trademarks and service marks, as well as to goods or services that are not similar to the well-known mark.[20]

When applied correctly, the well-known marks doctrine promotes the same goal of free trade that registration fosters. In this manner, the well-known status of a mark does not provide a separate basis for protection of a trademark but acts as a safety valve. Allowing entrepreneurs to take advantage of the fame garnered by a foreign trademark in member nations where it has not been registered or used would disincentivize entities from expanding abroad. For example, if the South African courts had recognized a local entrepreneur's registration of MCDONALD'S, other foreign entities would likely not have attempted to enter the South African market.[21] In essence, the correct level of protection for well-known trademarks protects the "global trading system through the prevention of piracy and unfair exploitation of well-known marks"[22] without undermining the registration and territoriality norms of the system.

While there is some guidance that assists member nations in determining how to decide whether a foreign mark is well known in a particular jurisdiction, as I will argue below, much of the guidance promotes a "passive perception" theory of well-known marks. This theory has been persuasive at times, as it is promoted by influential

---

[19]   Paris Convention, *supra* note 8, at art. 6*bis*(1).

[20]   *See* TRIPS, *supra* note 10, at art. 16.

[21]   In the landmark South African well-known marks case McDonald's Corporation v. Joburgers Drive-Inn Restaurant (Pty.) Ltd., the Appellate Division of the South African Supreme Court found in favor of McDonald's. 1996 (4) SA 1 (SCA) (S. Afr.), *available at* http://www.saflii.org.za/za/cases/ZASCA/1996/82.pdf. This case was upheld on appeal to the South African Supreme Court. *See South Africa – Appeal Upholds McDonald's Trademarks*, LADAS & PARRY – INTELL. PROP. L. (July 1997) (on file with author). For example, The Gap began business in South Africa around the time that the South African courts decided the McDonald's decision in the 1990s. *See* A.M. Moolla Grp. Ltd. v. The Gap, Inc., 2005 (6) SA 568 (SCA) (S. Afr.) (discussing the timeframe for The Gap's entry into the South African market).

[22]   ITC Ltd. v. Punchgini, Inc., 482 F.3d 135, 165 (2d Cir. 2007).

organizations and practitioners, and, as I will argue in Part III, is also embedded in the requirements of TRIPS and in the guidance established by the World Intellectual Property Organization. Unfortunately, this theory is faulty on a number of grounds, and therefore I argue that an "interactional" theory of well-known marks should be adopted by all member nations. Before I discuss the two different theories and their applications, it is important to first address how a trademark acquires consumer recognition, as this is the core of what makes a foreign mark well known.

III TRADEMARKS AND CONSUMER RECOGNITION

Consumer recognition is the linchpin of what turns an ordinary word, sign, picture, or other object into a trademark.[23] A trademark is only considered as such if consumers recognize that the mark is intended to denote its product source, and, as such, consumers can rely on the trademark as a way to find the same product they previously enjoyed.[24] Over time, courts and legislatures have come to grant trademarks that have gained high levels of consumer recognition, or fame, heightened protection.[25] Due to their high levels of fame, judges (and later legislatures) believed that consumers would likely be more confused than otherwise. And since the likelihood of consumer confusion is the evil that trademark protection seeks to prevent, the correlation between the scope of trademark protection and the level of trademark fame has grown. A trademark holder whose trademark has a moderate level of consumer recognition may enjoin the use or registration of the same or a similar trademark within the same category of products. For example, the holder of "FAMILY CIRCLE," a trademark for a women's magazine, can enjoin third parties from using FAMILY CIRCLE with women's clothing or food (as featured in the magazine), but not for a discount store.[26] For those trademarks that have acquired a high level of fame, such as

---

[23] *See, e.g.*, James Burrough, Ltd. v. Sign of Beefeater, Inc., 540 F.2d 266, 274, 276 (7th Cir. 1976).

[24] William M. Landes and Richard A. Posner, *The Economics of Trademark Law*, 78 TRADEMARK REP. 267, 271 (1988).

[25] For example, the United States provides extra protection to "famous" trademarks. *See* Trademark Dilution Revision Act of 2006, Pub. L. No. 109-312, § 2, 120 Stat. 1730, 1730 (2006).

[26] *See* Family Circle, Inc. v. Family Circle Assocs., 332 F.2d 534, 540 (3d Cir. 1964).

"TIFFANY," its holders can enjoin third party uses of similar products (jewelry), but also unrelated product categories (automobiles).[27]

However, in order to be granted a wide scope of protection, the trademark holder is required to prove that its trademark has achieved such high levels of consumer recognition.[28] One of the problems with proving consumer recognition is that direct evidence (typically consumer surveys) is resource-intensive and, depending on how the evidence is structured or gathered, not necessarily considered reliable or probative.[29] Therefore, in lieu of survey evidence, courts and administrative agencies in many jurisdictions rely on proxies to test for consumer recognition, such as the length of time the trademark has been used, the geographical use of such trademark, as well as sales and advertising.[30] The assumption is that the longer the mark has been in use, the wider the geographical territory it has been used in, and with a progression of sales over the years, along with large amounts of money spent on advertising, the higher the level of consumer recognition it will have.

These assumptions were valid at the turn of the century when a shift in advertising from merely conveying product information to commercials that advertised a "lifestyle" was quite successful in increasing sales. An example of this success is cigarette advertising, where in the late nineteenth century cigarette ads focused on the "taste, smell, and price."[31] By 1915, these same ads focused more on the consumer's "desire for

---

[27]   *See* Tiffany & Co. v. Classic Motor Carriages, Inc., 10 U.S.P.Q.2d (BNA) 1835, 1842 (T.T.A.B. 1989).

[28]   *See* Champions Golf Club, Inc. v. Champions Golf Club, Inc., 78 F.3d 1111, 1117 (6th Cir. 1996). "Trademark strength" refers to consumer recognition. *See* James Burrough, Ltd. v. Sign of Beefeater, Inc., 540 F.2d 266, 276 (7th Cir. 1976); *see also* J. Thomas McCarthy, MᴄCᴀʀᴛʜʏ ᴏɴ Tʀᴀᴅᴇᴍᴀʀᴋs ᴀɴᴅ Uɴꜰᴀɪʀ Cᴏᴍᴘᴇᴛɪᴛɪᴏɴ § 11:73 (4th ed. 2010).

[29]   *See* Graeme W. Austin, *Trademarks and the Unburdened Imagination*, 69 Bʀᴏᴏᴋ. L. Rᴇᴠ. 827, 831–32 (2003–2004); *see also* Coach Leatherware Co. v. AnnTaylor, Inc., 933 F.2d 162, 169 (2d Cir. 1991).

[30]   For example, in the United States, six factors have generally been considered: "(1) advertising expenditures, (2) consumer studies linking the mark to a source, (3) unsolicited media coverage of the product, (4) sales success, (5) attempts to plagiarize the mark, and, (6) length and exclusivity of the mark's use." Genesee Brewing Co. v. Stroh Brewing Co., 124 F.3d 137, 143 n. 4 (2d Cir. 1997) (quoting Centaur Commc'ns v. A/S/M Commc'ns, 830 F.2d 1217, 1222 (2d Cir. 1987)).

[31]   *See* Robert G. Bone, *Hunting Goodwill: A History of the Concept of Goodwill in Trademark Law*, 86 B.U. L. Rᴇᴠ. 547, 581 (2006).

romance, adventure, and sophistication."[32] Modern trademark law's construction of consumer recognition is based on these assumptions that visual stimuli lead to an automatic increase in sales, and therefore, an increase in consumer recognition.[33]

Recent advances in media and technology have called into question the soundness of these assumptions. Unlike the early twentieth century, advances in media have created a twenty-first-century society where advertisements and other visual stimuli advancing the sales of consumer products and services are ubiquitous. These days, consumers are presented with ads everywhere they look, from billboards to television, public bathrooms, and even while checking their email, Facebook, or playing games on their smartphones. As one scholar has so aptly stated, "With all that clutter, it's hard to catch a consumer's attention."[34] Scientific studies support the observable phenomenon that consumers are not paying attention to visual promotions of products: studies using magnetic resonance imaging to measure the amount of brain activity during commercial viewings have shown that "a third to a half of commercials do not generate any brain reaction at all."[35] This supports the argument that the continued reliance on visual stimuli in proving consumer recognition is faulty: the length of time a mark has been in use, the mark's geographical territory, or even the amount spent on advertising does not necessarily correlate to levels of consumer recognition.[36]

In fact, evidence from the consumer psychology field shows that reliance on product sales and other forms of evidence that can show consumers are provided with contextual details of products would better correlate to levels of consumer recognition. Studies in this field demonstrate that the physical presence of a product increases cognitive response more intensely, versus simply viewing the product visually.[37] The purchase of the product may not be necessary; rather, it may be enough that the product is used by a person in order to increase cognitive responses.[38] The use of a product means the consumer has initiated a direct experience, which leads to the increased cognitive response. I would argue that trademark holders are already cognizant of this evolution in the manner of gaining consumer recognition: think of all the "sampling" that is done

---

[32] *Ibid.*
[33] *See* Austin, *supra* note 29, at 829.
[34] Tushnet, *supra* note 6, at 512.
[35] Chang, *supra* note 5.
[36] *See* Tushnet, *supra* note 6, at 547.
[37] *See* Kardes et al., *supra* note 5, at 136.
[38] *Ibid.*

at grocery stores, or "free samples" of products that are given away at fairs or festivals. Trademark holders are attempting to initiate a physical experience between their products and consumers in the hopes of raising consumer recognition and, by extension, increasing their sales. Unfortunately, the law has not yet kept up with modern marketing and still relies upon, to a large extent, evidence of visual stimuli to prove levels of consumer recognition. Where foreign well-known marks are concerned, this heavy reliance on visual stimuli is inappropriate.[39] Although the level of consumer recognition to qualify a foreign trademark as "well known" is not well established in any jurisdiction, I argue in the next part that various international materials have an embedded bias toward visual stimuli, which has supported a "passive perception" theory of consumer recognition.

IV   DIFFERING THEORIES: PASSIVE PERCEPTION AND INTERACTIVITY

The addition of Article *6bis* to the Paris Convention in 1925 left a number of open issues, many of them focused on how foreign marks could become well known without registration or use in other jurisdictions.[40] In the run up to the 1958 Revision Conference of Lisbon ("Lisbon Conference"), influential commentators began to publicly stress a perspective that I have termed a "passive perception" theory of how a foreign mark becomes well known to consumers in a jurisdiction where the mark has been neither used nor registered.[41] Although this perspective was not initially adopted at the Lisbon Conference,[42] as will be discussed below, this view was adopted by later international documents.[43] However, this perspective is not necessarily the normatively appropriate one to apply to the well-known marks doctrine, nor is it the one that accurately reflects the acquisition of consumer recognition. Instead, I propose an adoption of a different theory, one that I term an "interactional" theory of well-known marks. After outlining the passive perception theory and its shortcomings in section A below, I will turn to a

---

[39]   I would further apply this argument to questions of secondary meaning, but this issue is outside the scope of this chapter.

[40]   *See* Bodenhausen, *supra* note 18, at 91.

[41]   *See, e.g.*, Stephen P. Ladas, *International Protection of Well-Known Marks*, 41 TRADEMARK REP. 661 (1951).

[42]   *See* Bodenhausen, *supra* note 18, at 91.

[43]   *See infra* Part II.A.1.

discussion of my proposed interactional theory in section B, which I argue is a more normatively appropriate approach to the well-known marks doctrine.

A Passive Perception Theory

1 Overview of the theory

Although commentators and trademark holders who advocate for greater protection of foreign well-known marks have not explicitly endorsed the passive perception theory, I believe the theory effectively encapsulates these advocates' beliefs. These commentators and trademark holders begin from the premise that globalization and technology have created an interconnected world of brands and consumers.[44] As early as 1951, influential commentators stressed this point; "commercial radio broadcasting featuring new marks transcend boundaries ... large magazines and periodical publications circulate internationally and ... air transportation bring people quickly from country to country and enable them to look at publications of many countries."[45] Based on this premise, these commentators and trademark holders believe that once a mark has obtained a sufficient level of consumer recognition in one part of the world, such recognition is likely the same in other parts of the world as well.[46] All that is needed for the flow of consumer recognition is for these other jurisdictions to have had the opportunity to be exposed to the advertising of these well-known (in their home jurisdiction) marks.

The effort to adopt this theory at the international level was not at first successful, with the 1958 Revision Conference of Lisbon of the Paris Convention ending without an adoption of an amendment that would have incorporated this theory into Article 6*bis*.[47] Later efforts, however, were more successful, and this theory can be found embedded in Article 16 of TRIPS and in the Joint Recommendation Concerning Provisions on the Protection of Well-Known Marks ("Joint Recommendation") issued by WIPO.[48] Article 16(2) of TRIPS states: "In determining whether a

---

[44] *See* Mostert, *Harmony, supra* note 2, at 103 n. 102.
[45] Ladas, *supra* note 41, at 662.
[46] *See supra* notes 1–3.
[47] *See* Bodenhausen, *supra* note 18, at 91.
[48] ASSEMBLY OF THE PARIS UNION FOR THE PROT. OF INDUS. PROP. & GEN. ASSEMBLY OF THE WORLD INTELL. PROP. ORG., WIPO JOINT RECOMMENDATION CONCERNING PROVISIONS ON THE PROTECTION OF WELL-KNOWN MARKS (Sept. 20–29, 1999), *available at* http://www.wipo.int/about-ip/en/development_iplaw/pdf/pub833.pdf [hereinafter WIPO JOINT RECOMMENDATION].

trademark is well[ ]known, Members shall take account of the knowledge of the trademark in the relevant sector of the public, including knowledge in the Member concerned which has been obtained as a result of the *promotion* of the trademark."[49] In specifying that knowledge obtained through "promotion" of a foreign trademark, TRIPS is in effect encouraging member nations to allow advertising to be the evidentiary proof for foreign well-known marks. One influential commentator has interpreted this language as follows:

> Article 16(2) of the TRIPS Agreement goes on to facilitate the proof of well-known status through *advertising*. ... In other words, awareness of the mark may be gauged against the relevant universe of people in the marketplace who are exposed to the mark through advertising. Proof of well-known status through advertising is particularly important in those instances where the mark has not yet been used in the local jurisdiction.[50]

In addition, Article 16(2) does not require that promotion of the foreign trademark occur *within* the member nation, but simply allows for knowledge in the member nation to arise through the promotional efforts. This knowledge may occur as a result of promotions inside *or outside* the member nation.[51] Commentators and trademark holders have seized upon this ambiguity to argue that the potential for knowledge to arise through "spillover advertising" – advertising outside the relevant member nation that filters in through satellite television, the Internet, or periodicals – supports a finding of sufficient consumer recognition for well-known status determinations.[52]

The Joint Recommendation provides additional support for the passive perception theory. WIPO, the international entity responsible for oversight of the Paris Convention, issued the Joint Recommendation in 1999, which lists six factors member nations should consider when deciding whether a mark is well known:

> (1) the degree of knowledge or recognition of the mark in the relevant sector of the public; (2) the duration, extent and geographical area of any use of the mark; (3) the duration, extent and geographical area of any promotion of the mark, including advertising or publicity and the presentation, at fairs or

---

[49]   TRIPS, *supra* note 10, at art. 16(2) (emphasis added).
[50]   Frederick W. Mostert, FAMOUS AND WELL-KNOWN MARKS 1–40 (Frederick W. Mostert ed., 2nd ed. 2004).
[51]   *See* Daniel Gervais, THE TRIPS AGREEMENT: DRAFTING HISTORY AND ANALYSIS 277 (3rd ed. 2008).
[52]   *See* Mostert, *supra* note 50, at 1–41.

exhibitions, of the goods and/or services to which the mark applies; (4) the duration and geographical area of any registrations, and/or any applications for registration, of the mark, to the extent that they reflect use or recognition of the mark; (5) the record of successful enforcement of rights in the mark, in particular, the extent to which the mark was recognized as well known by competent authorities; (6) the value associated with the mark.[53]

All the factors, with the exception of the first, provide support for the passive perception theory.[54] The second through sixth factors all direct member nations to focus on visual evidence that may not even relate to the member nation's own consumers.[55] For example, the second factor, "the duration, extent and geographical area of any use of the mark," when read in conjunction with one of the Joint Recommendation "prohibitions" in Article 2(3)(i), directs a nation to take into account the "use" conducted outside the nation.[56] Although the Joint Recommendation does not define "use," the term has traditionally meant sales or advertising or a combination of the two.[57] However, the foreign trademark holder is not required to show that these consumers were ever exposed to such use

---

[53] WIPO JOINT RECOMMENDATION, *supra* note 48, at art. 2(1)(b)(1)–(6).

[54] The first factor examines the actual consumer recognition in the member nation; however, as discussed earlier, this type of evidence is often not obtained by litigants, and most litigants base their cases on circumstantial evidence, like the items the remaining factors suggest. *See supra* note 30.

[55] For example, the only way the fifth factor, "successful enforcement of rights in the mark," could have any bearing on whether consumers recognize the foreign mark is if the mark holder publicized the enforcement actions. Most large corporations do in fact publicize successful enforcement actions through press releases and other media; however, this is "promotional" activity. As with advertising, if the press release does not issue inside the member nation, the competent authority there would need to assume that such a press release had "spilled over" into the member nation, creating the requisite consumer recognition. *See, e.g.*, Charles E. Webster, *The McDonald's Case: South Africa Joins the Global Village*, 86 TRADEMARK REP. 576, 588 (1996).

[56] This prohibition states:

Member State shall not require, as a condition for determining whether a mark is a well-known trademark: that the mark has been used in, or that the mark has been registered or that an application for registration of the mark has been filed in or in respect of, the Member State.

See WIPO JOINT RECOMMENDATION, *supra* note 48, at art. 2(3)(i).

[57] *See* New Eng. Duplicating Co. v. Mendes, 190 F.2d 415, 417–18 (1st Cir. 1951).

outside the member nation. Rather, historical global uses of a trademark may be sufficient to prove that a trademark has become well known.[58]

2 Problems with the passive perception theory

One of the main problems with the passive perception theory is that it sets a low evidentiary burden for meeting the elements of Article 6*bis*. An illustration of how the passive perception argument works in practice may be helpful, and an example from the advocacy efforts of the International Trademark Association ("INTA"), the self-described world's largest trademark organization, is useful. INTA commonly cites the "FERRARI" trademark as an example of how courts should implement the low evidentiary burden of the passive perception theory.[59] INTA's argument is as follows: as a result of FERRARI's international well-known status, consumers in any country – even where FERRARI cars are not sold and the trademark is not registered – have come to recognize the FERRARI trademark through global advertisements and promotion of FERRARI.[60] These global advertisements and promotions need not be directed at the member nation where a well-known trademark holder seeks protection; that advertisements or promotions likely "spilled over" into that nation suffice.[61] Proof that consumers in the member nation have access (but not necessarily proof that the consumers in fact viewed them) to certain magazines where FERRARI advertises, or to satellite television broadcasting the Ferrari-sponsored Formula One race series, would also suffice.[62]

Trademark holders also advance this theory; in fact, Ferrari itself seemingly used this theory in its litigation against a Chinese department

---

[58]   *See, e.g.*, Brief for Int'l Trademark Ass'n as Amici Curiae Supporting Appellants, Prefel SA v. Fahmi Babra (Sup. Ct. Oct. 2, 2002) (Indon.) [hereinafter Brief for INTA in Prefel] (on file with author).

[59]   *See* Brief for Int'l Trademark Ass'n as Amicus Curiae Supporting Appellants at 12, Tungsway Food & Beverage Holdings, Pte., Ltd. v. PT Istana Pualam Kristal (Sup. Ct. Aug. 15, 2005) (Indon.) (on file with author); Brief for Int'l Trademark Ass'n as Amici Curiae Supporting Appellants at 5, Davidoff & Cie S.A. v. N.V. Sumatra Tobacco Trading Co. (Sup. Ct. Apr. 11, 2003) (Indon.) (on file with author); Brief for Int'l Trademark Ass'n as Amici Curiae Supporting Appellants at 6, Intel v. PT Panggung Elec. Inds. (Sup. Ct. Oct. 2, 2002) (Indon.) [hereinafter Brief for INTA in Intel] (on file with author); Brief for INTA in Prefel, *supra* note 58.

[60]   *See* Brief for INTA in Intel, *supra* note 58, at 6.

[61]   *See* Mostert, *Harmony, supra* note 2, at 118.

[62]   *See* Brief for INTA in Prefel, *supra* note 58, at 7–8.

store that had registered Ferrari's "Prancing Horse design" for use on apparel.[63] Ferrari argued that its Prancing Horse design was a well-known mark in China and, even though it had not been registered in China, should be granted protection. To support its argument, Ferrari brought evidence that was primarily visual in nature, such as catalogs, advertisements, and worldwide registrations of its Prancing Horse design. Ferrari did not use any evidence of how Chinese consumers interacted with the Prancing Horse design – for example, through use of its cars (Ferrari sold its first car in China in 1993) in China or abroad.[64] If the court in the *Ferrari* case were to have found for Ferrari based on such evidence, the finding would have been one that did not reflect the Chinese consumer's perception of the Prancing Horse design and would have put an end to the Chinese department store's clothing line featuring the Prancing Horse design. Perhaps surprising to Western observers (viewing this case through the lens of a passive perception theory), the Chinese courts hearing the case all found in favor of the Chinese department store.[65]

Unfortunately, this low threshold for protection of the passive perception theory causes foreign mark holders (like Ferrari) to expect protection where their marks are well known outside the jurisdiction in which they are seeking protection. This expectation of protection raises another serious issue with the passive perception theory: a possible disincentivization of international registration, which has been one of the pillars of the international trademark system that fosters an atmosphere conducive to free trade. Financial burdens already disincentivize registration; the process can cost upwards of $30 000 for one trademark application filed through the Madrid System.[66] Large business entities typically use multiple trademarks at once, which may mean multiple payments of $30 000.[67] In addition to the registration costs, the introduction of a new

---

[63]   Ferrari v. Jiajian, (Beijing 1st Intermediate People's Ct.), as reported in Guo Jing-Xia, *Ferrari's Trademark – "Prancing Horse" Is Not Constituted as a Well-Known Trademark*, July 7, 2007 [hereinafter Jing-Xia] (translation on file with author).

[64]   *Ibid.*

[65]   *See* Jing "Brad" Luo and Shubha Ghosh, *Protection and Enforcement of Well-Known Mark Rights in China: History, Theory and Future*, 7 Nw. J. Tech. & Intell. Prop. 119, 147–48 (2009).

[66]   *See International Application Simulator*, World Intell. Prop. Org., http://www.wipo.int/madrid/en/madrid_simulator/ (last visited Dec. 26, 2012).

[67]   *See generally* Baroncelli et al., *supra* note 10.

trademark requires substantial resources.[68] A business entity may spend upwards of $40 000 in the first year to launch a new trademark.[69]

By providing a broad exception, the passive perception theory creates a viable alternative to registration, because promotion in these member nations is simpler and cheaper than registration. Although companies may incur long-term expenses litigating well-known marks cases in different member nations, various incentives exist to delay this expense, such as the correlation to return on investment. If an entity waits to acquire trademark rights in a member nation based on its well-known trademark status, it knows that the litigation expenses correlate to the potential return from product sales in that market. This correlation does not exist where product sales are uncertain. From this perspective, rather than acting as a safety valve to the strictures of territoriality, this grant of broad rights threatens to become a new basis for investing trademark rights to holders of well-known marks and is therefore an inappropriate manner in determining whether a foreign mark is well known.

B   Interactional Theory

1   Overview of the interactional theory

In contrast, the interactional theory depends on consumer recognition within the member nation and sets a higher threshold for foreign well-known mark protection. Of course, the interactional theory does not completely ignore the well-known status a foreign mark has achieved outside the member nation when it washes ashore through spillover advertising. Rather, evidence of such consumer exposure is unlikely to be found effective if the foreign litigant has no additional evidence that the advertising actually reached consumers. The interactional theory of well-known marks attempts to walk the fine line between territoriality and the reality that trademarks can and do transcend borders and cultures. The theory does this by requiring a showing of some type of consumer "interaction" with the foreign trademark, such as purchases, inquiries, or website activity. This evidence of local consumer interaction ties the foreign well-known mark to the consumers of the particular jurisdiction in which protection is sought. While there are no trademark holders advocating for the interactional theory, I argue that a number of cases from different jurisdictions, including the United States and China,

---

[68]   *See* Russell L. Parr, *The Value of Trademarks, in* Am. Law Inst. – Am. Bar Ass'n, *Trademarks, Copyrights, and Unfair Competition for the General Practitioner,* C913 A.L.I.-A.B.A. 229, 246 (1994).
[69]   *Ibid.*

appear to utilize interactional-like theories of well-known marks, or at the very least, they can be explained through the lens of the interactional theory.

In the U.S., several decisions regarding foreign well-known marks in the last decade have indicated that courts demand exposure and consumer interaction with the foreign trademark before deeming it well known.[70] In one of the more recent federal appellate cases discussing the well-known marks doctrine, *ITC Limited v. Punchgini, Inc.*,[71] the Second Circuit appears at first glance to simply decide that the doctrine was never incorporated into American trademark law. The foreign plaintiffs were owners of an international restaurant based in Delhi, India, named "BUKHARA." The U.S. defendants were former employees of the plaintiff (who at one point operated two Bukhara restaurants in the U.S.[72]) and who had opened a restaurant in New York City named "BUKHARA GRILL." Although the Second Circuit rejected the foreign plaintiffs' argument of an incorporated federal well-known marks doctrine, the court did analyze its substantive well-known marks claim under New York state law.[73] In its analysis, the Second Circuit arguably looked for interaction between New York City consumers and the original BUKHARA restaurant. Although the foreign plaintiffs had provided evidence of various BUKHARA outlets in Ajman, Bangkok, Hong Kong, Kathmandu, Montreal, and Singapore, as well as global advertising from a variety of international sources, this evidence was not connected to

---

[70] Due to space limitations, I can only discuss one recent case from the U.S. and China. For additional cases and discussions, please see Grinvald, *supra* note 13, at 28–34.

[71] ITC Ltd. v. Punchgini, Inc., 482 F.3d 135 (2d Cir. 2007).

[72] The foreign plaintiff needed to rely on the well-known marks doctrine in order to gain protection in the U.S. because the court ruled that it had abandoned any prior U.S. rights in its mark. *See* ITC Ltd. v. Punchgini, Inc., 373 F. Supp. 2d 275, 276–78 (S.D.N.Y. 2005), *aff'd*, 518 F.3d 159 (2d. Cir. 2008).

[73] ITC Ltd. v. Punchgini, Inc., 518 F.3d 159 (2d Cir. 2008). The Second Circuit previously held that the foreign plaintiffs were not entitled to well-known trademark protection. *See* ITC Ltd. v. Punchgini, Inc., 482 F.3d 135, 164–65 (2d Cir. 2007). This previous decision was based on the Second Circuit's finding that the well-known marks doctrine was not incorporated into federal law. *Ibid.* at 163–65. However, the Second Circuit certified to the New York Court of Appeals the question of whether New York state law recognized the well-known marks doctrine. *See ibid.* at 166. After the New York Court of Appeals answered the certified questions, the Second Circuit examined the merits of the foreign plaintiff's well-known marks argument and again held for the defendants. *See* ITC Ltd., 518 F.3d at 163–64.

New York consumers.[74] In addition, while the plaintiffs provided 14 comment cards written by various dignitaries and executives, including Bill Gates and President Clinton, to show that a large number of high-powered and influential Americans had knowledge of BUKHARA, none of the 14 were actually New Yorkers.[75] The Second Circuit carefully sifted through all of this evidence proffered by the foreign plaintiffs and concluded that it could not find any connection between the plaintiffs' BUKHARA and New Yorkers.[76]

China, too, has seemingly applied an interactional theory of well-known marks to cases involving foreign well-known trademarks. In the *Ferrari* case discussed above in Part III, I noted that Ferrari apparently relied on a passive perception theory of well-known marks, submitting evidence that was visual in nature: registration certificates, catalogs, etc. However, the Beijing First Intermediate People's Court held in favor of the defendant, seemingly based on an interactional theory. Similar to the holders of BUKHARA, Ferrari failed to demonstrate the grounds upon which Chinese consumers would recognize the Prancing Horse design as that of Ferrari.[77] While Ferrari could have brought evidence of Chinese consumers attending car shows (either in China or abroad) or visiting Ferrari dealerships (either in China or abroad), they did not, and therefore, the likelihood of proving that Chinese consumers recognized the Prancing Horse design – divorced from FERRARI – was slim.

2   Benefits of an interactional theory

Under the interactional theory, foreign well-known trademark holders bear an extremely heavy burden to acquire protection. In this manner, the interactional theory limits the well-known marks obligation to its intended purpose: a safety valve to an overly rigorous application of territoriality. This serves to make it more costly for an entity to rely on the doctrine as an alternative method of protection in foreign juris-dictions. To succeed in a well-known marks argument in litigation, the foreign mark holder would need to collect information on various consumer activities that arise within jurisdictions it has not yet targeted. Although technological advances, such as a system that automatically captures Internet protocol addresses and their country of origin or social

---

74   ITC Ltd., 373 F. Supp. 2d at 277.
75   *Ibid.* at 289.
76   *Ibid.* President Clinton did not move to New York until after his presidency term ended in 2000. *See* Adam Nagourney, *With Some Help, Clintons Purchase a White House*, N.Y. TIMES, Sept. 3, 1999, at A1.
77   *See* Jing-Xia, *supra* note 63; Luo and Ghosh, *supra* note 65, at 142–43.

media accounts, can make this less burdensome, the initial investment in this type of information-collecting system may prove more expensive than multinational registration. In a cost comparison, registration may be the cheaper option, especially where expansion into particular regions is likely. This would incentivize participation in the multinational registration system.

In addition, while the cognitive psychology research discussed in Part II does not necessarily invalidate the passive perception theory, the results should raise doubts about relying on a theory that bases the creation of consumer recognition on the potential for visual exposure to advertising.[78] While some consumer recognition through visual exposure may be possible, the threshold level of consumer recognition necessary for an application of the well-known marks doctrine is less likely. This is especially true where spillover advertising is the only way in which consumers would see the foreign trademark. In addition, these studies suggest that any memory of a mark, and hence its source, created through advertising alone may not withstand the assault created by the physical presence of a competing product at the point of sale.[79] This significantly weakens the argument that visual exposure to a foreign trademark can alone cause consumers to be confused at the point of sale by a similar mark for a similar product. On the contrary, these studies provide some validation of the interactional theory. The more sensory-related experience a consumer has with a trademarked product, the more likely the consumer will recall, and even prefer, that brand in the future. This lends support to the heavy burden that the interactional theory of well-known marks places on foreign trademark holders.

V CONCLUSION

The well-known marks doctrine should be available as a safety valve for those foreign trademarks that have become well known in foreign jurisdictions but without registration or use there. To achieve this, I posit that an interactional theory, rather than the passive perception theory, is the more appropriate justification on which to base a foreign well-known mark determination. Empirical evidence shows that consumers best acquire recognition through conscious activity and therefore suggests that the passive perception theory is a flawed metric for measuring a foreign

---

[78] *See* Kardes et al., *supra* note 5, at 141–42.
[79] *Ibid.* at 136.

mark's well-known status among local consumers. In addition, a narrower application of the well-known marks doctrine under an interactional theory supports the proactive international policy goal of an effective multinational registration system. By requiring both effective exposure and conscious consumer activity before finding a trademark well known, judicial and administrative agencies will apply the doctrine only where truly warranted.

4. The Pan-American Trademark Convention of 1929: a bold vision of extraterritorial meets current realities

Christine Haight Farley[*]

I INTRODUCTION

In 1990, the Federal Circuit reaffirmed the principle of territoriality, a central tenet of U.S. and international trademark law. That principle holds that trademark rights are bound by national borders. This non-controversial principle led to a harsh result for a sympathetic plaintiff in *Person's Co. v. Christman*.[1]

Larry Christman, a U.S. citizen and an employee of a sportswear wholesaler, took a business trip to Japan. While there, he visited a Person's Co. clothing store. Christman purchased several items of clothing bearing the Person's logo. When he returned home, he developed a clothing line based on the products he purchased from Person's Co. Many items were copied wholesale. The resulting clothing items were marked with the Person's logo bearing the same globe design used by the Person's Co. Christman obtained a registration for the Person's mark in the U.S. a few years later.

During that same period, the Japanese Person's mark had become a well-known mark in Japan. Additionally, Person's Co. was in the process of expanding its business to the U.S., apparently unbeknownst to Christman. Significantly, Christman's goods made it to market seven

---

[*] Professor, American University Washington College of Law. I wish to dedicate this chapter to the memory of Debra Evenson, one of the few U.S. trademark attorneys who was an expert on the Inter-American Convention. I am indebted to American University law students Kavita DeVaney and Ellie Atkins for their superb research assistance. I am also grateful for the helpful comments received at scholarly colloquia at Arizona State University, Marquette Law School and American University.

[1] 900 F.2d 1565 (Fed. Cir. 1990).

months before the Japanese goods, and Christman preceded the Person's Co. to the trademark office. Nevertheless, Person's Co. sought to cancel Christman's Person's mark based on its prior foreign use, and due to the registrant's bad faith.

The Federal Circuit refused to cancel Christman's mark, finding that the Person's Co. use of the mark in Japan did not establish its priority.[2] Citing the principle of territoriality, the court held that neither foreign trademark registration nor use can form the basis for U.S. priority. Additionally, the court held that the territoriality of trademark law also negated Person's Co.'s argument of bad faith since Christman is the senior user in the U.S. and the senior user cannot be charged with bad faith. The court stated that "[k]nowledge of a foreign use does not preclude good faith adoption and use in the United States."[3]

While the result may seem severe for Person's Co., it is founded on settled trademark principles. The concept of territoriality – that trademark rights exist country by country according to the laws of that country – is fundamental in trademark law.

But even fundamental principles sometimes have exceptions. And when they do, they often involve interesting rationales and pose significant tensions.

The primary purpose of this chapter is to reveal an intriguing and important exception to the principle of territoriality in U.S. trademark law. That exception can be found in the little-known 1929 General Inter-American Convention for Trade Mark and Commercial Protection ("Pan-American Convention").

The curious fact that the convention is unfamiliar to most U.S. trademark practitioners and scholars should first be noted. Since there are very few substantive trademark treaties in existence, this one is certainly not getting lost in the crowd. Moreover, this convention has neither been superseded nor denounced. It remains valid and in force today in the United States and in all of the original contracting countries.[4] Furthermore, this convention is self-executing. This means that the convention's substantive provisions can be given legal effect in U.S. courts. But what makes it most remarkable that the Pan-American Convention is unfamiliar, is that this convention provides some fairly radical trademark rights, especially its exceptions to territoriality.

---

2   *Ibid.*
3   *Ibid.* at 1570.
4   U.S. Dep't of State, Treaties in Force (2013).

II HISTORY OF THE INTER-AMERICAN CONVENTION

The historical context of the treaty helps explain some of its unusual features. The first major trademark treaty was, of course, the Paris Convention. The Paris Convention is a multilateral treaty that sets out substantive minimum rights of protection for trademarks and other industrial property. On the heels of the ratification of the Paris Convention of 1883[5] – a mere six years later – international negotiations began for a regional trademark agreement for the Americas. These negotiations were not swift. Between 1889 and 1930, six international meetings were convened and five separate conventions were adopted with an aim toward this objective.[6] These efforts were undertaken by the governments of the American countries toward the larger goal of creating a customs union in the Americas. The culmination of these meetings was the final adoption of the Pan-American Convention, which occurred on February 20, 1929, at Washington, D.C.

The Pan-American Convention was initially negotiated in the shadow of the Paris Convention. Since the large majority of Latin American states were not members of the Paris Union,[7] the primary objectives were to provide national treatment within the new union and to create a uniform system for the protection of foreign trademarks.

---

[5] Paris Convention for the Protection of Industrial Property, Mar. 20, 1883, last revised at Stockholm July 14, 1967, 21 U.S.T. 1583, 828 U.N.T.S. 305.

[6] The first *Pan*-American conference was held in 1889 in Washington, D.C.

[7] Only Brazil, Cuba and Mexico became members of the Paris Union by 1929. Brazil ratified the Paris Convention in 1883, Mexico ratified in 1903, and Cuba ratified in 1904. The U.S. ratified the Paris Convention in 1887. A few other Latin American states ratified the Paris Convention only to denounce the treaty shortly thereafter. For instance, the Dominican Republic ratified in 1884, but denounced in 1888. Likewise, Guatemala ratified in 1883, but denounced in 1894. Ecuador denounced in 1885. During the 1929 Pan-American conference it was stated that Brazil and Cuba intended to withdraw from the Paris Convention. PAN-AMERICAN TRADEMARK CONFERENCE, MINUTES OF THE PLENARY SESSIONS AND OF THE COMMITTEES OF THE CONFERENCES, 5 (1929). Brazil, Cuba, and Mexico were also members of the Madrid Agreement of 1891.

In 1906 Argentina invited the U.S.T.A. to comment on its domestic trademark law. Similarly, in 1908, Ecuador asked the U.S.T.A. to propose a trademark law which was to become the model for other Latin American countries. *About INTA History*, INTERNATIONAL TRADEMARK ASSOCIATION, www.inta.org/history/pages/history.aspx (last visited Jan. 22, 2013).

In 1889, at the International Congress of American States at Montevideo, the first Inter-American trademark treaty was signed.[8] The main feature of this convention was to secure reciprocal national treatment for trademark owners in the contracting countries. A second Inter-American trademark convention was adopted in Mexico City in 1902. The text of the 1902 convention largely reproduced the previous text, but added some language taken from the Paris Convention on national treatment and priority. One thing that this text did not borrow was the principle of independence. The 1902 convention provided that any state that cancelled a mark had to inform all of the contracting states so that they could decide if they too would cancel the mark.

The 1906 convention in Rio de Janeiro incorporated the 1902 convention and added a number of important new features. The 1906 convention established a registration regime modeled on the 1891 Madrid Agreement for the international registration of trademarks whereby registration offices were set up in Havana and Rio. In the establishment of these bureaus, the 1906 convention followed the Madrid arrangement, yet it went much further in purporting to centralize the registrations of trademarks as well as literary and artistic works, patents, and designs and models.[9]

The next convention that was adopted in 1923 in Santiago was not a general agreement for the protection of trademarks in the way that the Paris Convention is. Instead, its objective appears to duplicate the Madrid Agreement for the Americas. As such, unlike previous Pan-American Conventions, it contained no provisions concerning the national treatment of foreign trademark owners or a right of priority for filing applications for the registration of trademarks in the contracting countries.[10]

Since none of the conventions succeeded in securing widespread adoption in the region,[11] a final attempt was made. The 1929 convention

---

[8]   Stephen P. Ladas, THE INTERNATIONAL PROTECTION OF TRADE MARKS BY THE AMERICAN REPUBLICS 11 (1929). The contracting countries of this convention were Argentina, Bolivia, Chile, Paraguay, Peru, and Uruguay. Bolivia and Chile did not ratify. A corollary patent treaty was also adopted that gave patent owners a one-year priority.

[9]   Stephen P. Ladas, THE INTERNATIONAL PROTECTION OF TRADE MARKS BY THE AMERICAN REPUBLICS 13 (1929).

[10]   Stephen P. Ladas, THE INTERNATIONAL PROTECTION OF TRADE MARKS BY THE AMERICAN REPUBLICS 20, 29 (1929). The Pan-American Convention of 1923 remains in effect between Brazil, Chile, Cuba, the Dominican Republic, Guatemala, Haiti, Paraguay, and the United States.

[11]   Stephen P. Ladas, 3 PATENTS, TRADEMARKS, AND RELATED RIGHTS: NATIONAL AND INTERNATIONAL PROTECTION at 1752 (1975) (stating that despite

ultimately had 19 signatory countries: Bolivia; Brazil; Chile; Colombia; Costa Rica; Cuba; Dominican Republic; Ecuador; Guatemala; Haiti; Honduras; Mexico; Nicaragua; Panama; Paraguay; Peru; United States; Uruguay; and Venezuela. The convention entered into force on April 2, 1930. Ten states ultimately ratified the convention: Colombia; Cuba; Guatemala; Haiti; Honduras; Nicaragua; Panama; Paraguay; Peru; and the United States. The convention remains in force today in each of these countries.

In contrast to the Paris Convention, which was essentially negotiated by the European states, the Pan-American Convention was negotiated between the United States and 18 Latin American states. Whereas the Paris Convention negotiating states were largely in harmony in their approach to protecting trademarks and in their appreciation of what the problems were, the foundation for the Pan-American Convention negotiations was vastly different.

A major conflict between the U.S. and the other American countries was over the fundamental source of rights in trademarks. The view of the U.S. was that the common law created the right based on use of the mark and that the registration of the mark was merely evidence of that right.[12] In contrast, throughout Latin America, the registration creates the trademark right. Important corollaries of that principle are that unless and until the mark is registered, it is available for use by anyone, and if it is

---

repeated attempts for more than 40 years to create an American union for the protection of industrial property, the American states had yet to arrive at a workable resolution, acceptable to all states), *see also* Ladas, 3 PATENTS TRADEMARKS AND RELATED RIGHTS: NATIONAL AND INTERNATIONAL PROTECTION at 1745–51 (providing that the following states recognized the precedent conventions: Montevideo Conventions of 1889 – Argentina, Bolivia, Brazil, Chile, Paraguay, Peru and Uruguay; Second Pan American Convention of 1902 – Argentina, Bolivia, Colombia, Costa Rica, Chile, Ecuador, El Salvador, Guatemala, Haiti, Honduras, Mexico, Nicaragua, Paraguay, Peru, Dominican Republic and Uruguay; Pan-American Convention of 1906 – Honduras, Guatemala, Salvador, Nicaragua, Costa Rica, Chile, Ecuador, Brazil and Panama; Pan-American Convention of 1919 – Brazil, Costa Rica, Cuba, the Dominican Republic, Ecuador, Guatemala, Haiti, Honduras, Nicaragua, Panama, Paraguay, the United States and Peru; however, the governments of Costa Rica, Guatemala, Honduras, and Nicaragua subsequently denounced the trademark convention which resulted from this meeting; Pan-American Trademark Convention of 1923 – Brazil, Cuba, Dominican Republic, Haiti, Paraguay, United States, and Uruguay).

[12] Edward S. Rogers, *Some Suggestions Concerning a Trademark Registration Act*, 43 ANN. REP. A.B.A. 412, 413 (1920).

registered, it is incontestable.[13] Apparently, some U.S. trademark owners believed that the different system existing in Latin America left their trademarks vulnerable.[14]

In the early 1900s, there was not a vibrant trademark practice in any of the Latin American states involved in the Pan-American Convention negotiations. As a result, some of the negotiators lamented the lack of expertise they were able to bring to the table.[15] Representing the United States in these negotiations were Stephen P. Ladas and Edward S. Rogers. Ladas and Rogers were two of the foremost experts in both U.S. and international trademark law. They would have had a perfect under-standing of how the rights established in this convention would have extended protection beyond existing U.S. law.

Stephen Ladas published an influential book in advance of the 1929 Washington Conference in an effort to "facilitate the work of the conference of trade mark experts and specialists of the American countries, meeting at Washington, February 11, 1929."[16] Ladas was a member of the firm that eventually became known as Ladas & Parry. Not only was the firm specialized in intellectual property, but it was initially focused on seeking protection for American inventions and trademarks in foreign countries. In addition to practicing law, Ladas worked as a business consultant for the Coca-Cola Company. Stephen Ladas wrote several books on the international protection of trademarks including *The International Protection of Trademarks by the American Republics* (1929), *The International Protection of Industrial Property* (1930), and *Patents, Trademarks and Related Rights – National and International*

---

[13]   *Ibid.*

[14]   A 1920 article written for the A.B.A. by Edward Rogers mentions "much loose talk condemnatory" of the Latin American trademark system, and "[h]or-rible examples [] cited where valuable marks owned ... by American citizens, have been pirated and appropriated by foreigners for their own benefit." *Ibid.* at 414. Rogers accuses these detractors as displaying "a singular insularity of view" and defends that system as efficient.

[15]   *See* Stephen P. Ladas, 3 PATENTS, TRADEMARKS, AND RELATED RIGHTS NATIONAL AND INTERNATIONAL PROTECTION at 1753 n. 34 (1975) (citing the Argentine delegate as stating that he had never encountered a case involving trademarks during his career).

[16]   Stephen P. Ladas, THE INTERNATIONAL PROTECTION OF TRADE MARKS BY THE AMERICAN REPUBLICS (1929).

Protection (1975).[17] Ladas participated in the 1958 revision of the Paris Convention as a member of the United States delegation.[18]

Edward Rogers, one of the chief architects of the Lanham Act, acted as the most engaged delegate to the conference that drafted the Pan-American Convention. In 1914, Rogers published *Good Will, Trade-Marks and Unfair Trading*, which became for many decades the leading text in trademark law. By the 1920s, Rogers had become known as the "Dean of the Trademark Bar." He began drafting a new federal trademark law which eventually was enacted as the Lanham Act. Rogers' firm, which has come to be known as Pattishall McAuliffe, also developed a reputation in international trademark practice and worldwide brand protection programs. Ladas and Rogers continued their interest in this convention beyond its ratification and, in a joint publication in 1950, proposed a revision in order to attract additional parties.[19]

Because this treaty followed the Paris Convention, the rights contained were anticipated to go beyond the minimum protections mandated by the Paris Convention. In an article published in 1950, Ladas and Rogers state that the Pan-American Convention is "in some respects superior to that achieved by the [Paris Convention]."[20]

III EXCEPTIONS TO TERRITORIALITY

In these negotiations, the U.S. not only had the most expertise, but it also had the clearest objectives. The primary objective was to provide U.S. corporations with trademark rights in advance for when and if they should choose to do business in one of the contracting states. Specific-ally, it was desired that these corporations should have trademark rights in cases where they did not register, use or advertise their mark if the party they sought to enjoin had knowledge of their trademark rights in the U.S. Significantly, this was not a bad faith standard, but an entirely new right.

---

[17] He also wrote a book on international copyright protection: Stephen P. Ladas, THE INTERNATIONAL PROTECTION OF LITERARY AND ARTISTIC PROPERTY (1938).

[18] Ladas' partner, Lawrence Langner, was involved in the drafting of the trademark provisions of the Treaty of Versailles.

[19] Edward S. Rogers and Stephen P. Ladas, *Proposals for Uniform Trademark Laws* 40 TMR 8 (1950).

[20] *Ibid.* at 14.

Thus, the Pan-American Convention priority right was novel at the time and it remains unique in international trademark law today. Unlike the Paris Convention priority right, it is neither limited in time nor applied uniformly. It is also unlike the Paris Convention's "well-known marks" protection in that the senior user does not have to prove fame in the country in which it seeks protection, but may merely show that the junior user was aware of senior user's rights in any member country.

These priority provisions are found in Articles 7 and 8 of the convention. Article 7 provides:

> Any owner of a mark protected in one of the Contracting States in accordance with its domestic law, who may know that some other person is using or applying to register or deposit an interfering mark in any other of the Contracting States shall have the right to oppose such use, registration or deposit and shall have the right to employ all legal means, procedure or recourse provided in the country in which such interfering mark is being used or where its registration or deposit is being sought, and upon proof that the person who is using such mark or applying to register or deposit it, had knowledge of the existence and continuous use in any of the Contracting States of the mark on which opposition is based upon goods of the same class, the opposer may claim for himself the preferential right to use such mark in the country where the opposition is made or priority to register or deposit it in such country, upon compliance with the requirements established by the domestic legislation in such country and by this Convention.[21]

Thus, Article 7 provides the owner of a mark in a contracting state the right to challenge the use and registration of an interfering mark in another contracting state upon proof that the interfering party had knowledge of the existence and continuous use of the mark and upon compliance with the domestic requirements in that contracting state. Article 7 entitles the owner of the mark to "the preferential right to use such mark ... or priority to register ... ."

In terms of the relationship with U.S. statutory law, Article 7 merely establishes as a prerequisite to assertion of a claim or defense under Article 7 compliance with the domestic legislation in the country where the actionable conduct takes place.

So the elements required in order to prevail on the issue of priority pursuant to Article 7 of the Pan-American Convention are as follows: (1) plaintiff is the owner of a mark protected in one of the member states; (2) defendant is using or applying to register an "interfering mark" in the

---

[21]   General Inter-American Convention for Trade Mark and Commercial Protection, Feb. 20, 1929, 46 Stat. 2907, 124 L.N.T.S. 357, art. 7.

United States; (3) defendant had knowledge of the existence and continuous use in a member state of plaintiff's mark in connection with goods in the same class, prior to its use of the mark in the United States; and (4) plaintiff has complied with the requirements of the domestic law in both member states.

This new right first appeared in 1929 – it had not been discussed in connection with any previous treaty. The "Cuban draft" that was presented at the 1929 Washington conference first introduced the rights that later were developed into Articles 7 and 8. Article 5 of that draft provided that:

> Any owner of a mark legally protected in one of the contracting States in accordance with its domestic legislation who may know that some other person or entity is using or endeavoring to register or deposit a mark substantially the same as his or likely to cause confusion … shall have the right to object to the use, registration or deposit … upon proving that the person who is using it or attempting to register or deposit it had knowledge of the existence and use of the marks on which the opposition is based, in any of the contracting States … and may claim for himself the right to use his mark preferentially … .[22]

Similarly, the draft Article 6 provided that "the owner of a mark" has the right to cancel a conflicting registration if his mark enjoyed legal protection in a contracting state at the filing date, and the registrant had knowledge of the use or registration in a contracting state for the same goods, or that his goods have circulated in the country of registration by the filing date.[23]

Edward Rogers, serving as a U.S. delegate to the Washington conference,[24] made numerous amendments to the draft text in the first meeting, some of which were rejected.[25] One of his interventions concerned the knowledge standard in what became Articles 7 and 8. Mr. Rogers proposed that either actual or constructive knowledge should be sufficient and that to require both would be unnecessarily burdensome. The Cuban

---

[22] PAN AMERICAN TRADEMARK CONFERENCE, MINUTES OF THE PLENARY SESSIONS AND OF THE COMMITTEES OF THE CONFERENCES, 17 (1929).

[23] *Ibid.* at 18.

[24] Rogers published an article in 1920 that lambasted the current U.S. Trademark Act as "a slovenly piece of legislation." "Its draftsmen had a talent for obscurity amounting to genius." At 414. "A virtuoso in vagueness must have conceived it." At 416. "Possibly the whole thing was intended as a practical joke." At 417.

[25] PAN AMERICAN TRADEMARK CONFERENCE, MINUTES OF THE PLENARY SESSIONS AND OF THE COMMITTEES OF THE CONFERENCES, 46–47 (1929).

delegate who authored the provision pushed back just a bit and reminded Mr. Rogers of the great stretch it was for Latin American states to recognize use, but quickly accepted the proposal.[26]

Article 8 extends the priority right of Article 7 to the context of cancelling an interfering mark. Article 8 provides:

> When the owner of a mark seeks the registration or deposit of the mark in a Contracting State other than that of origin of the mark and such registration or deposit is refused because of the previous registration or deposit of an interfering mark, he shall have the right to apply for and obtain the cancellation or annulment of the interfering mark upon proving, in accordance with the legal procedure of the country in which cancellation is sought, the stipulations in Paragraph (a) and those of either Paragraph (b) or (c) below:
>
> (a) That he enjoyed legal protection for his mark in another of the Contracting States prior to the date of the application for the registration or deposit which he seeks to cancel; and
> (b) that the claimant of the interfering mark, the cancellation of which is sought, had knowledge of the use, employment, registration or deposit in any of the Contracting States of the mark for the specific goods to which said interfering mark is applied, prior to adoption and use thereof or prior to the filing of the application or deposit of the mark which is sought to be cancelled; or
> (c) that the owner of the mark who seeks cancellation based on a prior right to the ownership and use of such mark, has traded or trades with or in the country in which cancellation is sought; and
>
> that goods designated by his mark have circulated and circulate in said country from a date prior to the filing of the application for registration or deposit for the mark, the cancellation which is claimed, or prior to the adoption and use of the same.[27]

Perhaps the approach of Articles 7 and 8 may sound sensible to many U.S. trademark holders. This policy would prevent intermeddlers who try to preempt trademark owners' rights in order to force a transaction. Moreover because of the knowledge requirement, it does not create a trap for the "innocent filer" as the Paris Convention priority right does.[28]

Whether or not this may be an effective strategy to deal with a pernicious problem, it must be noted that these articles advance rights

---

[26]   *Ibid.* at 65.

[27]   General Inter-American Convention for Trade Mark and Commercial Protection, Feb. 20, 1929, 46 Stat. 2907, 124 L.N.T.S. 357, art. 8.

[28]   *E.g.*, SCM Corp. v. Langis Foods Ltd., 539 F.2d 196 (D.C. Cir. 1976) (the "LEMON TREE case" is the seminal case enforcing Paris Convention priority against the "unaware" U.S. applicant).

that are anathema to the fundamental principles of U.S. trademark law. First, trademark rights are territorial. As was seen in the *Person's* case, the doctrine of territoriality means that rights to a mark in a foreign country do not create rights in other countries. The Pan-American Convention priority provisions represent a major exception to territoriality under which trademark rights exist according to each country's statutes. Second, at least in the U.S., there are no rights in gross for trademarks.

The chances that these rights would be asserted by a Latin American party in U.S. court were nonexistent at the time the convention was adopted. The preemption problem was only occurring in the south. Perhaps it was not anticipated that these provisions would ever need to be encountered in a U.S. court. One may wonder why Latin American countries would ratify this convention if it only addressed the concerns of U.S. trademark holders. Much like north–south IP treaty negotiations today, perhaps these Latin American countries thought that by providing these rights, they would be successful in attracting U.S. businesses to the region. At the time, the dominant economic interest in Latin America, which was largely comprised of raw material exporters, was commercial trade with the United States.[29]

The Pan-American Convention can be viewed as providing a novel approach to the protection of well-known marks. Because it is not a further iteration of the Paris Convention's well-known marks protections, there is no requirement that fame of the mark be demonstrated. This strategy to protect well-known marks also has the advantage that there is no bad faith element that must be proven.

IV IMPLEMENTING TREATIES IN THE U.S.

This treaty is more than mere historical curiosity. The Pan-American Convention is self-executing. Or to be more precise, certain of the treaty provisions are "self-executing," meaning that these rights are immediately operative in U.S. courts.

Self-executing treaties become applicable in domestic courts upon ratification. The legislature does not need to act in order to make the

---

[29] Tulio Halperin Donghi, THE CONTEMPORARY HISTORY OF LATIN AMERICA 159 (John Charles Chasteen ed. and trans., 1993); AN ECONOMIC HISTORY OF TWENTIETH-CENTURY LATIN AMERICA: VOLUME 1 THE EXPORT AGE: THE LATIN AMERICAN ECONOMIES IN THE LATE AND EARLY TWENTIETH CENTURIES, 4 (Enrique Cardenas, Jose Antonio Ocampo and Rosemary Thorp eds., 2000).

treaty operative in that jurisdiction. Thus, self-executing treaties become the law of the land upon ratification, as if Congress has passed the law. Therefore, if a treaty dealing with trademarks is self-executing, it would behoove a trademark lawyer to be familiar with the rights therein.

Sometimes treaties contain language indicating that they are not self-executing. There is no language in the Pan-American Convention suggesting that it is not self-executing. In addition, with respect to the priority provisions, the rights are so specific and detailed that legislative implementation is not necessary.

In addition to reliance on the convention's status as self-executing, a provision in the Lanham Act could be utilized to give effect to the Pan-American Convention's priority provisions. Specific language in section 44 (b) of the trademark act, the "international law section," would appear to grant treaty rights to members of treaty countries if those treaty rights are more extensive than the U.S. trademark act otherwise provides.

Section 44 (b) of the Lanham Act provides:

> Any person whose country of origin is a party to any convention or treaty relating to trademarks, trade or commercial names, or the repression of unfair competition, to which the United States is also a party, or extends reciprocal rights to nationals of the United States by law, shall be entitled to the benefits of this section under the conditions expressed herein to the extent necessary to give effect to any provision of such convention, treaty or reciprocal law, in addition to the rights to which any owner of a mark is otherwise entitled by this chapter.[30]

Previously, this provision had made explicit reference to the Pan-American Convention and the Paris Convention. That language was omitted in 1962 when subsection (b) of section 44 was amended in a housekeeping revision. Nevertheless, the meaning – and the relationship with the Pan-American Convention – remains unchanged. Thus, under the Lanham Act section 44, any signatories of the Pan-American Convention receive not only the rights granted under the Lanham Act but also any additional rights granted under the convention.

Moreover, further language in that section extends the benefits of these external treaty rights to U.S. parties. Section 44 (i) of the Lanham Act provides: "Citizens or residents of the United States shall have the same

---

[30]   15 U.S.C. § 1126 (2000) (governing international conventions and the registration of foreign marks in the United States).

benefits as are granted by this section to persons described in subsection (b) of this section."[31]

This chapter may therefore provide a good litigation strategy to foreign and domestic parties in the U.S. However, should the revelation of this strategy result in large-scale application of the convention in U.S. courts, it would have the effect of turning U.S. trademark law on its head.

Under the Supremacy Clause of the Constitution, self-executing treaties and federal statutes have essentially equal status under U.S. law. Moreover, federal statutes must be construed so as not to conflict with international law.[32] The Supreme Court has long held that in the event of a conflict between a treaty and a federal statute, the latter in time will prevail under U.S. law.[33] In the event that a seemingly conflicting federal statute is the last in time, courts will always endeavor to construe a treaty and federal law on the same subject so as to give effect to both if that can be done without violating the language of either.[34] Thus, it is a solid canon of statutory interpretation that a court will not construe an act of Congress to be inconsistent with international law if another construction is possible.[35]

Moreover, a state cannot get out of its treaty commitments simply by overriding them with conflicting domestic legislation. A state cannot invalidate a treaty by passing an inconsistent federal statute. Such an act does not terminate the international obligations of the state to its treaty partners. That state's obligations remain intact. Rather, a state can free itself from obligations under a treaty by withdrawing from it, according to the treaty's provisions. A treaty will not be deemed to have been abrogated or modified by a later statute unless such purpose on the part of Congress has been clearly expressed.

The United States cannot ignore its obligations under this treaty. Renunciation by silence is not an option under international law. The Pan-American Convention used to have a Protocol. That Protocol was later denounced by the U.S. So evidently the U.S. does know how to properly denounce a treaty. Finally, the last alternative is for the U.S. to maintain its obligations under the Pan-American Convention, but not give

---

[31]   15 U.S.C. § 1126 (i).
[32]   Murray v. The Schooner Charming Betsy, 6 U.S. 64, 118 (1804) ("It has also been observed that an act of Congress ought never to be construed to violate the law of nations if any other possible construction remains …").
[33]   Breard v. Greene, 523 U.S. 371 (1998).
[34]   Whitney v. Robertson, 124 U.S. 190, 194 (1888).
[35]   Murray v. The Schooner Charming Betsy, 6 U.S. 64 (1804).

them effect in U.S. courts. Clearly, this would be a breach of the bargain struck in 1929.

V U.S. DISPUTES THAT HAVE INVOKED THE CONVENTION

Although the convention remains unfamiliar to most U.S. litigants, three Trademark Trial and Appeal Board decisions have been decided on the merits under the Pan-American Convention. To this date, no federal district court has ruled on the merits under the convention, although two courts have ruled on the convention.

A T.T.A.B. Cases

The first case in the United States to be decided under the Pan-American Convention was in 2000, and it was in the Trademark Trial and Appeal Board. In *British-American Tobacco Co. Ltd. v. Philip Morris Inc.*[36] the board held that the Inter-American Convention is self-executing and has the same force of law as the Lanham Act. It furthermore held that the Pan-American Convention is independent of the Lanham Act and gives the board the jurisdiction to cancel a registration for being in violation of the convention.

In this case, a Panamanian company sought to cancel BELMONT for cigarettes based on priority in Panama under Article 8 of the Inter-American Convention. The marks were incontestable in the U.S. The board also concluded that it had jurisdiction to consider a claim (for cancellation) brought under Article 8 of the convention.

The next case came seven years later, and was also decided by the Trademark Trial and Appeal Board. In *Diaz v. Servicios De Franquicia Pardo's S.A.C.*[37] the applicant for the mark Pardo's was the junior user of the mark in the U.S., but asserted priority under Article 7 of the Inter-American Convention based on prior use of the mark in Peru. The application was opposed by the senior user of the mark who had used the mark in Florida previous to the November 2002 application.

The board held that the clear purpose of the convention is to protect the foreign trademarks that fall within the treaty's purview; and the intent of the treaty is to confer a substantive right to the protection of the foreign mark. It held that its jurisdiction over the matter did not violate

---

[36] 55 U.S.P.Q.2d 1585, 2000 WL 1005433 (T.T.A.B. 2000).
[37] 83 U.S.P.Q.2d 1320, 2007 WL 549241 (T.T.A.B. 2007).

the doctrine of territoriality because the convention explicitly created an exception to the doctrine.

As to the knowledge requirement, the board held that pursuant to Article 7, the applicant is not required to establish that the opposer knew that the applicant was the owner of the foreign mark, only that the opposer had knowledge of the continuous use and existence of the mark. In this case, there was no evidence of actual knowledge of the use of the mark in Peru, but instead evidence of constructive knowledge satisfied the board. The evidence showed that Applicant Diaz is a Peruvian citizen born in Peru, who lived in Peru prior to moving to the United States, and who has travelled to Peru in the past ten years. He lived in Peru at an address less than 20 blocks from one of Applicant's restaurants. And prior to opening his restaurant in Florida, Diaz erected a sign bearing the words PARDO'S CHICKEN in the same stylization and color as that used by Applicant in Peru. The board therefore concluded that there was no genuine issue of material fact regarding Diaz's knowledge of Applicant's use of the PARDO'S CHICKEN mark in Peru prior to his first use in the U.S.

In the third case, *Corp. Cimex S.A. v. D.M. Enterprises & Distributors Inc.*,[38] the board granted the Opposer's motion for summary judgment in the application for CUBITA for coffee under Article 7 of the Inter-American Convention. Opposer owned the mark in Cuba. In this case, Applicant conceded that it knew of the existence and use of the CUBITA mark in Cuba by Opposer and its predecessor.

In addition to these three T.T.A.B. cases, there is a fourth T.T.A.B. case that deals with a related convention. In *Franpovi S.A. v. Wessin*[39] the board held that the Santiago Convention of 1923, a predecessor to the Pan-American Convention, is in effect with a state that did not ratify the Inter-American Convention. In this case, Opposer sought to prevent the registration of Applicants' mark POLLOS VICTORINA based on Opposer's alleged rights under the Santiago Convention. The parties filed cross-motions for summary judgment on Opposer's claim under the Santiago Convention. The board explained that one of the Santiago Convention's conditions for such an opposition was that the party must apply for protection through an Inter-American Bureau ("I.A.B."). However, the I.A.B. closed in 1949. Because this condition could not be satisfied, the board found that Opposer could not bring an opposition

---

[38]   2008 WL 5078739, at. *2. (T.T.A.B. 2008) (not precedential).
[39]   89 U.S.P.Q.2d 1637, 2009 WL 353299 (T.T.A.B. 2009).

based on the Santiago Convention in the United States, and granted summary judgment for Applicants on that claim.

B   Federal Court Cases

Only three federal court cases have ruled on the Pan-American Convention. None of these cases, however, have dealt with the convention on the merits.

In 1940, the U.S. Supreme Court – in dictum – indicated that the Pan-American Convention is self-executing. In *Bacardi v. Domench*,[40] the Supreme Court stated that a central goal of the Pan-American Convention was to create uniform trademark protection among countries.[41] The Court found this treaty to be self-executing, saying it bound Puerto Rico and could not be overridden by the Puerto Rican legislature, even where the Puerto Rican rule was applicable to its own citizens and not just foreigners.[42] The Puerto Rican law's hostility toward the treaty and discrimination against foreign parties was clear, and thus the court found the legislation invalid.[43]

In a dispute between a Cuban and a U.S. rum producer over the rights to the "Havana Club" trademark and trade name in the U.S., a federal court had its first opportunity – in 1997 – to consider the application of the Pan-American Convention. In two of its four opinions in *Havana Club Holding, S.A. v. Galleon, S.A.*, the district court for the Southern District of New York considered claims under the Pan-American Convention.[44] The district court ultimately held that section 211 of the Omnibus Appropriations Act[45] explicitly prevented it from recognizing any rights to which plaintiffs would otherwise be entitled under any treaty, including the Pan-American Convention.[46] Thus, the court did not reach the merits of the treaty claim. The court did, however, unambiguously state:

---

[40]   Bacardi Corp. of America v. Domenech, 311 U.S. 150 (1940).
[41]   *Ibid.* at 157–58.
[42]   *Ibid.* at 161–63.
[43]   *Ibid.* at 166.
[44]   Havana Club Holding, S.A. v. Galleon, S.A., 974 F. Supp. 302, 309 (S.D.N.Y. 1997). In its first ruling on the convention, the court ruled that the Cuban Assets Control Regulations are a temporary substitute for the Pan-American Convention rights with regard to the effect of trademark assignments in member states.
[45]   Pub. Law 105-277 (1998).
[46]   Havana Club Holding, S.A. v. Galleon, S.A., 62 F. Supp. 2d 1085, 1092 (S.D.N.Y. 1999), *cert. denied*, Havana Club Holding, S.A. v. Bacardi & Co., 531 U.S. 918 (2000).

"The Inter-American Convention, which was adopted at a special conference held in February 1929, is a self-executing treaty, and thus it became law in the United States without the necessity for implementing legislation."[47]

On appeal, the Court of Appeals for the Second Circuit affirmed holding that the plaintiffs' Pan-American Convention rights were abrogated by the Cuban Assets Control Regulations, and that the statute precluded it from enforcing its treaty rights under the Pan-American Convention.[48] The Second Circuit did express one further statement about the Pan-American Convention that went beyond what the district court had held. It held that a plaintiff must assert its rights under the Pan-American Convention "pursuant to section 44 (b) of the Lanham Act."[49] This suggests that a plaintiff asserting rights under the Pan-American Convention must make its claim for relief under the Lanham Act.

In addition to trademark and trade name claims, the plaintiff asserted unfair competition claims under section 44 (h) of the Lanham Act and the Pan-American Convention. Because these claims were not addressed by the Omnibus Appropriations Act, the court was free to enforce these treaty rights. Instead, the court found that plaintiff's "section 44 (h) claim amounts to little more than the re-assertion of its section 43 (a) claim because article 21 (c) of the [Pan-American Convention] prohibits a subset of the conduct already effectively prohibited under American law by section 43 (a)."[50] The court held that the same standing rules applicable to a 43 (a) claim were required for a 44 (h) claim. Additionally, the court held that the plaintiff was not entitled to the substantive provisions of Article 23 of the convention, concerning "Repression of False Indications of Geographical Origin or Source" because section 44 (h) of the Lanham Act only reaches substantive provisions of the Pan-American Convention that are "related to the repression of unfair competition."[51]

Just a couple of years after the Second Circuit's opinion in *Havana Club*, the Southern District had another opportunity to consider claims

---

[47]   Havana Club Holding, S.A. v. Galleon, S.A., 62 F. Supp. 2d 1085, 1092 (S.D.N.Y. 1999), *cert. denied*, Havana Club Holding, S.A. v. Bacardi & Co., 531 U.S. 918 (2000) (citing Bacardi Corp. of America v. Domenech, 311 U.S. 150, 161 (1940)).

[48]   Havana Club Holding, S.A. v. Galleon, S.A., 203 F.3d 116 (2d Cir. 2000).

[49]   *Ibid.* at 128.

[50]   *Ibid.* at 135.

[51]   *Ibid.*

under the Pan-American Convention. Again, the dispute involved competing claims to a U.S. mark by Cuban and U.S. traders – this time for COHIBA cigars. Closely following the Second Circuit's opinion, the district court in *Empresa Cubana Del Tabaco v. Culbro Corp.* narrowly construed the plaintiff's viable treaty claims to be those that related to the repression of unfair competition. Finding no meaningful way to determine that the claims under Articles 7 and 8 of the Pan-American Convention could be construed as claims related to the repression of unfair competition, and finding the implication of these rights to be counter to U.S. trademark policy, the court held that they "are not 'related to the repression of unfair competition' and are not within the ambit of Section 44 (h)."[52]

In a subsequent opinion, the court added some clarification and precision to its earlier ruling on the Pan-American Convention. It stated quite plainly that "a party must enforce its rights under an international convention through Section 44 (b) and some other subsection of Section 44."[53] It suggested that rather than section 44 (h), "there are other provisions of the Lanham Act under which Articles 7 and 8 of the IAC may be enforced."[54] Then it advised that as Articles 7 and 8 are related to the priority of marks, section 44 (d) is the appropriate vehicle. The court reasoned that since the treaty grants rights in these articles "upon compliance with the requirements established by the domestic legislation in such country ..." a claimant under Articles 7 or 8 must comply with section 44 (d). According to the court, "[b]ecause Articles 7 and 8 mandate compliance with the domestic legislation, i.e. Section 44 (d), the United States would be out of compliance with those convention articles only if it refused to recognize the rights of parties that had duly complied with Section 44(d)."[55]

These two Second Circuit cases constrain the import of the Pan-American Convention. Rather than simply finding the convention self-executing as the T.T.A.B. did, the Second Circuit resorted to section 44. And rather than reading section 44 as mandating the applicability of the substantive rights of the convention, the Second Circuit held that section 44 limited the claims that could be made under the convention.

---

[52]   Empresa Cubana Del Tabaco v. Culbro Corp., 213 F. Supp. 2d 247, 282 (S.D.N.Y. 2002).
[53]   Empresa Cubana Del Tabaco v. Culbro Corp., 2002 U.S. Dist. LEXIS 21731, *7 (S.D.N.Y. Oct. 8, 2002).
[54]   *Ibid.*
[55]   *Ibid.* at *9.

As a result of the *Cohiba* and *Havana Club* cases, there may be additional obstacles to asserting a Pan-American Convention claim in the Second Circuit. Nevertheless, it would appear that unless these embargo-laden cases are followed, these claims will at least be viable in other circuits.

VI APPLICATION OF THE EXTRATERRITORIAL PROVISIONS

What would be the effect of asserting a claim under the convention? Consider the *Person's* case with one fact changed. Imagine the foreign company was located not in Japan, but in Peru. In this hypothetical, U.S. citizen Larry Christman took his business trip to Peru, where he visited a Person's Co. clothing store. Again Christman purchased items of clothing bearing the Person's logo, and upon his return, he developed a clothing line by copying the products he purchased. He then sold his clothing with the same Person's logo and registered the Person's mark in the U.S. Subsequently, the foreign Person's Co. sold its goods in the U.S. and applied to register the mark in the U.S.

Now consider an action brought by the Peruvian Person's Co. in the U.S. If brought under Articles 7 and 8 of the Pan-American Convention, the Peruvian company could seek to cancel Christman's registration and "oppose" Christman's use of the mark in the U.S. The Peruvian company should be successful because it can establish that (a) Christman's mark is an "interfering mark;" (b) it is the owner of a mark protected in a member state (Peru) prior to the date of the application for registration in the U.S.; (c) Christman had knowledge of the use of the mark in Peru for the specific goods for which he applied prior to the filing of his application; (d) it has sold goods designated by the mark prior to its application for registration; and (e) it has complied with the requirements of the domestic law in both member states. So under the same facts with only the foreign location being changed to a member state, the heretofore vital principle of territoriality, which was the basis of the Federal Circuit's holding, is immaterial.

VII CONCLUSION

This revelation of the Pan-American Convention should not only become part of the toolkit of any U.S. trademark attorney who faces issues of territoriality originating from Latin America, it should provide a sledge-hammer. As the protections achieved under the convention go beyond those of the Paris Convention, the priority rights contained in Articles 7 and 8 can provide protections for U.S. marks even when the mark would not qualify as a well-known mark. The substantive rights offered under Article 8 would also offer U.S. trademark owners concrete protections against acts of unfair competition that occur in Latin America. Additionally, through the knowledge requirement under Article 7, innocent filers of previously registered trademarks in signatory countries could avoid the liabilities imposed upon them by the Paris Convention.

At a more macro level, this reminder of the Pan-American Convention should signal courts and policymakers that the U.S. does have an obligation under the convention to recognize the international obligations assumed by the U.S. at the time of the signing of the treaty. While the limited use of the convention has perhaps precluded policymakers from considering the impact of the convention, they should be mindful that international norms mandate either that the convention be fully applied or that it needs to be properly denounced.

PART II

Protecting quality and identity in the global economy

5. Marks and more(s): certification in global value chains

Margaret Chon*

Law and economics scholars understand trademarks as devices that reduce consumer search costs by signaling the source of a product or service. But scholars in fields as diverse as anthropology and business management suggest that signaling source is just the beginning of the complex social and cultural work that brands and logos do.[1]

I INTRODUCTION

Ever since the Lanham Act was enacted in 1946, and especially since the World Trade Organization (WTO) came into existence in 1995, private standard-setting has increasingly interconnected with public regulation, to form a dense network some call global governance.[2] Increasingly as well, trademarks, service marks, collective marks, and certification marks (CMs) (collectively, marks)[3] denote specific standards such as fair trade.[4] In this context, trademark and unfair competition law (collectively,

* Donald and Lynda Horowitz Professor for the Pursuit of Justice, Seattle University School of Law. This chapter is adapted from an article entitled *Marks of Rectitude*, originally published in the FORDHAM L. REV. (2009), *available at* http://papers.ssrn.com/sol3/papers.cfm?abstract_id=1369922.

1 Brand New World: Distinguishing Oneself in the Global Flow, University of California, Davis (October 4–5, 2012), *available at* http://www.law.ucdavis.edu/news/event.aspx?id=2779.

2 Tim Büthe and Walter Mattli, THE NEW GLOBAL RULERS, THE PRIVATIZATION OF REGULATION IN THE WORLD ECONOMY (2011); Fabrizio Cafaggi, *Private regulation, supply chain and contractual networks: The case of food safety*, EUROPEAN UNIVERSITY INSTITUTE, EUI WORKING PAPER RSCAS 2010/10 (2010).

3 A "trademark" in this chapter denotes trademarks and service marks, registered or not. Collective marks and certification marks are treated as separate categories, unless otherwise noted.

4 Through this chapter, global "North" is used interchangeably with the term "developed countries" and global "South" with "developing countries."

trademark law)[5] can and already does mediate among various stake-holders and standards in the global marketplace. However, the territorially constrained nature of trademark law limits its effective signaling functioning within global frameworks. This chapter considers the need for a more developed account of the trust function of marks for consumers in light of these regulatory trends.

Trademark law, typically territorial in its reach, is nonetheless part of a greater global regulatory regime. Links between marks and significant international standard-setting and harmonizing organizations, such as the International Organization for Standardization (ISO),[6] or agreements, such as the WTO Agreement on Technical Barriers to Trade (TBT),[7] can contribute to objectives such as development-oriented trade, sustainable global production, regulatory harmonization of private standards and the curbing of potential market abuses across borders.[8] At best, standards can discipline markets by maintaining a floor or even raising the ceiling of potentially beneficial social activity. For example, private labor standards can attempt to reinforce International Labour Organization baselines.[9]

---

[5]   As used in this chapter, the term "trademark law" covers federal law as well as the common law of trademarks and unfair competition.

[6]   International Organization for Standardization, Discover ISO 26000, *available at* http://www.iso.org/iso/discovering_iso_26000.pdf. Because the acronym for "International Organization for Standardization" would vary across languages, its founders also gave it the short, "all-purpose" name "ISO." The official U.S. representative to ISO is the American National Standards Institute (ANSI), and its documents indicate reliance on certification marks without much elaboration of their role in standard-setting. AMERICAN NATIONAL STANDARDS INSTITUTE, NATIONAL CONFORMITY ASSESSMENT PRINCIPLES FOR THE UNITED STATES 8 (2002), *available at* http://publicaa.ansi.org/sites/apdl/Documents/News%20and%20Publications/Brochures/NCAP%20second%20edition.pdf.

[7]   Final Act Embodying the Results of the Uruguay Round of Multilateral Trade Negotiations, Apr. 15, 1994, Agreement on Technical Barriers to Trade, Annex 1A, Legal Instruments – Results of the Uruguay Round, 33 I.L.M. 1125 (Oct. 22, 1994) [hereinafter TBT Agreement].

[8]   Douglas A. Kysar, *Preferences for Processes: The Process/Product Distinction and the Regulation of Consumer Choice*, 118 HARV. L. REV. 525, 550, 558–62 (2004).

[9]   Margaret M. Blair, Cynthia A. Williams and Li-Wen Lin, *The Roles of Standardization, Certification and Assurance Services in Global Commerce* 3–4 (Vand. L. and Econ., Research Paper No. 08-16), *available at* http://ssrn.com/abstract=1120503.

This standard-setting activity relies heavily on soft law[10] within a loose treaty framework.

Standards potentially restructure markets in the global supply or value chains, through the value added to products from social mores or premiums.[11] Because they attempt to shape the market according to norms and principles other than reduction of tariffs, some argue that they have the potential to create a sustainable and possibly more ethical alternative to mainstream trade.[12] Consumers drive this decentralized global regulatory environment – by their choices of what to buy, based on labels and marks.[13] Whether within mainstream or alternative trade channels (such as fair trade), consumers require more accurate information in order for these sorts of transactions to have integrity – whether expressed as a consumer's right to information, a right to participate meaningfully in a civic realm or as a right of expression.[14] The vulnerability of consumers to misleading quality assurance within global

---

[10]   Mary E. Footer, *The Role of "Soft" Law Norms in Reconciling the Antinomies of WTO Law* 2–3 (Soc'y of Int'l Econ. Law, Working Paper No. 54/08, 2008), *available at* http://papers.ssrn.com/sol3/papers.cfm?abstract_id= 1159929.

[11]   Douglas Murray, Laura T. Raynolds and Peter Leigh Taylor, *One Cup at a Time: Poverty Alleviation and Fair Trade Coffee in Latin America* 27 (2003), *available at* http://www.colostate.edu/depts/sociology/FairTradeResearchGroup/ doc/fairtrade.pdf; *see generally* FAIR TRADE: THE CHALLENGES OF TRANSFORM-ING GLOBALIZATION (Laura T. Raynolds, Douglas L. Murray and John Wilkinson eds., 2007) [hereinafter FAIR TRADE].

[12]   The International Trade Centre, a joint agency of the WTO and the United Nations, views this trade paradigm as a viable alternative to the pure WTO model. Its slogan is "Export Impact for Good." *See generally* International Trade Centre, Export Impact for Good, http://www.intracen.org/ (last visited April 10, 2013). Other agencies, such as the Food and Agriculture Organization, support this view. *See generally* Alice Byers, Daniele Giovannucci and Pascal Liu, *Value-Adding Standards in the North American Food Market: Trade Opportunities in Certified Products for Developing Countries* (Food and Agriculture Organization of the United Nations Commodities and Trade Technical Paper, 2008), *available at* ftp://ftp.fao.org/docrep/fao/010/a1585e/a1585e.pdf.

[13]   Gavin Fridell, FAIR TRADE COFFEE: THE PROSPECTS AND PITFALLS OF MARKET-DRIVEN SOCIAL JUSTICE 63 (2007).

[14]   Tom Roterham, TRADE KNOWLEDGE NETWORK LABELLING FOR ENVIRON-MENTAL PURPOSES: A REVIEW OF THE STATE OF THE DEBATE IN THE WORLD TRADE ORGANIZATION 12–14 (2003) (expressing a right of information); Peter S. Menell, *Structuring a Market-Oriented Federal Information Policy*, 54 MD. L. REV. 1435, 1445 (1995) (framing the issues as one of informed consumer choice); Kysar, *supra* note 8 at 610–17 (positing a right to expression and participation in civic life through consumer choices).

supply chains is highlighted by the recent exposés involving horsemeat in the European Union[15] or sushi in the United States.[16] And the recent fire in a Pakistani clothing factory illustrates the utter vulnerability of producers at the other end of the value chain, particularly the factory workers who produce goods that are certified as complying with fair labor standards.[17]

Standard law and economic accounts posit that marks provide a signaling function to consumers, that is, a cognitive shortcut that facilitates market transactions through distilled and accurate information. However, marks are increasingly unsuccessful at fulfilling this function, at least for processes and other hidden quality attributes. For example, it is still an open question as to whether they can convey effective signals regarding minimum price supports, democratic decision-making, ecological practices, gender equity and so on, to the consumer. This suggests that a major piece is missing from the prevailing theoretical frameworks in this area. A fuller account of trademarks in global value chains would focus on their trust function as mediated by third-party certifications, to guarantee to consumers that the hidden process attributes within the goods or services are in fact what they appear to be.

Trademark law to date has focused on what will be called here first-party certifiers, that is, the firm itself that markets a particular brand of good or service, and that signals source of manufacturing origin directly to consumers via trademarks within a particular territorial (or national) space. The classic trademark paradigm of first-party certifiers assumes that a firm will act in its own self-interest to maximize quality assurance (often measured by consumers through consistency of its product or services, rather than necessarily a high level of quality). In this conventional narrative, the roles of second-party certifiers (voluntary industry associations or buyer firms in a value chain)[18] or third-party

---

[15]   Michael Holden, *EU ministers to hold meeting on horsemeat* (February 12, 2013), *available at* http://uk.reuters.com/article/2013/02/12/uk-britain-food-horsemeat-idUKBRE91B13R20130212.

[16]   Kimberly Warner, et al., WIDESPREAD SEAFOOD FRAUD FOUND IN NEW YORK CITY, Oceana Reports, December 2012, *available at* http://209.183.226.238/sites/default/files/reports/Oceana_NYC_Seafood_Fraud_Report_FINAL.pdf.

[17]   Declan Walsh and Steven Greenhouse, *Certified Safe, A Factory in Karachi Still Quickly Burned*, *available at* nytimes.com, December 7, 2012, accessed 3 March 2013, *available at* http://www.nytimes.com/2012/12/08/world/asia/pakistan-factory-fire-shows-flaws-in-monitoring.html?pagewanted=all.

[18]   Laura T. Raynolds and John Wilkinson, *Fair Trade in the Agriculture and Food Sector: Analytical Dimensions*, *in* FAIR TRADE, *supra* note 11, at 41.

certifiers (independent third-party, nongovernmental standard-setting, inspection, assurance, and certification services[19]) has not been rigorously evaluated. Whether provided through first-, second- or third-party certifiers, the quality assurance function of trademarks is mediated throughout the numerous steps and corresponding stakeholders in the global value chain.

Typically an entity (often a third party) will certify that a good or service conforms to a standard, which can be set privately – through a firm itself, a civil society organization, a trade association, or a combination of some or all of the above. This certification then may be communicated to a buyer or consumer through a marketing campaign such as a firm's corporate social responsibility (CSR) literature, or implicitly through a trademark's assurance of quality, or more explicitly through adherence to the standards required by a CM. Marks can inform intermediate buyers (variously referred to as buyer or purchaser firms, or second parties) or, more typically, end-consumers of product qualities related to the largely opaque steps of the process leading to the product to which they are affixed. These process standards include not only quality assurance standards, which are within the classic trademark mandate, but also a multitude of other process measures.

Marks now express – whether implicitly or explicitly – environmental, human rights, and labor characteristics, as well as classic health and safety standards (for example, Underwriters Laboratory). These marks place a proverbial stamp of ethical approval upon standards developed largely outside public view. While usually viewed as an inconsequential backwater of trademark law, CMs are playing an ever-expanding role in the certification of goods in the U.S. and elsewhere, such as "organic" commodities that are certified to meet certain standards, or services such as "LEED" certifications of the U.S. Green Building Council.[20] These certified goods are then delivered into the stream of global commerce.

This chapter canvasses some major issues in this complex emerging global governance framework. Ultimately it suggests a renewed focus on Article 10*bis* of the Paris Convention as a way of mediating among

---

[19]   U.S. CONGRESS, OFFICE OF TECHNOLOGY ASSESSMENT, GLOBAL STANDARDS: BUILDING BLOCKS FOR THE FUTURE 2 TCT-512 (Washington, D.C.: U.S. Government Printing Office, March 1992) [hereinafter OTA Report].

[20]   U.S. Green Building Council LEED Certified USGBC, U.S. Trademark Serial No. 77199311 (filed June 6, 2007).

different national laws, between the international intellectual property and international trade regimes, as well as between private governance and public frameworks.

II   PRIVATE REGULATION AND ITS DISCONNECTS

Many have observed that virtually no overarching entity, whether public or private, is monitoring certification quality.[21] And consumers may be removed from this process altogether, or at the very least, several steps from quality control. Immediately apparent are the regulatory gaps consisting of lack of accountability and transparency within private certifying firms. This gives rise to a newer kind of consumer confusion (or what might accurately be called ignorance) created by lack of information as well as its opposite – informational clutter about standards.[22] This section walks through the various aspects of these private regulatory dilemmas.

A   Transnational Governance

Private standards – taxonomized in the next section – function as normative technical components of a transnational regulatory system.[23] Standard-setting organizations (SSOs) are often composed of private actors, such as industry, producer, or trade associations and/or non-governmental organizations (NGOs) representing particular perspectives or interests. Standard-setting, certification, and labeling have major

---

[21]   *See* Blair et al., *supra* note 9, at 10; Daniele Giovannucci and Stefano Ponte, *Standards as a New Form of Social Contract? Sustainability Initiatives in the Coffee Industry*, 30 FOOD POL'Y 284, 289 (2005); OTA Report, *supra* note 19, at 9–10.

[22]   Errol Meidinger, *Multi-Interest Self-Governance Through Global Product Certification Programs*, *in* RESPONSIBLE BUSINESS? SELF-GOVERNANCE IN TRANSNATIONAL ECONOMIC TRANSACTIONS 259 (Dilling et al. eds., 2007), at 270–73; *see also* Michael Lewis and David Einhorn, Op-Ed., *The End of the Financial World as We Know It*, N.Y. TIMES, Jan. 4, 2009, at 9 (recommending checks on misleading ratings created by credit agencies Moody's and Standard & Poor's); Gay W. Seidman, BEYOND THE BOYCOTT: LABOR RIGHTS, HUMAN RIGHTS, AND TRANSNATIONAL ACTIVISM (2007).

[23]   Meidinger, *supra* note 22, at 268 ("Labeling requirements, rather than being mere technical matters, are forums for policy debate and competition."); Margaret Jane Radin, *Online Standardization and the Integration of Text and Machine*, 70 FORDHAM L. REV. 1125 (2002) (noting that standards are simultaneously technical and legal).

implications with respect to global trade and trademark law, supposedly driven by consumer choice. As Douglas Kysar states, "consumer process preferences can be understood not from the standpoint of their effect on the external world or their utility as mechanisms for public expression, but rather simply from the premise that consumption often is an intensely personal activity with significant moral consequences."[24]

But private standards are simultaneously a decentralized form of market regulation and a vehicle of market manipulation. To the extent that the mark is opaque and the consumer may not know what he or she is getting, consumer trust can be breached through indifference to conformity with standards or even by outright deceit. The transaction costs associated with these consumer choices come in two major forms, both informational. The first form is of subtle market positioning, where a firm may play upon consumer perceptions of social responsibility and other amorphous measures represented by a mark. Here, the potential for abuse is large and even consumers seem to be aware of this. Consumer surveys indicate that the public is skeptical of ethical claims by companies, retailers, and even governments.[25] Consumers are not often in a position to be able to assess the truthfulness of a claim made about a product's qualities. Yet the issue of consumer trust is central to the legitimate functioning of this regulatory regime. The second type of transaction cost could be viewed as the failure of success. Certain standards have proliferated to the point that consumers are unable to differentiate among them.[26] This may be an artifact of multi-stakeholder governance, which encourages and indeed celebrates a market-driven, bottom-up promulgation of standards.[27]

---

[24] Kysar, *supra* note 8, at 617.

[25] Harriet Lamb, *Fairtrade: Working to Make Markets Fair, in* TRADE – WHAT IF? NEW CHALLENGES IN EXPORT DEVELOPMENT: CONSUMERS, ETHICS AND ENVIRONMENT 99, 100 (International Trade Centre 2008) [hereinafter TRADE – WHAT IF?].

[26] This issue of proliferation has also affected agricultural producers, who find it hard to "keep up with and even to understand the standards. [One researcher] finds that many standards and codes of practice have been driven by Northern consumer and NGO perceptions of business responsibility and have been more *ad hoc* rather than comprehensive and consultative." Daniele Giovannucci, *How New Agrifood Standards Are Affecting Trade, in* TRADE – WHAT IF?, *supra* note 25, at 106.

[27] Meidinger, *supra* note 22.

B   Transnational Standards-setting

What is a standard? In a broad sense, it can be described simply as a "norm for market-based activity."[28] Indeed, Radin supports this expansive definition by including language (such as English) as a kind of standard.[29] As these definitions imply, standards can be set by any entity. Indeed, SSOs can be intergovernmental organizations (for example, the contracting states of the WTO, which set the minimum standards of TRIPS),[30] a government, or a combination of these and other regulatory entrepreneurs, including but not limited to civil society organizations such as NGOs, trade groups, or even individuals such as activist law professors.[31]

In the United States, standard-setting typically is more decentralized and privatized than in many other parts of the world.[32] But part of the impetus for the growth of private standards globally is the expansion of international markets, which rely on longer value chains and outsourcing,[33] along with a greater complexity of products and division of labor.[34] One observer claims that the typical commodity transaction

---

[28]   Steve Charnovitz, *International Standards and the WTO* 13–14 (George Washington Univ. Law Sch. Pub. Law and Legal Theory, Working Paper No. 133, 2005), *available at* http://papers.ssrn.com/so13/papers.cfm?abstract_id= 694346, at 25–26 at 2 ("The broad definition pursued here should be contrasted with the narrower definition of 'standard' used in the WTO Agreement on Technical Barriers to Trade (TBT). In TBT, a standard is defined as a: Document approved by a recognized body, that provides, for common and repeated use, rules, guidelines or characteristics for products or *related* processes and production methods, with which compliance is *not* mandatory. It may also include or deal exclusively with terminology, symbols, packaging, marking or labelling requirements as they apply to a product, *process or production method*" (emphasis added) (citing TBT, *supra* note 7, at Annex 1, para. 2)). *Ibid.* at 4.

[29]   Radin, *supra* note 23, at 1126–27.

[30]   Final Act Embodying the Results of the Uruguay Round of Multilateral Trade Negotiations, Apr. 15, 1994, Agreement on Trade-Related Aspects of Intellectual Property Rights, Annex 1C, Legal Instruments – Results of the Uruguay Round, 33 I.L.M. 1125 (1994), arts. 22–24 [hereinafter TRIPS Agreement]; *see* discussion *infra* Part I.

[31]   Ian Ayres and Jennifer Gerarda Brown, *Privatizing Employment Protections*, 49 Ariz. L. Rev. 587 (2007) (proposing a certification mark that allows employees and applicants to enforce the Employment Non-Discrimination Act, prohibiting discrimination on the basis of sexual orientation).

[32]   *See ibid.* at 14.

[33]   *See* OTA Report, *supra* note 19, at 11.

[34]   *See ibid.* at 11–12.

involves no fewer than 18 links.[35] Driving factors are also the international institutions that facilitate trade and development. Among these is ISO, which is a "world-wide federation of national standards bodies from over 100 countries."[36] It is a NGO where "[s]tandards are developed by a consensus process in order to be inclusive of the views of all stakeholders. They represent industry-wide interests, seek to promote global solutions and are voluntary."[37] Yet despite ISO's growing influence "there are only limited opportunities for public involvement."[38]

The so-called ISO 9000 standards of quality management, promulgated in 1987, were a huge leap forward with respect to third-party certification and standard-setting. An early observer noted:

> ISO 9000 represented a departure from conventional ISO work products in two ways. First, ISO 9000 was the first international standard that did not simply harmonize existing, uniform national standards. Second, the standards were applicable to a wide range of industries and services, rather than to a specific product, process, or plant.

> The ISO 9000 quality control standards, published in 1987, contain guidelines for companies to use both in their own implementation of a quality assurance system and in specifying contract requirements for suppliers and subcontractors. *The explicit goal was to harmonize quality assurance requirements to facilitate international trade.*[39]

These ISO 9000 standards resulted in "certification [becoming] rapidly a *de facto* requirement for doing business in Europe and other parts of the world."[40]

Another important driving factor behind standard-setting is international trade law – in particular, the WTO Agreement on Technical Barriers to Trade (TBT).[41] Some major SSOs such as the International

---

[35] Jacqueline DeCarlo, FAIR TRADE: A BEGINNER'S GUIDE 14 (2007) (citing Michael Barratt Brown, FAIR TRADE: REFORM AND REALITIES IN THE INTERNATIONAL TRADING SYSTEM (1993)).

[36] Michael J. Trebilcock and Robert Howse, THE REGULATION OF INTERNATIONAL TRADE 151 (2nd ed. 1999).

[37] Trebilcock and Howse, *supra* note 36, at 151.

[38] Charnovitz, *supra* note 28, at 25–26.

[39] Naomi Roht-Arriaza, *Shifting the Point of Regulation: The International Organization for Standardization and Global Lawmaking on Trade and the Environment*, 22 ECOLOGY L.Q. 479, 499 (1995) (emphasis added) (footnotes omitted).

[40] *Ibid.* at 500.

[41] *See ibid.* at 10.

Social and Environmental Accreditation and Labelling (ISEAL) Alliance, have adopted all or some of its provisions, including ones that are voluntary as well as mandatory.[42] Despite these non-binding principles and voluntary initiatives, the process by which the private standards themselves come into being is largely shielded from public view. The "fair trade" standards are an example of a stated grassroots collaborative approach towards relatively open standards, deliberately involving producers (farmer associations) as well as the third-party certifier, Fairtrade Labelling Organizations (FLO International), the non-profit international fair trade certification consortium.[43] By contrast, purely proprietary standard-setting by a firm, such as the C.A.F.E. standards set by Starbucks, may not necessarily involve regulatory entrepreneurs or stakeholders other than the firm itself and also may be less transparent.[44]

C Certifications

Third-party certifications of conformance to standards are key components of this private form of regulation. As Meidinger explains:

> A central actor in implementing multi-interest self-governance is the certifier, who is conceived as a trustworthy expert who can verify for outsiders that a firm is performing to standard. The certifier is directly analogous to a government inspector or hearing officer in a traditional regulatory scheme, except that the firm, rather than the state, chooses and pays the certifier.[45]

Firms providing ISO 9000 quality assurance certification grew rapidly from roughly 28 000 in 1993 to 670 400 in 2004.[46] After the advent of environmental certification in 1996 (the ISO 14000 environmental management standards), the number of firms and facilities meeting those

---

[42] ISEAL Alliance, ISEAL Code of Good Practice for Setting Social and Environmental Standards 4 (Jan. 2006) (Public Version 4), *available at* http://www.fairtrade.net/fileadmin/user_upload/content/P005_ISEAL_Code_PD4_Jan_06.pdf.

[43] Fairtrade Labelling Organization, http://www.fairtrade.net/ (last visited April 10, 2013).

[44] STARBUCKS CORP., CORPORATE SOCIAL RESPONSIBILITY, FISCAL 2007 ANNUAL REPORT: OUR COMMITMENT TO ETHICAL COFFEE SOURCING 11 (2007) [hereinafter STARBUCKS CSR REPORT].

[45] Meidinger, *supra* note 22, at 267.

[46] OTA REPORT, *supra* note 19, at 6.

standards rose to 90 569 in 2004.[47] Currently the ISO 26000 standard, published in 2010, provides "Guidance on Social Responsibility."[48]

Certification is also fueled by a growing demand for products that embody workplace safety, labor, and environmental minimum standards by, for example, Socially Responsible Investment (SRI) funds.[49] This demand for socially responsible trade also correlates with the decided rise in NGO activity during the 1990s.[50] Some of these NGOs catalyze the standard-setting process; others are involved as third-party certifiers; some are mark holders; a few engage in all three activities.

A number of social responsibility-oriented certifying firms came into existence in the 1990s. One major firm specializing in third-party social accountability certification is Social Accountability International (SAI), which is a U.S.-based, non-profit organization that promulgates "an auditable certification standard [SA8000] based on international and workplace norms."[51] Socially responsible trade is evident as well in voluntary CSR standards adopted by second-party certifiers such as industry associations.[52] For example, the Kimberley Process Certification Scheme is a system administered through the diamond industry, and functions both to certify diamonds in accordance with a U.N. resolution to address the problem of conflict diamonds[53] and to meet demand for conflict-free diamonds by wealthy, socially aware consumers.[54] FLO International is a non-profit, multi-stakeholder association established in

---

[47]   Blair, *supra* note 9, at 7.

[48]   Andrew Johnston, *ISO 26000: Guiding Companies to Sustainability Through Social Responsibility?* (June 13, 2012). European Company Law, Kluwer Law International, Special Issue on CSR and SRI, 2012, volume 9, issue 2, 110–117; University of Oslo Faculty of Law Research Paper No. 2012-11, *available at* SSRN: http://ssrn.com/abstract=2083479 or http://dx.doi.org/10.2139/ssrn.2083479.

[49]   Blair, *supra* note 9, at 8.

[50]   *Ibid.*; *see also* James McGann and Mary Johnstone, *The Power Shift and the NGO Credibility Crisis*, INT'L J. NOT-FOR-PROFIT L., Jan. 2006, at 65, 67 ("*The Economist* estimates that the number of international non-governmental organizations rose from 6,000 in 1990 to 26,000 in 1996. According to the 2002 UNDP Human Development Report, nearly one-fifth of the world's thirty-seven thousand INGOs (international non-governmental organizations) were formed in the 1990s.").

[51]   Overview of SA8000, *available at* www.sa-intl.org/index.cfm?fuseaction=Page.viewPage&pageId=473 (last visited April 10, 2013).

[52]   OTA REPORT, *supra* note 19, at 20.

[53]   *See* G.A. Res. 55/56, U.N. Doc. A/RES/55/56 (Jan. 29, 2001).

[54]   Footer, *supra* note 10, at 17–18 (discussing the 2003 WTO waiver covering conflict diamonds).

1997, which bills itself as the leading standard-setting and certification organization for labeled Fairtrade.[55] Because it separates the certification process from the standards-setting process, it complies with the ISO standards.[56]

Whether within or without the ISO framework, certification itself is ironically not an area that is carefully supervised. Within a third-party certification framework generally, the potential for abuse of consumer trust exists because supplier firms requiring certification to do business with purchaser firms may pick the third-party certifier – resulting in an obviously less than a fully disinterested certifier.[57] This problem is quite apparent in the financial services industry where credit rating agencies such as Moody's or Standard & Poor's have contributed to the misleading nature of financial viability on Wall Street.[58] There may be other issues related to misreporting of information by producers to the third-party certifier.[59] And the third-party certifiers themselves may be under-resourced, be untrained or unable to check for certain standards and/or engage in less than due diligence.

D Marks

The growth of standards and certifications raises the question of what type of quality assurance is represented by their accompanying labels and marks, if any. How are these labeling initiatives understood by the

---

[55]   Fairtrade Labelling Organizations, supra note 43.

[56]   Stephanie Barrentios and Sally Smith, *Mainstreaming Fair Trade in Global Production Networks*, *in* FAIR TRADE, *supra* note 11, at 118–19; FAIR TRADE, *supra* note 13, at 19 (referencing International Organization for Standardization, ISO/IEC Guide 65: 1996 (1996)).

[57]   Blair et al., *supra* note 9, at 5; Meidinger, *supra* note 22, at 267 (noting that certification programs do not seem to have focused very carefully on this risk thus far, but rather they have dealt with it by primarily relying on professionalism in accreditation standards and, in some cases, random external auditing); Roht-Arriaza, *supra* note 39, at 534 (pointing to evidence of massive industry violations of a voluntary code of conduct with respect to the use of pesticides).

[58]   Lewis and Einhorn, *supra* note 22 (describing how short-term interests of credit rating agencies led to dubious ratings, and recommending reforms so that issuers do not pay for ratings).

[59]   Giovannucci and Ponte, *supra* note 21, at 291–92 (listing issues ranging from inspections that may take place only once to the employment of untrained college students to verify standards).

various market actors?[60] I posit that the current meaning-making environment for trademarks and CMs is highly dynamic. It involves overt interplay among the usual suspects: domestic courts and agencies such as the U.S. Patent and Trademark Office (USPTO), competitors in the realms of products and standards, mark holders and consumers. But, in a global governance framework, the discourse also expands to include multiple other stakeholders: SSOs like ISEAL; third-party certifiers (which may or may not be the same as the mark holders); other actors in the value chain; competing standards-setting bodies and their constituents, such as industry associations, consumer organizations, other NGOs, other intergovernmental agencies;[61] and government agencies across multiple jurisdictions. Current U.S. trademark law funnels all these perspectives through the proxy of the consumer confused with respect to the claims of competing firms. However, the consumer confusion being generated by standards is of a very different sort than envisioned through a simpler, more territorially bounded lens.

1 Quality

The conventional narrative of trademark law is that the firm's trademark functions to indicate the source of manufacturing origin of a product, so as to provide cognitive shortcuts to a consumer who will then re-purchase the same product if satisfied with the product's quality.[62] At least in countries that have adopted Anglo-American principles of unfair competition, the underlying rationale of trademark protection is based upon a decentralized and privatized consumer protection scheme, where enforcement is provided by competitors, who act as proxies for the consumers. Liability attaches to "passing off" – that is, a competitor's labeling that "is likely to cause confusion, or to cause mistake, or to deceive"[63] so as to mix up the quality assurance signal performed by the mark.

But as the Office of Technology Assessment (OTA) has noted,

> [t]he concept of "quality" of a product has become more complex over the last decade, incorporating aspects of product differentiation, health, safety, social and environmental implications of both products and processes, trends

---

[60] Graeme B. Dinwoodie and Mark D. Janis, *Confusion Over Use: Contextualism in Trademark Law*, 92 Iowa L. Rev. 1597, 1604 (2007).

[61] The International Trade Centre (ITC) and the U.N. Conference on Trade and Development (UNCTAD) have been active in promoting ethical trade via standards.

[62] *See generally* Deven R. Desai and Sandra L. Rierson, *Confronting the Genericism Conundrum*, 28 Cardozo L. Rev. 1789 (2007).

[63] 15 U.S.C. § 1114(1)(a) (2006).

that would otherwise seem to require more managerial involvement and thus movement of production into vertically-integrated firms. Yet ISO and other reliable standards have been developed that permit standardization of these otherwise complex phenomena, including the management systems to address them, permitting clear communication to industrial buyers and consumers through third-party assurance and *certification to credible quality standards*.[64]

The assumptions underlying the "credible quality standards" upon which the OTA's description rests are dubious. They do not account for, or even anticipate, the possible miscommunication resulting from a global marketplace characterized by longer value chains, greater outsourcing, growing complexity of products, and increased division of labor.

The traditional trademark guarantee of quality is not typically mediated by third parties – rather, the consumer directly experiences the quality of the good or service bearing a mark. By contrast, as described in previous sections, standards and certifications inevitably make what is being signaled by the mark quite intricate and opaque. And, the consumer is located a fair distance in the value chain from an entity (certifier) that creates a potentially false signal. The quality guaranteed by a certifying firm may or may not be reflected in a mark *per se*; many standards are used in addition to a mark as part of an overall marketing strategy.[65] A consumer is not going to be able to tell whether a firm claiming that its products are not tested on animals has in fact tested its mascara on bunnies, and must simply trust the certifier.

Compared with trademarks, the purpose of certification marks is to guarantee characteristics of the goods or services, rather than to brand the goods and services themselves.[66] Indeed, the conventional wisdom is that

---

[64]   Blair et al., *supra* note 9, at 16 (emphasis added) (citing Peter Gibbon and Stefano Ponte, *Quality Standards, Conventions and the Governance of Global Value Chains*, 34 ECON. & SOC'Y 1, 5 (2005)).

[65]   *See, e.g.*, Against Animal Testing, http://www.thebodyshop.com/_en/_ww/values-campaigns/against-animal-testing.aspx? (last visited April 10, 2013) (owning a registered mark in its business name and having a well-honed reputation for sustainable business practices); *see also* Milk and Cream, http://www.benjerry.com/activism/mission-statement (last visited April 10, 2013).

[66]   Both collective marks and certification marks were added to the U.S. trademark statute in 1938 in order to comply with obligations under the Paris Convention for the Protection of Industrial Property art. 7*bis*, Mar. 20, 1883, 21 U.S.T. 1583, 828 U.N.T.S. 305 (done as revised at Brussels on December 14, 1900, at Washington on June 2, 1911, at The Hague on November 6, 1925, at London on June 2, 1934, at Lisbon on October 31, 1958, and at Stockholm on July 14, 1967, and as amended on September 28, 1979) [hereinafter Paris Convention]; *see Hearing on S. 2679 Before the J. Comm. on Patents*, 68th

CMs are the appropriate vehicle within the Lanham Act to represent standards and certifications. For example, the USPTO has advocated the use of CMs as geographical indications, which are often based upon standards developed by regional producer associations. Upon closer examination, however, CMs have numerous drawbacks, preventing them from being a consistent basis for oversight of this complex area.

It is not clear whether firms have incentives to invest in or market CMs under U.S. law, unless standards are already widespread or a firm wants to encourage the adoption of new standards. On the one hand, CMs can generate revenue for a CM holder (especially where standards are *de facto* requirements for legitimate business). On the other hand, the CM holder is obligated to license the mark to all firms that meet the standard and may not market its own products bearing a CM.[67] Until a standard is dominant in a market or unless the mark holder is committed to something other than profit, there may be little motivation to nurture a CM to maturity. When the mark holder is a non-profit or NGO, marketing may not be as high a priority as developing standards or working with producers.

Even if a firm does invest in and register a CM, the same issue arises as discussed above in the context of a trademark generally. Again, the relevant consumer confusion in a global marketplace may be due more to the lack of transparency of characteristics guaranteed by the CM than to the inability to distinguish between a real and a fake mark (the classic passing-off scenario). For these and other reasons, conflicts may exist between objectives of a certification program and that of marketing or licensing a trademark affiliated with the CM.[68]

Cong. 153–54 (1925) (statement of Bernard A. Kosicki, Bureau of Foreign and Domestic Commerce, Department of Commerce), *reprinted in* 3 TRADEMARK PROTECTION AND PRACTICE: SECTION BY SECTION LEGISLATIVE HISTORY OF THE LANHAM ACT § 4, at 4–5 (Jerome Gilson ed., 1988) [hereinafter Gilson] ("That would also, I believe, meet with our international obligations, in article 7 1/2 [*sic*] of the Paris Convention of 1883, which provides for the registration of association trade-marks. So far we have not given effect to that measure because no machinery was available.").

[67] 15 U.S.C. § 1064 (2006).

[68] The Ethiopian Coffee Network, for example, decided to use a trademark licensing strategy rather than a CM approach to promoting Ethiopian coffees in Northern markets. *See* About the Trademark and Licensing Initiative, http://www.ethiopiancoffeenetwork.com/about6.shtml (last visited April 10, 2013); *but see* Justin Hughes, *Coffee and Chocolate: Helping Developing Country Farmers Through Geographical Indications* (unpublished paper on file with author) (divining contradictory reasons for Ethiopia's decision).

The flip side of opacity is too much information. Consumers may face a confusing proliferation of certifications, labels, and marks.[69] While competition among standards can lead to innovation and increased quality of goods, it can also lead to the transactional costs associated with informational clutter in the market. Plainly stated, consumers are faced with multiple competing standards whose differences are not readily ascertainable. The plethora of certified organic standards[70] has led to a recent successful effort on the part of UNCTAD, FAO, and IFOAM to harmonize organic agriculture.[71] Outside this type of intergovernmental cooperation, standards may coalesce when a single standard-setting firm becomes dominant or if firms are encouraged to cooperate towards umbrella standards in the public interest (with or without the cooperation of a public agency) without fear of being accused of anticompetitive conduct.[72]

In an ideal system, firms would be rewarded for making standards more transparent. A strong incentive could be provided to link standards to CMs, which then could be licensed broadly, whether for a royalty or on a royalty-free basis.[73] Conversely, firms should be discouraged from developing completely private, proprietary standards that are problematically opaque and potentially unlicensed. These changes would address the twin dangers of lack of accountability and lack of transparency, explored at greater length below.

---

[69] Daniele Giovannucci, Oliver von Hagen, Joseph Wozniak, Corporate Social Responsibility and the Role of Voluntary Sustainability Standards *in* VOLUNTARY STANDARDS SYSTEMS – A CONTRIBUTION TO SUSTAINABLE DEVELOPMENT (Carsten Schmitz-Hoffmann, Michael Schmidt, Berthold Hansmann and Dmitry Palekhov eds., 2013).

[70] Meidinger, *supra* note 22 at 270.

[71] INTERNATIONAL TASK FORCE ON HARMONIZATION AND EQUIVALENCE IN ORGANIC AGRICULTURE, COMMUNIQUÉ FROM THE 8TH INTERNATIONAL TASK-FORCE MEETING (2008).

[72] The Standards Development Organization Advancement Act of 2004, Pub. L. No. 108-237, § 102, 118 Stat. 661, 661–62, provides for a number of incentives and safe harbors for SSOs, including the evaluation of their conduct under an antitrust rule of reason. 15 U.S.C. § 4302 (2006).

[73] Giovannucci and Ponte, *supra* note 21, at 289; *accord* Karen Ellis and Michael Warner, Research Fellows, Overseas Dev. Inst., IS THE TIME RIPE FOR A GOOD FOR DEVELOPMENT PRODUCT LABEL? 1 (Oct. 2007), *available at* http://www.odi.org.uk/resources/odi-publications/opinions/88-karen-ellis-michael-warner-good-for-development.pdf.

2 Accountability and transparency

It is theoretically possible that competing standards (through competing marks) can stake out differential semiotic values *vis-à-vis* each other.[74] However, without dominant industry standards, consumers can experience lack of accountability and transparency in at least two ways: lack of accessible information about the substance of standards and informational clutter when many competing standards exist. The challenge of navigating between these two transactional costs can be illustrated through the example of GIs (geographic indications).

In the wake of TRIPS, commentators have focused on GIs as a specific type of CM.[75] Both kinds of CMs – whether GIs as source of "regional ... origin" or CMs generally as a source of "other origin, material, mode of manufacture, quality, accuracy, or other characteristics,"[76] are deeply implicated in global trade.[77] While this chapter is not about GIs *per se*, the treatment of GIs – particularly the standard-setting process underlying designation of a particular food, wine, or spirit as a GI – is pertinent. One issue is whether the proliferation of GIs actually assists rather than confuses consumers in the marketplace.[78] A challenge of "too much information" faces both standards embedded within marks and GIs.

Article 22 of the TRIPS Agreement establishes minimum standards for the protection of GIs in member countries.[79] Article 22 defines geographic indications as "indications which identify a good as originating in the territory of a Member, or a region or locality in that territory, *where a given quality, reputation or other characteristic of the good is essentially attributable to its geographical origin*."[80] Under Article 22(2) of the TRIPS Agreement, TRIPS members are required to provide the "legal means" for interested parties to prevent:

---

[74]   Barton Beebe, *The Semiotic Analysis of Trademark Law*, 51 UCLA L. REV. 621, 643 (2004).

[75]   *See, e.g.*, Justin Hughes, *Champagne, Feta, and Bourbon: The Spirited Debate about Geographical Indications*, 58 HASTINGS L.J. 299 (2006); Tomer Broude, *Taking "Trade and Culture" Seriously: Geographical Indications & Cultural Protection in WTO Law*, 26 U. PA. J. INT'L ECON. L. 623 (2005).

[76]   15 U.S.C. § 1127 (providing the definition of CM).

[77]   As McCarthy puts it, "[w]ith a growing world market in foodstuffs, accurate identification of the geographic origin of food and beverages has become of increasing importance." McCarthy, *supra* note 24, § 14:1.

[78]   *See, e.g.*, Hughes, *supra* note 75, at 346.

[79]   *See* TRIPS Agreement, *supra* note 30, art. 22.

[80]   *Ibid.*, art. 22, para. 1 (emphasis added).

    (a) the use of any means in the designation or presentation of a good that indicates or suggests that the good in question originates in a geographical area other than the true place of origin in a manner which misleads the public as to the geographical origin of the good;

    (b) any use which constitutes an act of unfair competition within the meaning of Article 10*bis* of the Paris Convention (1967).[81]

With regard to paragraph b above, Article 10*bis* of the Paris Convention for the Protection of Industrial Property ("the Paris Convention") prohibits the use of any act of competition that "in the course of trade is liable to mislead the public as to the *nature, the manufacturing process, the characteristics, the suitability for their purpose*, or the quantity, of the goods."[82] Parallels between GIs and other types of certification suggest that Article 10*bis* can and should be used more aggressively to prevent misleading use of standards. When standards enter the picture, the tension between not providing enough information through a mark and providing too much information requires careful calibration, in order to provide for optimal regulatory accountability and transparency.

E   Regulatory Entrepreneurs within Global Value Chains

Decentralized rather than top-down approaches towards promoting social welfare are encouraged by the neoliberal trade framework, characterized by the "decline of state intervention and of market regulation and the rise of NGO-led development projects."[83] As stated earlier, effective functioning of this model depends on the motivation of regulatory entrepreneurs, who may consist of a variety of stakeholders including consumers. However, there are also possible costs and pitfalls to this decentralized model, including where to locate points of meaningful participation, such as accountability and transparency, within this heavily privatized framework.

From a consumer perspective, specific certification standards can be found on the websites of the larger SSOs, but they are not available in a

---

[81]   *Ibid.*, art. 22, paras. 2(a)–(b). The TRIPS Agreement also provides heightened protection for wines and spirits. Specifically, under Article 23, geographic indications may not be used for wines and spirits even if the public would not be deceived. *See ibid.*, art. 23, para. 1.

[82]   *See* Paris Convention, *supra* note 66, art. 10*bis*, para. (3)3 (emphasis added); *see also* Hughes, *supra* note 75, at 317.

[83]   Fridell, *supra* note 13, at 94.

form that provides meaningful shorthand to consumers.[84] Thus, a consumer will have to engage in a fair amount of research to compare and contrast the various standards. Currently, consumer trust in certified goods and services can only operate at the *caveat emptor* level, because so much of the standard-setting and certification process is beyond public oversight. At the same time, standard-setting activities can result (and have indeed resulted) in different, inconsistent regimes governing the same area.

Adequate global accountability may be lacking among *all* of the institutions engaged in global governance, and accountability itself should be looked at as a comparative phenomenon. Thus, one should expect the attributes of accountability for non-state actors to be different than for states or others.[85] In regard to standards, the OTA has stated that:

> [d]ue process ... is not a constant. Agreement about what is a fair and open standardization process changes over time and in different circumstances. Today, the rapid advance of technology, the shift to a global economy, the rise of user groups, and the desire to substitute voluntary standards for regulation will likely put the issue of due process into much starker relief.[86]

As Meidinger notes, these multi-stakeholder governance systems "are best understood as *compound* accountability systems, resting on ... open and transparent decisional procedures, and dynamic competition among certification programs for business and public acceptance."[87]

Nonetheless, while accountability may be different for non-state actors than for public agencies, many observers have noted that the nature of standard-setting may leave too much discretion in the hands of self-interested firms. While it makes sense for standards to be set in part by the firms involved in the relevant industries, it is not equally sensible that

---

[84]   Table of Fair Trade Coffee Standards (unpublished and on file with author). My very able and motivated research assistants spent many hours discerning the differences among coffee standards, based on publicly available information on the Internet.

[85]   Ruth W. Grant and Robert O. Keohane, *Accountability and Abuses of Power in World Politics*, 99 AM. POL. SCI. REV. 29 (2005).

[86]   OTA Report, *supra* note 19, at 18 (emphasis omitted); *see also ibid.* ("Due process issues are inherent in standardization. Safeguards must be built into the process, because manufacturers and users can use standards to set prices and constrain trade. In a pluralistic society such as the United States, competition and countervailing forces provide such safeguards. It is assumed that no one party can dominate the standards setting process because it is transparent and everyone can participate.").

[87]   Meidinger, *supra* note 22, at 284.

they should be the only actors involved in enforcement through certification. Additionally, meaningful opportunity for consumer as well as producer involvement in the standards must be provided.

Private standards and CSR alternatives not only raise questions about industry capture, but also of clutter in the signals, which Trebilcock and Howse view as a type of "regulatory inefficiency."[88] Private standard-setting in the sustainable forestry area has led to regulatory competition between one major NGO and an industry substitute, resulting in regulatory convergence.[89] By contrast, the multiplicity of signals in most areas regulated through certification suggests possible limits to alternative governance. The proliferation of signals raises questions not only of what we mean by alternative trade but also what we mean by civil society. The general history of private standard-setting within the United States shows domination by corporate interests, and even a relatively recent OECD report expressed ongoing unease with the possibility of private capture of *de facto* regulation.[90] A truly robust system of private regulation should account for consumers as regulatory entrepreneurs in their own right, with meaningful replacements for the principles of due process (notice and opportunity to be heard) that are essential design components of its public regulatory counterparts.

III   CONCLUSION: THINKING AND ACTING GLOBALLY

The ascendancy of standards is part of a discernible pluralistic trend in global intellectual property.[91] This chapter suggests that the nature of pluralism in standards extends very deeply into the nongovernmental or private side of norm-setting, involving non-state actors such as NGOs,

---

[88]   *Ibid.* at 278.

[89]   *Ibid.* at 261 (alliances centered around FSC versus PEFC); *see also* Misty L. Archambault, *Making the Brand, Using Brand Management to Encourage Market Acceptance of Forestry Certification*, 81 N.Y.U. L. REV. 1400, 1408 (2006) (explaining differences between Forestry Stewardship Council (FSC) and the Sustainable Forestry Initiative (SFI)). FSC is a certification promulgated by the NGO sector as opposed to SFI being pushed by trade associations. *See ibid.*

[90]   Trebilcock and Howse, *supra* note 36, at 228–29 (citing the OECD Report on Regulatory Reform, 1997).

[91]   Margaret Chon, *Global Intellectual Property Pluralism and the Domains of Development, in* WORKING WITHIN THE BOUNDARIES OF INTELLECTUAL PROPERTY (Rochelle Dreyfuss, Harry First and Diane Zimmerman eds., 2009), *available at* http://papers.ssrn.com/sol3/papers.cfm?abstract_id=1743803.

industry or producer associations, regional or international coalitions and other stakeholders.[92] Consumers' interests have been underemphasized in this expanding private regulatory scheme.

Soft law initiatives such as standardization through certification and labeling involve the increasing intertwining of private and public, national and international, as well as commercial and social justice domains of law. Either explicitly or implicitly, standard-setting and certifications in these global value chains operate under the shadow of the law of unfair competition, and should be viewed as an integral part of that long-standing body of common law, for which an international hard law norm exists (Article 10*bis* of the Paris Convention). A more vigorous deployment of these existing legal tools may shift the territorial focus of trademark law more effectively and successfully onto the global plane and provide a public law method of steering private regulation.

As suggested in the introduction, marks are thought to provide a signaling function to consumers through their significant roles in pro-viding informational shortcuts for consumers in market transactions. However, this chapter suggests that another account of trademarks – what might be called their trust function – deserves to be explored more fully, particularly in the context of global trade.[93] This further investigation I will leave to future efforts.

---

[92]   Meidinger, supra note 22, at 273–76.

[93]   Ariel Katz, *Beyond Search Costs: The Linguistic and Trust Functions of Trademarks*, Brigham Young Univ. L. Rev. 1555 (2010), *available at* SSRN: http://ssrn.com/abstract=1497103 ([T]rademarks perform two main functions that are related yet distinct: they reduce search costs by condensing complex meanings into concise and unequivocal terms, and they allow buyers to trust and rely upon the signals conveyed by sellers as guarantees for quality, thus helping to prevent the lemonization of markets for goods with experience and credence attributes. Let us call the first function the *linguistic function* of trademarks and the second the *trust function* of trademarks.).

6. Branding the land: creating global meanings for local characteristics

Doris Estelle Long[*]

I INTRODUCTION

Despite the power of global brands[1] to dominate the market, local brands remain strong competitors, particularly when the goods reflect local tastes and culture. "Branding the land" strategies that use geographic designators[2] to promote locally produced goods, provide useful tools for expanding their market.[3] In the era of "long tail"

---

[*] Professor of Law, Director of the Center for Intellectual Property Laws and Chair, Intellectual Property, Information Technology and Privacy Group, the John Marshall Law School, Chicago, Illinois. This chapter is based on ideas first contained in my article *Is Fame All There Is?: Beating Global Monopolists at Their Own Marketing Game*, 40 GEO. WASH. INT'L L. REV 123 (2008). Thanks to Irene Calboli and Edward Lee for the invitation to expand those initial ideas into the growing debate over the role of territoriality in global brand protections. As always, any errors in this chapter belong solely to me.

[1] I use the term "global brands" advisedly. No mark is ever truly "global," but many brands play such a dominant role in diverse geographic markets as to warrant a designation more powerful than the contested terms "well-known" or "famous." The brands are generally owned by multinational corporations and often rely on brand loyalty to leverage market share. See Doris Estelle Long, *Is Fame All There Is?: Beating Global Monopolists at Their Own Marketing Game*, 40 GEO. WASH. INT'L L. REV 123 (2008) (hereinafter "Long, FAME").

[2] I am using the term "geographic designator" to refer to the use of a geographic term that refers to the territorial origin of the associated good where such location provides some unique quality, characteristic, or reputation for that good. Such geographic designators include geographical indications, appellations of origin, denominations of origin, and geographic marks, including culture authentication marks, certification marks, and collective marks. For definitions of these diverse geographic designators, *see infra* notes 9, 27, 28, 67 and 76, respectively.

[3] *See infra* note 12.

economics,[4] where such goods have a perceived uniqueness based on qualities or characteristics derived from the local environment (terroir) or from the use of traditional production techniques (handicrafts), "branding the land" can help secure a potentially sustainable domestic industry. But achieving success in such efforts requires more than stamping local goods with a "geographic designator." To the contrary, efforts to create successful niche markets may be undermined by the evolving nature of the territorial relationship between "geographic designators" and the wide range of products sought to be brought under their imprimatur. Assuring that goods maintain the special territorially centered features that assure their uniqueness in the marketplace, while simultaneously conveying meaningful information to consumers about such features requires more than the simple addition of a geographical indication,[5] appellation of origin,[6] certification mark,[7] collective mark,[8] or other trademark that contains a geographic reference to the territorial origin of the associated goods.[9] It requires a nuanced approach that combines the assurance of production control by those most interested in maintaining product uniqueness with a carefully crafted legal regime that assures that the nature and meaning of the geographic designators used in connection with such goods provide consumers with meaningful information about this uniqueness. Present international regimes must be revised to assure that geographic designators contain adequate safeguards to assure the quality they signify and the consumer meaning they convey are the same. Without such revisions, "branding the land" strategies could become yet another failed economic experiment of the twenty-first century.

II BRANDING THE LAND

Despite the power of global brands, such as Starbucks, McDonald's, and Coca-Cola, to dominate the market in the twenty-first century, local marks have survived. The Coca-Cola and Pepsi-Cola brands are among the most dominant soft drink companies in the world. Yet despite this

---

[4] *See, e.g.*, CHRIS ANDERSON, THE LONG TAIL: WHY THE FUTURE OF BUSINESS IS SELLING LESS OF MORE (2006).

[5] *See infra* note 27.

[6] *See infra* note 28.

[7] *See infra* note 67.

[8] *See infra* note 76.

[9] These include culture authentication marks, discussed *infra* Section III.

dominance, notable local brands remain capable of maintaining a sustained market share. Inca Kola in Peru maintains approximately a 31 percent dominant market share.[10] Similarly, the Peruvian franchise Bembos Burger Grill maintains a strong local presence in Lima despite the increasing popularity of Burger King and McDonald's.[11] These examples demonstrate that local tastes may still form the basis for a strong market presence.

When local tastes are combined with product features derived from human traditions (handicrafts) or local environmental factors (terroir), the ability to create a viable local industry may be strengthened.[12] Thus,

---

[10] *Inca Kola*, INCA KOLA, http://www.solarnavigator.net/solar_cola/inca_ kola.htm (last visited Apr. 21, 2013); *see also* Eric J. Lyman, *In the Company of Giants ... Inca Kola*, ERICJLYMAN.COM (Oct. 1998), http://www.ericjlyman.com/ incakola.html (last visited May 5, 2013). Part of this dominance, however, may be due to its subsequent purchase by the Coca-Cola Company and its promotion as a regional alternative. *See* John Tagliabue, *U.S. Brands Abroad Are Feeling Global Tension*, N.Y. TIMES, Mar. 17, 2003, at C3.

[11] Luz Marina Garcia et al., *Bembos Burger Grill*, 1 J. OF INT'L BUS. EDUC. 111, 112 (2004), *available at* www.neilsonjournals.com/JIBE (last visited May 5, 2013); John S. Wolfe, *Peru: Bembos Outcooks McDonalds* (March 7, 2010), http://www.johnswolfe.com/business/peru-bembos-outcooks-mcdonalds (last visited May 5, 2013).

[12] *See, e.g.*, Cerkia Bramley, *A Review of the Socio-economic Impact of Geographical Indications: Considerations for the Developing World*, WORLD- WIDE SYMPOSIUM ON GEOGRAPHICAL INDICATIONS, LIMA, JUNE 22–24, 2011 (WIPO 2011) (discussing the positive economic impact of the use of geographical indications on diverse products), *available at* www.wipo.int/edocs/ mdocs/geoind/en/wipo_geo_lim_11/wipo_geo_lim_11_9.pdf (last visited May 5, 2013); Astrid Gerz, Dominique Barjolle and Denis Sautier, *Geographical Indications (GIs): A Way Forward for Local Development: International Training Module* (UMR Innovation 2007) (providing economic frameworks and analyses of the positive impact of the use of geographical indications on diverse goods), *available at* www.intergi.org/Geographical_Indications.pdf (last visited May 5, 2013); Alexandra Basak Russell, *Using Geographical Indications to Protect Artisanal Works in Developing Countries: Lessons from a Banana Republic's Misnomered Hat*, 19 TRANSNAT'L L. & CONTEMP. PROBS. 705 (Spring 2010) (describing the economic impact of protection for the geographical indication for the Montecristi hat from Ecuador). *But cf.* Dwijen Rangnekar, *The Socio- Economics of Geographical Indications: A Review of the Empirical Evidence from Europe* (UNCTAD and ICTSD 2004) (examining the differential economic impact of the use of geographical indications on diverse goods); Tim Josling, *The War on Terroir: Geographical Indications as a Transatlantic Trade Conflict*, 57 J. AGRIC. L. 337 (2006) (describing the adverse effect the geographical indication CHIANTI CLASSICO had on the ability of Italian wine producers to market a

sparkling wine produced locally in the Champagne region of France may have certain qualities derived from the soil, weather, and other environmental conditions in which the grapes are grown that make its production a potentially valuable domestic industry.[13] Similarly, silk produced in Mysore, India using traditional practices and designs may appeal to consumers seeking the unique qualities of handcrafted goods.[14] By employing "geographic designators" to market such products, industry can "brand the land," making geography a selling point, thereby helping to promote local industries. Sparkling wine becomes "champagne" and silks become "mysore." Simply using geographic designators in connection with locally produced goods, however, does not assure the development of a viable niche market. To the contrary, without domestic laws that assure that quality control of such geographically "branded"[15] goods is maintained in ways that supplement the consumer meaning embued in the selected geographic designator, "branding the land" strategies may only add to existing consumer confusion with regard to many geographic and other territorially linked[16] designators.

"modified" Chianti wine; the wine was later successfully marketed under the "Super Tuscan" designator).

[13] Admittedly, claims to a special terroir relationship between the soil and the vine of certain French wines may be somewhat attenuated as a result of the use of American roots to combat Phylloxera in the nineteenth century. *See Franc de Pied and Historical Reconstruction,* HTC EXPERIMENTS (December 20, 2012), http://htcexperiments.org/2012/12/20/franc-et-pied-and-historical-reconstruction (last visited May 5, 2013). The presence of such roots, however, arguably does not alter the impact that different climates and other environmental factors may have on the wine produced.

[14] *See* Press Release, 28 Products Registered as Geographical Indications, Government of India, Department of Commerce (November 9, 2006) (Mysore registered as GI for silk in India in 2006), *available at* commerce.nic.in (last visited May 5, 2013).

[15] I am using the term "brand" in the broader generic sense in which businesses use the term. *See* Long, FAME *supra* note 1. Thus, "champagne" serves as a "brand" since it promotes an arguably unique sparkling wine to consumers, even if it does not qualify as a "trademark" in the legal sense due to lack of distinctiveness.

[16] Such territorially linked designators include culture authentication marks placed on goods created by indigenous peoples, using traditional knowledge. *See* discussion *infra* Section III.

III SUPPORTING THE CREATION OF LOCAL INDUSTRIES

Some local industries capable of a "branding the land" marketing strategy arise through historical practices, such as the local brewery that uses traditional processes to create its beer. But others, such as craft-based industries, may require more than the creation of an appropriate legal regime to protect the geographic designators they will use to market their products. They need domestic laws that assure that the quality of such goods remains authentically unique. In creating such laws, countries must look beyond traditional trademark procedures and develop a legal regime for the protection of indigenous arts and practices, which could form a commercial base for new products and "brand the land" identities. Such "traditional knowledge," including protected folk art, may ultimately provide brand identities that have the potential to compete on a global scale because of the unique qualities of the goods associated with the application of such traditional knowledge.

The protection of traditional knowledge seeks to recognize and protect the creative and innovative works of indigenous groups, even if such works do not fit within current categories of traditional intellectual property. There is no presently agreed upon definition for the concepts of "traditional knowledge" or "traditional cultural expressions" – the copyright related subset of "traditional knowledge." Generally, however, to qualify as a potentially protectable form of traditional knowledge, the practice or work in question must be based on traditions that have been transmitted from generation to generation.[17] These are not necessarily works that represent "snapshots" of indigenous culture. To the contrary, part of the nature of traditional knowledge is that such traditions continue to evolve in response to a changing environment.[18] Generally, traditional knowledge includes a wide variety of spiritual and cultural beliefs and practices. Works based on traditional knowledge are most often currently considered part of the public domain because of their long existence or

---

[17] *See, e.g.*, Cathryn A. Berryman, *Toward More Universal Protection of Intangible Cultural Property*, 1 J. INTELL. PROP. L. 293, 297 (1994); Doris Estelle Long, *Traditional Knowledge and the Fight for the Public Domain*, 5 J. MARSHALL INTELL. PROP. L. REV. 316, 321 (2006) ("Long, FIGHT"); Angela R. Riley, *"Straight Stealing": Towards an Indigenous System of Cultural Property*, 80 WASH. L. REV. 69 (2005). *See generally* WIPO, THE PROTECTION OF TRADITIONAL CULTURAL EXPRESSIONS: DRAFT ARTICLES (2012); WIPO, THE PROTECTION OF TRADITIONAL KNOWLEDGE: DRAFT ARTICLES (2012).

[18] *See* MICHAEL F. BROWN, WHO OWNS NATIVE CULTURE? 42–68 (2003).

their present identification as part of a nation's cultural patrimony. Such forms would include (but not be limited to) fables, stories, myths, rituals, costumes, folk medicine, and other elements of pre-literate society that combine to form cultural "expression" or heritage.[19] Because most folklore and ritual lack identifiable creators or holders of rights, their protection poses unique problems for intellectual property regimes.[20] Such protection, however, under domestic *sui generis* or expanded intellectual property regimes would allow local groups to develop local industries to commercialize those aspects of traditional knowledge that the relevant rights holders want to commercialize.[21]

The sale of authentic, traditional knowledge-based works not only supports the development of local industries, it provides a strong basis for developing local marks that can compete without the large resource expenditures required to challenge a global mark. Traditional knowledge holders can avoid these expenditures, because generally no global mark can be associated with the same types of goods. By their very nature, being based on the practices of a particular tribe, authentic goods utilizing traditional knowledge should be relatively unique. This uniqueness should help prevent legitimate producers from marketing competing goods under a globally famous non-indigneous-based brand.

---

[19] *See, e.g.*, Berryman, *supra* note 17, at 310; Paul Kuruk, *Protecting Folklore Under Modern Intellectual Property Regimes: A Reappraisal of the Tensions Between Individual and Communal Rights in Africa and the United States*, 48 AM. U. L. REV. 769, 776–80 (1999); Long, FIGHT *supra* note 17, at 318–21; Riley, *supra* note 17, at 77.

[20] *See, e.g.*, Doris Estelle Long, *The Impact of Foreign Investment on Indigenous Culture: An Intellectual Property Perspective*, 23 N.C. J. INT'L L. & COM. REG. 101, 269 (1998); Kuruk, *supra* note 19, at 788–99; Riley, *supra* note 17, at 80.

[21] Not all traditional knowledge is protected for purposes of commercialization. To the contrary, sacred works are often protected to avoid such commercialization. *See* Daniel Gervais, 11 CARDOZO J. INT'L & COMP. L. 467, 469 (2003) (defining sacred traditional as "the opposite of profane or secular, the extreme forms of which are commercially exploited"); Peter Yu, *Traditional Knowledge, Intellectual Property, and Indigenous Culture: An Introduction* 4 n. 16 (describing the confidential nature of many sacred ceremonies), *available at* http://www.peteryu.com/tk.pdf (last visited May 5, 2013). A complete traditional knowledge protection scheme would need to address such works, as well as those for which commercialization is permitted. *See* Doris Estelle Long, *Trade Secrets and Traditional Knowledge: Strengthening International Protection of Indigenous Innovation,* in THE LAW AND THEORY OF TRADE SECRECY, CH. 19 (Rochelle Cooper Dreyfuss and Katherine Strandberg eds., 2011) ("Long, TRADE SECRETS").

Authentication is a critical component in developing local brands and industries. It prevents locally produced goods from being "hijacked" by non-local producers and helps prevent de-culturalizing uses of cultural goods. Many countries, including India, Mexico, and Brazil, have successfully utilized geographic designations to support the marketing of tradition-based local goods.[22] The issue presented in crafting an adequate legal regime that assures that the meaning of such designators adequately communicates the true nature and quality of those goods to consumers is discussed more thoroughly below in Section IV. Tradition-based goods, however, create a separate problem of authentic meaning that exists outside the scope of any geographic designator that may be used to market the products. It is the problem of cultural authentication, including an assurance of adequate respect for the traditions and culture used to create such goods.

In commercializing traditional knowledge-based goods, authentication marks must be created that assure that culture and tradition-based goods are offered in a manner that respects the culture and traditions of the holders of the traditional knowledge represented by the associated goods.[23] "Culture authentication" marks can serve as powerful tools for enhancing local identity brands. The value of culture authentication marks, however, must be secured by limiting the use of traditional symbols to authentic goods and other uses approved by the legitimate holders of the incorporated traditional knowledge. These limits are required on two grounds. First, such restrictions help secure the value of local brand identities in the marketplace by maintaining both their uniqueness as well as their relationship to tradition-based works (further enhancing their value as authenticating signifiers). Second, these limits ensure that any traditional symbols will not be used in contravention of cultural traditions. While this latter goal is not directly related to the commercial valuation of culture authentication marks, establishing a procedure that provides an adequate balance between the rights of indigenous peoples and the needs of the marketplace furthers both the

---

[22]   *See supra* note 12.

[23]   *See* Terri Janke, *Minding Culture: Case-Studies on Intellectual Property and Traditional Cultural Expressions, Case Study Eight: Indigenous Arts Certification Mark* 3–4 (2003), *available at* http://www.wipo.int/tk/en/studies/cultural/minding-culture/studies/finalstudy.pdf (discussing main objectives of an authentication system); Mariana Annas, *The Label of Authenticity: A Certification Trade Mark for Goods and Services of Indigenous Origin*, 3 ABORIGINAL L. BULL., Mar. 1997, at 4. Often the holders of such traditional knowledge are the tribe itself. *See* Long, TRADE SECRETS, *supra* note 21.

goals of respect for the human rights of traditional knowledge holders and the needs of developing countries for viable branded goods that can compete successfully in the global marketplace.

Culture authentication marks may not necessarily comprise geographic designators, but they nonetheless represent designators linked to precise territorial areas (homelands) and present the same issues of meaning and signification as other geographic designators. For example, the Maori historically have inhabited New Zealand. Maori-made goods, therefore, have a strong land connection to New Zealand. Marks associated with the Maori, such as the toi-iho mark to indicate authentic Maori-made goods,[24] therefore represent products with a geographic connection to New Zealand. So long as such goods remain authentic, then the geographic and quality significations incorporated in the culture authentication mark should be conveyed to consumers (assuming adequate promotion of the significance of the mark as meaning "Maori-made goods").[25] Other culture authentication marks, however, are not so transparent in their meanings. Consider the example of two indigenous groups located in the United States: the Cherokee Nation and the Iroquois (the Haudenosaunee). Members of the Cherokee Nation have traditionally been located within the geographic boundaries of the United States. By contrast, members of the Iroquois live in two countries, the United States and Canada, due to an historical division of territory in which the Iroquois had no voice. Similar to the issues of conflicting geographies for purely geographic designators discussed below in Section IV, the award of rights to a culture authentication mark must be crafted with regard to reducing the potential consumer confusion that may arise. A designator of "Iroquois" for tradition-based goods created by members of the Canadian Iroquois and marketed in the United States would not accurately portray the true geographic origin of the goods in question or the nature of those goods. Such lack of clarity is particularly critical where practices between geographically dispersed tribes have diverged, as in the case of the some Iroquois-produced goods. While the U.S. Iroquois forbid any commercialization of ceremonial "False Face Masks,"[26] Canadian Iroquois offer hand-carved versions for sale on the

---

[24] The "toi-iho" mark, registered in New Zealand by the Maori, is used "to promote and sell authentic, quality Maori arts and crafts." *Welcome to toi iho*, Toi Iho, http://www.toiiho.co.nz (last visited Apr. 21, 2013).

[25] *See* discussion *infra* Section III.

[26] *See* Chief Leon Shenandoah, *Haudenosaunee Confederacy Policy on False Face Masks* (2001), *available at* http://www.peace4turtleisland.org/pages/maskpolicy.htm (last visited May 5, 2013).

Internet. In Canada, "Iroquois" false face masks would be an accurate designator of the geographic and cultural characteristics of the goods. In the United States, it would be misleading.

IV GEOGRAPHICAL INDICATIONS AND THE STRENGTHENING OF LOCAL IDENTITY

Local brand values are also enhanced through a rationalized system of protection for geographical indications,[27] appellations of origin,[28] and other geographic signifiers that represent local characteristics.[29] Trademarks are source identifiers that by their very nature are generally owned

---

[27] Geographical indications are generally geographic terms and other indicators of the geographic origin of a particular good where a given quality, reputation, or other characteristic is attributable to the geographic source of the product. *See, e.g.*, TRIPS, art. 22(1) (defining geographical indications as "indications which identify a good as originating in the territory of a Member, or a region or a locality of that territory, where a given quality, reputation or other characteristic of the good is easily attributable to its geographical origin"); Council Regulation 510/2006, art. 2(1)(b), 2006 O.J. (L 93) 12, 14 (EC) (defining a "geographical indication" as "the name of a region, a specific place or, in exceptional cases, a country, used to describe an agricultural product or a foodstuff: originating in that region, specific place or country, and which possesses a specific quality, reputation or other characteristics attributable to that geographical origin, and the production and/or processing and/or preparation of which take place in the defined geographical area").

[28] An "appellation of origin" has been defined as "the geographical name of a country, region or locality which serves to designate a product originating therein, the quality and characteristics of which are due exclusively or essentially to the geographical environment, including natural and human factors." Lisbon Agreement for the Protection of Appellations of Origin and their International Registration art. 2(1), Oct. 31, 1958, last amended Sept. 28, 1979, 923 U.N.T.S. 205 [hereinafter Lisbon Agreement] (emphasis added); *see also* Council Regulation 510/2006, art. 2(1)(a), 2006 O.J. (L 93) 12, 14 (EC) (defining a "designation of origin" as "a name of a region, a specific place or in exceptional cases, a country, used to describe an agricultural product or a foodstuff: originating in that region, specific place or country, the quality or characteristics of which are essentially or exclusively due to a particular geographical environment with its inherent natural and human factors, and the production, processing and preparation of which take place in the defined geographical area").

[29] Other geographic signifiers include protected "designations of origins" and geographic indicia of production, such as "made in Greece."

by a single holder and represent a privately owned business asset.[30] By contrast, geographical indications and other geographic designators represent collective signifiers.[31] They are used by the producers of a particular good from a particular region as a consumer signal for geographically linked qualities. CHAMPAGNE for sparkling wines,[32] IDAHO for potatoes,[33] KALAMATA for olives,[34] DARJEELING for tea,[35] and ROQUEFORT for cheese,[36] all provide significant consumer information regarding the products with which they are associated. But beyond being information purveyors, geographical indications, like trademarks, may represent reputational quality that can have significant market value for the producers who use them. As Ludwig Baeumer points out:

> The reputation connected with geographical indications typically exists not only in the country where the geographical area to which the indication refers is located, but also in other countries, in many cases even worldwide. Indeed,

---

[30] Because valid trademarks must generally be subject to quality control to maintain their source designating function, *see, e.g.*, Dawn Donut Co. v. Hart's Food Stores, Inc., 267 F.2d 358, 367 (2d Cir. 1959), most marks are generally owned by a single holder that exercises control over the authorized use of the mark, *see* TRIPS, art. 15(1) (defining trademarks as "signs, capable of distinguishing the goods or services of *one undertaking* from those of other undertakings") (emphasis added).

[31] Geographical indications are generally registrable by a group of producers of the relevant product. *See, e.g.*, Council Regulation 510/2006, art. 5, 2006 O.J. (L 93) 12, 14 (EC) (specifying that "[o]nly a group shall be entitled to apply for registration"). Similarly, collective marks are registered by a collective entity. *See* United States Trademark Law, 15 U.S.C. § 1127 (2006) (defining a collective mark as one "used by the *members* of a cooperative, an association or other collective group or organization") (emphasis added). Collective marks, and their role in protecting local characteristics, are discussed more fully *infra* Section IV. Certification marks, when used to certify the geographic origin of a product are also generally owned by collective entities, including governmental organizations, since these are most likely to have the critical ability to exercise the appropriate level of control over the certification of qualifying goods. *See* US Trademark Manual of Examining Procedure (TMEP) § 1306.02(b) (April 2013 edition).

[32] *See* Lisbon Registration No. 231 (registered Dec. 20, 1967).

[33] *See* IDAHO POTATOES GROWN IN IDAHO, Registration No. 2,914,309.

[34] *See* Door Database, ec.europa.edu/agriculture/quality/door/list.html (kalamata registered in Greece in 1996 as PDO) (last visited May 5, 2013).

[35] *See* DARJEELING, Registration No. 2,685,923.

[36] *See* ROQUEFORT, Registration No. 571,798.

many of the products for which geographical indications are used are marketed in many countries of the world and represent a substantial share of the volume of exports of certain countries.[37]

Despite the useful role that geographical indications may play in establishing local market identities, they remain among the most contested rights in international intellectual property law. At the center of the dispute is the relationship between local geographic identities and global trademarks. Currently, the global protection of geographic designators is based on two distinctive and contradictory theories of protection. As protected under TRIPS, "geographical indications" are a particular category of geographic designators that are generally protected against misleading uses.[38] To qualify for protection, the designators must be "indications which identify a good as originating in the territory of a Member, or a region or locality in that territory, where a given quality, reputation or other characteristic of the good is essentially attributable to its geographical origin."[39] By definition, a protectable geographical indication can arise simply due to reputation, with no need for any unique environmental causation. Moreover, the use of the term "indication," as opposed to "name," potentially allows protection for symbols and other geographic depictions, thereby providing a broader range of choices for local "brand the land" efforts.[40]

TRIPS, however, poses significant impediments to the use of local identities as a counterbalance to the power of global marks. First, the so-called "first in time, first in right" rule provides that trademarks take precedence over subsequently adopted geographical indications.[41] When a trademark has been applied for or registered in good faith, or rights have been acquired through good faith use before the related geographical indication is protected in its country of origin, the right of use or registration of the mark cannot be "prejudiced" by the geographical indication.[42] This first-in-time right assures that geographical indications remain subsidiary to trademarks because the best they can hope for is coexistence when conflicts arise. At worst, trademarks may well take

[37] Ludwig Baeumer, *The International Protection of Geographical Indications*, WIPO Symposium on the International Protection of Geographical Indications (1991).

[38] TRIPS, art. 22.

[39] *Ibid.* art. 22.

[40] Daniel Gervais, The Trips Agreement: Drafting History and Analysis 190–91 (2nd ed. 2003).

[41] TRIPS, art. 24(5).

[42] *Ibid.*

precedence, at least in those instances when a likelihood of confusion exists between the two.[43]

Most significantly, Article 24 of TRIPS allows member countries to decline to protect geographical indications if the indication is "identical with the term customary in common language as the common name for such goods or services in the territory of that Member."[44] This "country of use" veto explains why "Chablis" is a protected geographical indication in France but is an unprotected generic term for white wine in the United States.[45] Finally, while TRIPS requires an absolute prohibition against the use of geographical indications for wines and spirits that did not originate in the specified location,[46] subject to a relatively circumscribed grandfather clause,[47] it allows all other geographical indications to remain unprotected unless their use misleads the public as to the geographical origin of the good or constitutes an act of unfair competition.[48]

By contrast, the Lisbon Agreement for the Protection of Appellations of Origin and their International Registration (Lisbon Agreement) provides for heightened protection, yet for a narrower range of protected geographic designators. Under the Lisbon Agreement, protected appellations are limited to the "geographical *name* of a country, region or locality, which serves to designate a product originating therein."[49] Protected appellations are further limited to those geographic designators

---

[43]   *See, e.g.*, Florent Gevers, Conflicts Between Trademarks and Geographical Indications – The Point of View of the International Association for the Protection of Industrial Indications (AIPPI), in SYMPOSIUM ON THE INTERNATIONAL PROTECTION OF GEOGRAPHICAL INDICATIONS 143, 152–53 (1995) (contending that if geographical indications qualify as signs under TRIPS, art. 16, they are prohibited from co-existence if they cause a likelihood of confusion with a pre-existing trademark); *see also* Council Regulation 2081/92, art. 14, 1992 O.J. (EC) (rejecting co-existence as a sufficient remedy to potential conflicts between geographical indications and trademarks).

[44]   TRIPS, art. 24(6).

[45]   Institut Nat'l Des Appellations D'Origine v. Vinters Int'l Co., 958 F.2d 1574, 1581 (Fed. Cir. 1992); see also Vine Products Ltd. v. MacKenzie & Co., Ltd., [1969] R.P.C. 1, 25–26 (Ch.) (finding sherry is generic in the United Kingdom).

[46]   TRIPS, art. 23.

[47]   *Ibid.* art. 24(4) (permitting members to allow continued use of geographical indications for wines and spirits where such indications were used "in a continuous manner ... for at least 10 years preceding 15 April 1994 or ... in good faith preceding that date").

[48]   *Ibid.* art. 22(2).

[49]   Lisbon Agreement, art. 2 (emphasis added).

that indicate a "quality and characteristics ... due exclusively or essentially to the geographical *environment*, including natural or human factors."[50] Similar limitations are contained in the European Union's Regulation on the Protection of Geographical Indications and Designations of Origin for Agricultural Products and Foodstuffs.[51]

At the heart of the major disputes between those who follow TRIPS and those who follow the Lisbon approach is the ability of non-originating countries to eliminate protection for geographic designators based on the generic nature of the term in the country of use. While TRIPS allows such genericide, Lisbon does not. Under Lisbon, so long as the appellation remains protected in its country of origin, it must be protected in any country of use, regardless of its local significance.[52]

The precedence of local meanings over country-of-use meanings would make geographic designators potent sources for "branding the land" strategies. The assurance of a single global identity, which could not be lost through over-popularization such as when trademarks become generic, would give owners of such geographic designators a powerful incentive to create strong quality significations. But under TRIPS, such precedence is absolutely precluded.[53] The permitted country-of-use veto under TRIPS makes the development of strong local value identities problematic on a global scale. Even more problematic is the limited scope of protection for exclusive geographic designators. Because TRIPS only requires absolute protection for indications relating to wines and spirits,[54] the ability to develop a strong competitive market based on geographical indications remains limited.

The rationalization of the global protection for geographical indications has been slow. Yet such rationalization is absolutely required to strengthen the value of local identities. Current efforts to expand the categories of absolute protection beyond wine and spirits, or to create a global register of protected designators, have faltered. The strengthening of local brand values represented by geographic designators cannot continue without a rationalized system for protection. This rationalized system should eliminate the major points of conflict between the Lisbon

---

[50]   *Ibid.* (emphasis added).

[51]   Council Regulation 2081/92, art. 2(a), 1992 O.J. (L 208) 2 (EC). The regulation also contains the identical definition for a "geographical indication" as in TRIPS. *Ibid.* art. 2(b); *see also* Decision No. 344 on Common Provisions on Industrial Property, para. 129, Oct. 21, 1993, 34 I.L.M. 1635 (Andean Cmty.).

[52]   Lisbon Agreement, art. 6.

[53]   TRIPS, art. 24(6).

[54]   *Ibid.* art. 23.

and TRIPS systems of protection in a manner that assures a strengthening of the value of such indications as an alternative to well-known marks and other global brands. Such strengthening, however, must also maintain the appropriate balance between geographic designators and trademarks to assure consumers receive accurate information from the use of geographic designators.

Because geographic designators serve a local branding function, their protection should be based upon the same general principles as those governing international trademarks. These principles include recognition of the need for exclusive rights, limitation of protection to those designators that have a quality-differentiation value, and prevention of consumer confusion regarding the quality/source of designated products. Geographic designators by their descriptive nature – at a minimum, they *describe* the geographic origin of the goods – are relatively weak brands. Protection should be limited to those designators that have acquired some level of marketplace significance. Such significance may not necessarily rise to the level of "distinctiveness" required to qualify as a trademark,[55] but it should have some level of recognition as a quality, characteristic, or reputation signifier in the marketplace. Without such significance, there seems little reason to protect an indicator because it has no relative value in the marketplace.[56]

For local brands to compete effectively in the global marketplace, such brands must represent some level of quality to consumers, or they will not affect consumer choice in the absence of emotional or other non-market-driven bases. While requiring a level of quality distinctiveness would most likely necessitate a certain level of reputational expenditures (probably through some form of advertising), such expenditures would be useful in strengthening the brand value of local identities. Like trademarks, use of a geographic designator, or its registration, is not *alone* sufficient to imbue the designator with value on a practical level. Without commercialization of the *meaning* of the geographic designator, including the characteristics of the goods associated with it, such designator will have a limited impact on the ability of the producers to broaden the market for their goods.

---

[55] Trademarks must be "distinctive" to be protected. *See, e.g.*, TRIPS, art. 15; Paris Convention for the Protection of Industrial Property, art. 6*quinquies*; United States Trademark Law, 15 U.S.C. § 1052 (2006).

[56] *See* Doris Estelle Long, *Branding the Land: Geographic Indications and the Limits of Territoriality* (2007) (draft on file with author) ("Long, BRANDING"); Kal Raustiala and Stephen Munzer, *The Global Struggle Over Geographic Indications*, 18 EUR. J. OF INT'L L. 337 (2007).

Heightened consumer protection is a critical component of a rationalized system for protection of geographic designators. The determination of the accuracy of a geographic designator is not always easy, particularly when the product has been processed or prepared in one region using raw materials from another region, such as Tequila produced in Texas from imported blue agave cactus[57] and Parma hams produced in London from Parma-raised pigs.[58] Consumer confusion may also arise regarding the nature of the designated goods from the use of homonyms,[59] or from cross-border geographic regions. Many geographic regions extend beyond national borders, giving rise to potentially conflicting claims. The most famous may be the dispute between Peru and Chile regarding the right to use the term "pisco" in connection with a particular liquor. While both claim to be derived from the practices of the Inca in this region of South America, the two "piscos" have distinctly different tastes.[60]

Perhaps most problematic of all, despite the relationship between the geographic designation and physical territory, not every name for a geographic region is unique. To the contrary, immigrants from one country often named new locations after their former homes. Thus, when immigrants settled in the United States and established breweries using traditional techniques from their home countries, conflicts over the use of the geographic designators were inevitable. The fights between the holder of the Budweiser mark in the United States[61] and the Budweiser Budvar

---

[57] Tequila Rose described as "a combination of strawberry cream liquor with a splash of tequila" at *Tequila Rose – Strawberry*, MCCORMICKDISTILLING.COM, http://mccormickdistilling.com/tr/strawberry.php (last visited Apr. 21, 2013). *But cf.* Railean "Silver Agave" described as an "American Agave Spirit" that is "perfect for Authentic Texas Margaritas" at *Premium Blue Agave | El Perico Silver | American Agave*, RAILEAN.COM, http://www.railean.com/products/el-perico-silver.html (last visited Apr. 21, 2013).

[58] Case C-108/01, Consorzio del Prosciutto di Parma and Salumificio S. Rita SpA v. Asda Stores, Ltd. and Hygrade Foods, Ltd. (2003) (use of Parma for ham that was obtained from Parma but packaged in the UK violated rights under protected desgination of origin).

[59] TRIPS expressly provides that homonymous geographical indications may be protected for wines except where the indication "falsely represents to the public that the goods originate in another territory." TRIPS, arts. 22(4) and 23(3).

[60] *See generally* Gonzalo Gutierrez, *El Pisco: Apuntes para La Defensa Internacional de la Denominacion de Origen Peruana* Fondo Editorial del Congreso del Peru (2005); Pisco Liquer [*sic*] Dispute between Chile and Peru, http://www1.american.edu/ted/pisco.htm (last visited May 5, 2013).

[61] U.S. Reg. No. 0064125.

mark in the Czech Republic have been epic in nature. They include the registration in 2005 of Budweiser as a protected geographical indication in the European Union.[62]

Similarly, when Portugal officially recognized a new region called "Torres Vedras" in 1989, a potential conflict with the well-known TORRES mark for wine (owned by a Spanish wine producer) arose. Under the governing European Wine Regulation, the subsequently adopted geographic designator would take precedence over the TORRES trademark.[63] The Regulation was subsequently changed to avoid this result by providing that a well-known "brand name" may coexist with an identical geographic designator for wine provided the "brand name" was registered at least 25 years before the official recognition of the geographic designator and used without interruption.[64] A contrary rule giving precedence to geographical indications would undeniably have supported local identity in Portugal. Neither the former rule, nor its present incarnation, however, resolves the problem of consumer signification in the case of conflicting geographic designators.

In the era of globalization, a rule that automatically threatens trans-border commerce should be disfavored. While the first-in-time precedence rule of TRIPS[65] might arguably have the benefit of predictability,[66] such a principle does not necessarily serve the needs of the marketplace for a viable method for securing greater market share for locally produced goods while simultaneously providing accurate consumer significations connected to geographic designators. Where potentially conflicting geographic designators arise, quality differentiation combined with confusion reduction warrants protecting the term with the greatest identification value. If the previously existing trademark continues to maintain its role as a distinctive source identifier, then such

---

[62] Budejovikcy Budvar: Label Protection as per place of origin at www.budejovickybudvar.cz/en/o-spolecnosti/znacky/ochrana-oznaceni.html (last visited May 5, 2013).

[63] *See* Council Regulation 1576/89, art. 40(3), 1989 O.J. (EC) (providing that when a "brand name" of a wine conflicts with a geographical indication, the name can continue to be used only until December 31, 2002, and only if it was registered no later than December 31, 1985).

[64] *See* Council Regulation 3897/91, 1991 O.J. (L 368) 5 (EC).

[65] TRIPS, art. 24(5).

[66] Such predictability, however, is doubtful given the lack of clear rules on how to determine precedence and the right of coexistence in certain instances. *See* WTO Panel Report, European Communities – Protection of Trademarks and Geographical Indications for Agricultural Products and Foodstuffs, WT/DS174/R paras. 7.614, 7.619, 7.625 (2005).

distinctiveness should *not* be eroded by a subsequently adopted geographic designator for a similar or related good. Continued protection, however, makes little sense from a policy basis if the trademark owner has not taken reasonable efforts to protect the mark against the loss of distinctiveness posed by a geographical indication, including reasonable policing efforts. Furthermore, prior registration should not grant a trademark owner pre-emptive rights if the mark itself was adopted in a bad faith attempt to gain pre-emptive rights to a developing geographic designator. In the case of a valid dispute between a legitimate trademark and a good faith geographic designator, the effectiveness of alternative methods for resolving the conflict, including disclaimers, should be considered. In all cases, the goal should be to protect the legitimate expectations of brand owners while ensuring that the public receives accurate information about the products at issue. Without a process for insisting on such distinctions, the value of geographic designators as meaningful consumer signifiers remains problematic and "branding the land" remains uncertain at best.

V TRADEMARKS: THE "OTHER" GEOGRAPHIC DESIGNATOR

There is no question that geographical indications and appellations of origin can serve the role of recognizable consumer "brands" to support geographically sourced goods. These indications can authenticate geographically sourced goods and can be used by all qualifying producers/sellers/providers of such goods. Certification marks serve a similar purpose where such marks are used to "certify" the geographic origin of the goods.[67] They can also help assure that branded goods contain the necessary geographically based qualities to support successful "branding the land" strategies since they require the specification of the qualities

---

[67] *See* TMEP §1206.01 (defining certification marks under US law as including marks that "certify that goods or services originate in a specific geographic region"). A certification mark is used to certify that a product meets certain specifications and can serve as a valuable means of protecting signifiers that certify regional source or quality, including geographic designators. *See* United States Trademark Law, 15 U.S.C. §1127 (2006) (defining a certification mark as "any word, name, symbol or device or any combination thereof" used "to certify regional or other origin, material, mode of manufacture, quality, accuracy or other characteristics of such person's goods or services or that the work or labor on the goods or services was performed by members of the union or other organization").

that are being certified. In the United States, certification marks have largely assumed the place of geographical indications,[68] protecting such diverse geographic designators as DARJEELING,[69] ROQUEFORT,[70] and JAMAICAN BLUE MOUNTAIN COFFEE.[71]

For geographic designators registered as certification marks, the registering entity has a strong interest in maintaining the certification obligations that assure the branded goods retain the necessary geographically sourced features to assure continued uniqueness in the marketplace. While there is no absolute prohibition against altering these obligations, there is a limitation to the degree of change that can be made. Fundamentally, a cheese cannot be certified "Roquefort" unless it is produced in Roquefort, France. Certain qualities may be altered if such changes do not alter the fundamental nature of the certification.[72]

Although certification marks facially appear capable of protecting the authentication and consumer signification needs of geographic designators, they, nevertheless, remain somewhat disfavored in many countries.[73] This disfavor may arise from the perception that heightened use demands, including advertising, exist to secure trademark protection. These heightened use demands generally arise from the need to prove that an arguably descriptive term, such as a geographic indicator of origin, has achieved a level of consumer recognition to qualify as a distinctive source designator.[74] As a practical matter, geographical indications also require use to

---

[68] *See* US Patent and Trademark Office, Geographical Indication Protection in the United States (undated).

[69] DARJEELING, Registration No. 2,685,923.

[70] ROQUEFORT, Registration No. 571,798.

[71] JAMAICAN BLUE MOUNTAIN COFFEE, Registration No. 1,414,598.

[72] *See* TMEP § 1306.06(g)(i) (providing under U.S. law that the statement of specifications "does not have to include details of the specifications of the characteristic being certified" but urging the inclusion of more detailed specifications in the application file "if practicable").

[73] Among the countries that do not presently provide protection for certification marks, *per se*, are the European Union, Japan, Mexico, Russia and the Czech Republic.

[74] *See Geographical Indications and TRIPS: 10 Years Later ... A Roadmap for EU GI holders to get protection in other WTO Member Countries*, COMMISSION OF THE EUROPEAN UNION COMMUNITIES (2007) (describing diverse problems posed by countries using a certification mark system of protection for geographical indications). The United States, however, does not require distinctiveness for certification marks. *See* TMEP, §13-6.02; United States Trademark Law, 15 U.S.C. §1052(e)(2) (2006).

become effective "brands."[75] But legal protection of such indications has no distinctiveness obligation.

Certification marks also pose a potential issue with regard to the ownership of the mark. There is no obligation that the mark owner represent the producers of the goods, merely that it have the capability of certifying compliance by those who seek to apply the mark with the applicable specifications. In fact, in many countries, governmental agencies often hold such registrations. By contrast, collective marks[76] not only provide branding and signification benefits similar to geographical indications; they also provide marketing and producer control possibilities that are not necessarily available under certification mark regimes. Collective marks also allow the costs of marketing a new good, or at least popularizing that good, to be spread over a larger number of interested parties.

Although legally certification marks, geographical indications, and the like may be protectable upon use, as noted above,[77] in reality goods bearing such indications are only successfully marketed if the consuming public is made aware of the special value which goods bearing such indications provide. For example, although "champagne" may be a protectable geographical indication for sparkling wine from the Champagne region of France, the term itself has gained a certain cachet among consumers in the United States as a result of a *concerted advertising campaign* designed to encourage them to choose French sparkling wine over local equivalents.[78]

In the real-world marketplace, simply attaching a geographical indication (or a collective mark) does not generate sales. Informing consumers of the desirable nature of the good bearing such indication does. The costs of advertising, however, can be prohibitive for smaller or locally based industries. Collective marks, or more specifically the organizations

---

[75] *See* Long, BRANDING *supra* note 56; Raustiala, *supra* note 56; Robert Brauneis and Roger E. Schechter, *Geographic Trademarks and the Protection of Competitor Communication*, 96 TRADEMARK REP. 782, 817 (2006) (arguing that the majority of geographic terms used as marks are "neither clearly descriptive nor clearly arbitrary" due to consumers' lack of knowledge of the qualities associated with products from a particular geographic area).

[76] Collective marks are generally used to promote goods or services rendered by a specified group, such as a union or franchise. See United States Trademark Law, 15 U.S.C. § 1127 (2006) (defining a collective mark as one "used by members of a cooperative, an association, or other collective group").

[77] *See* discussion *supra* Section III.

[78] *Champagne only comes from Champagne*, CHAMPAGNE BUREAU USA, http://www.champagne.us (last visited Apr. 21, 2013).

which own such marks, provide the immediate potential for both the creation of necessary advertisements to promote the new collective "brand" and the spreading of costs among the members of the collective organization who will be the direct beneficiaries of such advertising. They also provide a critical basis for the development of investment clusters, which can be used to organize and promote local handicraft industries. For example, the village of Cumbe in Peru sought to promote the Chirimoya fruit raised by the villagers through the registration of the collective mark "Chirimoya Cumbe." According to a report on the issue by Luis Alonso Garcia Muñoz-Najar, the village chose a collective mark as opposed to an appellation of origin because the village itself wanted to be the owner of the mark and in control of its use, including the rules governing the application of the mark to the Chirimoya.[79]

While the definition of a collective mark may vary among those countries that recognize this type of mark, at the heart of a collective mark is the collective organization that is the owner of the mark. Quite simply, a collective mark, by its very definition, cannot exist without such an organization. The need for such a collective organization makes the ownership of a collective mark essentially a four-step process. First, the organization to own the mark must be created. Second, once the organization is established, a collective mark must be selected. For geographic designators, the mark can be as simple as the geographic term that describes the origin of the goods or may also contain images or symbols designed to enhance its attractiveness to potential consumers. Third, advertising to enhance the use of the collective mark as an authenticator of desirable goods is required. Finally, registrations to protect the new collective mark to be featured prominently in such advertisements must be filed in appropriate countries. Despite these initial start-up costs, collective marks can serve as a critical component in marketing handicrafts and other local goods.

Many holders of geographical indications have the potential ability to spread the costs of brand advertising over potential users of the mark. Yet such "licensing" fees may run counter to local laws governing the use of such geographical indications.[80] By contrast, collective marks, by their very nature, are held by collective entities composed of members who can be charged membership fees, portions of which can be targeted for

---

[79] *See Chirimoya Cumbe – The Value of a Name*, WIPO, http://www. wipo.int/sme/en/case_studies/chirimoya.htm (last visited Apr. 21, 2013).

[80] *See* Peruvian Framework Law on Regulatory Boards for Denominations of Origin (Law No. 28331), art. 3 (2004) (no fees established for authorization of right to use registered denomination of origin).

brand marketing. Moreover, such collective organizations can serve a vital commercial development role by helping to bring together clusters of related businesses that can use their expertise to create a chain of value with the potential to enhance the market placement of their goods. By bringing together experts in a given field, the collective organization has the potential to organize competitive groups that can craft valuable production standards for the associated goods provided by their membership. More importantly, such a collection of experts potentially has the ability to assure that any such rules are enforced so that branded goods retain their market value. Absent specific legal prohibitions against such activities under domestic association laws, collective organizations provide a ready source of both expertise and funding to create and promote new brand identities.

Theoretically, geographical indications provide consumers with information about the geographic origin of the associated goods and, consequently, the unique qualities or characteristics of such goods. For example, the term "tequila" tells consumers that the clear liquid that they are drinking came from the tequila region of Mexico and has a slightly smoky taste. By contrast, a collective mark may not necessarily be a "brand" mark *per se*, although most countries, including the United States, allow collective marks to be used by members on goods.[81] At its heart, a collective mark is a mark of association. It authenticates the associated goods because they are affiliated with a collective entity which itself certifies (through membership) the quality or characteristic of the goods. Thus, a collective mark assures consumers of the quality of the good *because the collective entity authenticates the goods through its membership qualifications and use regulations for control of its mark.*

Furthermore, collective marks are not limited to the narrow "uniqueness" that may be imposed on certification marks or geographical indications. Briefly, appellations of origin are limited to certifying qualities or characteristics that arise from environmental factors due to the geographic source of the good.[82] Geographical indications are similarly restricted although they may be applied to goods that have achieved a certain reputation based on geographic location without the need for any particular environmentally based quality or characteristic.[83] Certification marks are generally required to certify some aspect of the good

---

[81] *See* United States Trademark Law, 15 U.S.C. §1127 (2006) (defining a collective mark as being "used by the members of a cooperative, an association or other collective group or organization").

[82] *See supra* note 6.

[83] *See generally* TRIPS, art. 22.

that is quantifiable. For example, in the United States, certification marks must be used "to certify regional or other origin, material, mode of manufacture, quality, accuracy, or other characteristics of such person's goods or services or that the work or labor on the goods or services was performed by members of a union or other organization."[84]

Collective marks, by contrast, can create a brand identity from the simple banding together or clustering of producers and sellers who have decided to create a market based on their collectivity alone. Subject to the limits of unfair competition and related laws, a collective organization can create a market demand for a product even if the only unique aspect of that product is that a member of the organization produced it. It is, thus, the only one of the geographically based designators that can be used to create market demand based on a reputation for quality, potentially without the need for any particular unique geographically based characteristic. In essence, a collective mark can be used to gain an economic and market advantage for the collective based on its ability to signify that goods bearing such marks are *of a particular quality because they are produced by the collective according to its regulations*, even if such quality is not otherwise locally derived.

Collective marks also provide a significant basis on which to assure that tradition-based goods are authentic because they have the potential to grant the holders of the traditional knowledge used in creating the goods the right to control its commercialization. Some countries, such as Mexico, limit the members of a collective to "legally incorporated associations of *producers, manufacturers, merchants or providers of services*" who use the mark "to distinguish in the market the products or services of their members from products or services of non members."[85] These more limited enumerations do not expressly prevent indigenous groups from qualifying as an appropriate collective organization, although they do appear to limit membership to those members of the tribe who actually participate in the production of the goods themselves.

---

[84] *See* United States Trademark Law, 15 U.S.C. §1127 (2006) (defining a certification mark as including certifications of "regional or other origin" of the good).

[85] Trademark Law of Mexico, Article 96 (emphasis added).

VI RECONFIGURING ENFORCEMENT POLICIES TO PROTECT LOCAL IDENTITIES

To give local identities the support they need to create broader market appeal, it is not enough to create strong cultural authentication and geographic designator regimes. The power to enforce those rights must also be enhanced. A critical legal tool in enhancing such enforcement efforts is a well-staffed and well-supported domestic trademark office. This office is the logical repository for registration activities for the full panoply of geographic quality signifiers, including geographical indications (and their associated designators including appellations of origin), culture authentication marks, collective marks, and certification marks. These source and quality signifiers represent valuable business assets and potential investment opportunities. They can serve as potential security for commercial growth and development. On the public side of the balance, they also serve as guarantors of quality for the goods and services with which they are associated. But to serve as investment tools, governments must quickly and, even more importantly, correctly grant registration rights.

Finally, the creation of strong local identities cannot be secured unless mark owners are protected against unauthorized uses. In addition to depressing the price for goods below a competitive rate for producers of new goods, counterfeiting undermines consumer confidence in the marketplace. Counterfeiting activities are not limited to well-known marks. To the contrary, if a product is perceived to have some level of market power, it will be counterfeited. Counterfeiting denies the local brand owner any financial reward for his or her efforts and places the less well-established brands at risk of being unable to overcome any reputational harm in the marketplace that counterfeit goods might cause. Such harm may be particularly problematic for local producers using "branding the land" strategies since the reputation of all locally produced goods can be harmed by an inauthentic counterfeit of inferior quality.

Achieving local brand-enhancing enforcement, however, requires local governments to reconfigure their enforcement policies to recognize the significance of geographic designator protection to domestic industrial and commercial growth. Under a reconfigured policy, registration and enforcement are no longer activities undertaken by developing countries to support the monopolizing efforts of global mark owners. To the contrary, they serve as critical steps in the creation of valuable and viable local identities, which in turn serves the domestic growth that is at the heart of sustainable economic development. This reconfigured policy, however, must go beyond merely authorizing greater funds for enforcement or training of appropriate enforcement officials. Enforcement policies that would include protection of all geographic designators must be part of the country's overall domestic development agenda. Local governments should combine these policies with domestic policies regarding consumer education and financial and training assistance for local entrepreneurs, so that local values can be protected and enhanced. This requires a reconfiguration of the mission of domestic trademark offices. Instead of serving as mere registries for source designators, domestic offices must expand their role. Trademark offices should coordinate to provide educational programs and support to local businesses regarding the value of their local identities and the methods for enhancing global marketing efforts.

In Peru in the 1990s, for example, the Peruvian Intellectual Property Office (INDECOPI) served as a liaison between local business persons and members of the local financial community to assist both sides in realizing the economic and legal value of source designators used on privately owned commuter van lines in the city of Lima. Such assistance not only helped the van owners successfully combat third parties who used their marks on gypsy vans, but also encouraged local investment in a growing industry. Similarly, enforcement should be viewed as an arm of commercial development. Such reconfigurations are critical to ensuring the necessary domestic support for the growth of local identity values as a branding tool to expand the market potential for locally produced goods.

VII CONCLUSION

A "branding the land" strategy is no guarantor that locally produced goods will secure a wider market appeal. Geographic designators may be imbued with unclear meanings of quality that make their use as brand identities problematic. Terms such as "Virupakshi Hill" for bananas and "Dongshan bai lu sun" for asparagus may have little meaning beyond the geographic borders of the originating country at present. Others, such as "champagne," may be more evocative of a certain lifestyle than the true nature of the associated goods. But where adequate advertising and other informational activities are used to promote clear consumer meanings, geographic designators can serve as powerful "brands" in the "long tail" economy of the twenty-first century.

To achieve their potential, "branding the land" strategies must be supported by legal regimes that actually encourage the creation of geographically or culturally unique goods that can be marketed under a geographic designator. This includes goods that embody the traditional knowledge of indigenous peoples. International protection regimes must be revised to strengthen the consumer signification of geographic designators and to reduce consumer confusion when conflicting uses arise. Fortunately, in crafting "branding the land" strategies, there are numerous geographic designators to choose from. Geographical indications and appellations (denominations) of origin are obvious choices. For groups such as the holders of traditional knowledge, who seek even stronger control over the goods bearing such designators, collective marks may be a more desirable choice. But until legal regimes are better rationalized, any "branding the land" scheme will remain an uncertain strategy at best.

7. Signs beyond borders: moving from commodity to differentiated exports in the coffee industry

Daphne Zografos Johnsson[*]

I INTRODUCTION

This chapter examines how coffee producers in developing countries can use intellectual property, or intellectual property-related rights as differentiation tools, to move from pure commodity exports to higher-price exports in niche markets and create value. It takes into account the influence of new consumption patterns in the coffee industry and analyses the various differentiation techniques that have been proposed, such as single-origin and sustainable coffees. This topic is particularly relevant to the territoriality debate, as it provides tangible examples of the added value that signs and brands can have beyond national borders, whether those are trademarks, geographical indications, certification or collective marks, or other labels.

Coffee is the single most important tropical commodity traded worldwide. It is produced in over 50 developing countries, and it is estimated that some 20 million rural families,[1] or 125 million people,[2] depend on

---

* Legal Officer, Traditional Knowledge Division at the World Intellectual Property Organization. The views expressed in this chapter are the author's own and do not necessarily reflect the views of WIPO or any of its member states. A version of this chapter was presented at the 3rd Global Forum on Intellectual Property, Singapore (January 6–7, 2011). A longer version of this chapter was first published as part of the International Intellectual Property Scholars Series, *see* Daphne Zografos Johnsson, *Using Intellectual Property Rights to Create Value in the Coffee Industry*, 16 MARQ. INTELL. PROP. L. REV. 283 (2012).

[1] *See* UNITED NATIONS DEVELOPMENT PROGRAM (UNDP), HUMAN DEVELOPMENT REPORT 2005: INTERNATIONAL COOPERATION AT A CROSSROADS. AID, TRADE AND SECURITY IN AN UNEQUAL WORLD 139 (Charlotte Denny ed., 2005) [hereinafter UNDP].

[2] *See* Nestor Osorio, The Global Coffee Crisis: A Threat to Sustainable Development (2002).

growing coffee throughout the world for their livelihoods. Over the past decade, coffee producers have been facing considerable difficulties because of low and unstable coffee prices. In 2002, coffee prices collapsed to 100-year lows in real terms, leading to a world coffee crisis. Meanwhile, the coffee economy in high-income countries has been moving in the opposite direction, and the crisis is hardly visible from Starbucks-type Western coffee chains. Since 2005, prices have started to recover, reflecting a greater balance between supply and demand. In 2008, coffee prices reached their highest level in more than a decade, and since then, they have flattened out, but remain well above the average prices recorded over the course of the past two decades.[3] While conditions for producers have improved, this does not signal the end of their problems. Further, it is argued that price recovery is likely to be only temporary, given the cyclical nature of the coffee market.[4]

II THE DECOMMODIFICATION OF COFFEE

A   Changes in Consumer Consumption Patterns

For a long time, coffee was seen as a commodity, priced according to the New York or London exchanges,[5] with coffee-producing countries being the suppliers of the raw material. Much of the discussion around the coffee crisis has revolved around the themes of oversupply and increased production efficiency, and while coffee-producing countries are actively trading, they are not making much profit from trade and are stuck in a commodity problem.

Over the past two decades, the act and symbolic association of coffee drinking have evolved, and new consumption patterns have emerged with the growing importance of differentiated coffees, usually either by geographic origin, quality, or cultivation processes. In addition, the ways in which coffee is drunk have changed dramatically, and the coffee

---

[3]   FOOD AND AGRICULTURE ORGANIZATION, THE MARKET FOR ORGANIC AND FAIR TRADE COFFEE 6 (2009) [hereinafter FAO].

[4]   *See* Bryan Lewin et al., *Coffee Markets: New Paradigms in Global Supply and Demand*, 3 WORLD BANK AGRIC. & RURAL DEV. xiv (2004).

[5]   Coffee is a traded commodity on major futures and commodity exchanges, most importantly London for Robusta coffee and New York for Arabica coffee.

market has gone through a "latte revolution"[6] with the emergence of coffee bars and café chains at every street corner. Coffee lovers can now custom order their drink, with choices at every level of the formulation, including bean origin, brewing and grinding methods, concentration, flavouring, packaging, social content, and ambiance.

With the advent of differentiated coffee sectors and an increased interest on the part of consumers in coffee's symbolic attributes, consumers have also started to become more conscious about the social and ecological dimensions for coffee consumption. These emerging trade paradigms may offer producers opportunities to pursue strategies independent of commodity pricing at the exchanges and capture value by asking for higher prices for better quality coffee and more sustainable cultivation and trade practices.

B   Differentiated Coffees

Differentiated coffees are types of coffees that can be clearly distinguished because of distinct geographical origin, defined processes, or exceptional characteristics such as superior taste or zero defects. They are often characterised by a closer and sometimes direct relationship between a producer and a roaster or buyer, rather than being traded in bulk or via the commodity market. In contrast, mainstream coffees are usually pre-ground blends of unidentified origin and are normally distributed through mainstream channels, such as supermarkets.[7]

There is a growing interest in the economic, social, and environmental benefits of differentiated coffees, as they can provide producers with alternative trading opportunities and help them move from pure commodity exports to higher-price exports in niche markets such as single-origin and sustainable coffees such as organic, fair trade, or shade, bird or eco-friendly coffees. Over the past few years, differentiated markets have been growing steadily. This is due to consumers' interest and increasing demand from gourmet and/or ethical consumers, but also to the industry's interest in their high growth rate, their contribution to producer stability, and their ability to command higher prices.

---

   [6]   BENOIT DAVIRON AND STEFANO PONTE, THE COFFEE PARADOX, GLOBAL MARKETS, COMMODITY TRADE AND THE ELUSIVE PROMISE OF DEVELOPMENT xvi (2005).
   [7]   *See* Lewin et al., *supra* note 4, at 99.

III SINGLE-ORIGIN COFFEES

Single-origin coffees are coffee varieties with a single known geographical origin, which can be a country, a region, or even a single farm or plantation. Single-origin coffees are viewed by consumers as synonymous with quality or special characteristics associated with the climate or soil composition of their geographical origin. Protection of single-origin coffees with intellectual property tools can take the form of geographical indications, trademarks, or certification and collective marks.

A Geographical Indications of Origin

"Geographical indications", as defined in Article 22(1) of the Agreement on Trade-Related Aspects of Intellectual Property Rights (TRIPS Agreement) are indications which identify a good as originating in the territory of a member, or a region or locality in that territory, where a given quality, reputation or other characteristic of the good is essentially attributable to its geographical origin. In other words, under the TRIPS definition, geographical indications communicate important information on: (i) the name of the product; (ii) the area of geographical origin of the product; and (iii) its given quality, reputation or other characteristics, which are essentially attributable to that geographical origin.

Article 22(2) of the TRIPS Agreement establishes the general standard of protection that must be available for all geographical indications. It provides that "legal means" must be provided to interested parties to prevent the use of geographical indications which mislead the public as to the geographical origin of the goods. It also requires that legal means must be provided to prevent use which constitutes an "act of unfair competition" within the meaning of Article 10*bis* of the Paris Convention. However, while it is mandatory for member states to provide protection to geographical indications, they are free to determine the appropriate method of protection, when implementing the provisions of the Agreement within their own legal system and practice.[8]

There are many examples where geographical indications have been chosen as a tool to differentiate single-origin coffees, such as Hawaiian

---

[8] Agreement on Trade-Related Aspects of Intellectual Property Rights art. 1 para. 1, Apr. 15, 1994; Marrakesh Agreement Establishing the World Trade Organization, Annex 1C, THE LEGAL TEXTS: THE RESULTS OF THE URUGUAY ROUND OF MULTILATERAL TRADE NEGOTIATIONS 320 (1999), 1869 U.N.T.S. 299, 33 I.L.M. 1197 (1994), *available at* http://www.wto.org/english/docs_e/legal_e/legal_e.htm#agreements [hereinafter TRIPS Agreement].

Kona and Guatemalan Antigua coffee. But perhaps one of the most publicised examples is the registration and marketing of the indication Café de Colombia.

Colombia has a long history of developing strategies to protect and promote its coffee. This is mainly due to the marketing strategies developed by the National Federation of Coffee Growers of Colombia (FNC)[9] to differentiate and market Colombian single-origin coffee. Initially, the FNC's marketing strategy relied on trademark protection. In the early 1980s, with the help of a New York advertising agency, it developed and registered the Juan Valdez logo featuring Juan Valdez (the typical *cafetero*), his mule, and the Colombian mountains in the background. The purpose of the logo is to identify and serve as a seal of guarantee to the brands that consist of 100 per cent Colombian coffee as approved by the FNC. In order to obtain the right to use the logo, the product must meet certain minimum standards. A trademark licence will only be granted for use on whole bean or ground roast coffee, whether caffeinated or decaffeinated, and without flavour enhancers. These coffee brands are subsequently subject to quarterly quality control tests by the FNC. Failure to pass these tests can lead to the revocation of the trademark licence.

In addition to its trademark strategy, the FNC took steps to register the words "Café de Colombia" as a geographical indication. In December 2004, the FNC presented the Colombian government with an application to recognise Café de Colombia as a national geographical indication, which was granted in February 2005. In addition, Café de Colombia was registered as a certification mark in the United States and Canada, as a Denomination of Origin in Ecuador and Peru, and as a Protected Geographical Indication (PGI) under the European Union system. The latter, which was granted in 2007, was the first non-EU agri-food product to be granted a PGI.

Another example of differentiation through geographical indications comes from Indonesia. Arabica coffee was first introduced in Indonesia by the Dutch at the end of the seventeenth century. In the 1880s, most plantations were wiped out by coffee rust disease. This led to the widespread introduction of the more disease-resistant Robusta type of coffee around 1900.[10] Today, coffee is one of the most important

---

[9] The FNC is a non-profit and non-political cooperative that tries to stabilise the market for Colombian coffee, and undertakes research, social assistance and promotion programs on behalf of the small, independent *cafeteros*.

[10] *See* JON THORN AND MICHAEL SEGAL, THE CONNOISSEUR'S GUIDE TO COFFEE 147 (2009).

agricultural commodities for Indonesia, and Indonesia has become one of the world's top producers of Robusta, with less than 10 per cent of total coffee production being of Arabica beans. Most of the coffee is produced on small plantations, which account for about 90 per cent of the total production. Today, Indonesia is the fourth biggest coffee exporter in the world, and in 2007, it was estimated that over 1.5 million people depended on coffee for their livelihoods.[11]

In 2002, the Indonesian Coffee and Cocoa Research Institute (ICCRI), in cooperation with CIRAD, a French agricultural research organisation, initiated a pilot project on the geographical indication protection of Kintamani Bali Arabica coffee. The Kintamani pilot was to be a model on the use of geographical indication as a tool to promote other types of coffees, and other products in Indonesia, and to take advantage of its rich indigenous culture. Kintamani coffee was chosen for the pilot project after careful consideration of several of its features: (i) its reputation: Bali coffee is well known worldwide for its quality and distinctive taste; (ii) the use of uniform planting materials; (iii) the farmers' organisation: Arabica coffee farmers in Kintamani are, mostly, organised in traditional structures of farmers' organisations founded on Hindu philosophy, which can easily be established into a rural cooperative; (iv) the use of uniform application of farming techniques including organic farming, single-stem pruning, the use of shade trees on 30–50 per cent of the land, as well as diversification with tangerine trees which all contribute to the unique taste of that coffee; (v) strong efforts on quality improvement over the past five years; and finally (vi) an optimal altitude: Kintamani coffee is grown at an altitude of 1000–1500 meters, and this high altitude also contributes to the formation of a better aroma and taste.[12]

On 5 December 2008, Kintamani Bali Arabica coffee was the first geographical indication to be registered in Indonesia. Since then, a number of domestic and foreign applications have been received by the DGIPR, including applications for Flores Bajawa Arabica coffee from the island of Flores and Gayo Arabica coffee from the area of Aceh in northern Sumatra. At the start of the geographical indication pilot project, the price of Arabica coffee, including that of the Kintamani Bali variety, was on average US$0.70 per kilo of unsorted green coffee, which was

---

[11] *See* SURIP MAWARDI, ESTABLISHMENT OF GEOGRAPHICAL INDICATION PROTECTION SYSTEM IN INDONESIA, CASE IN COFFEE 4 (2009) [hereinafter WIPO DOCUMENT].

[12] *See* SURIP MAWARDI ET AL., DEVELOPING GEOGRAPHICAL INDICATION PROTECTION IN INDONESIA: BALI KINTAMANI ARABICA COFFEE AS A PRELIMIN-ARY CASE 1–4 (2005).

less than the price of Indonesian Robusta coffee. By 2006, Kintamani Bali Arabica coffee was one of the most expensive in Indonesia, and in 2008, its average price reached US$3.10 per kilo of unsorted green coffee.

B Trademarks

Trademarks are signs which distinguish goods or services of one undertaking from those of other undertakings and convey information about the source or trade origin of the goods or services in respect to which they are used. In addition to their distinguishing function, trademarks also have an advertising function. They play a pivotal role in the branding and marketing strategies of companies, contributing to the definition of the image and reputation of the company's products in the eyes of consumers. The image and reputation of a company create trust, which is the basis for establishing a loyal clientele and enhancing a company's goodwill. Finally, they provide information about, amongst other things, the quality of the goods and services which consumers need to make informed purchasing decisions. Trademarks provide an incentive for companies to invest in maintaining or improving the quality of their products in order to ensure that products bearing their trademark have a positive reputation. Consumers who are satisfied with a product are likely to buy or use that product again in the future.

Trademark registration, combined with an appropriate marketing strategy, can increase consumer recognition of single-origin coffees and in turn increase commercial benefits for coffee producers as the addition of a trademark on a good adds to its value. There are many examples of trademarks being used to market single-origin coffees. One of the most significant is the Ethiopian fine coffee trademarking and licensing initiative.

Ethiopia is one of the poorest countries in the world. In 2007, it ranked 171st out of 182 countries in the Human Development Index.[13] Causes for poverty include recurrent droughts, low levels of agricultural technology and rural infrastructure, and an unstable political environment. In 2008, agriculture accounted for 43 per cent of GDP and employed 85 per

---

[13] The Human Development Index looks beyond GDP and provides a composite measure of three dimensions of human development: life expectancy, adult literacy, and standard of living.

cent of the active population, while industry and services respectively represented 13 per cent and 45 per cent of GDP.[14]

With coffee being its single most important export product, Ethiopia is one of the countries that has been most affected by the coffee crisis. Coffee provides more than 60 per cent of foreign exchange earnings and 10 per cent of government revenue. About one-quarter of the population is involved directly or indirectly in producing and marketing coffee.[15] While exports have increased by two-thirds between 1998 and 2003, export earnings have fallen dramatically as a result of the coffee crisis, and the price shocks absorbed by coffee producers have been enormous.[16]

Solutions proposed to maximise Ethiopia's export earnings and the price received by coffee farmers include increasing the quantity of national production through extensification (new plantings) and/or intensification (higher productivity), improving quality, increasing the proportion of coffees selling at significant premiums, such as differentiated coffees, and raising demand for Ethiopian coffee through promotion.[17] With regard to product differentiation, Ethiopia already benefits from an impressive selection of distinctive coffees such as Harrar, Sidamo, Yirgacheffe, Limu, and Wollega. However, due to the country's wealth of genetic resources and large areas with optimal growing conditions, there is potential to increase the proportion of specialty coffee exports, if quality and consistency are guaranteed.[18] In addition, in the field of sustainable coffees, Ethiopia could benefit from the market for organic coffee as over 95 per cent of exported coffee is organic.[19]

In 2004, the Ethiopian Intellectual Property Office (EIPO) started working with partners to identify mechanisms to capture the intangible value of selected single-origin coffees. Following extensive studies and consultations, a consortium of stakeholders, including representatives of farmers' cooperatives, coffee exporters, and government bodies, agreed

---

[14]   *Key Development Data & Statistics for Ethiopia*, WORLDBANK.ORG, http://www.worldbank.org/en/country/Ethiopia (last visited May 6, 2013) [hereinafter WORLD BANK].

[15]   *See* UNDP, *supra* note 1, at 140.

[16]   *Ibid.* at 140–41.

[17]   Nicolas Petit, *Ethiopia's Coffee Sector: A Bitter or Better Future?*, 7 J. OF AGRARIAN CHANGE 225, 252 (2007).

[18]   *Ibid.* at 253.

[19]   Ethiopian organic coffee is the product of subsistence farmers who do not use chemicals, fertilisers or pesticides in the production process. TADESSE MEKURIA ET AL., ETHIOPIAN ORGANIC COFFEE: HOME OF THE BIODIVERSITY OF *COFFEA ARABICA L.*, THE FIRST AND FINEST COFFEE OF THE WORLD (2004).

that their objective was to achieve wider recognition of the distinctive qualities of these specific types of Ethiopian coffees as brands and to position them strategically in the expanding coffee market, while at the same time protecting Ethiopia's ownership of their coffee names so as to prevent their misappropriation.

While the large majority of coffee-producing regions tend to seek protection for single-origin coffees with geographical indications, the stakeholders opted for a trademark-based solution and identified a selection of three coffee designations: Harrar/Harar, Sidamo, and Yirgacheffe. The EIPO then began filing applications to register the names in key foreign market countries. This move was combined with the offer of royalty-free licences to foreign coffee companies to create a network of licensed distributors, who, in return, would actively promote Harrar/Harar, Sidamo, and Yirgacheffe to consumers in the specialty coffee market. This would eventually allow producers to ask for a higher price for their coffee, once demand for Ethiopian coffee grew.

From 2005–2007, the EIPO filed trademark applications for Harrar/Harar, Sidamo, and Yirgacheffe in 34 countries and was granted 27 titles by mid-2007, including in Canada, the European Union, and Japan. However, in the United States, while the U.S. Patent and Trademark Office (USPTO) had approved the application to register Yirgacheffe, the National Coffee Association (NCA) strongly opposed the EIPO's applications to register Harrar/Harar and Sidamo. Both applications were refused by the USPTO on the ground that the proposed marks had become too generic a description for coffee. The EIPO filed rebuttals against the USPTO decisions with supporting evidence to demonstrate that the terms Harrar/Harar and Sidamo had acquired distinctiveness, and they were both registered as trademarks by the USPTO in June 2008 and February 2008, respectively.

According to the website of the Ethiopian Coffee Network, the Ethiopia Trademarking and Licensing Initiative is already producing an important impact both within Ethiopia and in the world coffee market. Several different stakeholders in the coffee sector have united, within Ethiopia, in a new grouping to support these trademarks and to prepare to invest in production for and promotion of these coffee brands. It is expected that better brand and supply management in Ethiopia, combined with strategic promotion, will help achieve higher returns for everyone in the coffee chain, and in particular increase the income of coffee farmers in Ethiopia.

C Certification and Collective Marks

Certification and collective marks are special types of marks. They inform the public about certain characteristics of the products or services marketed under the mark. Article 7*bis* of the Paris Convention provides for mutual obligation of registration and protection of collective marks in the countries of the Union. However, it leaves each country to be the judge of the particular conditions under which a collective mark shall be protected and provides that it may refuse protection if the mark is contrary to the public interest. Even though the Paris Convention only refers to collective marks, it is generally understood that the term also includes certification marks.[20] Certification and collective marks can be indications of geographical origin. As such, they can be protected under the TRIPS Agreement.

A certification mark is a mark that indicates the goods or services in connection with which it is used are certified by the proprietor of the mark in respect of geographical origin, material, mode of manufacture of goods, or performance of services, quality, accuracy, or other characteristics. In other words, they are indicia of conformity of goods or services to particular standards, stipulated by the proprietor of the mark. Any person or entity that authorises traders to use a certification in relation to certain products or services may apply for a certification mark. However, the applicant must be considered competent to certify the products concerned. The owner of the certification mark is ultimately responsible for controlling its use and for ensuring that the mark is not used on non-compliant goods. The applicant must also supply a copy of the regulations governing the use of the certification mark, which must indicate who is authorised to use the mark, the characteristics to be certified by the mark, how the certifying body is to test those characteristics and supervise the use of the mark, the fees to be paid in connection with the administration of the certification scheme and the procedures for resolving disputes. Unlike collective marks, certification marks are not confined to any membership. They can be used by anybody who complies with the standards defined by the owner of the certification mark.

A collective mark is a mark that distinguishes the goods or services of members of an association, which is the proprietor of the mark, from those of other undertakings, without any requirement for certification of

---

[20] *See* NORMA DAWSON, CERTIFICATION TRADE MARKS, LAW AND PRACTICE 13 (1988).

the goods or services. In most jurisdictions, applicants are required to supply a copy of the regulations governing use of the collective mark. These generally indicate who is authorised to use the mark, the conditions of membership of the association, any conditions for use of the mark, as well as sanctions against misuse. The cost, duration, and scope of protection applicable to collective marks are similar to those of ordinary trademarks. However, since the cost of registering a collective mark is divided between the members of the association, it becomes much cheaper for an individual member. This can be an attractive argument for small coffee producers for whom the cost of registering an ordinary trademark to market their products or services could be dissuasive.

An association of coffee producers can register a collective mark and authorise its members to use it in relation to their products or services. In that way, a collective mark can be used as a tool to help them obtain consumer recognition and customer loyalty and develop a joint marketing campaign for their products. Unlike certification marks, the proprietor association of a collective mark does not have to set standards to be met by its members in order to be able to use the mark. However, it may do so if it wishes. Consequently, collective marks may also perform a certification function. This is particularly relevant in countries that do not provide for registration of certification marks.

An example of use of a certification mark to differentiate single-origin coffee is the "Jamaica Blue Mountain Coffee" certification mark. Blue Mountain coffee is cultivated in three specific parishes of Jamaica (Portland, Saint Andrews, and Saint Thomas), and more than 7700 farmers work in these areas to produce this famous coffee. In 1982, the government of Jamaica decided to adopt an export-oriented agriculture strategy, and as a result, the Coffee Industry Board of Jamaica (CIB) launched a series of coffee development programmes. A definition and delimitation of the Blue Mountain Area was included in the Coffee Industry Regulation Act; however, the development of the Blue Mountain brand was a long process that took several decades. It began with an effort to achieve a consistent production of high-quality coffee, followed by the development of a target market,[21] and only later organised legal protection efforts.

---

[21] Most Blue Mountain coffee is sold to Japan, and exports of green coffee from Jamaica to Japan have grown steadily since the 1970s. However, even though the crop is quite limited, Jamaican exporters are keen to develop new markets, and the CIB has been working towards legal protetction in various other markets. *See* Kira Schroeder, *The Case of Blue Mountain Coffee, Jamaica, in*

The Blue Mountain indication is now protected under Jamaican law by a certification mark, and the CIB was designated the sole entity with the authority to grant the use of the Blue Mountain designation. The CIB certifies not only the geographical origin of the coffee, but also its quality and characteristics. In addition, the CIB has since registered the mark on other markets. Today, Blue Mountain is registered in approximately 51 countries, either as a certification mark where the law offers that option or, if not, as a trademark.[22]

IV SUSTAINABLE COFFEES

A Introduction

1 Sustainable development

Sustainable development was defined in the Brundtland Report on Environment and Development[23] as being development that meets the needs of the present without compromising the ability of future generations to meet their own needs.[24] In turn, sustainability in the coffee world means that a sustainable producer shall meet long-term environmental and social goals while being able to compete effectively with other market participants and achieve prices that cover his production costs and allow him to earn an acceptable business margin.[25]

Some sustainable coffees are sold as certified coffees, such as organic, shade, bird or eco-friendly, or fair trade, while others are sold under sustainability initiatives that are designed by private companies, with or without third-party monitoring.[26] So far organic, shade, bird or eco-friendly, and fair trade coffees have been the best attempts towards

---

GUIDE TO GEOGRAPHICAL INDICATIONS, LINKING PRODUCTS AND THEIR ORIGIN 170, 170–72 (2009).

[22] *Ibid.* at 172.

[23] The Brundtland Report is also known as the Report of the World Commission on Environment and Development: Our Common Future. The report is *available at* http://www.un-documents.net/wced-ocf.htm [hereinafter Brundtland Report].

[24] *See* Brundtland Report, ch. 2 para. 1. This definition was later endorsed by the 1992 Rio Summit and the 2002 Johannesburg World Summit on Sustainable Development.

[25] *See* DANIELE GIOVANNUCCI AND FREEK JAN KOEKOEK, THE STATE OF SUSTAINABLE COFFEE: A STUDY OF TWELVE MAJOR MARKETS 15 (2003).

[26] These include the Green Mountain Coffee Roasters' Stewardship Programme, Thanksgiving Coffee Company's Song Bird and Bat Magic Coffees,

sustainable production practices that meet the environmental, social, and economic needs of coffee producers. Very importantly, they all allow for reasonable verification of their claims. Indeed, as more firms adopt their own "sustainable" criteria, it is critical that they clarify their standards of certification and use third-party verification so as to ensure compliance with claims and reduce the risk of losing public confidence, which would be damaging for all market participants.[27]

Although sustainable coffee is still a small niche, it is growing rapidly, and the industry is generally optimistic about its future. The estimated size of certified sustainable coffees in 2001 was approximately 600 000 60-kg bags, which represents, on average, 1–2 per cent of the trade in the leading consuming countries.[28] Of these, organic and fair trade were the largest markets by volume.

2 Ethical consumerism

Sustainability should be linked with changing consumer preferences and the notion of ethical consumerism. Ethical consumerism is not new. From a historical and sociological perspective, researchers have identified four waves of consumerism culminating in ethical awareness. The first wave was the cooperative movement, which took off in England in 1844. It began as a working-class reaction to excessive prices and poor quality goods.[29] The second wave, which emerged in the 1930s, focused on value-for-money, basic product information, and reliable labelling. Its aims were to make the marketplace more efficient and inform and educate consumers. The third wave concentrated on consumer safety and manufacturer accountability. Finally, the fourth and most recent wave introduced environmental and ethical issues, linked to notions of corporate citizenship and social responsibility.[30] There are several factors that influence the growth of ethical consumer behaviour. They include (i) the globalisation of markets and the rise of transnational corporations

---

Starbucks' CAFE programme, and Rapunzel Pure Organics' E-Blend and E-Espresso. *See* DAVIRON AND PONTE, *supra* note 6, at 164.

[27] GIOVANNUCCI AND KOEKOEK, *supra* note 25, at 22.

[28] By adding estimates of non-certified coffees that were sold with claims of sustainable production practices, the global total of "sustainable" coffee sold in the leading consuming countries could reach 1.1 million 60-kg bags. *See* Lewin et al., *supra* note 4, at 119.

[29] *See* Tim Lang and Yiannis Gabriel, *A Brief History of Consumer Activism*, *in* THE ETHICAL CONSUMER 33, 41 (2005).

[30] ALEX NICHOLLS AND CHARLOTTE OPAL, FAIR TRADE: MARKET-DRIVEN ETHICAL CONSUMPTION 181 (2005).

and brands, (ii) a growing awareness of the social and environmental effects of technological advances because of campaigning pressure groups, and (iii) a shift in market power towards consumers.[31]

There are five main types of ethical purchasing, which can be either product-oriented or company-oriented. These are boycott; positive buying; full screening, which compares ethical ratings across a product area; relationship purchasing, where consumers seek to educate sellers about their ethical needs; and anti-consumerism or sustainable consumerism.[32] In relation to coffee, ethical consumerism can manifest itself in a variety of ways. Consumers may, for example, want to boycott a company as a sign of protest because of unfair working conditions of coffee farmers; they might choose a fair trade label due to concerns for developing countries, an organic label because of concerns for their own health or the effect of the use of pesticides on wildlife and the environment, or a shade, bird or eco-friendly label due to concerns for the environment. Ethical consumers do not ignore price and quality as they will probably not choose these products if they are prohibitively expensive or if they do not have a good taste, but they are applying some additional criteria in the decision-making process.

B   Organic Coffee

According to the International Federation of Organic Agriculture Movements (IFOAM), an umbrella organisation for the organic agriculture movement that unites more than 750 member organisations in over 100 countries:

> Organic agriculture is a production system that sustains the health of soils, ecosystems and people. It relies on ecological processes, biodiversity and cycles adapted to local conditions, rather than the use of inputs with adverse effects. Organic agriculture combines tradition, innovation and science to benefit the shared environment and promote fair relationships and a good quality of life for all involved.[33]

Although many producers grow coffee without the use of synthetic agrochemicals, this alone is not enough for coffee to be considered organic. Organic certification requires active cultivation practices on the

---

[31]   *See* Lang and Gabriel, *supra* note 29, at 5.

[32]   *See* Rob Harrison, Terry Newholm and Deirdre Shaw, *Introduction, in* THE ETHICAL CONSUMER 1, 3 (2005).

[33]   *Definition of Organic Agriculture*, IFOAM, http://www.ifoam.org/growing_organic/definitions/doa/index.html (last visited Apr. 10, 2013).

part of producers, which add to their costs of production. However, producers will usually receive price premiums for certified organic coffee, which will compensate for the extra production costs.

Organic standards are set up by government authorities, international organisations,[34] and IFOAM. Organic certification, on the other hand, is carried out by a number of accredited certification agencies, which monitor organic standards of production, processing, and handling. IFOAM unifies organic standards and verification practices and accredits certifiers, so that organic certification is assessed in the same way throughout the world.[35]

Over the past decade, organic coffee has been used as a marketing tool to attract new consumers, and the organic coffee market has experienced a substantial growth. Recent statistics of the ICO indicate that the growth is ongoing. They show that the value of organic coffee exported in 2008–2009 amounted to US$38.44 million compared with US$31.96 million in 2007–2008. This represents an increase of 20.3 per cent in revenue, whereas the increase in the corresponding volume was 22.4 per cent.[36]

Depending on the source, average price premium values vary between 10 and 40 per cent for the period of 2002–2008. This is due to the fact that premiums are difficult to estimate because they depend on the quality and origin of the coffee, the situation of the market at a given moment, the reputation of the producer, and the existence of additional certification, such as fair trade.[37] Although price premium values for organic coffee seem to have fallen in recent years, there may be further opportunities for producers of organic coffee carrying multiple certifications or for organic coffee of exceptional quality.[38]

---

[34]   *See, e.g.*, Codex Alimentarius Commission, *The Guidelines for the Production, Processing, Labelling and Marketing of Organically Produced Foods*, FOOD & AGRI. ORG. OF THE UNITED NATIONS (1999), *available at* http://www.codexalimentarius.net/web/more_info.jsp?id_sta=360.

[35]   *See ibid.*

[36]   *See* INT'L COFFEE ORG., WP STATISTICS 140/09 (2009), *available at* http://www.ico.org/show_doc_category.asp?id=16.

[37]   *See* FAO, *supra* note 3, at 9.

[38]   *Ibid.*

C Shade, Bird and Eco-friendly Coffees

Shade, bird and eco-friendly are coffee production systems that maintain and enhance wildlife habitat and biological diversity through effective management of the forest canopy on the farm and protection and restoration of surrounding natural environments.[39] In the mid-1990s, biologists discovered a marked decline in populations of tropical migratory songbirds linked to the trend in coffee technification, which uses modernised varieties that prefer sun, thus requiring the removal of traditional shade trees and the use of additional chemicals.[40]

Currently, there are two certification systems for these types of coffees: the Smithsonian Migratory Bird Center (SMBC) for "bird-friendly" coffee and the Rainforest Alliance for "Rainforest Alliance Certified" coffee.

The SMBC's bird-friendly certification is only granted to producers of organic coffee. This certification requires amongst other things that coffee be grown under multi-storey shaded forest settings that maintain and support ecosystem biodiversity. Coffee farms should include a minimum of ten native tree species, and the shade should cover a minimum of 40 per cent of the land at solar noon.[41]

The Rainforest Alliance Certified seal combines environmental and social criteria. On the one hand, it guarantees that coffee is grown on farms where forest is protected and rivers, soils, and wildlife are conserved. On the other, it certifies that farmers are treated with respect, paid decent wages, are properly equipped, and given access to education and medical care. However, it does not require coffee to be organic to be certified, and the shade criteria are not as strict as those of the SMBC.[42]

The growth of shade, bird and eco-friendly coffee in the late 1990s represented a significant development in coffee-related activism. Whereas the primary market driver for organic coffee was the drinker's personal health concerns about agrochemicals, the motivation to buy shade, bird or

---

[39] *See* Lewin et al., *supra* note 4, at 102.

[40] *See* NINA LUTTINGER AND GREGORY DICUM, THE COFFEE BOOK, ANATOMY OF AN INDUSTRY FROM CROP TO THE LAST DROP 193 (2006).

[41] *See Shade-Grown Coffee Plantations,* SMITHSONIAN MIGRATORY BIRD CENTER – NATIONAL ZOO, http://nationalzoo.si.edu/SCBI/MigratoryBirds/Coffee/ (last visited Apr. 10, 2013).

[42] The Rainforest Alliance is a New York-based environmental group. *See Rainforest Alliance Certified Coffee,* RAINFOREST ALLIANCE, http://www. rainforest-alliance.org/agriculture.cfm?id=coffee (last visited Apr. 10, 2013).

eco-friendly coffees is fuelled by environmental concerns. In that way, rather than boycotting a company, consumers can show support by buying an alternative product.[43] Although the production and export volumes are much smaller than those of the organic and fair trade sustainable coffees, future market growth assessments for shade, bird and eco-friendly coffees are 10–20 per cent per year.[44] These coffees have achieved quick success, especially in North America, Taiwan, and Japan, and it is anticipated that they could have the greatest potential for mainstream distribution, as these certification systems are not limited to smallholders.

D Fair Trade Coffees

1 Fair trade: definition, philosophy, and principles
Fair trade is an alternative approach to conventional international trade. It may be defined as:

> ... a trading partnership, based on dialogue, transparency and respect, which seeks greater equity in international trade. It contributes to sustainable development by offering better trading conditions to, and securing the rights of, marginalised producers and workers – especially in the South. Fair Trade organisations (backed by consumers) are engaged actively in supporting producers, awareness raising and in campaigning for changes in the rules and practice of conventional international trade.[45]

As a philosophy, fair trade attempts to correct market failures by promoting empowerment and improved quality of life for producers through an integrated and sustained system of trade partnerships amongst producers and retailers. Minimum wages and the payment of a social premium are the primary mechanisms for achieving this goal. Fair trade relies on the assumption that consumers are willing to pay a premium price for fair trade products because of the moral satisfaction they derive from the assurance that the fair trade label provides. It contends that a "survival of the fittest model" on an international scale is neither moral nor defensible in modern society and argues that producers should be paid "as much as possible" rather than "as little as possible", thus

---

[43] *See* LUTTINGER AND DICUM, *supra* note 40, at 193, 195.

[44] *See* DAVIRON AND PONTE, *supra* note 6, at 180.

[45] Definition of the FINE alliance. FINE brings together the Fair Trade Labelling Organisation International (FLO), the International Federation for Alternative Trade (IFAT), the Network of European World Shops (NEWS) and the European Fair Trade Association (EFTA).

providing a dramatic contrast with mainstream business models in which attention is directed towards meeting consumer demand and expanding shareholder profits.[46]

Generally, fair trade principles can be summarised as follows:

Trade with producers

Importers must, wherever possible, buy directly from producers. While estates, plantations, and large-scale producers have historically enjoyed access to export markets, small-scale producers are typically isolated from direct export access unless organised into cooperatives or similar group-selling structures. Coffee farmers in developing countries often live in isolated rural areas and are therefore reliant on middlemen to come to their farms and buy their product. They have a very limited bargaining power, as competition by buyers is rarely achieved. Middlemen will often agree not to compete with each other on price, so that farmers receive only one price offer.[47] In order to develop an alternative approach to these trading practices, ATOs established a practice whereby they would buy directly from and build relationships with producers in developing countries. They set up business and supply chain structures that allowed them to ship the coffee from producer to customer via their own warehousing and often through their own shops.[48]

Long-term trading relationships

The aims behind the long-term trading relationship principle are to allow for long-term planning and sustainable production practices.[49] Long-term trading relationships allow farmers to benefit from a predictable income flow and to correct market information failures by allowing information exchange to take place between producers and importers regarding supply and quality requirements.

---

[46] *See* MARY ANN LITTRELL AND MARSHA DICKSON, SOCIAL RESPONSIBILITY IN THE GLOBAL MARKET: FAIR TRADE OF CULTURAL PRODUCTS 5 (1999); Andy Redfern and Paul Snedker, *Creating Market Opportunities for Small Enterprises: Experiences of the Fair Trade Movement* 4 (SEED, Working Paper No. 30, 2002).

[47] *See* ALEX NICHOLLS AND CHARLOTTE OPAL, FAIR TRADE: MARKET-DRIVEN ETHICAL CONSUMPTION 33–34 (2005).

[48] *See* Redfern and Snedker, *supra* note 46, at 21.

[49] *See Aims of Fairtrade Standards*, FAIRTRADE INTERNATIONAL, http://www.fairtrade.net/aims_of_fairtrade_standards.html (last visited Apr. 10, 2013).

Minimum price and social premium

The fair trade minimum price is calculated to cover the costs of sustainable production,[50] the cost of sustainable livelihood, and the cost of complying with fair trade standards.[51] The application of a minimum price to the fair trade model was inspired by the Keynesian model of economics where price should be more closely linked to the cost of production. According to Keynes, one should not pay less for a product than the cost of its production plus the cost of a decent standard of living for the producer.[52] The additional social premium on the other hand is intended for investment in social, commercial, or environmental development projects. It guarantees that producers earn a little extra to invest in improving their social condition or the quality of their natural environment. In other words, the social premium represents the "development agenda" of fair trade.[53]

Fair trade labelling

Fair trade labelling works as a certification system. It provides an independent guarantee to consumers that producers and traders have abided by all fair trade conditions, that fair trade products have been produced and traded according to pre-defined social, contractual, and sometimes environmental standards, and that fair trade workers and artisans benefit from a higher price, stable income, fairer trading relations and decent production conditions.

2 Fair trade coffee facts

In 2003, worldwide sales of all fair trade products amounted to approximately $895 million, up from an estimated $600 million in 2002. In 2006, consumers worldwide spent $2.2 billion on fair trade certified

---

[50] The costs of production include land, labour and capital costs of sustainable production. They are calculated based on surveys of producers. *See* NICHOLLS AND OPAL, *supra* note 47, at 40.

[51] *See ibid.* The costs of complying with fair trade standards include, for example, those of belonging to a cooperative, organising a worker's assembly, paperwork associated with inspections and reporting to FLO. *Ibid.*

[52] *See* Redfern and Snedker, *supra* note 46, at 4; NICHOLLS AND OPAL, *supra* note 47, at 41–42.

[53] *See* NICHOLLS AND OPAL, *supra* note 47, at 47.

products.[54] Despite these figures, fair trade still represents a tiny percentage of the volume of international trade. However, its social and economic impact should not be underestimated. Fair trade involves more than 827 certified producer organisations in 58 countries in Asia, Africa, and Latin America, representing over 1.2 million farmers and workers and their families, and there are over 100 fair trade import organisations working with producer groups providing goods to consumers via 45 000 sales outlets worldwide, so that overall, 6 million people are benefiting from fair trade.[55]

Coffee is the fair trade product with the highest sales volume. Although the market share for fair trade coffee was estimated at only 1 per cent of worldwide coffee sales in 2009, worldwide sales of fair trade coffee reached 14 per cent between 2007 and 2008, for a total value of US$1.6 billion. It is estimated that global fair trade coffee sales generated an additional income of US$30 million for nearly 400 producer organisations in 2008.[56]

For the June 2008 to June 2010 period, the FLO system guarantees a Fairtrade Minimum Price or floor price of US$1.01 to US$1.45 per pound, depending on the type of coffee, and a further US$0.10 Fairtrade Premium that goes into communal funds for farmers to improve social, economic, and environmental conditions. In addition, when the coffee is also certified organic, an extra minimum US$0.20 higher per pound is applied to the Fairtrade Minimum Price.[57]

Figures 7.1 and 7.2 compare the Fairtrade and New York price for Arabica, and the Fairtrade and London LIFFE price for Robusta respectively during the period 1989–2008. They show that the Fairtrade Minimum Price proved highly effective when world market prices fell below a sustainable level, like, for example, during the coffee crisis of the late 1990s to early 2000s. While in recent years the difference between the Fairtrade Minimum Price and the New York or London LIFFE prices

---

[54] Press Release, Fairtrade Labelling Organisation International, 7 Million Farming Families Worldwide Benefit as Global Fairtrade Sales Increase by 40% and UK Awareness of the Fairtrade Mark Rises to 57% (Aug. 10, 2007), *available at* http://www.fairtrade.org.uk/press_office/press_releases_and_statements/archive_2007/aug_2007/global_fairtrade_sales_increase_by_40_benefiting_14_million_farmers_worldwide.aspx.

[55] *See* Fairtrade Foundation statistics *available at* http://www.fairtrade.net/facts_and_figures.html.

[56] *See* FAO, *supra* note 3, at 10.

[57] *Coffee*, FAIRTRADE INT'L, http://www.fairtrade.net/coffee.html (last visited Apr. 10, 2013).

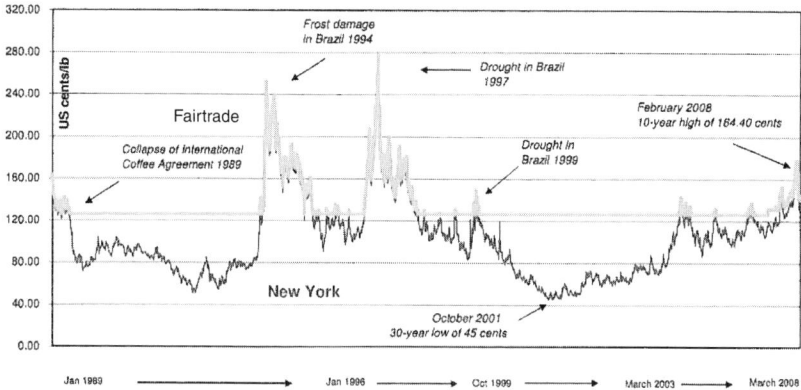

Source: Fairtrade Foundation 2009

*Figure 7.1   Comparison of New York and fair trade prices for Arabica
coffee, 1989–2008*

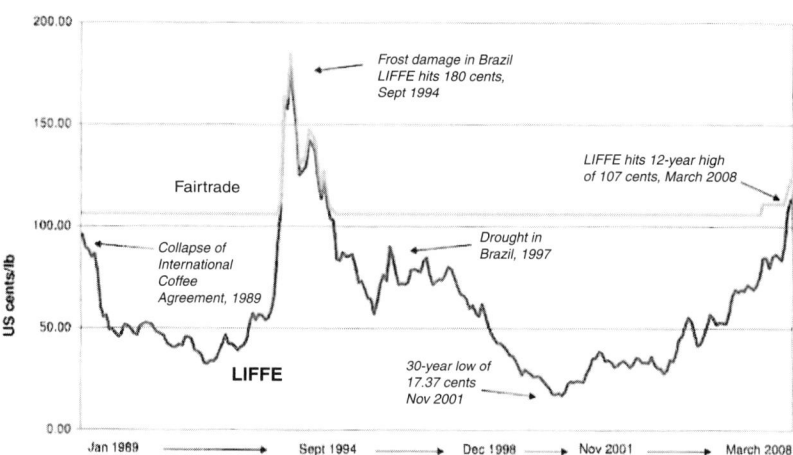

Source: Fairtrade Foundation 2009

*Figure 7.2   Comparison of London LIFFE and fair trade prices for
Robusta coffee, 1989–2008*

has been more modest, the fair trade system still provides a safety net and the certainty of receiving a guaranteed price in a typically highly volatile commodity market.[58]

E Industry-driven Certification Initiatives

Following the success of some sustainable coffee initiatives in the late 1990s, some large roasters, retailers, and food service providers recognised the potential of certification schemes and codes of practices and began their own internal "sustainability programs". Key coffee industry initiatives now include the Global Partnership for Good Agricultural Practice protocols (Global-GAP); the Utz Kapeh certification, now called Utz certified; the Common Code for the Coffee Community (4C); and Starbucks' CAFE Practices (Coffee and Farmer Equity) Program. For the most part, these schemes comprise a diversity of partnership models between NGOs or some independent schemes, like the Rainforest Alliance and the corporate coffee sector. Some other companies have shown their commitment to sustainable coffee, agreeing to purchase third-party-certified coffees.[59]

While these initiatives have the potential to include very large volumes of coffee in a short amount of time, raise awareness in the marketplace, and positively impact more of the world's coffee growers,[60] they raise some serious concerns. First, producers increasingly find that being enrolled within corporate-driven sustainability programs and traceability systems can be a requirement to market access. Yet it remains unclear whether producers actually receive financial benefits from their participation in these schemes. Second, many of these corporate-driven certification schemes offer lower social standards than fair trade and lower environmental criteria than organic certification.[61] Finally, it is feared that the proliferation of these parallel systems will confuse consumers, erode

---

[58] *See* FAO, *supra* note 3, at 11.

[59] For example, in 2006, Nespresso announced an intention to source 50 per cent of its coffee from the AAA Sustainability Program, and by 2010, McDonald's UK announced that all coffee served in its stores would be from Rainforest-certified farms. *See* Jeff Neilson, et al., *Challenges of Global Environment Governance by Non-State Actors in the Coffee Industry: Insights from India, Indonesia and Vietnam, in* AGRICULTURE, BIODIVERSITY AND MARKETS: LIVELIHOODS AND AGROECOLOGY IN COMPARATIVE PERSPECTIVE 178 (Stewart Lockie and David Carpenter eds., 2010).

[60] *See* GIOVANNUCCI AND KOEKOEK, *supra* note 25, at 56.

[61] *See* Neilson et al., *supra* note 59, at 179.

their confidence, and reduce their willingness to pay for these coffees, which will ultimately weaken the entire field.

V CONCLUSION

Over the past decade, the acts and symbolic association of coffee drinking have evolved, and new consumption patterns have emerged. There has been an increasing demand on the part of consumers for quality coffee with identifiable characteristics, such as geographical origin. At the same time, ethical considerations are increasingly involved in consumers' purchasing decisions, whether these are linked with concerns about health and food safety or the environmental and social implications of coffee production. These emerging tendencies offer producers opportunities to pursue cross-border branding strategies independent of commodity pricing at the exchanges and capture value in foreign markets by asking for higher prices for better quality coffee and more sustainable cultivation and trade practices. The examples presented in this chapter therefore highlight the capacity of signs and brands to empower local and sometimes small-scale producers to capitalise on branding strategies beyond a given national territory.

The choice of a differentiation strategy should be reached on a case-by-case basis, considering several factors. These include: (i) the existence of goodwill and reputation in a product; (ii) the existence of an appropriate legal system within the country of origin, or the country where protection is sought (this can be a decisive factor behind the choice of using a geographical indication, a trademark, or a certification mark for the protection of single-origin coffees); (iii) the manner in which coffee is produced, such as small-scale production or plantation systems (whereas fair trade will only be granted to small-scale producers, the organic, shade, bird or eco-friendly coffees are not limited to smallholders); (iv) the trends in market demand for specialty or sustainable coffees; and (v) the costs and time needed to reach the legal or certification requirements. For example, where a country has heavily invested in a low-cost/high-volume model of exploitation, it may be prohibitively expensive and time-consuming to move into niche markets.

In recent years, the market share for differentiated coffees has grown considerably, and in 2008, it was estimated that differentiated coffees accounted for 6 per cent of worldwide coffee production. With sales of conventional coffee stagnating both in Europe and the United States, differentiated coffees are one of the few segments of the coffee market registering sales growth.[62] As such, it is starting to attract the attention of large roasters, retailers, and food service providers who seek to meet consumers' demand for ethical products and give the image of socially responsible corporations.[63]

With the existence of multiple certification schemes and labels, and a recent increase in private voluntary ethical certification schemes, there are concerns that consumers may be confused as to what they stand for.[64] Also, some of these schemes, such as the SMBC's bird-friendly and the Rainforest Alliance certification marks seem to overlap to some extent and cause uncertainty. This may erode consumer confidence and reduce their willingness to pay for these coffees. Ultimately, it is up to the industry and regulatory bodies to educate consumers and ensure that the coffees using these labels are certified by an independent third party according to clearly defined standards.

---

[62] *See* FAO, *supra* note 3, at 15.

[63] *Ibid.* at 16.

[64] *See* Lewin et al., *supra* note 4, at 101; GIOVANNUCCI AND KOEKOEK, *supra* note 27, at 21.

PART III

Territoriality, exhaustion of rights, and gray
market products

8. The (avoidable) effects of territorially different approaches to trademark and copyright exhaustion

Irene Calboli[*]

I INTRODUCTION

In March 2013, the Supreme Court of the United States made copyright history when it issued its decision in *Kirtsaeng v. Wiley & Sons*[1] and ruled that the principle of copyright exhaustion as provided in section 109(a) of the Copyright Act applies equally to products manufactured and lawfully distributed in the United States as well as in foreign countries. It took over two decades of litigation for the Court to reach this position and clarify that genuine (non-counterfeit) books, pictures, software, and other copyrighted products can be freely imported into the United States not solely by copyright owners but also by independent third parties – the so-called gray marketers – regardless of where the products were "lawfully made" and first sold in the global market. The impact of the decision in *Kirtsaeng*, however, goes beyond international trade in books, pictures, and other communicative products, which are traditionally the subject matter of copyright protection. It directly extends to international trade in many other consumer products such as

* © 2014 Irene Calboli, Professor of Law, Marquette University Law School; Visiting Professor, Faculty of Law, National University of Singapore. This chapter draws on research from, and adapts parts of the author's publications in the volume INTELLECTUAL PROPERTY AT THE CROSSROADS OF TRADE (Jan Rosen ed., 2012), the *Northwestern Journal of Technology and Intellectual Property Law*, and the *International Review for Intellectual Property and Competition Law*.

[1] Kirtsaeng v. John Wiley & Sons, Inc., 133 S.Ct. 1351 (2013).

shampoos, watches, and chocolate.[2] Even though these products cannot be copyrighted in their entirety because they are non-copyrightable articles, they frequently carry "incidental features" such as decorations, product design, product packaging, creative labels, logos, and so forth that can qualify for copyright protection. In recent years, copyright protection for these incidental product features has become increasingly popular in the business world.

Why this trend? Because by securing copyrights in these product features, intellectual property owners could benefit from the effects of both trademark and copyright protection for their products. As I recount in this chapter, until the Supreme Court's decision in *Kirtsaeng*, the possibility to turn to copyright protection, and claim copyright infringement, proved particularly useful in order to prevent parallel imports of gray market products.[3] In general, businesses oppose gray market products because, even though these products are genuine and businesses themselves distributed the products into foreign markets, the sales of these products by independent parties disrupt businesses' ability to control product distribution and pricing in separate national markets.[4] Still, businesses in the United States have generally not been able to rely on trademark law in order to block parallel imports. Under the rule of trademark law, genuine products carrying a registered trademark can be imported into the national market after they have been lawfully sold and purchased elsewhere, including in a foreign market – in other words, the

---

[2] *See* Quality King Distribs., Inc. v. L'anza Research Int'l., Inc., 523 U.S. 135 (1998); Costco Wholesale Corp. v. Omega S.A., 131 S.Ct. 565 (2010); Euro-Excellence, Inc. v. Kraft Canada, Inc., [2007] 3 S.C.R. 20 (Can.).

[3] *See* Irene Calboli, *Corporate Strategies, First Sale Rules, and Copyright Misuse: Waiting for Answers from* Kirtsaeng v. Wiley *and* Omega v. Costco (II), 11 Nw. J. Tech. & Intell. Prop. 221, 227 (2013) [hereinafter Calboli, *Copyright Misuse*]. In this chapter, I use the terms "parallel imports" and "gray market goods" interchangeably as synonyms.

[4] The corporate opposition to gray market products is well summarized in the position adopted by the International Trademark Association (INTA). *See Trademark Owner's Guide to Parallel Imports in the United States* Int'l Trademark Ass'n (Feb. 2012), *available at* http://www.inta.org/Advocacy/Documents/INTA%20Trademark%20Owners%20Guide%20to%20Parallel%20Imports%20in%20the%20United%20States.pdf [hereinafter INTA, *Parallel Imports*] (advocating in favor of a system of national exhaustion in the best interest of trademark owners).

United States follows the principle of international trademark exhaustion.[5] Absent the possibility to invoke trademark law, businesses turned to copyright law. Several courts in the United States supported the position that section 109(a) of the Copyright Act only applied to national and not to foreign sales – that is, that the United States followed the principle of national copyright exhaustion. Accordingly, businesses started to seek copyright protection for their products, or most frequently for the incidental features of these products that could be copyrighted. In turn, businesses started to enforce this protection against parallel imports by claiming that parallel imports amounted to copyright infringement. Ultimately, the Supreme Court's decision in *Kirtsaeng* stopped this trend, when it explicitly stated that section 109(a) and the principle of copyright exhaustion applies to all copyrighted works after their first lawful sale in the market regardless of where this sale has taken place, domestically or internationally. After *Kirtsaeng*, businesses can no longer turn to copyright law, nor to trademark law, in order to prevent the importation of gray marketed products.

In previous works, I have extensively analyzed the principle of trademark and copyright exhaustion pre-*Kirtsaeng*[6] and criticized the corporate trend of exploiting territorially different exhaustion regimes to block the importation of otherwise legitimate products, which I argued amounts to copyright misuse.[7] Building upon these works, in this chapter I analyze the decision in *Kirtsaeng* and its impact on parallel imports, that is, the shift towards a system of international copyright exhaustion in the United States. In particular, in Part II, I briefly outline the alternative approaches that can be adopted with respect to the territorial application of the principle of intellectual property exhaustion – national, international, and regional exhaustion. In Part III, I recount the approaches followed by the United States with respect to trademark and copyright exhaustion pre-*Kirtsaeng*, and the resulting corporate trend of copyrighting incidental product features in order to prevent parallel imports. In

---

[5] *See* discussion *infra* Part III.

[6] *See, e.g.,* Irene Calboli, *An American Tale: The Unclear Application of the First Sale Rule in United States Copyright Law (and its Impact on International Trade)*, *in* INTELLECTUAL PROPERTY AT THE CROSSROADS OF TRADE 67 (Jan Rosen ed., 2012) [hereinafter Calboli, *First Sale in Copyright Law*]; Irene Calboli, *Market Integration and (the Limits of) the First Sale Rule in North American and European Trademark Law*, 51 SANTA CLARA L. REV. 1241 (2011) [hereinafter Calboli, *First Sale Rule in Trademark Law*].

[7] Calboli, *Copyright Misuse, supra* note 3, at 229–32.

Part IV, I analyze the Supreme Court's decision in *Kirtsaeng*, including the concurring and dissenting opinions that were issued along with the opinion of the majority. In Part V, I warn that the effect of *Kirtsaeng* may be short-lived in light of the heralded calls for copyright reforms made in the weeks immediately following the decision. Even though these calls did not mention *Kirtsaeng* directly, it would be naïve to underestimate the intensive lobbying activity that is taking place to overrule the decision. Yet should Congress overrule *Kirtsaeng*, this would recreate a system of territorially different exhaustion regimes in copyright and trademark law, and in turn the incentive for businesses to claim copyright protection in order to prevent the importation of gray market products. This does not need to be the case, however. As I conclude in Part V, courts and Congress could adopt appropriate mechanisms in order to prohibit the corporate games that took place pre-*Kirtsaeng*. In particular, as I have argued before, courts could explicitly rule that claims for copyright infringement concerning incidental product features amount to copyright misuse. Similarly, Congress could follow the example of countries such as Australia and Singapore, and adopt an ad hoc legislative amendment prohibiting, or rendering unenforceable, copyright protection for these features in the context of parallel imports.[8]

II ALTERNATIVE TERRITORIAL APPROACHES TO INTELLECTUAL PROPERTY EXHAUSTION

As I have analyzed in detail before, courts and legislators in the United States developed the principle of intellectual property exhaustion to balance the exclusive rights granted to businesses, inventors, and creators in their products and works with the rights of retailers, consumers, and second-hand dealers to freely resell or dispose of these products and works after having lawfully acquired them in the market.[9] Theoretically, the principle of exhaustion finds its rationale in the assumption that intellectual property rights must not be used as a tool to control market distribution or as a means of market division contrary to the respective functions of the various intellectual property rights – to provide incentive for inventors and creators for patents and copyrights, and to protect

---

[8] *See* discussion and references *infra* Part V. For a detailed proposal in this respect, *see* Mary LaFrance, *Avoiding Mutant Trademarks: A Statutory Exclusion for Copyrighted Accessories to Parallel Import*, Chapter 9 in this volume.

[9] *See* Calboli, *First Sale Rule in Trademark Law, supra* note 6, at 1250–51; Calboli, *First Sale Rule in Copyright Law, supra* note 6, at 71–72.

consumers against confusion and competitors against unfair market competition for trademarks. The principle of exhaustion of rights is additionally justified under the traditional rule against the restraint of the alienation of private property.[10] Under this rule, lawful purchasers of any products, including products carrying or embodying a given intellectual property right, should have the right to fully enjoy the possession of these products, which includes the right to re-sell or otherwise dispose of the products after their first sale.[11] As scholars have noted, this position directly responds to the pressing need to delineate "a necessary demarcation line between two colliding properties: the intellectual property right of the producer and the common proprietary right of the owner of [the] product he has bought."[12] To avoid overextending intellectual property rights, the proprietary owner of a product "should [thus] remain free to enjoy the specific privileges of traditional ownership: he should be free to resell or otherwise dispose of his property."[13]

Even though intellectual property owners frequently attempt to resort to other means to control post-sale product distribution (such as contractual limitations to product resale), the application of the principle of intellectual property exhaustion has been generally straightforward with respect to products manufactured and sold within the territory of individual countries. National legislators and the judiciary, however, have frequently struggled with the question of whether the principle of intellectual property exhaustion should also apply to products imported into the national territory from foreign countries without the consent of the owners of the various intellectual property rights embodied in the

---

[10] *See e.g.*, Columbia Pictures Industries, Inc. v. Redd Horne, Inc., 749 F.2d 154, 160 (3d Cir. 1984). H.R. 987, 98th Cong., 2d Session (1984) (highlighting that the first-sale doctrine is rooted in the rule against restraint on alienation of property).

[11] *See* 2–8 MELVILLE B. NIMMER AND DAVID NIMMER, NIMMER ON COPYRIGHT (2011) §8.12[A] (stating that "[the] continued control over the distribution of copies is not so much a supplement to the intangible copyright, but is rather primarily a device for controlling the disposition of the tangible personal property that embodies the copyrighted work" and that "the policy favoring a copyright monopoly for authors gives way to the policy opposing restraints of trade and restraints on alienation.").

[12] Herman Cohen Jehoram, *International Exhaustion versus Importation Right: A Murky Area of Intellectual Property Law*, 4 G.R.U.R. INT'L 280 (1996) (recounting that "[t]he dogmatic explanation of this exhaustion rule ... has been provided by the patriarch of intellectual property law: Josef Kohler").

[13] *Ibid.*

products.[14] Corporations, for instance, oppose parallel imports, as parallel importers usually engage in international arbitrage from low-cost to high-cost countries and ultimately sell the imported products at a lower price in the national markets where corporations also distribute the same products. On the other side, importers, wholesalers, and other distributors support parallel imports as the primary activity of these businesses precisely comprises in distributing the imported products to retailers, or in selling the products to the public, usually at a lesser price than the official distributors. Governments in several countries also favor parallel imports because of the advantages that parallel imports may provide to their economies, in terms of lower product prices and, in some instances, access to products that otherwise may not be distributed into their countries. Not surprisingly, based on the different interests at stake, national positions on the issue vary. Precisely because of these differences, Article 6 of the Agreement on Trade-Related Aspects of Intellectual Property Rights (TRIPS) recites that nothing in the Agreement can "be used to address the issue of the exhaustion of intellectual property rights."[15] In the absence of a common international standard, countries have adopted different territorial approaches with respect to the principle of exhaustion.[16]

Notably, national approaches with respect to the exhaustion of intellectual property rights can be grouped into three categories: national,

---

[14] On the relationship between intellectual property protection and international trade, see Herman Cohen Jehoram, *Prohibition of Parallel Imports Through Intellectual Property Rights*, 30 I.I.C. 495 (1999); Christopher Heath, *Parallel Imports and International Trade*, 28 I.I.C. 623 (1997); Charles Worth, *Free Trade Agreements and the Exhaustion of Rights Principle*, 1 E.I.P.R. 40 (1994); John C. Hilke, *Free Trading or Free-Riding: An Examination of the Theories and Available Empirical Evidence on Gray Market Imports*, 31 WORLD COMPETITION L. & ECON. REV. 75 (1988).

[15] Article 6, Agreement on Trade-Related Aspects of Intellectual Property Rights, April 15, 1994, Marrakesh Agreement Establishing the World Trade Organization, Annex 1C, LEGAL INSTRUMENTS – RESULT OF THE URUGUAY ROUNDS Vol. 31, 33 I.L.M. 83 (1994). *See also* S.K. Verma, *Exhaustion of Intellectual Property Rights and Free Trade – Article 6 of the TRIPS Agreements*, 29 I.I.C. 534, 539 (1998).

[16] *See, e.g.*, Vincent Chiappetta, *The Desirability of Agreeing to Disagree: The WTO, TRIPS, International IPR Exhaustion, and a Few Other Things*, 21 MICH. J. INT'L L. 333 (2000).

international, and regional exhaustion.[17] Undoubtedly the most protectionist position, the principle of *national exhaustion* provides that national intellectual property rights are considered exhausted only when the products have been distributed for sale in the domestic territory by intellectual property owners or with their consent by, for example, an affiliated company, a licensee, distributor, or agent.[18] Under this principle, intellectual property owners cannot object to the future commercialization of their products within the domestic market. They can still oppose as infringement, however, the importation (or re-importation) into the domestic market of genuine goods that have been first distributed outside the national territory. Under the principle of *international exhaustion*, which is more favorable toward free trade, national rights are instead considered exhausted after the products have been distributed for sale by intellectual property owners or with their consent anywhere in the world.[19] In countries adopting international exhaustion, intellectual property owners cannot object to the importation of gray market goods that were first marketed outside the national market or to the re-entry of genuine goods that were exported abroad after their first domestic sale. Lastly, as a hybrid solution, a third type of trademark exhaustion has emerged in the past half century – *regional exhaustion*. Under this principle, national rights granted by each member of a regional agreement, such as the European Union, are exhausted after the products are put into the market in any of the national territories of the members of the agreement.[20] Under this regime, intellectual property owners cannot object to the further circulation of their products within the boundaries of the region, regardless of the country where the first sale of the products occurred within the region. Intellectual property owners, however, may still oppose the importation (or re-importation) of gray market products that have been introduced into the market from outside the national territory of the members of the region.

---

[17]   *See generally* Jesper Rasmussen, *The Principle of Exhaustion of Trade Mark Rights Pursuant to Directive 89/104 (and Regulation 40/94)*, 4 E.I.P.R. 174 (1995) (describing the effects of the different types of trademark exhaustion).

[18]   *See* Calboli, *First Sale Rule in Trademark Law*, *supra* note 6, at 1256.

[19]   *Ibid.* at 1257.

[20]   *Ibid. See also* Irene Calboli, *Trademark Exhaustion in the European Union: Community-Wide or International? The Saga Continues*, 6 MARQ. INTELL. PROP. L. REV. 47 (2002).

The United States, in particular, follows a system of national exhaustion with respect to patent law and patented products.[21] The scope and extent of patent exhaustion, however, is not addressed in this chapter, which focuses on the analysis of the principle of exhaustion in trademark and copyright law. As I elaborate below, the United States follows a system of international exhaustion with respect to trademark law and trademarked products.[22] Yet, until the Supreme Court's decision in *Kirtsaeng*, it was unclear whether section 109(a) of the Copyright Act established a system of national or international copyright exhaustion, even though the majority of the courts seemed to favor an interpretation of the statute in favor of national exhaustion.[23] In *Kirtsaeng*, the Supreme Court clarified that the Copyright Act does not impose a territorial limitation on the application of the principle of copyright exhaustion, which brings the United States' position, at least for the time being, in line with the international exhaustion standard adopted under the rule of trademark law.[24]

III PRE-*KIRTSAENG* TRADEMARK AND COPYRIGHT EXHAUSTION (AND RESULTING CORPORATE GAMES)

As I mentioned in Part II, the United States has historically adopted a system of international exhaustion with respect to the enforcement of trademark rights. In other words, genuine goods carrying a mark that is protected in the United States can be imported into the domestic territory without the consent of the trademark owner regardless of where the goods were first sold, whether domestically or in a foreign market.[25] This

---

[21] In general, courts have consistently found that international sales do not exhaust patent rights. *See* Fuji Photo Film Co. v. Jazz Photo Corp., 394 F.3d 1368, 1376 (Fed. Cir. 2005) (noting that "[t]he patentee's authorization of an international first sale does not affect exhaustion of that patentee's rights in the United States ..." and that "foreign sales can never occur under a United States patent because the United States patent system does not provide for extra-territorial effect.").

[22] *See* Calboli, *First Sale Rule in Trademark Law, supra* note 6, at 1250–51 (summarizing the principle of trademark exhaustion in the United States).

[23] *See* Calboli, *First Sale Rule in Copyright Law, supra* note 6, at 71–73 (summarizing the ambiguities of the application of section 109(a) of the Copyright Act before the Supreme Court's decision in *Kirtsaeng*).

[24] Kirtsaeng v. John Wiley & Sons, Inc., 133 S.Ct. 1351 (2013).

[25] Originally, U.S. courts allowed parallel imports based on the principle of "universality" of trademark rights. *See* Hunyadi Janos Corp. v. Steger, 285 F. 861

approach rests on the position that, in the United States, trademarks are not protected as property, but as indicators of commercial origin and symbols of business goodwill.[26] Based on this premise, trademark law has generally permitted parallel imports of genuine products as long as consumers are not confused as to the origin and quality of the products.[27] In particular, trademark law permits the importation of gray market goods when "both the foreign and the United States trademark are owned by the same person or business entity."[28] To avoid strategic assignments between affiliated companies to circumvent this rule and block the importation of gray market products into the United States, courts have interpreted the concept of "same ownership" so as to also include "parent and subsidiary companies or [companies] otherwise subjected to common ownership and control."[29] The only exception to the general rule permitting parallel imports arises in the instance where the imported products, despite being genuine, are "materially different" from the products that trademark owners are selling in the domestic market under the same mark either directly or via authorized distributors – for instance, imported Coca-Cola products made with sugar instead of domestically distributed Coca-Cola products made with corn syrup.[30] As the D.C. Circuit ruled in the *Lever*

(2d Cir. 1922); Fred Gretsch Mfg. Co. v. Schoening, 238 F. 780 (2d Cir. 1916); Apollinaris Co. v. Scherer, 27 F. 18 (C.C.N.Y. 1886). However, in A. Bourjois & Co. v. Katzel, 275 F. 539 (2d Cir. 1921), *rev'd*, 260 U.S. 689 (1923), the Supreme Court affirmed that marks have separate existence in separate national territories, thus starting to follow the principle of "territoriality." *See also* American Circuit Breaker Corp. v. Oregon Breakers Inc., 406 F.3d 577 (9th Cir. 2005) (noting that in *Katzel* the Supreme Court "marked a dramatic change in trademark law by adopting the principle of 'territoriality' of trademarks and moving away from the rule of 'universality'").

[26] *See* Irene Calboli, *Trademark Assignment "With Goodwill": A Concept Whose Time Has Gone,* 57 FLA. L. REV. 771, 777–79 (2005) (recounting the history and theory of trademark law and policy in the United States).

[27] The U.S. Tariff Act prohibits the importation of a product "that bears a trademark owned by a citizen of ... the United States and is registered in the U.S. Patent and Trademark Office." *See* Tariff Act of 1930 § 526(a), 19 U.S.C.S. § 1526(a) (2006). The Lanham Act bars the importation of goods with a mark that will "copy or simulate" a registered trademark. Lanham Act § 42, 15 U.S.C. § 1124 (2006).

[28] K-Mart Corp. v. Cartier, Inc., 486 U.S. 281, 289 (1988).

[29] *Ibid.* (indicating that the "extraordinary protection" afforded by the Tariff Act § 526 is exclusively for domestic U.S. trademark owners that have no corporate affiliation with the foreign manufacturer).

[30] *See* J. THOMAS MCCARTHY, 5 MCCARTHY ON TRADEMARKS AND UNFAIR COMPETITION 10, § 29:50–51.75.

Brothers cases,[31] this exception is based upon the consideration that consumers could be confused if two products with identical appearance are sold in the United States under the same mark, but the products are of different quality. Still, not all products of materially different quality are destined to be blocked at the border. Notably, since the mid-1990s, the Customs Service Regulations were amended to permit the importation of materially different genuine products as long as importers have properly labeled the products with an ad hoc disclaimer alerting consumers about the different quality of the products compared with the products directly distributed by trademark owners.[32] The policy behind this exception rests again on the fact that, as long as the products are genuine and consumers are not confused as to the actual product quality, consumers should benefit from the lower prices and increased competition that gray market products may bring into the United States market.

Conversely, until the Supreme Court's decision in *Kirtsaeng*, the territorial application of the principle of copyright exhaustion was unsettled. Based on the interpretation of the majority of the courts, it seemed to lean towards an approach favoring national exhaustion.[33] Originally developed as a judicial doctrine in *Bobbs-Merrill v. Straus* in the early 1900s,[34] the principle of copyright exhaustion was first codified in the 1909 Copyright Act[35] and later confirmed in section 109(a) of the 1976 Copyright Act. Section 109(a) states that the owners of copyrighted works "lawfully made under this title" are entitled "to sell or otherwise

---

[31]   Lever Bros. Co. v. United States, 877 F.2d 101 (D.C. Cir. 1989) and Lever Bros. Co. v. United States, 981 F.2d 1330 (D.C. Cir. 1993). The court stated that when a mark is applied to physically different goods, the mark is not "genuine" despite the affiliation between producers, as this does not reduce the possibility of a likelihood of consumer confusion as to the product quality. *Lever Bros.*, 877 F.2d 101; *Lever Bros.*, 981 F.2d 1330. *See also* Societe Des Produits Nestle, S.A. v. Casa Helvetia, Inc., 982 F.2d 633, 639 (1st Cir. 1992).

[32]   19 C.F.R. § 133.23(b). "Goods determined by the Customs Service to be physically and materially different ... shall not be detained ... where the merchandise or its packaging bears a conspicuous and legible label ... " that indicates that "[t]his product is not authorized by the United States trademark owner for importation and is materially different from the authorized products." *Ibid.*

[33]   Calboli, *First Sale Rule in Copyright Law, supra* note 6, at 71–76.

[34]   Bobbs-Merrill Co. v Straus, 210 U.S. 339 (1908).

[35]   Quality King Distribs., Inc. v. L'anza Research Int'l., Inc., 523 U.S. 135, 141–42 (1998) ("Congress subsequently codified our holding in *Bobbs-Merrill* that the exclusive right to 'vend' was limited to first sale of the work.").

dispose of the possession of that [work]" without the "authority of the copyright owner."[36] Still, in neither the 1909 nor the 1976 Act did Congress clarify the territorial application of the principle of copyright exhaustion, that is, whether the principle of exhaustion applied to copyrighted products after their first sale anywhere in the world, or just in the United States. In the absence of such clarification, the question of the geographical application of the principle of copyright exhaustion became a question for the courts to clarify. Several courts thus supported the view that section 109(a) applied only to domestic and not to international sales.[37] In other words, they supported the view that the rights of copyright owners in copyrighted products first sold abroad were not exhausted, and copyright owners could prevent the importation of these products in the United States. These courts derived this position from the combined interpretation of sections 109(a) and 602(a)(1) of the Copyright Act. In particular, section 602(a)(1) provides that the "importation into the United States" of a copyrighted work acquired outside the United States "without the authority of the [copyright] owner" is "an infringement of the exclusive right [of] distribut[ion]."[38] In particular, these courts supported the notion that, by adopting section 602(a)(1), Congress intended to create a system barring the unauthorized importation of copyrighted products even when the products had been lawfully made and distributed abroad under the authority of copyright owners.[39] Only in a few instances, courts deviated from this interpretation. Most notably, the Third Circuit supported the position that section 109(a) limited the importation right in section 602(a)(1) and equally applied to national and international sales.[40] Regardless of these internal judicial disagreements, however, the United States consistently purported that national copyright exhaustion was the official national position on the matter while negotiating international agreements, both at the multilateral level, such as during the TRIPS negotiations, as well as the bilateral or

---

[36]   17 U.S.C. § 109(a) (2008).

[37]   *See, e.g.*, Denbicare U.S.A. Inc. v. Toys "R" Us, Inc., 84 F.3d 1143 (9th Cir. 1996); Parfums Givenchy, Inc. v. Drug Emporium, Inc., 38 F.3d 477 (9th Cir. 1994); BMG Music v. Perez, 952 F.2d 318 (9th Cir. 1991).

[38]   17 U.S.C. § 602(a)(1) (2008).

[39]   *See Parfums Givenchy*, 38 F.3d at 481.

[40]   *See, e.g.*, Sebastian International Inc. v. Consumer Contacts (Pty.) Ltd., 847 F.2d 1093 (3d Cir. 1988).

plurilateral level while negotiating free trade agreements (FTAs) with foreign countries.[41]

Still, due to the lack of express legislative guidance in section 109(a), ambiguities and conflicting interpretations remained as to the actual territorial application of the principle of copyright exhaustion in the United States. Not surprisingly, these ambiguities translated into litigation between copyright owners and parallel importers and distributors of gray market products. In the late 1990s, the Supreme Court attempted to provide some clarity in this respect and granted certiorari in *Quality King v. L'anza*, a case about gray market products re-imported into the United States.[42] Unfortunately, the Supreme Court's decision in *Quality King* did not resolve the existing doubts, but rather complicated the issue. The Court ultimately ruled in favor of the distributor, Quality King, and found that copyright in the products had been exhausted even if the products had been imported from overseas. Yet, the Court reached this conclusion only because the products at issue were made and first sold in the United States – only after this domestic first sale were the products exported overseas, and Quality King later re-imported them into the United States.[43] Moreover, the Court in this case did not explicitly address the issue of the territorial application of section 109(a) for *all* gray market products, in particular for those made and first sold abroad.[44] Absent such important clarification, the decision left many questions unanswered. To a certain extent, many read in the decision the confirmation that the United States followed a system of national copyright exhaustion, at least with respect to products manufactured and first distributed abroad. Justice Ginsburg concurred with the majority precisely on this premise.[45] More problematically, she stated that "lawfully made under this title" meant "lawfully made in the United States,"[46] which could imply that section 109(a) did not apply to foreign manufactured goods at all, even after these goods have been distributed in the

---

[41]   Kirtsaeng v. John Wiley & Sons, Inc., 133 S.Ct. 1351, 1384 (2013) (Ginsburg J. dissenting).

[42]   Quality King Distribs., Inc. v. L'anza Research Int'l, Inc., 523 U.S. 135 (1998).

[43]   *Ibid.* at 139.

[44]   *See generally* Calboli, *First Sale Rule in Copyright Law*, *supra* note 6, at 79 (highlighting that the "Supreme Court fell short of addressing the territorial extent of the first sale rule in copyright law").

[45]   *Quality King*, 523 U.S. at 153 (Ginsburg J. concurring).

[46]   *Ibid.* (Ginsburg J. concurring) (citing WILLIAM F. PATRY, COPYRIGHT LAW AND PRACTICE (1997 SUPP.) 166–70 and 10 PAUL GOLDSTEIN, COPYRIGHT (2nd ed. 1998) § 16.0, 16:1–16:2).

United States under the authority of the copyright owners. Not surprisingly, additional litigation followed. In 2010, the Supreme Court again attempted to resolve the issue in *Costco v. Omega*.[47] This case involved gray market watches manufactured and first distributed in Europe and later imported into the United States. Yet, the Court's decision was again disappointing. Justice Kagan recused herself due to her previous role as Solicitor General, and the remaining Justices equally divided and affirmed, without explanation,[48] the Ninth Circuit's ruling in favor of Omega, which supported the position that section 109(a) only applies to products after their first authorized sale in the United States.[49]

Amidst these judicial ambiguities, the interpretation favoring the position that the United States followed a principle of national copyright exhaustion continued to be prevalent. As indicated, national exhaustion was also the position straightforwardly supported by the United States internationally while negotiating with other countries. In this context, it was thus not surprising that the business world quickly realized that, compared with the rule of (international) trademark exhaustion, the rule of (national) copyright exhaustion could better assist businesses in their fight against gray market products.[50] As I noted, businesses could not turn to trademark law to stop gray market products due to the fact that the principle of trademark exhaustion applied, and applies, internationally. Yet businesses could stop these products by applying the principle of national copyright exhaustion under which the unauthorized importation of copyrighted products amounted to copyright infringement. To turn to copyright exhaustion, however, businesses first needed to secure copyright protection for their products, which frequently were uncopyrightable because the products constituted useful articles. Still, some of the features incorporated into these products, such as logos, labels, product packaging, or product instructions, could qualify for copyright protection, as these features were not useful and met a level of originality, which was sufficient for copyright protection.[51] Accordingly,

---

[47] Costco Wholesale Corp. v. Omega, S.A., 131 S.Ct. 565 (2010).

[48] *Ibid.*

[49] Omega S.A. v. Costco Wholesale Corp., 541 F.3d 982 (9th Cir. 2008). *See also* Samuel Brooks, *Battling Gray Markets through Copyright Law: Omega S.A. v. Costco Wholesale Corporation*, 2010 BYU L. Rev. 19 (2010).

[50] *See* Willie Skinner, *Preventing Gray Markets: Is Copyright Law the Answer?*, 26 Syracuse J. Int'l L. & Com. 315, 328 (1999).

[51] *See* INTA, *Parallel Imports*, *supra* note 4, at 23–24. "The Copyright Act allows the copyright owner exclusively to control the first sale of an authorized copy. Current U.S. jurisprudence provides that goods manufactured and first sold

businesses started to invoke copyright protection on these features and in many instances registered these features with the Registry of Copyright. Businesses then turned to section 602(a)(1) of the Copyright Act and claimed that the importation of gray market goods carrying those features infringed their national copyrights.[52] Both *Quality King* and *Costco* involved, for example, copyright claims concerning incidental copyrighted features of otherwise uncopyrightable products – copyrighted labels and designs of shampoo bottles in *Quality King*, and Omega watches carrying a tiny insignia (the Omega Globe) on the back of the watches in *Costco*. Interestingly, courts did not seem to be concerned by these "unusual" copyright claims. Instead, the judiciary, including the Supreme Court, addressed these claims, at least in appearance, as traditional copyright claims.[53]

IV GAME OVER? THE (POSITIVE) IMPACT OF *KIRTSAENG* ON GRAY MARKETS (AND THE RISKS AHEAD)

After the non-decision of the Supreme Court in *Costco v. Omega*, uncertainty continued to dominate the debate over the territorial application of the principle of copyright exhaustion, in particular with respect to foreign-made products. Additional litigation followed and, in 2012, the Court decided to grant certiorari again in *Kirtsaeng v. John Wiley &*

---

abroad cannot be sold again in the U.S. without the U.S. copyright owner's authorization." *Ibid.* at 24. "If a trademark owner obtains a U.S. copyright registration for some aspect of its product or product packaging (which requires that a requisite level of originality and creativity be shown), it may record its copyright registrations with the [Custom and Border Protection]." *Ibid.* "[T]rademark owners should seek relief through the district courts or the ITC to address gray market copyright infringement." *Ibid.*

    [52] *See, e.g.*, Omega S.A. v. Costco Wholesale Corp., 541 F.3d 982, 984 (9th Cir. 2008); L'anza Research Int'l., Inc. v. Quality King Distribs., Inc., 98 F.3d 1109 (9th Cir. 1996).

    [53] In *Quality King*, the Supreme Court noted that this was an "unusual" copyright case because L'anza was not seeking to prevent unauthorized copying of its copyrighted material but rather to protect "the integrity of its method of marketing." Yet the Court proceeded to address the claim at issue without further attention to this aspect. Quality King Distribs., Inc. v. L'anza Research Int'l, Inc., 523 U.S. 135, 140 (1998).

Sons[54] to hopefully settle the issue once and for all. This case concerned gray market books imported from Thailand, not copyrights for incidental features, as in *Quality King* and *Costco*. The Court was again set to address the issue of whether section 109(a) applies to copies made and distributed in a foreign country. The decision on appeal, issued by the Second Circuit, was particularly problematic.[55] By relying on Justice Ginsburg's concurrence in *Quality King*, the Second Circuit interpreted the language "lawfully made under this title" in section 109(a) as "lawfully made in the United States," that is, "as applying only to works manufactured domestically."[56] This position was strongly criticized, including by a dissenting opinion in the case authored by Judge Murtha.[57] The culprit of contention was, again, that the position of the Second Circuit discriminated between domestic and foreign manufactured products. Based upon the Second Circuit's decision, only domestically manufactured products were subject to copyright exhaustion – regardless of whether they were sold nationally or re-imported into the United States under the rule in *Quality King* – while section 109(a) did not apply to foreign-made products, even after their authorized sale in the United States.[58] Due to the large number of products manufactured abroad and in circulation in the United States, the implications of the decision were of important concern. If literally applied, the decision would result in prohibiting retailers, consumers, and even libraries and museums, from reselling, lending, or gifting goods manufactured abroad even after these goods had been lawfully acquired in the United States. Judge Murtha and others forcefully opposed a reading of the provision in this sense, which could paradoxically incentivize businesses to relocate their manufacturing facilities abroad to avoid the application of the

---

[54] Kirtsaeng v. John Wiley & Sons, Inc., 132 S.Ct. 1905 (U.S. 2012).

[55] John Wiley & Sons Inc. v. Kirtsaeng, 654 F.3d 210 (2d Cir. 2011).

[56] *John Wiley & Sons*, 654 F.3d at 221 (relying on Justice Ginsburg's concurrence in Quality King Distribs., Inc. v. L'anza Research Int'l, Inc., 523 U.S. 135, 154 (1998)).

[57] *Wiley*, 652 F.3d at 224–29 (Murtha J. dissenting). As later supported by the Supreme Court, Judge Murtha stated that to interpret the language "lawfully made under this title" as "made in the United States" was incorrect since section 109(a) of the Copyright Act does not make reference to the place of manufacture of the products, but instead focuses on whether the products are made "lawfully." *Ibid.*

[58] *Ibid.* at 221. The Second Circuit decided that "while perhaps a close call … in light of its necessary interplay with Section 602(a)(1), Section 109(a) is best interpreted as applying only to works manufactured domestically." *Ibid.*

principle of copyright exhaustion to their products also after the authorized importation of the products into the United States.[59]

In October 2012, the Supreme Court heard the oral arguments in the case.[60] Clearly, the Justices could hardly reconcile the outcome of the decision of the Second Circuit with the intention of the legislature in enacting section 109(a) of the Copyright Act. Notably, echoing the concerns expressed by many parties, the Justices posited that Congress could not have intended a "horrible" system wherein foreign manufactured goods would not be subject to the principle of copyright exhaustion.[61] Ultimately, in March 2013, with a majority of 6 to 3 votes, the Supreme Court reversed the Second Circuit's decision.[62] In particular, the Court held that the foreign sales of copies of copyrighted works lawfully made abroad do exhaust the rights in these works, thus clarifying that the United States follows a principle of international copyright exhaustion in which the unauthorized importation of copyrighted products into the United States does not amount to copyright infringement. In an opinion delivered by Justice Breyer for the majority, the Court rejected, in particular, any "geographical application" of section 109(a).[63] Wiley and other publishers had specifically advocated that "lawfully made under this title" meant that copies had to be "made" in the United States in order to fall within the scope of the provision, as Justice Ginsburg had suggested in *Quality King*. Instead, after a careful analysis of the legislative history of section 109(a) and the common law history of the principle of copyright exhaustion as it was adopted by the Court itself in *Bobbs-Merrill*,[64] Justice Breyer's opinion indicated that the language in section 109(a) does not refer to the actual place where the products are manufactured. According to the majority, the language in section 109(a) should be interpreted as applying to any copies that have been "made" in a manner that meets the requirement of national copyright law, notably

---

[59]   *Ibid.* at 226–27 (Murtha J. dissenting) (noting that it could not have been Congress's intent to provide more copyright protection to foreign goods than domestic ones).

[60]   Transcript of Oral Argument, Kirtsaeng v. John Wiley & Sons, Inc., No. 11–697 (S.Ct. argued Oct. 29, 2012), *available at* http://www.supremecourt. gov/oral_arguments/argument_transcripts/11-697.pdf.

[61]   *Ibid.* at 29–32.

[62]   Kirtsaeng v. John Wiley & Sons, Inc., 133 S.Ct. 1351, 1358 (2013) (providing that section 109(a) establishes a defense against a copyright infringement claim based on unauthorized resale "where, as here, copies are manufactured abroad with the permission of the copyright owner.")

[63]   *Ibid.* at 1355–56.

[64]   *Ibid.* at 1363–64.

that are "made" with the permission of, "in accordance with," "in compliance with," the copyright owners,[65] without any particular geographical limitation with respect to the actual place where these copies are made and first sold, whether nationally or internationally.

Furthermore, the majority did not seem particularly sympathetic to the argument brought forward by Wiley and others that a non-geographical interpretation of the provision would affect corporations and their international pricing strategies. Notably, Justice Breyer acknowledged that a "non[-]geographical interpretation" of section 109(a) would make it "difficult, perhaps impossible for publishers (and other copyright holders) to divide foreign and domestic markets" and that "a publisher may find it more difficult to charge different prices for the same book in different geographic markets."[66] Still, Justice Breyer stated that the majority of the Justices could not find a "basic principle of copyright law that suggests that publishers are especially entitled to such rights."[67] Moreover, the opinion emphasized that, at least at the national level, market segmentation is a practice that is inconsistent "with antitrust law that ordinarily forbids market division." Congress enacted the principle of copyright exhaustion following *Bobbs-Merrill*, Justice Breyer wrote, specifically to limit the ability of copyright owners to divide markets,[68] even though Congress did not elaborate whether the market at issue was solely the domestic or also the international market. Justice Breyer concluded by underlining that the Solicitor General himself had stated that the consequences of affirming the Second Circuit's decision ("perpetual downstream control") were worse than finding in favor of Kirtsaeng ("restriction of market segmentation").[69] He finally rejected the argument brought forward by Wiley that a system of international exhaustion was unprecedented in the United States. Instead, Justice Breyer noted that the Court had already stated in *Quality King* that section 109(a) "is a defense in U.S. courts even when 'the first sale occurred abroad',"[70] even though in that case the Court had referred only to goods made domestically, exported, and later re-imported into the United States.

---

65   *Ibid.* at 1358.
66   *Ibid.* at 1370.
67   *Kirtsaeng*, 133 S.Ct. at 1370.
68   *Ibid.* at 1371.
69   *Ibid.*
70   *Ibid.* Justice Breyer stated, specifically, that "our holding in Quality King that § 109(a) is a defense in U.S. courts even when 'the first sale occurred abroad' has already significantly eroded such principle." *Ibid.* (citation omitted).

Yet, a concurrence and a dissenting opinion were also issued in the case. In particular, in addition to joining the majority, Justice Kagan, joined by Justice Alito, submitted a concurring opinion wherein she explained that the majority decision was necessary in light of the Court's previous decision in *Quality King*.[71] According to Justices Kagan and Alito (neither of whom was sitting on the Court when it decided *Quality King*), *Quality King* may have been incorrectly decided and majority opinion in *Kirtsaeng* had rectified the ill effects of *Quality King*, especially the discrimination between domestically made and foreign-made products.[72] Still, Justice Kagan's opinion indicated that the majority decision in *Kirtsaeng* had reduced the importation rights as per section 602(a)(1) "to a fairly esoteric set of applications." Accordingly, the concurring Justices seemed open to a possible legislative review of the provision by Congress.[73] In particular, Justice Kagan wrote that "if Congress thinks copyright owners need greater power to restrict importation and thus divide markets, a ready solution is at hand" – to clarify in the statute that section 602(a)(1) applies to all products imported into the United States.[74] Justice Kagan nonetheless emphasized that, should Congress decide to restrict the importation of products sold abroad, Congress should clarify that the same rule applies to *all products* without discriminating based on place of manufacturing. In particular, she wrote that Congress should not follow the position supported by Wiley in the case (which was the same position that the Court had supported in *Quality King*) that section 109(a) only applies to products made in the United States. This position, Justice Kagan argued, would ultimately "impos[e] downstream liability on those who purchase and resell in the United States copies that *happen to have been manufactured abroad.*"[75] Instead, she concluded by saying that, should Congress review the territorial application of principle of copyright exhaustion, Congress's action should "target importers alone" and not the "the 'libraries, used-book dealers, technology companies, consumer-goods retailers, and museums' with whom the Court today is rightly concerned."[76] Ultimately, Justice Kagan and Justice Alito seemed to indicate that they had joined the majority primarily as a necessary measure to avoid the "parade of horribles" that a

---

[71] *Ibid.* at 1372–73 (Kagan J. concurring).
[72] *Kirtsaeng*, 133 S.Ct. at 1372 (Kagan J. concurring).
[73] *Ibid.*
[74] *Ibid.*
[75] *Ibid.* (emphasis added).
[76] *Ibid.*

discriminatory application of the principle of exhaustion – applicable only to domestically made products – could have entailed for the economy.

Lastly, in clear disagreement with the majority, Justice Ginsburg issued a dissenting opinion, which Justice Kennedy joined and Justice Scalia joined in part.[77] Repeating the position that she supported in the concurring opinion in *Quality King*, Justice Ginsburg stated that the majority's interpretation of section 109(a) in *Kirtsaeng* was "at odds with Congress' aim to protect copyright owners against the unauthorized importation of low-priced, foreign-made copies of their copyrighted works."[78] She also seemed to suggest that petitioner and the majority had exaggerated the "parade of horribles" that a reading of section 109(a) as suggested by Wiley would have on retailers, museums, and manufacturers. Instead, she emphasized that if the Court had applied the *Quality King* analysis in the case, the outcome would have favored Wiley because "lawfully made under [Title 17]" is a prerequisite for application of section 109(a). Since the copies in question were not "lawfully made under [Title 17]," section 109(a) would not apply because Kirtsaeng's unauthorized imports would have been correctly considered as infringing copies under section 602(a)(1).[79] Justice Ginsburg also noted that the position of the majority in the case was in conflict with the position repeatedly taken by the United States in international trade agreements, that copyright owners should have the right "to prevent the unauthorized importation of copies of their work sold abroad."[80] As I have mentioned before, Justice Ginsburg's observation in this respect is indeed correct, as the United States adopted provisions in favor of a system of national copyright exhaustion in some of the FTAs currently in force or that are being negotiated between the United States and other countries. In particular, the United States–Jordan Free Trade Agreement[81] and the

---

[77] *Kirtsaeng*, 133 S.Ct. at 1373 (Ginsburg J. dissenting).

[78] *Ibid.* (noting that "the Court's bold departure from Congress' design is all the more stunning, for it places the United States at the vanguard of the movement of 'international exhaustion' of copyrights – a movement that the United States has steadfastly resisted on the world stage").

[79] *Ibid.* at 1377.

[80] *Ibid.* at 1384.

[81] Article 4(11), Agreement Between the United States of America and the Hashemite Kingdom of Jordan on the Establishment of a Free Trade Area, U.S.–Jordan, Oct. 24, 2000, 41 I.L.M. 63 (2002), *available at* http://www.ustr.gov/assets/Trade_Agreements/Bilateral/Jordan/asset_upload_file250_5112. pdf [hereinafter U.S.–Jordan FTA].

United States–Morocco Free Trade Agreement,[82] and most recently the (leaked) drafts of the Intellectual Property Chapter of the Trans-Pacific Partnership Agreement[83] include a provision stating, with minimal variations, that members of the agreement shall provide to copyright owners "the right to authorize or prohibit the importation into that Party's territory of copies of the work, performance, or phonogram that are made without authorization, or made outside that Party's territory with the authorization of [copyright owners]."[84]

V   THE (AVOIDABLE) EFFECTS OF TERRITORIALLY DIFFERENT APPROACHES TO TRADEMARK AND COPYRIGHT EXHAUSTION

By clarifying that the territorial application of copyright exhaustion in the United States is international, the decision in *Kirtsaeng* thus eliminated (at least for the time being) the possibility of exploiting copyright protection against gray market products due to the lack of an equivalent rule in trademark law. Still, in the light of recent events, the effects of the decision may be short-lived. The same concurring opinion written by Justice Kagan seemed to point in this direction when the Justice almost explicitly called upon Congress to overrule the decision should Congress desire to (re)instate a system of national copyright exhaustion. Moreover, the very day after the decision in *Kirtsaeng*, Maria Pallante, the United States Register of Copyrights, publicly called upon Congress, stating that

---

[82]   Article 15.5(2), United States–Morocco Free Trade Agreement, U.S.–Morocco, June 15, 2004, 44 I.L.M. 544 (2005), *available at* http://www.ustr.gov/Trade_Agreements/Bilateral/Morocco_FTA/FInal_Text-Section_Index.html [hereinafter U.S.–Morocco FTA].

[83]   Article QQ.G.3, Trans-Pacific Partnership (TPP), Intellectual Property Rights (IP) Chapter Consolidated Text, August 30, 2013, *available at* https://wikileaks.org/tpp/static/pdf/wikileaks-secret-TPP-treaty-IP-chapter.pdf/ [hereinafter TPP, *2013 IP Chapter Consolidated Draft*]. *See also* Article 4.2, TPP IP Chapter Draft Agreement, Feb. 2011, *available at* http://keionline.org/site/default/files/tpp-10feb2011-us-text-jpr-chapter.pdf [hereinafter TPP, *2011 IP Chapter Draft*]. Interestingly, the August 2013 TPP Draft includes an additional provision, Article QQ.G.17, which is opposed by the United States and Australia, advocating that "[t]he parties are encouraged to establish international exhaustion of rights. *See* TPP, *2013 IP Chapter Consolidated Draft*, art. QQ.G.17. The TPP is currently being negotiated between Australia, Brunei Darussalam, Canada, Chile, Japan, Malaysia, Mexico, New Zealand, Peru, Singapore, Vietnam, and the United States.

[84]   *See* U.S.–Jordan FTA, art. 4(11); U.S.–Morocco FTA, art. 15.5(2); TPP, *2013 IP Chapter Consolidated Draft*, art. QQ.G.3.

the time had come for Congress to undertake important copyright reforms that would finally bring American copyright law in line with the needs and challenges, both technological and otherwise, brought forward by rapid changes of the twenty-first century.[85] This time, Congress did not wait long to respond to this call. Just a few weeks later, in April 2013, Representative Goodlatte heralded that Congress was considering a major and comprehensive review of the Copyright Act.[86] Although the decision in *Kirtsaeng* was not singled out by Ms. Pallante or Mr. Goodlatte (the timing of their intervention was perhaps a coincidence), the issue of the territorial application of the principle of copyright exhaustion will certainly be addressed in any proposal on copyright reforms. It also remains true that, following the decision of the Supreme Court, the position supported by the United States at the international level – so far national copyright exhaustion (at least for foreign-made products) – no longer aligns with the post-*Kirtsaeng* interpretation of sections 109(a) and 602(a)(1) of the Copyright Act.[87] As a result, it would not be surprising if the various parties interested in overruling *Kirtsaeng* would soon start arguing that Congress should (re)align the domestic position on copyright exhaustion with the obligation undertaken by the United States in international trade agreements.

Should Congress overrule the decision in *Kirtsaeng* and (re)instate a system of national copyright exhaustion, however, this would also (re)instate a territorially different system of intellectual property exhaustion for trademark and copyright – as was the case pre-*Kirtsaeng*. In turn, this would restore the incentive for corporations to recur to copyright protection for incidental product features in order to (again) circumvent

---

[85]   Maria Pallante testified, on March 20, 2013, before the House Subcommittee on Courts, Intellectual Property and the Internet. There, she urged Congress to begin seriously considering comprehensive legislation. *See* Statement of Maria A. Pallante, Register of Copyrights of the United States, Subcommittee on Courts, Intellectual Property and the Internet Committee on the Judiciary, United States House of Representatives 113th Congress, 1st Session March 20, 2013, *available at* http://judiciary.house.gov/hearings/113th/03202013/Pallante%20032013.pdf. Pallante's testimony was based on a public lecture that she delivered on March 4, 2013, at Columbia University Law School. *See* Maria A. Pallante, *The Next Great Copyright Act*, 37 COLUM. J.L. & ARTS 315 (2013).

[86]   On April 24, the House Judiciary Committee Chairman Bob Goodlatte (R-Va.) announced that the Judiciary Committee would conduct a comprehensive review of U.S. copyright law over the coming months. The announcement is *available at* http://judiciary.house.gov/news/2013/04242013_2.html.

[87]   *See* discussion and FTAs cited *supra* Part IV.

the rule of international trademark exhaustion and prevent the importation of gray market products that would otherwise be lawful imports under trademark law. Absent a specific prohibition to resort to copyright protection in the context of parallel imports, nothing in the current law could prevent businesses from securing copyright protection for incidental product features simply in order to exploit this protection against parallel imports. Hence, even though the exploitation of one type of intellectual property rights to expand other types of rights has become a normal occurrence in the business world – businesses routinely seek protection under different regimes in order to enjoy the highest protection for their products – this does not necessarily translate into the fact that the intellectual property system should accept, or even tolerate, a system where businesses turn to copyright protection to protect labels, warranty instructions, or the like – hardly the works of authorship that can promote the progress of science and useful arts to which the Constitution refers to justify intellectual property protection.[88] To the contrary, courts and Congress could, and should, put in place specific mechanisms (judicial doctrines or an ad hoc legislative prohibition) that would prevent this opportunistic exploitation of territorially different exhaustion regimes, which directly undermine the pro-competitive goals of trademark law and permit the ban of otherwise legitimate parallel imports.[89]

Notably, as I recently argued, courts could explicitly prohibit the practice of leveraging copyright protection for incidental product features to restrict the importation of these products into the national market as a type of copyright misuse.[90] In general, courts found copyright misuse primarily in two instances so far in the United States: (1) when a copyright holder uses rights granted under the Copyright Act in a manner that violates federal antitrust law or in a deliberately anti-competitive manner,[91] and (2) when copyright holders attempt to extend their copyright beyond the scope of the exclusive rights granted by Congress

---

[88]   U.S. Const., art. I, § 8, cl. 8.

[89]   Due to the limited scope of this chapter, I do not specifically address the solution adopted by the European Union (EU): a comprehensive regional harmonization of all types of intellectual property rights (IPRs). Notably, the EU follows the same territorial application to the principle of exhaustion, EU-wide regional exhaustion, with respect to all types of IPRs. By doing so, the EU promotes the free movement of products within the European internal market and prevents the enforcement of any type of IPRs acting as a barrier against the free movement of products. Yet, while promoting free trade at the regional level, the EU adopts an EU-protectionist position, prohibiting as infringement the parallel imports of gray market products from anywhere outside the EU/EEA.

[90]   Calboli, *Copyright Misuse*, *supra* note 3 at 229–32.

[91]   *See* Kathryn Judge, *Rethinking Copyright Misuse*, 57 STAN. L. REV. 901, 903, n. 4 (2004) (quoting *In Re* Napster, Inc. Copyright Litig., 191 F. Supp.2d

in a manner that violates the public policy embodied in copyright law, including by "leveraging their limited monopoly to allow them to control areas outside their monopoly."[92] Under these parameters, courts could explicitly rule that the exploitation of copyright protection to prevent parallel imports directly amounts to an additional type of copyright misuse. As I noted in Part III, courts have repeatedly stated that "the right of a producer to control distribution of its trademarked product does not extend beyond the first sale of the product."[93] The rule of trademark exhaustion was specifically designed so that the public could benefit from the further distribution of trademarked products once trademark owners realized the commercial value of their marks with the first sale of these products in the market, nationally or internationally. By contrast, attempts to circumvent this rule by turning to copyright protection of incidental product features directly amounts to "leveraging [the] limited [copyright] monopoly to allow [businesses] to control areas outside their monopoly."[94] Courts could thus explicitly prohibit these attempts as copyright misuse. One court in the United States has already followed this position, the California District Court in the case *Omega v. Costco*,[95] on remand after the 2010 Supreme Court case *Costco v. Omega*. Notably, this court found that "Omega misused its copyright of the Omega Globe Design by leveraging its limited monopoly in being able to control the importation of that design to control the importation of its watches."[96] An appeal on this case is currently pending in front of the Ninth Circuit. In my scholarship, I have extensively analyzed this case, and I advocated that the Ninth Circuit should affirm the District Court's finding that Omega misused copyright protection.[97]

Besides the judicial doctrine of copyright misuse, Congress could also enact an ad hoc legislative amendment in the Copyright Act as an additional mechanism to address the possible negative effects of territorially different exhaustion regimes. As I have also argued before, and as Mary LaFrance extensively elaborates in this volume,[98] the United States

---

1087, 1103 (N.D. Cal. 2002) as "one of the most thorough summaries available of the doctrine's history and current status").

[92]   *Ibid.* at 904.

[93]   Sebastian Int'l, Inc. v. Longs Drug Stores Corp., 53 F.3d 1073, 1074 (9th Cir. 1995).

[94]   Practice Mgmt. Info. Corp. v. Am. Med. Ass'n, 121 F.3d 516 (9th Cir. 1997).

[95]   Omega S.A. v. Costco Wholesale Corp., No. 04-05443, slip op. (C.D. Cal. Nov. 9, 2011).

[96]   *Ibid.* at 3.

[97]   Calboli, *Copyright Misuse, supra* note 3 at 235.

[98]   Mary LaFrance, *supra* note 8.

would not be the first country to adopt such a legislative measure. Countries such as Australia[99] and Singapore[100] have already introduced provisions prohibiting the enforcement of copyright protection for incidental product features in the context of international trade. Following the example of these countries, Congress could enact, as part of the soon-to-be-undertaken overall copyright reforms, a similar provision stating that "the importation or sale of an article does not infringe the copyright embodied in elements that are merely 'accessory' to the article." By enacting such a provision, Congress would, once and for all, eliminate the incentive for corporations to claim copyright protection on accessory features applied on consumer products, or their packaging, as corporations would not be able to enforce copyright protection on these features in order to block parallel imports of otherwise lawful gray market products. As under Australia and Singapore's Copyright Acts, Congress could also specifically list the product features that should be considered as "accessory" features.[101] This should include, in particular, features such as: labels or other insignias affixed to a product or to the

---

[99]   Copyright Act 1968 (Cth) ss. 10(1), 10(d), 44C, and 112 (Austl.). The original text of the Australian Copyright Act was amended in 1998, 2000, and 2001. In particular, with respect to the subject matter of this chapter, *see* Schedule 3, Copyright Amendment Bill 1997 (Cth) (Austl.). "[I]f the label or instructional material has already been approved by the manufacturer as an accessory to the product (say, for use in another country), then the importation into Australia of the product itself should not be stopped. The issue is that the force of copyright law was never meant to apply to the contents of the bottle of liqueur which is really the subject of the importation." Bill Digest 160 1996–97, Copyright Amendment Bill 1997, Main Provisions, Schedule 3, *available at* http://www.aph.gov.au/Parliamentary_Business/Bills_Legislation/bd/BD9697/97 bd160#Passage.

[100]   Singapore Copyright Act of 1987, §§ 7(1), 40A(1) (2006) (Sing.) (as amended by Copyright Amendment Act No. 14 of 1994).

[101]   Such a provision would also be compatible with a possible ratification of a final text of the TPP as it has been circulated in the current (leaked) draft. In fact footnote 135 to the proposed text of Article QQ.G.3, specifies that "[w]ith respect to copies of works and phonograms that have been placed on the market by the relevant right holder, the obligations described in Article [QQ.G.3] apply only to books, journals, sheet music, sound recordings, computer programs, and audio and visual works (i.e., categories of products in which the value of the copyrighted material represents substantially all of the value of the product)." TPP, *IP Chapter Consolidated Draft*, art. QQ.G.3, n. 135, *supra* note 83. However, the last part of footnote 135 concludes with the language, "[n]otwithstanding the foregoing, each Party may provide the protection described in Article [4.2] to a broader range of goods." *Ibid.* An identical provision was included in the 2011 TPP Draft. *See* TPP, *2011 IP Chapter Draft*, *supra* note 83.

product's packaging or container; the product packaging or container itself; the written instructions, warranties or other written information provided with a product. In general, Congress could introduce such a provision in the Copyright Act even in the event that Congress does not overturn the decision in *Kirtsaeng*, that is, even if the principle of international copyright exhaustion remains the applicable rule to be followed in the United States. Singapore, for example, currently follows a system of international copyright exhaustion, yet the Singapore Copyright Act also includes the prohibition against the enforcement of copyright protection for accessory copyright in the context of international parallel trade.[102]

Still, there is a high likelihood that Congress may simply overrule the decision in *Kirtsaeng* without contextually introducing a legislative amendment like the one for which Professor LaFrance and I advocate. Should this become the case, the responsibility would again rest primarily with the judiciary to safeguard the public policy objectives that are at the core of intellectual property rights. Notably, courts should assure that businesses do not exploit gaps in the system to increase their existing monopoly to the detriment of the public interest and market competition. This specifically includes preventing the degeneration of the intellectual property system into a system wherein businesses distort the framework constructed under the rule of trademark law by invoking copyright protection for the incidental (and frequently insignificant) product features such as decorative labels, packaging, or insignias affixed onto their products, or even warranties and product instruction with the sole intent of circumventing the rule of international trademark exhaustion and partitioning international markets. For these reasons, it remains fundamental that the Ninth Circuit affirms the District Court in the appeal currently pending in *Omega v. Costco* and confirms that segmenting the market by leveraging copyright for product accessories constitutes

---

Interestingly, this provision seems to have been suggested, and is supported by the United States as part of the TPP negotiations.

[102] To date, Singapore follows a rule of international first sale both in copyright and trademark law, thus Singapore courts have not addressed the issues of corporations leveraging copyright protection to circumvent the rule of trademark law. This may change, however, if the adoption of the TPP will eventually require a shift toward national exhaustion, as currently supported by the United States (and Australia). In that case, Singapore may need to modify its stance on copyright exhaustion according to the current text of art. QQ.G.3 of the TPP. TPP, *2013 IP Chapter Consolidated Draft*, art. QQ.G.3. Still, the current text of footnote 135 will allow Singapore to continue prohibiting the enforcement of accessory copyright. TPP, *IP Chapter Consolidated Draft,* art. QQ.G.3 n. 11.

copyright misuse. To the contrary, corporations would continue to exploit territorially different exhaustion regimes, segment the international market, and derive multiple rewards for the sale of the same products in different national markets. This is something that businesses cannot do under the rule of trademark law, and should also not be able to do under the rule of copyright law. Thus, appropriate mechanisms – at least the enforcement of the judicial doctrine of copyright misuse – should be put into place and consistently enforced in order to prevent businesses from opportunistically exploiting copyright protection simply in order to circumvent trademark law and policy.

VI CONCLUSION

As I elaborated in this chapter, the principle of exhaustion of intellectual property rights has been developed in order to prevent intellectual property rights from being used as a mechanism to control post-sale product distribution and in turn segment the marketplace. To the contrary, the enforcement of intellectual property rights with respect to post-sale distribution would trigger anticompetitive effects and result in unjustifiable restraints on the right of alienation of private property on the part of those who have lawfully purchased the products that embody these rights. While accepted within national markets, the international application of this principle has been very controversial at the international level as the international application of intellectual property exhaustion directly interferes with the ability of intellectual property owners to segment international markets by charging different prices in different jurisdictions. With TRIPS being silent on the issue, the various members of TRIPS have followed the territorial approaches – national, international, or regional exhaustion – that best suited their national or regional economies. The United States, in particular, has traditionally followed a system of international trademark exhaustion based upon the principle that, as long as consumers are not confused, trademarks cannot be used to partition the international market. Until the decision in *Kirtsaeng*, the position of the United States on copyright exhaustion was unsettled with a large part of the judiciary advocating that the combined text of sections 109(a) and 602(1)(a) of the Copyright Act established a system of national copyright exhaustion.

As a result of these different approaches, however, businesses turned to copyright law and claimed copyright protection for incidental product features of otherwise uncopyrightable goods in order to prevent parallel imports. For the time being, the decision in *Kirtsaeng* has put an end to this game. Following *Kirtsaeng*, unauthorized genuine gray market products can now enter the United States market as the first lawful sale of these products anywhere in the world exhausts both the copyright and trademark rights in the products. As I highlighted in this chapter, however, the effect of *Kirtsaeng* may be short-lived. Ultimately, the Justices proved deeply divided in the case, and two of the Justices, Justice Kagan and Justice Alito, seemed to join the majority mostly as a necessity to redress the previous ill effects of *Quality King*. Still, the concurring opinion almost invited Congress to legislate around the decision of the majority as long as Congress does not discriminate between domestic and foreign-made copyrighted products – the main issue addressed by *Kirtsaeng*. At the time this chapter is going to press, proposals for grand reforms of the Copyright Act have been heralded by Congress and the Register of Copyrights, and it would be naïve to think that such reforms would not consider (a possible revision of) the effects of *Kirtsaeng*. Moreover, the United States has ratified several FTAs that establish a rule of national copyright exhaustion for the signatories, at least with respect to the products "made outside the territory" of the respective members. A similar provision is currently being discussed as part of the Trans-Pacific Partnership Agreement. It would certainly not be long before interested parties start to push for the re-alignment of the United States' position on the issue at the international and national level.

Still, should Congress overrule *Kirtsaeng*, the United States would again find itself following a non-territorially harmonized system of intellectual property exhaustion – national exhaustion in copyright law and international exhaustion in trademark law. This, in turn, would restart the corporate game of claiming overlapping copyright and trademark protection for incidental product features in order to prevent parallel imports. This should not be the case, however, as this game undermines the pro-competitive objectives of trademark law and policy. Accordingly, appropriate mechanisms should be put into place to prohibit this game. In particular, courts should hold that copyright claims for incidental product features in the context of parallel imports amount to copyright misuse. As part of the announced copyright reforms, Congress could also introduce a provision prohibiting, or rendering unenforceable, copyright protection for "accessory copyright" against parallel imports following the examples of other jurisdictions such as Australia and Singapore. These mechanisms could prevent, once and for all, businesses from opportunistically exploiting territorially different exhaustion regimes to partition international markets with respect to the distribution of consumer goods – shampoos, watches, chocolate, or the like – against the rule of trademark law and the principle of international trademark exhaustion.

9. Avoiding mutant trademarks: a statutory exclusion for copyrighted accessories to parallel imports

Mary LaFrance[*]

I INTRODUCTION

In its 2013 decision in *Kirtsaeng v. John Wiley & Sons, Inc.*,[1] the Supreme Court disrupted the settled expectations of many copyright owners by adopting a rule of international exhaustion for copyrighted works. In so doing, it also disrupted a strategy that had proved beneficial to many trademark owners – using copyright law to block parallel imports that are otherwise permissible under federal trademark laws.

Prior to *Kirtsaeng*, United States trademark owners had increasingly turned to federal copyright law to prevent the importation and domestic resale of genuine goods that they had intended only for overseas sale. Under then-prevailing interpretations of the first-sale rule, embedding even a small amount of copyrighted material into merchandise or its packaging could enable a domestic copyright owner to block the importation of otherwise lawful goods. In some cases, the copyright would subsist in the trademark itself. However, even when a trademark is not itself copyrightable, copyright can protect a textual or design element of merchandise or its packaging, such as a label, ornamental design feature, instruction book, user manual, warranty card, or software. This end-run around the limitations of trademark law became popular with trademark owners who wished to block third parties from importing and reselling parallel imports that bore lawful trademarks but were manufactured

---

 * IGT Professor of Intellectual Property Law, William S. Boyd School of Law, University of Nevada, Las Vegas. This chapter is based on an article originally published in volume 20 of the *Michigan Telecommunications and Technology Law Review* (November 2013).
 1 Kirtsaeng v. John Wiley & Sons, Inc., 133 S.Ct. 1351 (2013).

abroad and intended for sale only outside the United States (usually at lower prices).

Trademark owners have used these strategies not only in the United States but in other countries, including Canada, Australia, Singapore, and South Africa. Both Australia and Singapore have responded by enacting statutory exemptions for copyrighted "accessories" that are imported along with non-infringing articles. In Canada and South Africa, courts have considered arguments for creating similar exemptions through judicial action, but have ultimately concluded that the question must be resolved through legislation.

If Congress overrules *Kirtsaeng* and reinstates the copyright importation ban, the efforts of these other nations to delineate an "accessories" exception to the copyright owner's exclusive importation rights will provide useful guidance for adopting a similar exemption in the United States.

II THE COPYRIGHT BARRIER TO PARALLEL IMPORTS IN THE UNITED STATES

Prior to *Kirtsaeng,* United States copyright owners had succeeded in using section 602(a) of federal copyright law[2] to block the importation and domestic resale of copies of their work that were manufactured outside the United States, even when those copies were made in full compliance with copyright laws in their country of manufacture. Trademark owners realized that they, too, could take advantage of this rule in order to block the importation and resale of genuine (that is, non-counterfeit) goods that cannot be excluded under federal trademark law. They could accomplish this by including foreign-made copyrightable material in their products or packaging whenever they wished to prevent those goods from entering domestic markets.

The use of copyrights as quasi-trademarks to block parallel imports gained steam after the Supreme Court's 1998 decision in *Quality King Distributors, Inc. v. L'anza Research Int'l, Inc.*[3] *Quality King* applied the first-sale rule of copyright law in holding that copyright law did not preclude the unauthorized importation of merchandise bearing copyrighted labels that were lawfully made in the United States.[4] The Court

---

[2] 17 U.S.C. § 602(a) (2006).

[3] Quality King Distribs., Inc. v. L'anza Research Int'l, Inc., 523 U.S. 135 (1998).

[4] *Ibid.* at 145. The first-sale rule appears in 17 U.S.C. § 109(a) (2006).

strongly implied, however, that the outcome would be different if the labels had been foreign-made, because the first-sale rule would not apply.[5] Although subsequent courts treated this interpretation as binding law,[6] it has been widely criticized for giving United States copyright owners more control over copies made abroad than over domestically made copies, thus encouraging them to shift their manufacturing operations overseas.[7]

Ten years after *Quality King*, watchmaker Omega successfully invoked copyright law to prevent the unauthorized importation and domestic sale of genuine Omega watches manufactured in Switzerland. In *Costco Wholesale Corp. v. Omega S.A.*,[8] Omega relied on its copyright in the "Omega Globe Design" that was engraved on the back of each watch. Omega began using this copyrighted design on the advice of its legal department, and under pressure from its authorized retailers, for the specific purpose of blocking parallel imports.[9] The Ninth Circuit held that the first-sale rule did not permit the importation of watches bearing the copyrighted design because those copies, while made with the consent of the United States copyright owner, were neither made in the United States nor sold in the United States with the copyright owner's consent.[10] Because the Supreme Court affirmed the Ninth Circuit's decision by a 4–4 vote,[11] the Court failed at that time to resolve the question whether foreign-made copies can ever be imported under the first-sale rule.

In *Kirtsaeng*, however, the Supreme Court held, by a vote of 6–3, that the first sale of a lawfully made copy of a work negates the copyright owner's exclusive importation and distribution rights with respect to that

---

[5]   *Ibid.* at 147–48.

[6]   *See, e.g.*, Omega S.A. v. Costco Wholesale Corp., 541 F.3d 982, 988–90 (9th Cir. 2008); Pearson Educ., Inc. v. Kumar, 721 F.Supp.2d 166, 176–78 (S.D.N.Y. 2010).

[7]   *See, e.g.*, PAUL GOLDSTEIN, COPYRIGHT, § 5.6.1.2.a. The Ninth Circuit responded to this concern in Denbicare U.S.A., Inc. v. Toys R Us, Inc., 84 F.3d 1143, 1150 (9th Cir. 1996), holding that once a United States copyright owner has consented to the first domestic sale of its foreign-made copies, the first-sale rule permits subsequent resales.

[8]   Costco Wholesale Corp. v. Omega S.A., 131 S.Ct. 565 (2010).

[9]   *Costco*, 2011 WL 8492716, at *1 (C.D. Cal. Nov. 9, 2011).

[10]   *Costco*, 541 F.3d 982, 990 (9th Cir. 2008). Because the copyright owner had not consented to the sale of these specific watches in the United States, the Ninth Circuit did not have occasion to apply the first-sale interpretation that it applied in *Denbicare*.

[11]   Justice Kagan was recused.

copy, regardless of whether the copy was made in the United States or abroad. The Court relied in part on its statutory analysis in *Quality King*, where it held that, because the section 602 importation right is subsumed within the section 106(3) public distribution right, the first-sale rule applies to importation as well as public distribution. Although the first-sale rule, by its own terms, applies only to copies "lawfully made under this title," *Kirtsaeng* concluded that Congress did not intend this phrase to discriminate against lawful copies made outside the United States. While focusing much of its analysis on the statutory language and history of the first-sale rule, the Court also emphasized the potential downstream effects of a contrary holding. If the first-sale rule did not apply to foreign-made copies, the Court observed, then used bookstores, libraries, and others who sell or lend copyrighted materials would have to determine where their copies were made and would need the copyright owner's permission to sell or lend any copies that might have originated outside the United States. This onerous burden would effectively shut down their operations.

This regime of international copyright exhaustion may be short-lived. Because the Court's opinion relied on statutory interpretation rather than constitutional imperatives, Congress can change the law simply by amending the statute. The influential copyright-intensive industries in the United States (book publishing, software, motion pictures, sound recordings, and video games) are likely to lobby for restoration of the importation ban. The Obama Administration will probably support such efforts, because the United States Trade Representative has consistently opposed international exhaustion in negotiating trade agreements with other countries. Failure to restore the ban will therefore mean that the United States has abandoned the very policy it has urged other countries to adopt. The United States has continued to adhere to this position in negotiating its prospective commitments under the Trans-Pacific Partnership Agreement (TPP). In the most recent leaked draft of the TPP, Article QQ.G.3 provides:

> Each Party shall provide to authors, performers, and producers of phonograms the right to authorize or prohibit the importation into that Party's territory of copies of the work, performance, or phonogram made without authorization, *or made outside that Party's territory with the authorization of the author, performer, or producer of the phonogram.*[12]

---

[12] Trans-Pacific Partnership Agreement (TPP), 2013 Draft (Aug. 30, 2013) (hereinafter "TPP 2013 Draft") art. QQ.G.3 (emphasis added).

The United States is one of the strongest backers of the TPP, and has included similar provisions in several free trade agreements.[13] However, the United States may be losing ground on this issue, as other TPP members appear to be aligning in favor of international exhaustion.[14]

Justice Kagan's concurring opinion in *Kirtsaeng*, in which Justice Alito joined, suggests one way in which Congress can restore the importation ban without triggering the parade of horribles that concerned the *Kirtsaeng* majority – by amending section 602(a) to clarify that the importation ban is not limited by the first-sale rule.[15] This would allow copyright owners to pursue infringement claims against unauthorized importers, but not against purchasers who subsequently sell or lend those imported copies within the United States.

If Congress reinstates the importation ban, then trademark owners will continue to add copyrightable features to their foreign-made products and packaging for the primary purpose of controlling parallel imports. In addition to the copyrightable elements in packaging, labels, tags, instructions, and owner's manuals, copyrightable designs can be embedded in the products themselves (like Omega's engraved design) so that the importer or domestic reseller cannot easily remove or cover up the copyrighted content. Copyright may also attach to the shape or overall appearance of a product, provided that (1) it possesses a minimal degree of originality,[16] and (2) the artistic element is physically or conceptually separable from the utilitarian function of the article.[17] A candy maker, for example, can assert federal copyright protection for the shape of a candy bar if it is more original than the ubiquitous rectangle

---

[13] U.S.–Jordan Free Trade Agreement art. 4(11) (Oct. 24, 2000); U.S.–Morocco Free Trade Agreement art. 15.5(2) (June 15, 2004).

[14] An identical provision appeared in the draft that was leaked in 2011. *See* Trans-Pacific Partnership Agreement, 2011 Draft (Feb. 10, 2011), art. 4.2. However, annotations to the 2013 draft indicate that the United States is now the only one of the twelve TPP countries that still endorses this provision. In addition, the 2013 draft contains a new and contradictory provision, endorsed by eight countries, which affirmatively favors international exhaustion. "The Parties are encouraged to establish international exhaustion of rights." TPP 2013 Draft, art. QQ.G.17. Canada has proposed yet another alternative, opposed by the United States and Australia, which would allow each TPP member to choose its own exhaustion policy. *Id.*

[15] *Supra* note 1, *Kirtsaeng*, 133 S. Ct. at 1372–73.

[16] Lamps Plus, Inc. v. Seattle Lighting Fixture Co., 345 F.3d 1140, 1146–47 (9th Cir. 2003).

[17] Brandir Int'l, Inc. v. Cascade Pacific Lumber Co., 834 F.2d 1142, 1143 (2d Cir. 1987).

or flattened cylinder shape and if the shape does not have an inseparable utilitarian component (such as making the candy bar easier to hold or to break into pieces). In addition, many consumer products include copyrighted software. Even if software is not strictly necessary to the functioning of a consumer product, adding even a small software component will give the trademark owner another method for blocking imports. Complex products such as automobiles, office equipment, computers, and large appliances will almost always contain a significant software component that can be invoked to block unauthorized imports.

III LEGISLATIVE RESPONSES IN AUSTRALIA AND SINGAPORE

Both Australia and Singapore have adopted legislation limiting the use of copyright law to block otherwise lawful parallel imports. While these statutes raise interpretative issues of their own, they offer useful guidance for crafting a legislative solution in the United States.

A Australia

Unless the goods are materially different, Australia generally permits the unauthorized importation of lawfully made trademarked goods.[18] During the 1980s, Australian trademark owners succeeded in using copyright law as an alternative avenue of relief. In *R. & A. Bailey & Co. Ltd. v. Boccaccio Pty. Ltd.*,[19] the Supreme Court of New South Wales held that, while importing bottles of genuine Bailey's Irish Cream was not a trademark infringement, it did infringe the rights of the party that owned the copyright in the labels.

After the *Bailey* decision, Australia's Copyright Law Review Committee recommended amending the copyright statutes to prohibit the use of copyright law to block the importation of non-copyrightable merchandise. The Committee's Report stated:

> [t]he Committee is strongly of opinion that distributors of goods should not be able to control the market for their products by resorting to the subterfuge of devising a label or a package in which copyright will subsist. The purpose of copyright is to protect articles which are truly copyright articles such as

---

[18]   *See, e.g.*, Atari Inc. v. Fairstar Elecs., 50 ALR 274 (FCA 1982).

[19]   R. & A. Bailey & Co. Ltd. v. Boccaccio Pty. Ltd., 84 FLR 232, 4 NSWLR 701 (1986).

books, sound recordings or films. If the simple expedient of affixing or attaching a label in which copyright subsists to any goods at all entitles the owner of the goods to exclude others from marketing similar goods, the sooner the practice is stopped the better it will be. However imaginatively labelled or packaged a bottle of liquor may be, the product is liquor. The same may be said of cigarettes, perfume and cosmetics.[20]

Although this recommendation led to no immediate changes, in the ensuing years Australia sought to reduce consumer prices by liberalizing its parallel import policies for many classes of copyrightable goods.[21] When the import restrictions on sound recordings were eliminated in 1998, the owners of sound recording copyrights faced competition from cheaper parallel imports. Because commercial CDs include copyrightable elements other than recorded music – such as cover art and liner notes – copyright owners might have been able to continue blocking parallel imports of CDs by asserting infringement of these other copyrightable components. Australia's Parliament sought to prevent this – and at the same time to put an end to the strategy that succeeded in the *Bailey* case – by adding section 44C to the Copyright Act.[22]

Section 44C provides that the importation or sale of an imported article[23] does not infringe the copyright in any non-infringing "accessory." To be non-infringing, the copyrighted content in the accessory must have been reproduced in a Berne or WTO country with the consent of the person owning the copyright *in that country*.[24] The statute defines

---

[20] COPYRIGHT LAW REVIEW COMMITTEE, THE IMPORTATION PROVISIONS OF THE COPYRIGHT ACT 1968 224 (AGPS, Canberra, 1988), *quoted at* Polo/Lauren Co. LP v. Ziliani Holdings Pty. Ltd., [2008] FCA 49, 75 I.P.R. 143, para. 53.

[21] *See* Copyright Amendment Act 1991 (assented to Dec. 23, 1991) (books); Copyright Amendment Act (No. 2) 1998 (assented to July 30, 1998) (sound recordings); Copyright (Parallel Importation) Act 2003 (assented to Apr. 15, 2003) (books, journals and music in electronic formats, and computer software).

[22] Copyright Amendment Act (No. 1) 1998 (assented to July 30, 1998) (amending § 10(1) and adding §§ 44C and 112C).

[23] While § 44C does not define the term "article," it has a specialized definition in two other sections of the Copyright Act. Section 38, which prohibits distribution of infringing articles, defines an article as "a reproduction or copy of a work or other subject matter, being a reproduction or copy in electronic form." Copyright Act 1968 (Cth) § 38(3). § 115, which authorizes injunctive relief in cases of electronic commercial infringement, uses the same definition. *Ibid.* § 115(7), (8). However, courts interpreting § 44C have not applied this definition, and the Copyright Act does not provide a general-purpose definition of the term.

[24] *Ibid.* § 10(1).

"accessory" to include labels, packaging, containers, instructions, warranties, or other information "provided with" the article, as well as instructional sound recordings or films "provided with" the article.[25] Had section 44C been in effect at the time of the *Bailey* case, the plaintiff could not have used the copyright in its label to prevent the importation of its product.

In interpreting section 44C, a significant challenge facing the Australian courts has been the meaning of "accessory." The Federal Court of Australia (FCA) has issued only two opinions interpreting this language. Nonetheless, they reveal the potential for additional interpretive challenges in the future.

The first and most significant case interpreting section 44C was the 2008 case of *Polo/Lauren Company LP v. Ziliani Holdings Pty. Ltd.*[26] The FCA held that the polo player logo that was woven into the plaintiff's shirts was a label, and therefore an accessory.[27] Accordingly, the plaintiff could not use the copyright in the logo to block importation of genuine Polo/Lauren shirts purchased outside Australia.

Although the definition of "accessory" included "a label incorporated into the surface of the article," the parties disputed whether the embroidered polo player logo was a label or a decorative feature of the article itself.[28] The court adopted a broad definition of the term "label," to include its usage as a synonym for "brand name, trade mark and the name by which a design or fashion house is generally known."[29] To determine whether the polo player image was a label or some other component of the product, the court applied a functionality test:

> The definition of an "accessory" in s 10(1) recognises a distinction between the article as a functional item of commerce, and a subsidiary constituent part of the article such as a label embroidered on to it. The embroidered component is functionally accessorial to the article's use. The function which an accessory performs is incidental to the use of the article as an item of commerce. The article can be used for its intended purpose regardless of whether the s 10 "accessory" is present on it or as part of it.[30]

---

[25] *Ibid.*
[26] 75 I.P.R. 143, [2008] FCA 49. The FCA opinion was upheld by the Full Court. 80 I.P.R. 531, 2008 FCAFC 195.
[27] *Ibid.* at para. 64.
[28] *Ibid.* at para. 44.
[29] *Ibid.* at para. 51.
[30] *Ibid.* at para. 58.

The court concluded that, even if the polo player logo was aesthetically pleasing, it functioned primarily as a label because it informed consumers of the "provenance" of the merchandise.[31] "[I]ts function is primarily to signify the manufacturer's identity, i.e. to act as a label."[32]

Three years later, in *QS Holdings SARL v. Paul's Retail Pty. Ltd.*,[33] a defendant had imported and sold both genuine and counterfeit apparel bearing the plaintiffs' registered trademarks. In addition to trademark claims, several plaintiffs also raised claims of copyright infringement based on the graphic designs on the clothing as well as images of the clothing reproduced in the defendant's sales brochures. With respect to the graphic designs on the non-counterfeit clothing, the Federal Court held that the unauthorized importation infringed the rights of the Australian copyright owners.[34] The defendants did not attempt to raise a defense under section 44C, presumably because they were unlikely to convince the court that the graphic designs on these garments were "accessories" rather than ornamental features of the products. Although the defendants did invoke section 44C with respect to the marketing brochures that reproduced the copyrighted designs,[35] the court ruled that section 44C did not apply because, inter alia, the brochures were not "accessories." In the court's view, an accessory must have "some physical relationship" with the merchandise to which it relates.[36]

Both of the copyrightable items in *QS Holdings* were ineligible for the section 44C exemption – the graphics on the shirt because (presumably) they were *not separate enough* to be an accessory, and the brochures because they were *too* separate to be an accessory. Future courts may find themselves searching for the happy medium of separateness necessary for an item to qualify as an accessory. Why is it that the logo woven into the *Polo/Lauren* shirt was an accessory, and the graphics on the *QS Holdings* shirts were not? Under the functionality test adopted in *Polo/Lauren*, the graphics on the *QS Holdings* shirts arguably played an important role in the functioning of the shirt, by making it more attractive, rather than communicating the provenance of the garment. Under this test, then, they were not accessories. However, some designs that serve a trademark function can also contribute to the aesthetic appeal

---

[31] *Ibid.* at paras. 62, 64.
[32] *Ibid.* at para. 63.
[33] QS Holdings SARL v. Paul's Retail Pty. Ltd., 92 I.P.R. 460, [2011] FCA 853.
[34] *Ibid.* at para. 92.
[35] *Ibid.* at para. 119.
[36] *Ibid.* at para. 124.

of the product incorporating them. The concept of what is an accessory is likely to continue to force Australian courts to make difficult line-drawing judgments. It is also likely to encourage trademark owners to avoid the "accessory" classification by incorporating copyrightable designs more fully into their merchandise, rather than limiting it to labels, regardless of whether the design also functions as a trademark.

B Singapore

Singapore's trademark law is especially liberal with respect to parallel imports, permitting the importation of unaltered goods that have been released into the market anywhere in the world with the express or implied consent of the owner of the Singapore trademark registration, even if that consent is conditional (for example, conditioned on distributing the goods only within a specified territory).[37]

Prior to 1994, it was unclear whether the importation of copyrighted works that were lawfully made in their country of manufacture required the consent of the Singapore copyright owner.[38] In 1994, however, the copyright law was amended in favor of parallel imports, by allowing importation of copies that were made with the consent of the person who owned the copyright in the country where the copies were made, even if that same person did not own the copyright in Singapore.[39] The same amendment also provides that the existence of consent is determined without regard to any "conditions as to the sale, distribution or other dealings in the article after its making."[40] Thus, even if the owner of a copyright in India consented to the copying and distribution of that work

---

[37] Singapore Trademark Act, §§ 29(1)–(2). *See* Burton Ong, *IPRs and Competition Law in Singapore*, *in* THE INTERFACE BETWEEN INTELLECTUAL PROPERTY RIGHTS AND COMPETITION POLICY 399 (Steven J. Anderman ed., 2007).

[38] Singapore Copyright Act §§ 32, 25(2).

[39] Singapore Copyright Act §§ 32, 25(3). If there is no copyright owner in the country of manufacture (that is, if the work is not protected by copyright in that country), then the consent of the Singapore copyright owner is required. *Ibid.* § 25(3). In Remus Innovation & Anor v. Hong Boon Siong & Ors, 1995-2 SLR 148, 1994 SLR LEXIS 621, the amended law prevented a manufacturer from blocking parallel imports of automobile exhaust systems that were made with the Singapore copyright owner's consent and obtained from an authorized distributor in the United Kingdom. The plaintiff had asserted that the importers infringed the copyright in certain drawings of the exhaust systems.

[40] Singapore Copyright Act § 25(4).

only in India, that consent would enable those copies to be imported into Singapore despite the objections of the Singapore copyright owner.[41]

Singapore's copyright law also includes a provision similar to Australia's "accessories" exemption.[42] Section 40A of the Singapore Copyright Act provides that the importation and distribution of an "accessory" does not infringe a copyright when the accessory is imported along with a non-infringing article.[43] The Singapore statute defines "accessories" to include labels, packaging, containers, leaflets, pamphlets, certificates, warranties, brochures, "written instructions or other information" that are incidental to the article, as well as instructional sound recordings and films that are incidental to the article.[44]

However, in several respects section 40A departs from its Australian counterpart. First, whereas the Australian statute specifies that the accessory must have been made with the consent of the party that owns the copyright in the country of manufacture,[45] section 40A contains no such requirement. In fact, it is silent on the question whether the accessory itself must be non-infringing.

In a second point of departure, section 40A defines "accessory" more narrowly than the Australian statute. Specifically, an "accessory" does *not* include:

---

[41]   *See* Ong, *supra* note 37, at 385.

[42]   Australia Copyright Act § 44C.

[43]   Singapore Copyright Act § 40A provides:

Accessories to imported articles 40A. – (1) The copyright in a work embodied in an accessory to an article is not infringed by a person who, without the licence of the owner of the copyright, imports the article into Singapore for a purpose mentioned in section 32 (*a*), (*b*) or (*c*) unless the article is an infringing copy.
(2) The operation of this Act in relation to a work embodied in an article shall not be affected by the operation of this section in relation to a work embodied in an accessory to the article.
(3) If an article is imported into Singapore for a purpose mentioned in section 32 (*a*), (*b*) or (*c*) and the importation is not, by reason of this section, an infringement of the copyright in a work embodied in an accessory to the article, the use of the accessory with the article for any such purpose shall not be an infringement of the copyright in the work, and section 33 shall not apply to the accessory.

[44]   Singapore Copyright Act §§ 7(1), 116A.

[45]   Australia Copyright Act 1968 (Cth) § 44C(1)–(2) (exempting only "non-infringing accessories), § 10(1) (defining "non-infringing accessory"). The country of manufacture must also be a member of the Berne Convention or a WTO member with TRIPS-compliant copyright laws. *Ibid.*

(i)   a copy of a work that is incorporated into the surface of the article and is a permanent part of the article;

(ii)   a copy of a work that cannot be separated from the article without rendering the article unsuitable for its ordinary use; [or]

(iii) a manual sold with computer software for use in connection with that software[.][46]

However, these exclusions from the "accessories" definition do not allow copyright owners to block parallel imports of these three embodiments of copyrighted works. Because Singapore allows importation of *all* copyrighted works provided that the copies were made with the consent of the copyright owner in the country of manufacture, these three categories of non-accessories, if non-pirated, would still be importable under that general rule.

Perhaps the true impact of these exclusions derives from section 40A's failure to expressly require that imported accessories be non-infringing. Section 40A(1) states that:

> [t]he copyright in a work embodied in an accessory to an article is not infringed by a person who, without the licence of the owner of the copyright, imports the article into Singapore for a purpose mentioned in section 32 (*a*), (*b*) or (*c*) *unless the article is an infringing copy.*[47]

If this language means what it says, then an accessory attached to a non-infringing article can be imported under section 40A, *even if the accessory is infringing.* Therefore, if an item (such as surface ornamentation) does not meet the statutory definition of an accessory, then the section 40A exemption does not apply, and the general rules of sections 32 and 25 – requiring the copyright owner's consent for importation – would apply. This means that the three copyrighted items excluded from the "accessory" definition cannot be imported unless they were made under license from the copyright owner in the country where the copies were made (or from the Singapore copyright owner if there is no copyright owner in the country of manufacture). In the case of the first two exceptions, the accessory is so physically integral to the article itself that it would make little sense to apply different rules to the article and the accessory. The rationale for the third exception is less clear, but may reflect the degree of intellectual effort involved in creating software manuals as well as the substantial value they contribute to the software. While not physically integral to the software, they are functionally integral.

---

[46] Singapore Copyright Act § 7(1).
[47] *Ibid.* § 40A(1).

Subjecting these three categories to the generally applicable rules for importing copyrighted works is itself unremarkable. What is remarkable, however, is that the items which *do* qualify as accessories are apparently exempt from the general rule for parallel imports and thus can be imported even if they are pirated. Such a result would be impossible under the Australian statute, which permits importation only of "non-infringing" accessories. It is unclear whether, or why, Singapore's lawmakers intended this result. It was probably not a drafting error; when the lawmakers created three exceptions to the definition of an accessory, they must have intended those exceptions to have some legal effect. If this was a deliberate choice, it suggests that the legislature did not believe that infringing accessories cause significant harm to copyright owners.

As was the case in Australia, Singapore's decision to prevent the use of copyright law to block otherwise lawful imports of genuine trademarked goods took place in the context of a broader decision to liberalize import restrictions on copyrighted works. Even in a country that maintains import restrictions, however, a specific exemption for accessories may be politically feasible and economically sound. Singapore's statute offers a second possible model for such legislation, albeit one that provides less protection for copyright owners than the Australian model.

IV ATTEMPTS TO CREATE A JUDICIAL EXCLUSION FOR ACCESSORIES

Neither Canada nor South Africa has a statutory exemption for copyrighted accessories accompanying imported goods. However, courts in both countries have considered arguments for a judicially created exception. In each case, they have ultimately concluded that the question should be left to the legislature. Nonetheless, their ruminations provide useful guidance for future legislation.

A Canada

As Pierre-Emmanuel Moyse has recounted,[48] the Supreme Court of Canada held in *Euro-Excellence Inc. v. Kraft Canada Inc.*[49] that the copyright in a candy wrapper enables the Canadian copyright owner to

---

[48] Pierre-Emmanuel Moyse, *Las Confusion des Genres: Logos and Packaging as Copyrighted Works*, Chapter 10 in this volume.

[49] Euro-Excellence Inc. v. Kraft Canada Inc., [2007] 3 S.C.R. 20, 2007 SCC 37.

block the importation of the candy itself.[50] Several justices, however, would have been willing to adopt a judicially created exception for copyrighted content that is "merely incidental" to a product.[51]

These justices did not attempt a precise definition of "incidental" copyrights, and they acknowledged that the determination would not always be easy.[52] They suggested, however, that what constitutes "incidental" content should be determined from the consumer's perspective: "[i]f a reasonable consumer undertaking a commercial transaction does not think that the copyrighted work is what she is buying or dealing with, it is likely that the work is merely incidental to the consumer good."[53] Relevant factors in making this determination would include "the nature of the product, the nature of the protected work and the relationship of the work to the product."[54] The justices' examples of incidental works included an instruction booklet and "a small logo" on a shirt pocket.[55] In contrast, if a painting were reproduced on a t-shirt, the sale of that shirt would be treated as a sale of the copyrighted image.[56]

Five years after *Euro-Excellence*, the Copyright Modernization Act of 2012 amended Canada's copyright statutes to give copyright owners the exclusive right:

> in the case of a work that is in the form of a tangible object, to sell or otherwise transfer ownership of the tangible object, as long as that ownership has never previously been transferred in or outside Canada with the authorization of the copyright owner.[57]

---

[50] The majority ultimately permitted the importation, but on the narrow ground that Kraft Canada was only a licensee and not the owner of the Canadian copyright. *Ibid.* at paras. 49–51 (Binnie, Deschamps, and Rothstein JJ.). As illustrated in the *Frank & Hirsch* case which follows, a potential plaintiff can overcome this obstacle by obtaining an assignment of the copyright in the country of importation.

[51] 3 S.C.R. 20, at paras. 83–95 (Bastarache, LeBel, and Charron JJ.); *see also ibid.* at para. 56 (Fish J.) (expressing "grave doubt whether the law governing the protection of intellectual property rights in Canada can be transformed in this way into an instrument of trade control not contemplated by the Copyright Act").

[52] *Ibid.* at para. 94 (Bastarache, LeBel, and Charron JJ).

[53] *Ibid.*

[54] *Ibid.*

[55] *Ibid.* at para. 95.

[56] *Ibid.*

[57] Copyright Modernization Act, sec. 4, First Session, Forty-First Parliament, 60–61 Elizabeth II, 2011–12 (assented to June 29, 2012), adding section 3(1)(j) to the Copyright Act.

This provision simultaneously recognizes an exclusive distribution right and restricts that right by creating a rule of exhaustion. The Canadian courts will have to determine how the new exhaustion rule relates to the exclusive importation right. Does the exhaustion of the distribution right also exhaust the importation right? And if the work has different copyright owners in Canada and abroad, does a foreign owner's authorization of a foreign transfer exhaust the distribution right in Canada as well? Because Canada has recently joined the TPP negotiations, it has signaled its intention to preserve the exclusive importation rights of copyright owners. Like the United States, Canada will have to find a way to reconcile this position with the principle of exhaustion.

B   South Africa

In South Africa, a trademark is not infringed by importing goods to which the trademark has been applied with the consent of the trademark owner,[58] unless the goods have been materially altered.[59] However, in *Frank & Hirsch (Pty.) Ltd. v. A Roopanand Brothers (Pty.) Ltd.*,[60] the exclusive South African distributor of TDK tapes acquired the copyright in the trade dress (other than the trademarks) and the printed cardboard insert, and brought a copyright infringement claim to block the unauthorized importation of the tapes.[61] Although the Supreme Court ultimately

---

[58]   South Africa Trademarks Act, § 34(2)(d).

[59]   *See* Television Radio Centre (Pty.) Ltd. v. Sony Kabushki Kaisha t/a Sony Corporation, 1987 (2) SA 994 (Sony video recorders imported from Europe were no longer "genuine" because the importer had altered their tuners to pick up South African broadcasts).

[60]   Frank & Hirsch (Pty.) Ltd. v. A Roopanand Brothers (Pty.) Ltd., Case No. 580/91, 1993 ZASCA 90; 1993 (4) SA 279 (AD); 1993 (2) All SA 521 (A) (Appellate Division, Supreme Court of South Africa) (June 2, 1993), *available at* http://www.saflii.org/za/cases/ZASCA/1993/90.html.

[61]   Section 23 of the South African Copyright Act provides:

3. Infringement. –

(1) Copyright shall be infringed by any person, not being the owner of the copyright, who, without the licence of such owner, does or causes any other person to do, in the Republic, any act which the owner has the exclusive rights to do or to authorize.

(2) Without derogating from the generality of subsection (1), copyright shall be infringed by any person who, without the licence of the owner of the copyright and at a time when copyright subsists in a work –

(a) imports an article into the Republic for a purpose other than for his private and domestic use;

ruled in favor of the plaintiffs, the analysis of the lower court is of interest because it rejected the copyright claim, stating, in essence, that the copyright in the accessories was extinguished when they were attached to uncopyrightable goods:[62]

> [I]t is not an article the making of which constitutes an infringement if only the making of an accessory part of the article which has been made constituted an infringement. If the Legislature had meant to refer to such articles, it should have said so, e.g. by referring to an article or any part thereof. To hold otherwise would mean that the importer of a car which has components such as shock absorbers of another manufacturer fitted, upon which literary or artistic work is printed or painted, could be infringing copyright and be prohibited from importing the car. The remedies of the Copyright Act could not possibly have been meant to apply to such a situation. The short answer would be that the car is not an article the making of which infringed copyright. The car would not be a copy, reproduction or adaptation of the work. The reproduction work would merely be an accessory component thereof.
>
> It seems to me that these cassette tapes are also not articles the making of which would have constituted infringement of copyright. The physical reproductions of the artistic or literary works comprising the get-up were indeed accessory to the principal things, i.e. the cassette tapes and by *accessio* or *specificatio* became part of the cassette tapes, the articles in question.[63]

The Supreme Court rejected this interpretation because (1) it would effectively terminate a copyright in a manner inconsistent with the

---

> (b) sells, lets, or by way of trade offers or exposes for sale or hire in the Republic any article; [or]
>
> (c) distributes in the Republic any article for the purposes of trade, or for any other purpose, to such an extent that the owner of the copyright in question is prejudicially affected ... if to his knowledge the making of that article constituted an infringement of that copyright or would have constituted such an infringement if the article had been made in the Republic.

Copyright Act No. 98 of 1978, 1978 SA Commercial Law 98. The current version of section 23(2) is similar in all relevant respects. *See* Butterworths Statutes of South Africa, Commercial Law, Copyright Act No. 98 of 1978, 1978 SA Commercial Law 98.

[62] Frank & Hirsch (Pty.) Ltd. v. A Roopanand Brothers (Pty.) Ltd., 1991 (3) SA 240 (D & CLD).

[63] *Frank & Hirsch*, Case No. 580/91, 1993 ZASCA 90; 1993 (4) SA 279 (AD); 1993 (2) All SA 521 (A) (Appellate Division, Supreme Court of South Africa) (June 2, 1993) (*quoting* Frank & Hirsch (Pty.) Ltd. v. A. Roopanand Brothers (Pty.) Ltd., 1991 (3) SA 240 (D & CLD)).

termination provisions of the copyright statutes, and (2) its potential scope was too broad:

> It seems to be an inescapable consequence of the decision of the Court a quo that wherever the physical reproduction of a work in which A has the copyright becomes part of a "principal thing" (which itself is either not the subject-matter of copyright or over which A has no copyright) A loses his copyright and can have no claim for its infringement. If this were so, the protection afforded to an author by the copyright law would be nullified in a number of important instances. Thus, for example, an artist who painted an original artistic work would, presumably, not be entitled to sue under either part of sec. 23 if a reproduction of that painting were used without permission as a dust-cover for, or an illustration in, a book of which someone else was the author. Similarly, a writer or poet would have no claim against a publisher who unauthorizedly included his short story in a collection of short stories or his poem in an anthology of poetry.[64]

The lower court's analysis may indeed have gone too far in suggesting that the copyright in the accessory simply disappeared because it "merged" into the uncopyrighted article which it accompanied. Unlike Australia's statute, which requires that the accessory itself be non-infringing, the lower court's analysis in *Frank & Hirsch* could be read as eliminating all copyright protection for the accessory. However, the Supreme Court may have read the lower court's opinion too broadly; the lower court may have meant to apply its "merger" analysis only where the accessory itself was non-infringing. Imposing that condition would answer the Supreme Court's concern that authors and artists would have no infringement claim against someone who used their copyrighted work in an accessory without their consent. It would also have created a judicial exception that closely paralleled the Australian statute. Nonetheless, the Supreme Court's broad interpretation of the lower court's merger analysis led it to squarely reject that approach, opening the door for South African trademark owners to wield copyright law as a broad weapon against parallel imports.

A contemporaneous commentator noted that the principle of *Frank & Hirsch* could "be adapted so as to prevent parallel importation of equipment and all sorts of goods by relying on copyright in labels, get-up, instruction books and the like," and that, while "restraining the importation and dealing in peripheral items does not necessarily mean

---

[64] *Frank & Hirsch*, Case No. 580/91, 1993 ZASCA 90; 1993 (4) SA 279 (AD); 1993 (2) All SA 521 (A) (Appellate Division, Supreme Court of South Africa) (June 2, 1993).

that trading in the substantive items can be prevented. [I]n many cases it is not a commercial proposition to trade in the substantive items if they cannot be accompanied by the peripheral items in which copyright subsists."[65]

Since the *Frank & Hirsch* decision, South African trademark owners have brought successful claims of copyright infringement against gray market importers of hi-fi equipment, watches and other products, relying on the copyright in the design drawings on which these three-dimensional articles were based.[66]

V A LEGISLATIVE SOLUTION FOR THE UNITED STATES

In April 2013, the Chairman of the House Judiciary Committee announced the Committee's intent to conduct "a comprehensive review of U.S. copyright laws."[67] This review is likely to include a proposal to restore the exclusive importation right. If Congress adopts such legislation, it should also include an exception for copyrighted material that is merely incidental to non-copyrightable merchandise. A narrowly tailored statutory exception would preserve the balance of rights established under federal trademark law.

Importation exceptions for incidental copyrights may lead manufacturers to integrate their trademarks more fully into their designs – like Coke bottles and Toblerone bars – so that they can make the case that the trademark as a copyrightable design is an important part of the value to consumers. In some cases, this may be true, because sometimes the appearance of a product is more important than its other characteristics. Even if the trademark itself is not easy to integrate, other copyrightable features can be physically integrated into the product. In some of these cases, the exception for incidental copyrights should not apply, and the trademark owner should prevail. As a business strategy, "exploding" the

---

[65] Owen H. Dean, *South Africa – Copyright: Parallel Importation of Artistic Works*, 4 ENT. L. REV., No. 5, E99–101 (1993).

[66] Owen Dean, *South Africa: The South African Position on Parallel Importing* (Apr. 26, 2001), *available at* http://www.mondaq.com/article.asp?articleid=11258; *see also* Coenrad Visser, *Importing Grey Goods into South Africa*, 1 JUTA'S BUS. L. 187 (1993).

[67] Press Release, United States House of Representatives Committee on the Judiciary, Chairman Goodlatte Announces Comprehensive Review of Copyright Law (Apr. 24, 2013).

trademark to encompass a large part of the product design will succeed only if consumers find the resulting design appealing, and only if the design is nonfunctional in the trademark sense.[68] In addition, any copyrightable elements integrated into the product must have artistic features that are separable from the product's utilitarian features so as to retain their copyright protection.[69]

Drawing on the Australian and Singaporean models, a statutory exception for incidental uses of copyrighted works should include a non-exhaustive list of the types of uses that should be exempt from restrictions on importation and subsequent distribution. This will eliminate much of the uncertainty that would arise under a more general statutory test for "incidental uses." Concern over such uncertainty troubled the Canadian Supreme Court in *Euro-Excellence*.[70] As illustrated by the Australian case law, however, relying entirely on a list of examples may force courts to engage in difficult line-drawing and strained interpretation in an effort to fit unanticipated uses under one of the delineated categories. Therefore, the exception should also include a catch-all exception for the occasional incidental use that falls outside the delineated categories.

While incidental uses may be difficult to define, one approach is to consider how much value the copyrighted feature contributes to the overall commercial value of the individual article.[71] Where the contribution is insubstantial, then the presence of the protected content should not preclude importation and sale of the article. Where the copyrighted feature also functions as a trademark, the value of the feature should be calculated *without regard to the value of the goodwill that it represents*. Because the plaintiff's claim is not for trademark infringement, but for

---

[68] *See* 15 U.S.C. § 1052(e)(5) (2006) (barring trademark registration for functional features); TrafFix Devices, Inc. v. Marketing Displays, Inc., 532 U.S. 23 (2001) (features of product design that were the subject of an expired utility patent are presumed functional and therefore cannot be protected by trademark law).

[69] *See* 17 U.S.C. § 101 (2006) (definition of useful articles); Brandir Int'l, Inc. v. Cascade Pac. Lumber Co., 834 F.2d 1142 (2d Cir. 1987) (applying § 101 to deny copyright protection where utilitarian aspects of useful article were inseparable from artistic aspects).

[70] *Euro-Excellence*, 3 S.C.R. 20, at para. 6 (Binnie, Deschamps, and Rothstein JJ.).

[71] This is similar to the approach suggested by Justice Bastarache in his minority opinion in *Euro-Excellence*, 3 S.C.R. 20, at paras. 94–95 (Bastarache, LeBel, and Charron JJ.).

copyright infringement, any reputational value adhering to the copyrightable subject matter is irrelevant. If the feature in question is copyrighted text, or an audiovisual or sound recording, it should be valued according to its informational, artistic, or entertainment value. Furthermore, the inquiry should focus not on the value of the copyright, but on the value to the consumer of possessing a single *copy* of the copyrighted material.[72] While the value contributed by the copyrighted feature may be easy to assess in many cases, in closer cases expert testimony may be required. In the case of a chocolate bar, for example, an especially appealing design might contribute more to the product's consumer appeal than the chocolate itself. Ordinarily, people do not buy a chocolate Easter bunny for its flavor.

By combining enumerated categories with a catch-all provision focused on relative value, the law can exempt accessories from the exclusive importation rights of copyright owners. Combining these ideas into a single statute, the proposed exemption would provide:

Where a copyrighted work is incorporated in an accessory to an article, the copyright embodied in the accessory is not infringed by importing the accessory with the article, or by the domestic distribution of the imported accessory with the imported article, provided that the accessory was made with the consent of the copyright owner in the country where it was made.[73]

For purposes of this section, an accessory is

(1) A label affixed to, displayed on, incorporated into the surface of, or accompanying, the article;
(2) The packaging or container in which the article is packaged or contained;
(3) A label affixed to, displayed on, incorporated into the surface of, or accompanying, the packaging or container in which the article is packaged or contained;
(4) A written instruction, a warranty, or other information provided with the article;

---

[72] For example, the copyright in a motion picture may be worth millions of dollars, but the value of a single DVD embodying the motion picture is likely to be less than twenty dollars.

[73] Alternatively, this proviso could be expanded to include any accessories the making of which did not constitute an infringement in the country where they were made, even if the copyright owner did not consent. This would encompass accessories made in countries where the copyright had already expired, where the work did not qualify for copyright protection, or where the copying was otherwise permitted by law. If this approach is adopted, it should apply only if the country of manufacture adheres to the minimum copyright standards and nondiscrimination rules of the Berne Convention and the TRIPS Agreement.

(5) A phonorecord embodying an instructional sound recording provided with the article;

(6) A copy of an instructional audiovisual work provided with the article; or

(7) Any feature of the article, its packaging or its container, or any accompanying object, that contributes an insubstantial part of the value of the combination, apart from the trademark value of the feature.[74]

An importation exception along these lines would not cause the United States to violate any of its obligations under multilateral international trade or intellectual property agreements, which are agnostic on the question of international exhaustion.[75] In addition, such a carve-out is expressly permitted by Article QQ.G.3 of the proposed TPP, even as it requires stricter protection against parallel imports of several categories of copyrighted works. As noted earlier, Article QQ.G.3 embodies the United States' proposal to include in the TPP a provision that requires signatories to give copyright owners the right to block parallel imports. However, a footnote clarifies the scope of this requirement:

> With respect to copies of works and phonograms that have been placed on the market by the relevant right holder, the obligations described in Article [QQ.G.3] apply only to books, journals, sheet music, sound recordings and audio and visual works (i.e., categories of products in which the value of the copyrighted material represents substantially all of the value of the product). Notwithstanding the foregoing, each Party may provide the protection described in Article [QQ.G.3] to a broader range of goods.[76]

Thus, even if the United States persuades other TPP members to allow copyright owners to block parallel imports, the signatories will be free to exempt products in which the copyrighted component does not represent "substantially all the value" of the product. This leaves ample room for the proposed exception for accessories.

---

[74] The proposed exemption could easily be modified to apply to design patents, 35 U.S.C. § 171 (2006), if trademark owners begin to use these as an alternative to copyright or trademark protection.

[75] Relevant agreements include the Berne Convention for the Protection of Literary and Artistic Works, the TRIPS Agreement, the WIPO Copyright Treaty, and, should a similar exception be created for design patents, the Paris Convention for the Protection of Industrial Property.

[76] TPP 2013 Draft, *supra* note 12, at n. 11. An identical footnote accompanied Article 4.2 in the 2011 draft. The same language appears in a side letter to the U.S.–Morocco Free Trade Agreement, *supra* note 13, *available at* http://www.ustr.gov/trade-agreements/free-trade-agreements/morocco-fta. However, no such language accompanies the U.S.–Jordan Free Trade Agreement, *supra* note 13.

VI CONCLUSION

In regulating parallel imports of trademarked goods, trademark law attempts to strike a balance between the interests of trademark owners and the interests of consumers. By resorting to copyright law to block otherwise lawful imports of genuine goods, trademark owners have succeeded in avoiding the limitations imposed by trademark law, and have created a kind of mutant trademark law. This scenario has been played out in countries around the world. Their judicial and legislative responses, though imperfect, have provided a valuable learning opportunity.

The legislation proposed here builds on that opportunity. It provides guidance to importers, distributors, and intellectual property owners, allows lawmakers to impose different parallel import regimes for copyrights and trademarks, and prevents trademark owners from substituting one regime for another by adding trivial content to their unprotected goods. This approach preserves the pre-eminence of trademark law as the proper mechanism for balancing the legitimate interests of trademark owners and consumers.

10. *"La confusion des genres"*: logos and packaging as copyrighted works

Pierre-Emmanuel Moyse*

I INTRODUCTION

On July 26, 2007, the Supreme Court of Canada rendered its long-awaited judgment in the case *Kraft v. Euro-Excellence*.[1] It displays themes and interrogations similar to those presented in the copyright case *Omega S.A. v. Costco Wholesale Corp.*, notably P.E.M. on the issue of misuse. *Omega* was decided by the Ninth Circuit Court of Appeals, affirmed by the United States Supreme Court in 2010, and is now pending before the Court of Appeals of the Ninth Circuit after the case had been remanded to the District Court of California.[2] Albeit obviously

---

* Associate Professor at the Faculty of Law of McGill University and Director of the Centre for Intellectual Property. I wish to thank Jacqueline Rowniak for her excellent research and collaboration.

[1] Euro-Excellence, Inc. v. Kraft Canada, Inc., [2007] 3 S.C.R. 20 (Can.) [Kraft SCC]. *See* Pierre-Emmanuel Moyse, *Kraft Canada c. Euro-Excellence : l'insoutenable légèreté du droit*, 53 MCGILL L.J. 741 (2008). Many comments have been written on the case, including: Teresa Scassa, *Using Copyright Law to Prevent Parallel Importation: A Comment on Kraft Canada, Inc. v. Euro Excellence, Inc.*, 85 CAN. B. REV. 409 (2007); Robert Tomkowicz, *Copyrighting Chocolate: Kraft Canada v. Euro Excellence*, 20 INTELL. PROP. J. 399 (2007); Mistrale Goudreau, *Commentaire d'arrêt: l'affaire Euro-Excellence Inc. c. Kraft Canada Inc. en Cour suprême*, 37 R.G.D. 499 (2008); Daniel S. Drapeau, *Marchandises d'importation parallèle: une Cour suprême divisée*, 20 C.P.I. 183 (2007); Cameron J. Hutchinson, *Which Kraft of Statutory Interpretation? A Supreme Court of Canada Trilogy on Intellectual Property Law*, 46 ALTA. L. REV. (2008), *available at* http://papers.ssrn.com/sol3/papers.cfm?abstract_id= 1151994; Carol Hitchman and Christopher Tan, *Case Commentary Euro-Excellence Inc. v. Kraft Canada Inc.*, 7 CAN. INT'L L. 118 (2007).

[2] Omega S.A. v. Costco Wholesale Corp., No. 11-57137 (9th Cir. July 25, 2012), *appealed from* Omega S.A. v. Costco Wholesale Corp., 2011 U.S. Dist. LEXIS 155893 (C.D. Cal. Nov. 9, 2011).

not subject to the exact same legislation, such grey market cases[3] universally question the scope of protection of copyright law. They certainly beg the same question: to what extent can copyright law be used to control the parallel importation of consumable goods where the genuine product was first put on the market with the consent of the initial rightholder and producer of the good? In both cases referred to above, the plaintiffs were authorized distributors who claimed copyright protection in a logo affixed to the product they had manufactured or distributed. These cases hardly concern creativity, unless one considers the imagination deployed by the lawyers in devising such strategy to be a creative exploit. The objective in both instances was simply to exclude the unauthorized importer in order to create a distribution monopoly. The copyright infringement here takes a particularly unusual form: it is indirect, rather than direct, and extends to the product. The act of importation does not, strictly speaking, imply an infringement in the first place as it typically concerns genuine products, not counterfeit ones. Some countries have stretched their reproduction right or adopted a distribution right to somewhat mimic the importation remedy. Some French scholars, for example, have vouched for an expansive notion of "*droit d'édition*," a notion introduced in French law by the Act of 1793,[4] which bestowed control over the distribution of the tangible object embodying the work.[5] However, overarching legal principles underpinning property law, coupled with abolitionist movements, forced intellectual property to retract and yield to the free circulation of goods. Clearly, the act of importation

---

[3] *See* W.A. ROTHNIE, PARALLEL IMPORTS (Sweet & Maxwell 1993); *see also* PIERRE-EMMANUEL MOYSE, LE DROIT DE DISTRIBUTION (Yvon Blais 2007).

[4] *Décret du 19ᵉ Juillet 1793 relatif aux droits de propriété des auteurs d'écrits en tout genre, des compositeurs de musique, des peintres et des dessinateurs.* The vague formulation "*droit d'édition*" was replaced by technical-oriented reproduction right in 1957.

[5] FRÉDÉRIC POLLAUD-DULIAN, LE DROIT DE DESTINATION: LE SORT DES EXEMPLAIRES EN DROIT D'AUTEUR (LGDJ 1989). The doctrine is examined and rejected in the case Théberge v. Galérie d'Art du Petit Champlain Inc. by the Canadian Supreme Court:

> Under the civiliste tradition, and particularly in France, the right of reproduction was interpreted to include not only the right to make new copies of the work (reproduction stricto sensu) but also what is called by French jurists the "right of destination" (droit de destination). The right of destination gives the author or artist the right to control to a considerable extent the use that is made of authorized copies of his or her work.

Théberge v. Galerie d'Art du Petit Champlain Inc., [2002] 2 S.C.R. 33 at para. 63 [Théberge].

does not fall under the ambit of well-known copyrights such as the right of public performance or communication to the public, but rather belongs to a class of its own. Selling, marketing, or distributing a cultural product is clearly not an act of public performance, although its copy played on a mechanical device could lead to a public execution of the work,[6] a distinction that was not always well understood in the early twentieth-century copyright context.

The locus of this chapter is the evolution of the concept of distribution in copyright law throughout Canadian jurisprudence and legislation. This field, arguably the most obscure place of the copyright cosmos, is in constant evolution. The Copyright Modernization Act, in force since 2012, has amended the Copyright Act's section 3(1) by adding a new paragraph, subsection 3(1)(j), which creates a right to "sell or otherwise transfer ownership of tangible objects, as long as that ownership has never previously been transferred in or outside Canada with the authorization of the copyright owner."[7] The explicit reference to the place of first sale "outside Canada" certainly calls for international exhaustion; however, it remains to be seen how this amendment will interact with the importation provisions which, as we will see, allow for some control over international distribution. The U.S. legislator long ago codified the author's right to first sell a copy of a work, a solution known as the "first-sale doctrine," but is struggling, due to a lack of precision, with various interpretations relating to its international application.[8] 17 U.S.C. section 109(a), read in conjunction with section 107, which creates a distribution right, is to the same effect: "... the owner of a particular copy or phonorecord lawfully made under this title, or any person authorized by such owner, is entitled, without the authority of the copyright owner, to sell or otherwise dispose of the possession of that copy or phonorecord."[9] There exist a number of justifications behind the restriction operated by the so-called "first-sale doctrine." First, it offers a rule of conflict in situations where intellectual property laws risk encroaching upon the right of the owner of a tangible copy of a legally acquired

---

[6]   Discussing the application of copyright law to the operation of a mechanical piano, *see* White-Smith Music Publ'g Co. v. Apollo Co., 209 U.S. 1 (1908).

[7]   Copyright Modernization Act, S.C. 2012, c. 20 [*Act*].

[8]   *See* Irene Calboli, *An American Tale: The Unclear Application of the First Sale Rule in United States Copyright Law (and its Impact on International Trade)*, in INTELLECTUAL PROPERTY AT THE CROSSROADS OF TRADE (Jan Rosen, ed., Edward Elgar, 2012).

[9]   Limitations on exclusive rights: Effect of transfer of particular copy or phonorecord, 17 U.S.C. § 109(a) (2006).

work.[10] Second, it constitutes a jurisdictional and constitutional rule that articulates the division of powers between the state and federated states. The commerce of tangible property is, for the most part, governed by state or provincial law. Allowing copyright or any intellectual property right to be the instrument of control of tangible property would be seen as clearly impinging upon provincial or state powers, if not blatantly having an ultra vires reach. Third, by revealing the limits of copyright – its "*épuisement*" (exhaustion)[11] – we preserve the public and users' (purchaser of a cultural product) interests in balancing copyright law. The exhaustion principle used to explain this neutralization process is, in this sense, the product of a free market or anti-monopolistic approach.

This chapter commences with a personal and therefore subjective, though not necessarily unscientific, account of the *Kraft v. Euro-Excellence* case. Beginning in 2002, I acted as lead counsel for the defendant when the action was initiated and finally argued the case in 2007 before the Supreme Court. This portrait of a singular case will comprise Part II of this chapter. Part III will discuss the importation remedy in light of the Supreme Court opinion. Finally, Part IV will tackle the most challenging issue, an issue largely side-tracked or eclipsed by the Supreme Court: that of abuse of right or misuse. The abuse of right argument was made repeatedly and forcefully at every stage of the proceedings, and yet the courts were shy to engage with it. The American companion case *Omega S.A. v. Costco Wholesale Corp.* has revived the argument and, hopefully, will strengthen the place and role of this mighty doctrine in copyright law. It is timely as the general public is becoming increasingly weary of copyright overreach and excess.

---

[10] Only tangible objects are subjected to importation and distribution mechanisms. The Agreed Statement under Articles 6 and 7 of the WIPO Copyright Treaty 1996 specifies that the notion of "copies" used in the provision regarding the distribution "refer exclusively to fixed copies that can be put into circulation as tangible objects." WIPO Copyright Treaty, Geneva, Dec. 20, 1996.

[11] Stig Strömholm, *Le "droit de mise en circulation" dans le droit d'auteur – Étude de droit comparé*, 80 D.A. 279 (1967); Franz Gotzen, Het bestimmingsrecht van de auteur (Larcier 1975); Jaap H. Spoor, William R. Cornish and Peter F. Nolan, Copies in Copyright (Sithoff & Noordhoff 1980).

II *KRAFT V. EURO-EXCELLENCE:* A PERSONAL JOURNEY

Act I: The Parties

After having skimmed through the statement of claim, I remained unshaken and confident that I could find an expedient way to have this application rejected at the interlocutory stage. I was more impressed by its inherent procedural qualities than by the claim itself which, prima facie, appeared to me clearly abusive. Filed together with the official copyright registrations delivered by the Canadian Intellectual Property Office, the claim sought injunctive reliefs, as well as damages for copyright infringement of the wrappers of chocolate products, notably the "Côte d'Or Elephant" and the Toblerone "Bear in the Mountain" works. Euro-Excellence, the evidence would show, was indeed a victim of its own success. Although mainly operating in Québec, it had over the years, and under the envious eyes of its competitors, built a multi-brand and robust retail distribution business for food products. In fact, it performed so well that Kraft Canada saw in Euro-Excellence the reason for its stagnant performance in Canada. Kraft Canada, a subsidiary of Kraft International and based in Ontario, had been recently constituted to boost the sales of the newly acquired Toblerone and Côte d'Or lines in Canada. Kraft Canada's mission was to relay the expansionist and diversification ambitions of the mother company. In the war over chocolate and premium products, Euro-Excellence was a serious competitor. As the court judgments show, Euro-Excellence had only sold in Québec almost $3 million worth of Côte d'Or chocolates imported from Europe between 2002 and 2004, a number from which the $300 000 damages were disgorged.[12] The copyright infringement claim was the immediate result of failing negotiation between the parties and, of course, as the legal representative of Kraft Canada duly admitted in court, the irreducible resistance to commercial oppression displayed by Euro-Excellence. Kraft overlooked the tenacity of a man who, like the Galician Obélix, fell into the cauldron of chocolate. André Clémence, the real hero of this story, had something else in common with Obélix: he was French. His business was not simply a profitable activity; it was a French chapter in the North American way of life. He was the culinary version of the tale of the

---

[12] Kraft Canada Inc. v. Euro Excellence Inc., 2004 F.C. 652, 252 F.T.R. 50 [Kraft FC]; Kraft Canada Inc. v. Euro Excellence Inc., 2005 F.C.A. 427, [2006] 3 F.C.R. 91 [Kraft FCA]; Kraft SCC, *supra* note 1.

paper delivery boy who climbs his way to the top. In ten years, he went from delivering chocolate bars imported from Europe to local Québec retailers himself, driving his Renault 5, the last relic of the French automotive hopes on North American soil, to a multi-million-dollar medium-sized, family-owned enterprise.

The asymmetry of means and objectives between the parties became starker as the proceedings progressed. From where they stood, nothing was personal, and only numbers were important. I felt like I was taking part in a sequel of *The Corporation*. The Kraft Canada product manager I cross-examined prior to the Federal Court hearing had very little or no knowledge of the history of Côte d'Or or Toblerone she worked so ardently to assert. On the contrary, André Clémence was an encyclopedia on chocolate. He was quick to engage in lengthy stories about its origins, confection, and the Matterhorn (the mountain which forms part of the Toblerone logo), tales which would inevitably end with the ceremonial display of a picture of him published in a late 1970s issue of *Playboy* magazine, not as a centerfold, but as a chef chocolatier at the newly opened Lenôtre boutique in Berlin.

Act II: The Subterfuge and the Lower Courts

The case proceeds due to the unavailability of two legal grounds: contract and trademark law.[13] Contractual remedies are out of reach for the activities of the parallel importer or grey marketer as an independent distributor. This is for obvious reasons: the unauthorized distributor is, in essence, free from any contractual ties. No quotas, exclusivity, restrictions as to the conditions of distribution, account of profit or royalties can be imposed by the franchisor or the manufacturer. The parallel importer finds itself outside the traditional scope of trademark law as its activities are unlikely to cause confusion in the consumer's mind as to the origin of the products. Whether distributed by an authorized or unauthorized distributor, authentic products bear evidence of their provenance. This is where Kraft thought copyright would be useful. Because copyright protection can be obtained at little or no cost on elements of packaging, easily satisfying the loose requirement of originality, it can be used to

---

[13]   In favour of a generous interpretation of the importation provisions to remedy this situation, *see* William L. Hayhurst, *Intellectual Property as a Non-Tariff Barrier in Canada, With Particular Reference to "Gray Goods" and "Parallel Imports"*, 31 C.P.R. (3d) 289 (1990); *see also* W. Lee Webster, *Restraining the Gray Marketer Policy and Practice*, 4 CIPR 211 (1987).

control the product through the underlying work as an object of owner-ship. Since a consumable product cannot easily be marketed without its commercial outfit, comprising labels, logos, and text of all sorts, alleging copyright infringement in one of these elements would achieve the desired effect of recreating a distribution right over the product itself. At its core, this is what the *Kraft* case is about. In the courtroom of the Supreme Court of Canada, that cold day of February 2007, there were only distributors of food products, retailers and importers. Kraft Canada was first and foremost a distributor; it had acquired a license from the copyright owner in Canada – Kraft Belgium – for the sole purpose of suing Euro-Excellence. Using copyright as the way to control distribution of products was, as Justice Harrington, the trial judge, put it, "an interesting strategy":[14]

> Kraft has developed an interesting strategy in an effort to thwart Euro Excellence's distribution of these chocolate bars in Canada. To better appre-ciate the strategy, I should first say what it has not done. If it put distribution restrictions on Euro Excellence's supplier, it has not invoked them. Nor does it rely on trade-mark protection, although it alleges, and it is not contested, that it is the owner in Canada of the trade-marks "Côte d'Or" and "Toblerone." What it has done is take Canadian licensing rights in the artworks on the chocolate bar wrappers which have been copyrighted in Canada. It does not seek to enjoin Euro Excellence from distributing Toblerone and Côte d'Or chocolate bars. Rather, it seeks to enjoin it from distributing the copyrighted artwork on the wrappers. The idea is that the cost of re-wrapping or covering over the copyrighted artwork would act as a major disincentive. The entire Toblerone line is covered by wrappers which have some copyrighted artwork on them. In the case of Côte d'Or, some of the products distributed by Euro Excellence do not contain copyright material. *Kraft is not trying to interfere with the distribution of those products* (emphasis added).[15]

This was not the first time such strategy was deployed in a commercial case; however, it was the first in Canada to be decided on the merits. In fact, by the time the *Kraft* case had commenced, a similar copyright case was already registered on the Federal Court roll by a plaintiff represented by the same firm as Kraft. In the case, *Volkswagen Canada Inc. v. Access International Automotive*,[16] instituted in 1999, the plaintiff Volkswagen

---

14 Kraft FC, *supra* note 12, at para. 4.
15 *Ibid.*
16 Volkswagen Canada Inc. v. Access Int'l Auto. Ltd., [1999] F.C.J. No. 1016, 171 F.T.R. 311; Volkswagen Canada Inc. v. Access Int'l Auto. Ltd. [1999] 174 F.C.J. No. 529, 174 F.T.R. 161.

Canada filed a statement of claim alleging that the defendant, an importer of auto parts, infringed its copyright in the Volkswagen and Audi logos and requested that Access International cease dealing in parts and accessories bearing either logo on the Canadian market. The case was ultimately settled.

Of all common law countries, it was Australia that pioneered most of the doctrinal work on the issue of parallel importation. Due to its size and geographical situation, the Australian market depends heavily on importation, which has resulted in high prices for books, CDs, etc. Foreign manufacturers long ago resorted to copyright and trademark law to maintain control over the domestic market, a situation which was soon aggravated by the use of copyright on instructions booklets and graphic trademarks of non-cultural products. The Australian case *Bailey v. Boccaccio*, decided by Justice Young in 1986,[17] caused tremendous concern as he concluded that the unavailability of a trademark does not necessarily eliminate copyright protection. According to Justice Young, the selling or, by way of trade, offering or exposing for sale bottles with labels without the authorization of the rights holder in the original work (consisting of the label) constituted copyright infringement. This case, which Justice Harrington described later as "squarely on point"[18] to decide our case, led to a series of legal and impact studies. Ultimately, upon the recommendation of the Copyright Law Review Committee of Australia on importation,[19] which characterized the subterfuge as an inappropriate use of copyright, the Australian Copyright Act 1968 was amended to remove further possibilities of resorting to copyright protection in artistic works on packages and labels to prevent legitimate importation of products.[20]

Justice Harrington of the Federal Court gave Canada its own *Bailey* case, but, despite our intervention in 2010 before Bill C-32 Committee (a Bill that was replaced by Bill C-11, tabled by the actual government and

---

[17] R. & A. Bailey & Co. Ltd. v. Boccaccio Pty. Ltd. (1986), 84 FLR 232.

[18] Kraft FC, *supra* note 12, at 55.

[19] COPYRIGHT LAW REVIEW COMMITTEE, THE IMPORTATION PROVISIONS OF THE COPYRIGHT ACT 1968 (Australian Government Publishing Service 1988), *available at* http://www.worldlii.org/au/other/clrc/8/ [IMPORTATION PROVISIONS AUS].

[20] *Copyright Amendment Act (No. 1) 1998*, Schedule 2. Labeling and packaging etc. of imported goods, has been in force since 2000. For similar developments in New Zealand, *see* Louise Longdin, *Parallel Importing Post TRIPS: Convergence and Divergence in Australia and New Zealand*, 50 ICLQ 54 (2001).

passed by Parliament in 2012[21]), no copyright amendments have followed. Justice Harrington saw no legal rationale for preventing Kraft from using copyright law as a legal means to monopolize goods it acquired directly from the source in Belgium. In his opinion, "Kraft was simply taking care of business"[22] and rejected most of our arguments for being "philosophical,"[23] an adjective which I would take as a superlative in other circumstances, but which clearly had a negative ring in the wording of the opinion. The judgment is replete with *loci cummunes*:

> Although, of course, not binding, I find the Bailey's Irish Cream case persuasive and come to the same conclusion under our Act. I am not prepared to simply use the Copyright Act as a touchstone for an imaginative frolic of my own. The language is clear, and the very purpose of the Act is to prevent unauthorized distribution of copyrighted works.[24]

Justice Harrington condemned Euro-Excellence to $300 000 dollars in damages and granted the injunction against the copyrighted work in the chocolate bar wrappers. The injunction also ordered that the product be rendered non-infringing, a conclusion which led to a most absurd situation and turned the case into a copyright comedy. Unprepared to acknowledge any wrongdoing, the defendant challenged the Court and Kraft at their own game. André Clémence commissioned an engineering company to devise a computerized system that would cover up all the "Elephants" visible on the packaging. Red, brown, and black patches were placed on a transparent plastic film, which were subsequently applied by the machine on every chocolate bar. It is to this day the only "non-infringement" machine known to man. This excerpt of the decision on a motion to seek direction as to render the chocolate products non-infringing, so as to comply with the decision on the merits, is worth quoting:

> [4] There was, and is, no reason to assume that Euro Excellence will not abide by the order. It is not contrary to the Copyright Act to import into Canada and to possess Toblerone and Côte d'Or chocolate bars in wrappers that display the copyrighted artistic works. ... I did not intend to prohibit Euro Excellence from importing and possessing the chocolate bars in their

---

[21] *See* Transcript of Parliament, Legislative Committee on Bill C-32, 40th Parliament, 3rd Sess., No. 007 (Dec. 8, 2010), *available at* http://www.parl.gc.ca/HousePublications/Publication.aspx?DocId=4867858&Language=E.

[22] Kraft FC, *supra* note 12, at 46.

[23] Kraft FC, *supra* note 12, at 47 and 61.

[24] Kraft FC, *supra* note 12, at 60.

original wrappers. I certainly did not say that the wrappers had to be rendered non-infringing in Europe. As long as Euro Excellence renders the wrappers non-infringing, whether it does so in Canada or elsewhere, before it sells, distributes, exposes or offers for sale the product in question, it will not be in violation of section 27(2) of the Copyright Act.

[5] This brings us to the second issue, which is the manner in which the packaging can be rendered non-infringing. ...

[6] The only evidence on point is in the form of the affidavit of André Clemence, Euro Excellence's president. After consulting with a printing company, he proposes to cover up the copyright material with a self-sticking plastic film. The film would be translucent but the part which covers the Toblerone bear within a mountain and the Côte d'Or elephant would be opaque. At the hearing four prototypes were filed covering the Toblerone 100 gram bar, the Côte d'Or INTENSE 100 gram and 10 gram bars, and the Côte d'Or 47.5 gram banana snack bar.

[7] Kraft's concern is that the plastic film could be removed, say by a retailer who wanted to demonstrate he was selling the genuine product.

[8] It was left to me in open court to try and remove the plastic film. I could not remove the film with my fingernails. Perhaps it could be scraped away with a knife or other tool, or steamed off. I don't know why anyone would want to go to such trouble, or what shape the bear and elephant would be in after such an ordeal. Three of the four bars passed the test.[25]

Act III: Section 27(2)(e) of the Copyright Act

Strictly speaking, there is no right of importation. Section 3(1) of the Copyright Act contains a long list of prerogatives enjoyed by the rightholder, but does not comprise the right to import. One has to venture into the civil remedy section of the Act, and more precisely section 27(2)(e), to find it. A civilian would immediately interpret this distinction as conferring a special status to the right to prevent unauthorized import. It is, in fact, more of the nature of a remedy than that of a right, which would considerably restrict its scope and force. At the very least, it underlines its specificity, or perhaps an anachronism, as copyright law does not traditionally venture into the domain of the circulation of goods. True, some noticeable intrusions of copyright in the realm of distribution have recently been observed. For example, two specific distribution rights have been added in recent years to the list of substantial rights under section 3(1) for libraries: the right to rent out copies of software programs (article 3(1)(h)) and to rent out sound recordings (article

---

[25] Kraft Canada Inc. v. Euro Excellence Inc., 2004 F.C. 832 at paras. 4–8, [2004] F.C.J. No. 1015 [Kraft motion].

3(1)(i)). As they are exceptional in nature, these specific rights reaffirm rather than contradict the limits of copyright protection conveyed by the first-sale principle now enshrined in the new article 3(1)(j). What makes the copyright infringement recourse under 27(2)(e) so peculiar is that it is deprived of any fraudulent or intentional elements. In fact, it challenges the idea of infringement itself, such that the definition of infringement had to be adjusted to fit its extraordinary purpose. In fine and rather uneasy language, the definition of "infringement" specifies that it "includes a copy that is imported in the circumstances set out in paragraph 27(2)(e) and section 27.1 but does not otherwise include a copy made with the consent of the owner of the copyright in the country where the copy was made."[26] In fact, the activities captured by section 27(2)(e) are inherently at odds with copyright, and actually so much so that the law must rely on a hypothetical test to establish the condition of an otherwise improbable infringement situation. The importation remedy belongs to the indirect infringement class of actions and holds a unique place within it. To succeed under an indirect infringement claim, one must establish primary infringement, i.e. an act made in violation of one of the rights contemplated under 3(1) of the Act. Importation is an exception. As the Court of Appeal rightly noted, "primary infringement of copyright need not be proven in the case of paragraph 27(2)(e) of the Act."[27] The infringement it presupposes is not real, nor actual. It is an imaginary situation featuring a hypothetical maker. The importation remedy represents one of the greatest fictions of law. It posits that infringing is the importation of a copy of a work, which, if it had been made in Canada by the person who made it abroad, would constitute an infringement of the reproduction right of the Canadian rightholder:

> (2) It is an infringement of copyright for any person to
>   (a) sell or rent out,
>   (b) distribute to such an extent as to affect prejudicially the owner of the copyright,
>   (c) by way of trade distribute, expose or offer for sale or rental, or exhibit in public, ... or
>   (e) import into Canada for the purpose of doing anything referred to in paragraphs (a) to (c), a copy of a work, sound recording or fixation of a performer's performance or of a communication signal that the

---

[26] Copyright Act, R.S.C 1985, c. C-42 s. 2 "Infringement," *available at* http://laws-lois.justice.gc.ca/eng/acts/C-42/, [Copyright Act].

[27] Kraft FCA, *supra* note 12, at 59.

person knows or should have known infringes copyright or would
infringe copyright if it had been made in Canada by the person who
made it.[28]

Motives are immaterial since knowledge by the importer of the violation
is not a defense. As per section 27(2)(3), "knowledge of the importer"
indicates that:

> in determining whether there is an infringement under subsection (2) in the
> case of an activity referred to in any of paragraphs (2)(a) to (d) in relation to
> a copy that was imported in the circumstances referred to in paragraph (2)(e),
> it is irrelevant whether the importer knew or should have known that the
> importation of the copy infringed copyright.[29]

Act IV: Interpretation of Section 27(2)(e)

The courts below adopted a strict textual interpretation of the Act and the
licenses supporting Kraft's arguments. They moved away from any policy
considerations, rejecting most of our arguments as too philosophical,
teleological, and tended towards policy considerations. "I have found in
Kraft's favor," writes Justice Harrington, "because I think the Copyright
Act compels me to."[30] The Court of Appeal, in a rather lean opinion,
concurred. Once originality in the logos was found, the application of the
importation provision seemed perfectly logical. There was admittedly, as
the text requires, importation for the purpose of sale of a copy of a work.
The maker of the Côte d'Or chocolate was Kraft Belgium, and, had the
company made the copy of the work in Canada, it would have directly
impinged on the exclusive right to produce and reproduce the work
contractually granted to Kraft Canada by license. The nature of the
hypothetical infringement caused by the hypothetical maker was chal-
lenged and discussed before the Court of Appeal, but without insistence
as it diverted the Court from the central issue: the legitimacy of the
action itself. The exclusive license, we argued, could not establish the
grounds for the infringement sought under 27(2)(e) because the making
of copies by the licensor would defeat the very purpose of the license
itself which, subsidiarily, had no other function than to engage the
copyright protection. The mere fact that all products were packaged and

---

28 Copyright Act, *supra* note 26.
29 Copyright Act, *supra* note 26, at 27(2)–(3).
30 Kraft FC, *supra* note 12, at 61.

manufactured in Europe by the Kraft mother companies showed the true nature of the licensing arrangement with Kraft Canada. This arrangement was in essence an exclusive distribution agreement of products and not of copies of a work. Québec courts had already unmasked and re-qualified what it called such "contrived" or "devious" arrangements.[31]

Kraft Belgium could not make the chocolate (an act implied by the license obtained by Kraft Canada to produce and reproduce the work "Elephant") in Canada for the simple reason that it was sold as chocolate made in Belgium – even the wrapper was printed in Europe. Our defense on this point, admittedly, had little chance to succeed. The test of 27(2)(e) after all referred to a hypothetical situation. The reality was that we knew at the time there was a flaw in the plaintiff's argument and in Justice Harrington's reasoning: a breach of a license does not necessarily constitute an infringement. We did not push the argument further as we knew that the change from a license to an assignment, a simple change of wording, would have solved this point. We knew this because Kraft used an assignment and not an exclusive license in the Volkswagen case. This lacuna became the focal point of the opinion in the Supreme Court decision. The distinction between a breach and an infringement ultimately disposed of the case and, as anticipated, reopened a new case a few months later, but this time Kraft Canada, having learned its lesson, was named assignee of the copyright in the logo. We strived before all the courts to move away from the contractual conundrum for obvious reasons: we wanted the court to decide the issue on abuse of right, a principled base doctrine of civil law origin and which has made its way as a spreading and promising doctrine in the U.S.

The courts remained deaf to our arguments, refusing to venture outside the rigid and two-dimensional texture of the law and leaving the difficult decision of the ambit and role of copyright law and congruent matters to Parliament. Justice Harrington's words, filled with obedient and unnecessary deference, are truly remarkable: "Since copyright is a creature of statute, and the rights and remedies provided for in the Act are exhaustive, and given my view of the compelling language of the Act, it is not strictly necessary to mention the arguments advanced as to what the law ought to be."[32] This petition against court interventionism is a reaction of our insistence to embrace a more difficult role, that of interpreter and not simply reader of the law.

---

[31] Maison du Livre Français, De Montréal, Inc. v. Institut Littéraire du Québec Ltee, 31 CPR 69 73, 73–74 (1957).

[32] Kraft FC, *supra* note 12, at 61.

The Court of Appeal, with little effort, upheld the decision rendered by Justice Harrington, acceding to Kraft's demands. The Federal Court of Appeal expedited the matter swiftly without adding much to the analysis:

[R]eproductions of protected works that are made outside Canada, even by the copyright holders KFB (Kraft Belgium for Côte d'Or) and KFS (Kraft Schweiz, for Toblerone), may not be imported into Canada by Euro Excellence for the purpose of doing anything referred to in paragraphs 27(2)(a) to (c), without there being a secondary infringement of KCI's copyright, because KCI (Kraft Canada) has an exclusive right of reproduction for Canada, even as against KFB and KFS, and Euro Excellence knew that KCI's exclusive rights in the two works had been registered for Canada.[33]

By the day the Court of Appeal judgment was published, the situation for the defendant and his president had become dire. I had, as principal legal representative, been defeated twice before the courts judging on the merits of the case and countless times in motions and interlocutory proceedings. If *"impossible was not French,"* in the words of Napoleon, the task of pleading on high principles in statutory cases was Herculean. Later, I had the opportunity to share my experience with the protonotary sitting on many of the unsuccessful motions I had brought forward before the Federal Court. He admitted that the arguments underpinning my pleading – that of misuse of copyright law – intimidated the Court. Ill-at-ease with the case I was making, the Court simply retracted.

We sought leave to appeal before the Supreme Court of Canada. The most fundamental issue was left unanswered: does the plaintiff's use of copyright law constitute an abuse of right?

III JOURNEY TO THE SUPREME COURT

Scene I: Copyright Perplexity and Diversion

The hearing took place in Ottawa on February 16, 2007.[34] Since we received judgment granting leave to appeal in the interim, the Supreme Court had given two interveners the right to make written representations: the Retail Council of Canada (RCOC) and the Canadian Association of Manufacturers and Exporters (CAME). The former joined the ranks of the appellant, Euro-Excellence. When presenting our case, we

---

33   Kraft FCA, *supra* note 12, at 60.
34   Euro-Excellence Inc. v. Kraft Canada Inc. SCC Docket 31327, *available at* http://www.scc-csc.gc.ca/case-dossier/cms-sgd/dock-regi-eng.aspx?cas=31327.

considerably sharpened our arguments to explain in simple language why the court should seize this opportunity to discuss the abuse of right theory. We felt it was important to abandon other grounds we deemed less amenable to this objective. In particular, we departed from the contractual argument as we knew that this avenue would ultimately result in Kraft changing its licensing scheme in order to reinstitute a similar claim – which it did. Unfortunately for our discipline perhaps, the RCOC insisted in alleging that Kraft Belgium of Kraft Schweiz, the makers, lacked the necessary proprietary interests to enjoy the remedy contemplated under 27(2)(e) of the Act. The division or bisection of arguments on the Euro-Excellence side led to a split decision and no consensus. While we urged the court to consider natural or social justice principles, an open invitation to intervene in policy matters, our allies, the RCOC, relied on strict or literal interpretation of the statute. They submitted that the decisions of the lower courts were faulty not in the approach chosen by the judge, but simply by deciding wrongly on the issue of the hypothetical infringement. The Court was left without direction, and its fragmented judgment, which sets aside the question of abuse, clearly reflects its hesitations. The case was decided by a fragile majority on contractual grounds. Writing for the Court, Justice Rothstein writes:

[22] On the facts of this case, the Kraft companies have not made out all of the constitutive elements of a claim under s. 27(2)(e). Hypothetical infringement has not been established. The Kraft companies cannot prove that the impugned works imported and distributed by Euro-Excellence would have infringed copyright if the persons who made them in Europe had made them in Canada.

[23] The persons who made the impugned copies of the works in Europe were the Kraft parent companies, KFB and KFS. However, KFB and KFS would not have infringed copyright if they had produced the Côte d'Or and Toblerone logos in Canada.

[24] This is because KFB and KFS are, respectively, the owners of the Canadian copyright in the Côte d'Or and Toblerone logos. On the Kraft companies' argument, KFB and KFS would be the hypothetical copyright infringers. The Kraft companies argue that KFB and KFS would have infringed copyright if they produced the copyrighted works in Canada because they had licensed the Toblerone and Côte d'Or copyrights to Kraft Canada. Accepting this argument would mean that KFB and KFS have infringed their own copyrights – a proposition that is inconsistent with copyright law and common sense. Under s. 27(1), infringement arises when a person, without the consent of the owner, does something that under the Act

only the owner has the right to do. By definition, no person can simultaneously be owner and infringer of copyright.[35]

Dissenting, Justices Abella and McLachlin concurred with the Court of Appeal, refusing to render the application of section 27(2)(e) contingent on the transfer of ownership to the benefit of the Canadian rightholder. In their views, an exclusive license would be sufficient to vest in the licensee a copyright interest it can set up against its own licensor. If the latter were to impinge on the terms and conditions of the license, it would infringe in the meaning of the Act. Applied to the case at hand, the foreign owner of copyright – the makers – would not only breach their contractual obligations, they would also infringe the licensee's copyright. "In other words," concludes Justice Abella, "when the owner-licensor transfers an interest to the exclusive licensee, that licensee becomes, under the Act, the owner of a defined interest in the copyright."[36]

The discussion regarding the nature of the interest established and transferred by license occupied the center stage of the Supreme Court judgment and, as we anticipated, eclipsed the most fundamental question in law. It diverted the Court. A further remark is worth making. This case, an appeal from Québec, put on display two vibrant legal cultures and traditions. I pleaded in French, my friends in English. I exposed legal principles, called upon the functions and limits of the rights, their texture. My friends, on the other hand, descended into the details of the text, focusing on its microscopic variations in every subparagraph. My arguments must have been perceived as philosophical, if not metaphysical. My opponents' were technical. Civil law was meeting the common law on its own ground, and it shook. The two worlds do occasionally collide: in another famous Canadian copyright case, *Théberge v. Galerie d'art du Petit Champlain*,[37] the Court split perfectly along the dividing line separating the two legal traditions. The dissent was all civilian, while the majority was composed of common law lawyers.

Scene II: The Missing Points

By remaining fixated on the text, the Court fell short of addressing some issues raised in the factum. Two in particular would have deserved a better treatment. The first refers to a variation of what was known as the principle of accession under Roman law: accessory follows the principal.

---

[35] Kraft SCC, *supra* note 1, at 22–24.
[36] *Ibid.* at 120.
[37] Théberge, *supra* note 5.

Applied to the situation at hand, the argument is compelling. As a general rule, the law should only see the distribution of a product and not of a work when the latter is only a marketing or informational accessory to the good. It simply forbears the exercise of copyright. The argument was successfully made in a South African case brought by the exclusive distributor of blank TDK audio tapes against a parallel importer. The distributor, Frank & Hirsch, obtained the copyright by written assignment from the manufacturer of said blank cassette in "certain original artistic and literary works within the meaning of the Copyright Act of the Republic of South Africa No. 98 of 1978 in the nature of packaging, inserts, covers and the like for audio cassette and video cassette tapes."[38] The Court of First Instance found against the exclusive distributor on the ground that once the "certain original works" had been incorporated into the product as sold, they merged into the product and ceased to have an independent existence, which resulted in the packaged tapes no longer being copies of the original works. To the question,

> [w]hat is the position, though, if a physical reproduction of the work by *accessio* becomes part of a principal thing so that the thing thus made is not a reproduction, publication or adaptation of the work but a different thing altogether and what if such a physical reproduction of the work together with other physical things by *specificatio* becomes a new thing or article?

The first judge answers:

> It seems to me that the answer to this question must be that it is not an article the making of which constitutes an infringement if only the making of an accessory part of the article which has been made constituted an infringement. If the Legislature had meant to refer to such articles, it should have said so, e.g. by referring to an article or any part thereof. To hold otherwise would mean that the importer of a car which has components such as shock absorbers of another manufacturer fitted, upon which literary or artistic work is printed or painted, could be infringing copyright and be prohibited from importing the car.[39]

In 1993, the Court of Appeal disagreed and reversed the judgment, judging that it misplaced "[t]he reliance on the concepts of accessio and specificatio."[40]

---

[38] Frank & Hirsch (Pty.) Ltd. v. A Roopanad Brothers (Pty.) Ltd., [1993] I.P.R. 29 at 467 [Frank & Hirsch].

[39] *Ibid.* at 474 (cited by the Court of Appeal overturning the Court below). *See also* Exxon Corp. v. Exxon Ins. Consultants Int'l Ltd., [1982] R.P.C. 69.

[40] *Ibid.* at para. 33.

The argument was made once again before the Supreme Court of Canada. The copyrighted "Elephant" or "Bear in the Mountain" constituted only a *de minimis* or accessory part, at least quantitatively, of the product itself. During the hearing, the Court sought direction from the attorneys as to what was the real market or value of the wrapper displaying the artwork. This interrogation led to examining the relationship or overlap between trademark law, whose value is in capturing and securing the goodwill attached to the brand, and copyright law, whose beneficiaries are the authors or its assignees and the public. When one considers the nature and destination of the product, a chocolate bar, it becomes obvious that, even if we admit that a work eligible of protection is embedded in it, it should not follow that what is sold or distributed is a copy of a work. The lower courts clearly did not perceive the distinction as they were too busy making sense not of the law, but of its textual sophistication. The factum filed by the RCOC, written under the expert hand of Howard Knopf, perfectly articulated this point:

> S. 27(2)(e) refers to "copy of a work." However, the Respondent "strategy" consisted of arranging for licenses in the "Mountain" and "Elephant" artwork that clearly comprised only a portion of the product packaging. Quite apart from the artificiality of this "strategy", the packaging simply is not a copy or reproduction in an actionable way of the original art work – because that art forms only a part of a much larger "separate and distinct artistic work" – namely the packaging as whole – which in turn serves a very different purpose.[41]

The Supreme Court, in the words of Justice Rothstein, dismissed what he called the "incidental approach." It is, he posits, "skill and judgment – not the size of the work – that determines whether a work receives protection under the Copyright Act."[42]

---

[41] Kraft SCC, *supra* note 1 (Factum of the Intervener Retail Council of Canada at para. 28) (unpublished).

[42] *See quoted* J. Finlay, *Copyright Law: An Inappropriate and Ineffective Way to Control Distribution, in* COPYRIGHT REFORM 151–59 (H. Knopf ed., Insight Press, 1996).

> Distribution and marketing issues do not belong in a copyright act, it is not appropriate use of the copyright law. The free market place is a much more effective tool to resolve distribution and marketing issues. The historical development of the International Berne Convention on Copyright has, to this date, not supported the extension of copyright to distribution issues, and several proposals to add this right have been rejected.

The Court also felt it necessary to adequately frame the importation provision within its historical and economic context. If the modern iteration of the importation mechanism originates from the English Copyright Act of 1911, it had long been a subject matter of a legislation destined to regulate the book trade. The Australian Copyright Law Review Committee released a remarkable report on the history of the importation provision in Australian law, tracing its origin back to the early attempts to fight piracy. More on point, the reporters also concluded that:

> [a]lthough it is obvious that piracy is as old as copyright protection, the conception of what constitutes "unlawfully made" articles has changed over time. At one time unlawfully copied books included all books reproduced outside of England. Under present copyright laws the status of copied articles as unlawful is determined by the laws in the country of manufacture and the international relationship [of] that country with the country of importation. But, the older view that articles produced outside the country are unlawful has been maintained, to varying degrees, by the subterfuge of imposing a hypothetical place of manufacture on articles sought to be imported by persons other than the copyright owner.[43]

The test of the hypothetical maker received various interpretations in the English common law world leading to a mosaic of solutions amongst countries who implemented it. The English provision, as received in the former colonies, created the remedy for secondary infringement when copies of a work legitimately made abroad would have infringed copyright if, hypothetically, they had been made in the country of importation. But this provision, left open-ended until it was clarified, would achieve different results depending on who one considers to be the "maker." If the maker were the importer itself, virtually all importers would infringe the copyright absent a license to import. A similar conclusion would arise in cases where the maker was deemed to be the general public. These two positions lead to the rejection of international exhaustion. However, should the hypothetical maker be the maker of the legitimate copy abroad, international exhaustion would operate if the maker is the owner of the copyright in both countries, that of exportation and that of importation. In the Canadian context, the importation provision is aimed at encouraging the domestic making – manufacturing and printing – of books published abroad through copyright arrangement with foreign publishers. The law hence requires that the copyright owners in the

---

[43] IMPORTATION PROVISIONS AUS, *supra* note 19, at Appendix D – The Importation Provisions of the Copyright Act 1968 – A Historical and Comparative Analysis.

country of importation and exportation not be the same. Canada amended its legislation to this effect in 1997 to reflect this policy. First, it added section 27.1 to the Act, expanding the benefit of the importation provision to the exclusive distributors of books.[44] The mere fact that distributors enjoyed a special status highlights, in my opinion, the fact that distributors should not otherwise enjoy copyright protection. Secondly, the precision "had been made in Canada by the person who made it" was added to focus on the legal entitlement of the foreign manufacturer in Canada. If the latter has not departed from its copyright by assignment to a Canadian entity for the production of copies of a work, the Act provides the necessary remedy to prevent the importation of the copies into the Canadian market.

The Supreme Court judgment is certainly consistent with the political and historical developments of the importation provision, but the Court failed to recast its narrative in its continuum. There can also be no infringement, concluded the Supreme Court of Canada, where the actual maker has granted a license, even an exclusive license, to a Canadian entity, because, as Rothstein reiterated, the copyright owner cannot infringe its own copyright. But one has to look at the history of the provision to understand how significant it has been for countries who were importers of cultural goods. Until the early twentieth century, most countries were dependent upon the importation of books and later of vinyl as avid readers demanded international bestsellers while the local market was still emerging. It was clear to Parliament that, in order to promote the Canadian publishing industry and avoid the economic consequences of market asymmetries, priority and protection should be given to Canadian exclusive distributors and assignees of foreign publishers, again, asserting that books and other works should be made in Canada by Canadians.

IV FROM ABUSE OF RIGHTS TO MISUSE OF INTELLECTUAL PROPERTY RIGHTS

A   A Cornerstone of the Civil Law System

The doctrine of abuse of right is the coat of arms of private law in the civilian systems, its badge of honour. One of the earliest definitions

---

[44] Copyright Act, *supra* note 26, at S.27.1(4) ("an exclusive distributor is deemed, for the purposes of entitlement to any of the remedies under Part IV in relation to an infringement under this section, to derive an interest in the copyright in question by license").

comes from Porcherot at the turn of the twentieth century, writing "on abuse de son droit quand, restant dans ses limites, on vise un but différent de celui qu'a eu vue le législateur."[45] The new Civil Code of Québec proudly wears it under its article 7: "No right may be exercised with the intent of injuring another or in an excessive and unreasonable manner which is contrary to the requirements of good faith."[46] However, for those familiar with its legal historiography, and even for the most devoted servant of the civil law tradition, it remains an enigmatic spell, a powerful legal artifice which still today continues to attract, distract, and repulse. Ripert, an eminent French scholar and opponent of the abuse of right theory, describes it as a pure logomachy. Given its emphasis on the social function of rights, the doctrine would create a great deal of uncertainty in its application. In an open letter rejecting the theory he writes, "[a]ll the same, a vague sociological formula is not enough for the legal mind."[47]

Constantly under attack, the doctrine is, however, still alive and well. Evidence of this is the constant flow of literature expanding over its recurrent case law. The fascination of scholars for it, sometimes mixed with discomfort, balances the barristers' interests and hesitations to plead it. It is, for all intents and purposes, a residual and exceptional defense which applies indifferently to contract or property law. It often constitutes the ultimate card of a deck of legal mechanisms. The doctrine of abuse of right challenges our understanding of the law and the definition of right. It questions the very sense of entitlement, and our ability to act within our private sphere with impunity. It also brings within its purview the undisciplined and difficult idea of attributing a social function to a defined right, a right granted by statute for its exclusive enjoyment. This right, guaranteed by the state and vested in a legal person, being a natural person or a corporation, allows its holder the "*sujet de droit*" to emancipate itself in a free society. He or she will exercise all the prerogatives provided expressly by the law for its private interest, without constraints or state intervention, as long as he or she remains in the limits

---

[45] ERNEST PORCHEROT, DE L'ABUS DE DROIT 215 (L. Venot 1901). *See generally* P.E. Moyse, *L'anténorme : essai sur une théorie de l'abus en propriété intellectuelle, Partie I*, 57 McGILL L.J. 861 (2012) and *Part II*, 58 McGILL L.J. 3 (2012).

[46] Art. 7 CCQ.

[47] Georges Ripert, *Abus ou relativité des droits*, 49 REV. CRIT. LÉG. ET JUR. 33, 44 (1929) [Ripert]. For Josserand's response, *see* Louis Josserand, *À propos de la relativité des droits : Réponse à l'article de M. Ripert*, 49 REVUE CRITIQUE DE LÉGISLATION ET DE JURISPRUDENCE 277 (1929).

set by the law. There should be no wrongdoing, in principle, for an act otherwise accomplished legally, i.e. in compliance with the written prescription of the law. The theory of abuse of right challenges this proposition though. Tort can still be found when a right, defined by law, is taken too far. The wrong, however, is not to be found in the preconditions of the right as spelled out in the legislation – i.e. a statute – but in its realization. Hence, from a purely formalist point of view, the rightholder is simultaneously in compliance with the law and infringing it. To escape this apparent contradiction, one has to distinguish between the law in its textual expression and the Law, its metaphysical aspiration: the spirit of the rights. Under the abuse of right doctrine, all rights are relative. None are absolute. The rightholder's actions are reviewable by the courts and open to damages because they are contrary to the specific social function assigned to the right being misused. The discussion on abuse of right took place at the turn of the nineteenth century in Germany and in France. It announced the end of a certain formal, and at times too simplistic, legal rationality – early positivism – and opened onto a more modern and sophisticated set of normative and interpretative methods aimed at adjusting the law to address the increasingly complex socio-economic reality. It supports the instrumental or teleological methods. The first wave of French scholars interested in developing legal theories able to answer the multitude of new challenges posed by the post-industrial revolution were part of a group of intellectuals later called "*les juristes inquiets*." The doctrine of abuse of right marked a departure from legal classicism; it was the *nouvelle vague* in legal scholarship. It reintegrates the ideas of duties within the notion of right. It was mainly the lack of flexibility of the Napoleonic Code and its allegedly individualistic traits that prompted Josserand, "*maitre à penser*" to this abuse of right movement, and the group of "*juristes inquiets*" to revisit the theoretical foundations of the law.[48] They strove for a new legal and social order at a time of instable governments and heavy industrialization. Above all, they wanted to give private law the same social importance as the rising public and constitutional law. It was felt that the traditional formal legal thinking was not able to provide enough flexibility; ossification of the whole private law was looming in stark contrast to widespread social changes. Hayek would later condemn, in more extreme terms, the Cartesian method, the adoption of which influenced greatly the

---

[48]   Duncan Kennedy and Marie-Claire Belleau, *La Place de René Demogue dans la généalogie de la pensée juridique contemporaine,* 56 REV INTERDISCIPL ET JUR 163, 174 ff (2006); LOUIS JOSSERAND, DE L'ESPRIT DES DROITS ET DE LEUR RELATIVITÉ: THÉORIE DITE DE L'ABUS DES DROITS (Dalloz 2nd ed., 2006).

exegesis school and the codification projects.[49] Critics of the old classicism demanded a new method which would reconsider the role of the judiciary power in interpreting statutes in order to adjust the rights to a new reality. Law could not be read from a calcified or anachronistic text, transfixed by the overriding social movements. The courts, in the opinion of abuse of rights theorists, must attribute social functions to agnostic prescriptions when need be. For Geny, a contemporary of Josserand and one of the "worried," whose work influenced the great American jurists, the notions of social responsibility and the role of the Courts in making the law were central. For him, as for Josserand, entrusting the courts with this new responsibility to guard rights from being abused or hijacked necessarily implied a recalibration of the division of powers to the advantage of the judiciary.[50] So true is this statement that Josserand's theory would later be described as *"positivisme jurisprudentiel,"* or jurisprudential positivism. The Code ceased to be the sacred codex, as it ceased to be complete. It was felt, as it is now felt in assessing the intellectual property texture, that legislative enactments were too encumbered with details and undesirable sophistications. The exegesis task that fell upon the interpreter was the new Bastille, a jail made up of words. At the same time, the meta-norm of the "social," cultivated in the emerging field of sociology, would, it was advocated, ensure robust and unimpaired progress through innovative law. The seminal case on abuse of rights in French law, the Clement-Bayard spite and fence case decided in 1917 by the Cour de Cassation, symbolized the triumph of progress over the egoistic intention of an individual. The Court concluded that the installation of a 16-metre-high fence on one's property, topped by metal spikes, in order to harm the neighbour's operation of a landing ground for dirigibles, amounted to an abuse of ownership. This was notable despite ownership being defined in the Code, under article 544 of the French Code, as an absolute right.[51]

---

[49]   F.A. HAYEK, LAW, LEGISLATION AND LIBERTY: A NEW STATEMENT OF THE LIBERAL PRINCIPLES OF JUSTICE AND POLITICAL ECONOMY. RULES AND ORDER (University of Chicago Press 1973).

[50]   *See* FRANÇOIS GÉNY, MÉTHODE D'INTERPRÉTATION ET SOURCES EN DROIT PRIVÉ POSITIF: ESSAI CRITIQUE (Paris Librairie générale de droit et de jurisprudence 2nd ed., 1919); FRANÇOIS GÉNY, SCIENCES ET TECHNIQUE EN DROIT PRIVÉ POSITIF: NOUVELLE CONTRIBUTION À LA CRITIQUE DE LA MÉTHODE JURIDIQUE (Sirey 1921); RENÉ DEMOGUE, TRAITÉ DES OBLIGATIONS EN GÉNÉRAL (Rousseau ed., 1923).

[51]   Case Coquerel v. Clément-Bayard DP 1917. 1. 79.

If the consensus was easily reached on the fact that law, like wine, needed to be oxygenized, the method or process by which such design could be achieved remained uncertain and ardently debated. The classic deductive techniques were admittedly limited techniques that started from and within the text, within the law. The law was always subservient to the text. A teleological conception of the law, however, claimed the proponents of the new doctrine would keep the text attuned to its socio and economic reality. Not surprisingly, the various articulations of the contemplated social norm will later be catalogued as reminiscent of the natural law movement. Alongside other theories that drew on the same ideal of a superior law,[52] the abuse of right defenders offered an attractive avenue for refocusing attention on the social project. Its success resides in part due to the eloquence of Josserand's thoughts exposed in its landmark work *"De l'abus des droits,"* first published in 1905. Its influence in civil law is a matter of controversy partly because Josserand's ambitious theory was never fully adopted. Josserand's conception went as far as to deny any force to a right used in a manner contrary to the social or economic interest regardless of the intent of its rightholder or whether the user acted reasonably or not. "The goal and purpose of the theory of abuse of rights," writes Josserand, "is to ensure that the spirit of the rights prevails, and so to guarantee justice not only in statutory instruments and abstract formulas, this being relatively easy, but, what is a more substantial ideal, in their very application and even in daily life."[53] In a civil law case from Québec confirming the availability and application of the doctrine in contractual matters, the Supreme Court of Canada explained that:

> despite the lofty goals of Josserand's theory, it is met with several criticisms. According to some critics, it ignores the distinction between the judiciary and the legislature. It is for the judge to apply the laws created by the legislative

---

[52] For example, *see* RUDOLF VON JHERING, THE STRUGGLE FOR LAW 5 (translated by John J. Lalor) (Callaghan and Company, 2nd ed. 1915):

> Our theory of law, it is only too easy to perceive, is busied much more with the scales than with the sword of justice. The one-sidedness of the purely scientific standpoint from which it considers the law, looking at it now so much as it really is, as an idea of force, but as it is logically, a system of abstract legal principles, has, in my opinion, impressed on its whole way of viewing the law, a character not in harmony with the bitter reality.

[53] LOUIS JOSSERAND, DE L'ESPRIT DES DROITS ET DE LEUR RELATIVITÉ 11 (Dalloz 2nd ed., 1939).

branch, and for the latter to determine which acts are "anti-social", whether in private or criminal law.[54]

Most civil law systems, including Québec, met Josserand's ambitions midway. They subjected the application of the doctrine to the test of "unreasonableness" or to the demonstration of excessive exercise of a right with the intent to cause injury. As the Supreme Court explained in *Houle*:

> the concept of a "bon père de famille" or the reasonable and prudent person is well known to Quebec civil law. Derived from the pater familias notion in Roman law, this standard, most often applied towards delictual liability, requires that an individual act in a manner which is [TRANSLATION] "ordinarily prudent and diligent."[55]

Thus, it is not surprising that the standard of "reasonableness" has made inroads into the doctrine of abuse of rights. This position was later codified under section 7 of the Civil Code of Québec in 1994.

By narrowing its scope, jurists were able to preserve an important civil principle: the primacy of the law as the overarching source of rights. But Josserand's rhetoric left a profound impact on private law scholarship. Rights as social norms have a function and cannot be used as a vehicle for purely egotistical purposes. The theory contributed to emancipating the courts and revealing their inherent powers to relay the legislation should the legislators defect. The idea was finally accepted that private law is not simply about coordinating private interests but rather creating mechanics or instruments involved in the greater social engineering. The presentation of the new doctrine, that of abuse of right and of the social function of the rights, required a subtle new rhetoric.

B   From Abuse of Rights to Intellectual Property Law

The doctrine of abuse of right could in theory support a rich right-based approach to many difficulties experienced in a field occupied by statutory law, such as intellectual property. In particular, it may serve as a curative mechanism to prevent the degeneration or excessive use of intellectual property rights. It may temper its pervasive properties and regulate what Josserand called the *"mésusages*," literally the "misuses." In other words,

---

[54]   Houle v. Canadian National Bank, [1990] 3 S.C.R. 122, 74 D.L.R. (4th) 577 [Houle].

[55]   JEAN-LOUIS BAUDOUIN, LA RESPONSABILITÉ CIVILE DÉLICTUELLE (Éditions Yvon-Blais Inc. 3rd ed., 1989), *cited in* Houle, *supra* note 52.

the abuse of right doctrine could be deployed to discipline intellectual property rights and even, perhaps, prevent intellectual property overlaps. The task of transplanting such a civil law concept in statutory law, like intellectual property, whose origins are found in English common law can prove to be daunting, if not unrealistic. Admittedly, the doctrine of abuse of right has had very little traction in the common law systems.[56] In its very best light, it is presented as an interesting relic of the civil law system, an archaeological artefact or anecdotal manifestation of a foreign system. Its incantations are heard in common law systems as a mysterious hymn from beyond. At worst, it is a useless metaphysical stench or socialist slogan of another age. The words of Gutteridge on the doctrine of abuse of right are emblematic of its rejection in common law and capture the profound disdain for its utility amongst common law lawyers:

> It would seem that the theory of abuse in its entirety is open to grave objections which fall under two headings. In the first place, as we have seen, it may get out of hand and result in serious inroads on individual rights, thus becoming an instrument of dangerous potency in the hands of the demagogue and the revolutionary. It resembles a drug which at first appears to be innocuous, but may be followed by very disagreeable after effects. Like all indefinite expressions of an ethical principle it is capable of being put to an indefinite variety of uses, and it may be employed to invade almost any sphere of human activity for the purpose of subordinating the individual to the demands of the State. It also furnishes a convenient pretext to recalcitrant debtors who may use it in order to shelter themselves behind a plea that creditors are acting oppressively; in fact it embodies a "slogan" which is perpetually on the lips of everyone who maintains that he ought not to be compelled to recognize a right which is vested in some other person.[57]

In France and in other civil law countries, the doctrine of abuse of rights has also been criticized and even rejected by some as an unacceptable limitation to individual liberties. Ripert, in his critic of Josserand's book

---

[56] *See quoted* D.J. Devine, *Some Comparative Aspects of the Doctrine of Abuse of Rights*, in B. Beinart, Acta Juridica (1964).

English Law has, in a series of cases consistently rejected a general doctrine of abuse of right such as exists in French Law. The need for such doctrine was obviated by existing rules of Common law, e.g. the law of nuisance, abuse of process, the tort of conspiracy, the rules concerning abuse of qualified privilege in defamation and the rules concerning fair comment as a defence in defamation.

[57] H.C. Gutteridge, *Abuse of Rights*, 5 CAMBRIDGE L.J. 22, 44 (1935). *See also* A. Di Robilant, *Abuse of Rights: The Continental Drug and the Common Law*, 61 HASTINGS L.J. 687 (2010).

De l'esprit des droits et de leur relativité (1927), echoed some of Gutteridge's impressions in addition to revealing the political tensions underlying the controversy:

> However, the absolutism of the individual right cannot be condemned in itself for it is the jural translation of the soul's desire to conquer power and liberty, and this desire is legitimate. The enjoyment in acquiring is of spiritual order and not of a material one. To disarm rightholders is to level down the society by destroying a necessary aristocracy.[58]

Not so long ago, proponents of the theory were accused of bolshevism. In fact, Josserand's doctrine is more modestly an objection to the imperialism of some individual interests. His concern was not so much the fabrication of a new and more accurate system; he would have felt quite content with the operations of the law as he observed them in his time if the law had offered satisfactory solutions. His proposal, put more simply and elegantly, was to put a corset on private law and repair some unacceptable manipulations. Abuse certainly implied a greater set of value, and his detractors were right to see in his doctrine the return of the volatile notion of moral justice into the austere chambers of the law, though only in rare and exceptional situations. The Josserand compromise, that of empowering the courts to ensure rights given to safeguard specific interests are not misused, was and remains in fact a minor displacement in the economy of private law. This, we argued, is the reason why the principle of abuse of rights should not be resisted or resented.

The *Kraft v. Euro-Excellence* case illustrates how a rehabilitated abuse of rights doctrine may take effect. We have already presented the case. We should now turn our attention to the concurring opinion delivered by Justice Bastarache who, in his reasons, uses notions and reasons with which Josserand himself would be in agreement. Justice Bastarache, joined by JJ. Charron and Lebel, allowed the appeal on strikingly different reasons than Justice Rothstein, who composed the majority opinion. The two judges argued openly in the decision itself as to what should be the appropriate view, with neither of them making a concession. Bastarache referred to the notion of "legitimate interest" in his opinion to reject the use of copyright on incidental work to cover chocolate distribution. In his introductory remarks, he commented:

---

[58]   Ripert, *supra note* 47, at 62. *See also* H.C. Gutteridge, *Abuse of Rights*, 5 CAMBRIDGE L.J. 22 (1935).

Can a chocolate bar be copyrighted because of protected works appearing on its wrapper? In particular, can s. 27(2) of the *Copyright Act*, R.S.C. 1985, c. C-42, which prohibits parallel importation into Canada of copyrighted works, be used by the respondent Kraft Canada Inc. to prevent the appellant, Euro-Excellence Inc., from, in the words of s. 27(2), importing, for the purpose of selling, renting, distributing or trading, genuine Toblerone and Côte d'Or chocolate bars into Canada, without obscuring the logos of those chocolate bars, on the basis that the logos are copyrighted? I conclude that it cannot. Both s. 27(2) and the *Copyright Act* as a whole are about the protection of copyrighted works, not about the importation and sale of consumer goods in general. The merely incidental presence of the copyrighted works on the wrappers of the chocolate bars does not bring the chocolate bars within the protections offered by the *Copyright Act*.[59]

One cannot fail to recognize in Bastarache's language a notion dear to Josserand himself, that of the "illegitimate motives" criterion proposed in his work to characterize the abuse. We, in fact, argued the case using the exact same notion. Copyright, in this case, is used by Kraft Canada for motives foreign to its legislative purposes. Rothstein immediately deflects Bastarache's arguments, which appear only as the third opinion in the judgment. This unusual setting allows us to speculate on Rothstein's initial role in the adjudication process. He may not have been the person initially sought to write the majority opinion. More importantly, the response by Rothstein directly addresses the role of the court in cases dealing with an objectionable use of the law. Here the debate opens against the backdrop of the separation of powers principles. And Justice Rothstein is prompt to raise his guard against any rampant forms of court activism. Immediately after the second paragraph of his opinion, Justice Rothstein delves into a lengthy section placed under the revealing title "Concerns." Justice Rothstein writes that "Bastarache J.'s approach in this case is inconsistent with this Court's approach to statutory interpretation," and while "the 'modern' or 'purposive' approach requires that the words of the statute 'in their grammatical and ordinary sense' be read harmoniously with the objects of the Act," it does not, however, give judges licence to substitute their policy preferences for those of Parliament. This Court has consistently held that "copyright is a creature of statute and the rights and remedies provided by the *Copyright Act* are exhaustive."[60] This is reminiscent of Ripert's attacks in his famous open letter to Josserand, written in 1929: "Si les tribunaux ont le droit souverain de limiter l'exercice des droits individuels, la règle de droit

---

[59]   *Kraft SC supra* note 12, at 57.
[60]   *Ibid.*, at 3.

s'efface." [61] The problem of encroachment on the legislative power is not ignored or avoided by Josserand. Common sense and a certain "*sentiment de justice*" allow the judiciary to intervene only in cases where, to borrow modern phraseology of evidence law, "justice would be brought in[to] disrepute." Josserand's criterion of "illegitimate interests," which envelops both subjective (motives) and objective elements (asocial behaviour), escapes all definitional attempt, and rightly so. The review process therefore operates haphazardly in the continuum between legislative and judiciary jurisdictions, an area where none of the institutions can claim exclusive power but which law has not deserted. It is the purgatory of all rights, the last checkpoint for normative assessment. If the texture of substantive law in common law is less amenable to the transplant of abuse of rights doctrine, since its fundamental constitution does not fully expand upon the "right" element, it is nevertheless well acquainted with the excesses caused by certain forms of positivism. This is why, quite logically, abuse of rights may translate itself as abuse of process in those systems where "right" is not used nor seen as a mechanism for social policy. If the "social" does not penetrate the substance of the law as easily as in civil law, it may well infiltrate the normative system through various other mechanisms. More generally, even if the common law is extremely liberal and prudent on the question of "motives," which clearly would stop short any discussion on subjective examinations of individual behaviours, various legal techniques or principles exist, in common law or in equity, to contain undesirable forms of individual absolutism.[62] Besides, the American misuse doctrine in intellectual property law is generally accepted as being based on equity.[63] But the task of civil law countries, operating in an unsettled social context, was greater in the sense that they had to both create stability in the textual exposition of rights and find a corrective mechanism to prevent abuse of private authority secured by said texts. As the common law relied principally on a praetorian system, the risk of distortion has never been great. Excesses were treated as wrongs, if anything, but only when substantial damages to personal property could be evidenced. A metaphysical approach,

---

[61] Georges Ripert, *Abus ou Relativité des droits, à pros de l'ouvrage de M. Josserand : De l'esprit des droits et de leur relativité, 1927*, 49 REV. CRIT. 33, 41 (1929).

[62] Joseph M. Perillo, *Abuse of Rights: A Pervasive Legal Concept*, 1 PAC. L.J. 37, 38 (1995) (A number of the maxims of equity suggest some similarity between the concept of abuse of right and equity).

[63] Kathryn Judge, *Rethinking Copyright Misuse*, 57 STAN. L. REV. 901 (2004).

steering towards social destination of rights, was not even envisioned: to English lawyers the term "right" has no metaphysical significance.[64] The system does not guarantee, through precepts or other prescriptive norms, any immunity or unlimited authority. However, as statutory law slowly invaded the primary form of common law conceived as unwritten rules, it began to take precedence. The structure of common law became more complex as its sources multiplied, and the systematic institutional endorsement by the legislative and regulatory bodies came to be comparable to continental codified law. This statement is particularly accurate in specialized laws, often derived but distinct from the *ius communis* in the traditional sense. Copyright law, it is often taught, is a complete code. And it is precisely in the shadow of legal ossification, an effect of the strict interpretation of written law, that the abuse of rights doctrine has emerged. Recent developments and the need to realign intellectual property law to policy objectives seem to converge towards the creation of a superior "social" norm.

V CONCLUSION

As seen in *Kraft Canada v. Euro-Excellence*, the Canadian federal courts have been apprehensive about importing the abuse of rights doctrine, a civil law notion, to limit statutory rights, rights born under common law heritage. While Canadian jurisprudence remains stagnant on this issue, our American compatriots have certainly been more vocal. The doctrine of misuse has slowly evolved and emerged as a serious contender on the list of anti-monopolistic principles and has led to important doctrinal work and influential opinions.[65] Historically, the American legal system

---

[64]   F.H. Lawson, *"Das subjektive Recht" in the English Law of Torts* 176, in F.H. Lawson, 1 MANY LAWS: SELECTED ESSAYS (North Holland 1977).

[65]   Assessment Tech. of WI LLC v. Wiredata Inc., 350 F.3d 640 (7th Cir. 2003) (Posner. J.); Thomas F. Cotter, *Misuse*, 44:4 HOUS. L. REV. 901 (2007); John T. Cross and P.K. Yu, *Competition Law and Copyright Misuse*, in A COPYRIGHT COCKTAIL 55 (Y. Gendreau, Les Éditions Thémis, 2007); Victoria Smith Ekstrand, *Protecting the Public Policy Rationale of Copyright: Reconsidering Copyright Misuse*, 11:5 COMM. L. & POL'Y 565 (2006), Cory Tadlock, *Copyright Misuses, Fair Use, and Abuse: How Sports and Meida Companies Are Overreaching their Copyright Protections*, 7:3 J. MARSHALL REV. INTELL. PROP. L. 621 (2008); Ilan Charnelle, *The Justification and Scope of the Copyright Misuse Doctrine and its Independence of Antitrust Laws*, 9:2 UCLA ENT. L. REV. 167 (2002); Aaron Xavier Fellmeth, *Copyright Misuse and the Limits of Intellectual Property Monopoly*, 1 J. INTELL. PROP. L. 1, 6 (1998).

has developed a right-based conception of law with the notion of *right* being the pivotal and political element to articulate and adjust natural rights of the individual and prerogatives of the State. Canadian federal law, with its roots in British common law, has had a much more difficult time *working* with the notion of rights, hence its resistance to developing an *abuse of right* doctrine. However, with its proximity to the civil law system, there is no reason why Canadian federal law could not receive tools borrowed from the civil tradition. Let us hope that Canada will take advantage of its *bijuridicism* to at least nourish the discussion on this topic. The *Kraft Canada v. Euro-Excellence* case is a timid debut, but at least it has started the discussion. Justice Bastarache has indeed set the stage, inviting the Court to leave the chapter on abuse of rights open:

> As with the concept of *abus de droit*, my analysis renders an appeal to this developing doctrine unnecessary to deal with parallel importation of consumer goods. However, this is not to comment on the possible application of this doctrine in Canada; a determination on that issue is best left for another day.[66]

---

[66]   Para. 98.

PART IV

(National) trademark enforcement challenges

11. Territoriality (mis)understood: enforcing well-known foreign marks in the United States

Lee Ann W. Lockridge[*]

I INTRODUCTION

In 2007, the Second Circuit flatly denied the existence of federal protection for well-known foreign marks. It did so – unfortunately – by both overstating and underappreciating the significance and function of territoriality in United States trademark law.[1] In 2004, on the other hand, the Ninth Circuit expressly held that well-known foreign marks are protected by federal law, although it, too, may not have adequately assessed territoriality or articulated the source of federal protection.[2] Since 2007, the Trademark Trial and Appeal Board ("T.T.A.B.") has largely adopted the Second Circuit view, at least for a traditional likelihood of confusion claim.[3] The divergence of authorities has muddied the water

---

[*]   David Weston Robinson Professor of Law, Louisiana State University Law Center. This chapter is adapted from the 2011 article, Lee Ann W. Lockridge, *Honoring International Obligations in U.S. Trademark Law: How the Lanham Act Protects Well-Known Foreign Marks (and Why the Second Circuit Was Wrong)*, 84 ST. JOHN'S L. REV. 1347 (2011).
[1]   ITC Ltd. v. Punchgini, Inc., 482 F.3d 135, 142 (2d Cir. 2007).
[2]   *See* Grupo Gigante SA de CV v. Dallo & Co., 391 F.3d 1088, 1098–99, 1109 (9th Cir. 2004).
[3]   *See, e.g.*, Bayer Consumer Care AG v. Belmora LLC, 89 U.S.P.Q. 2d 1587 (T.T.A.B. 2009) (dismissing a foreign mark owner's claim for cancellation based on confusion but refusing to dismiss its claim based on misrepresentation of source due to the registrant's copying of its foreign packaging). For further discussion of several post-*ITC* T.T.A.B. decisions, see Lee Ann W. Lockridge, *Honoring International Obligations in U.S. Trademark Law: How the Lanham Act Protects Well-Known Foreign Marks (and Why the Second Circuit Was Wrong)*, 84 ST. JOHN'S L. REV. 1347, 1377 n. 127 (2011).

with respect to the availability of protection in the United States for well-known foreign marks neither registered nor used in U.S. commerce.

This chapter, following a brief summary of the international obligations of the United States to protect well-known foreign marks, provides an account of U.S. judicial decisions related to the protection of well-known foreign marks. The focus then becomes the meaning and value of "territoriality" within trademark law – the issue ultimately driving the current split in the courts. "Territoriality" takes on different meanings and represents different interests depending on the context. In trademark law, this term can be a shorthand reference to the geographic or geopolitical areas where a mark is entitled to legal protection. In international law, on the other hand, "territoriality" is used in connection with the presumptive jurisdictional principle used as a starting point for determining the reach of a country's laws. As a result, how "territoriality" should be defined and applied in relation to a matter of international trademark law depends on the context. One facet of "territoriality" generally refers to use-based rights in the United States and is largely derived from an analysis of the likelihood of confusion, while the other facet has primarily international political connotations and results from the territorial scope of each nation's authority to govern.[4] In evaluating Lanham Act protection for a foreign mark, then, each facet deserves separate recognition and analysis. Future decisions sensitive to a deeper understanding of territoriality could yield outcomes in harmony with both U.S. trademark law and U.S. international obligations.

II U.S. TREATY OBLIGATIONS RELATED TO WELL-KNOWN TRADEMARKS

Protection for "well-known marks" is required under the Paris Convention for the Protection of Industrial Property (the "Paris Convention")[5] as well as the Agreement on Trade-Related Aspects of Intellectual Property

---

[4] *See* Graeme B. Dinwoodie, *Trademarks and Territory: Detaching Trademark Law from the Nation-State*, 41 HOUS. L. REV. 885, 888 (2004); *see also* Graeme W. Austin, *The Territoriality of United States Trademark Law*, *in* 3 INTELLECTUAL PROPERTY AND INFORMATION WEALTH: ISSUES AND PRACTICES IN THE DIGITAL AGE 235, 236–40 (Peter K. Yu ed., 2007).

[5] Paris Convention for the Protection of Industrial Property, art. 6*bis,* Mar. 20, 1888, 13 U.S.T. 2, 828 U.N.T.S. 107, as revised at Stockholm on July 14, 1967, 21 U.S.T. 1583, 828 U.N.T.S. 305 [hereinafter Paris Convention].

Rights (the "TRIPS Agreement")[6] and several other international agreements of which the United States is a member.[7] The basic Paris Convention obligation is to allow an "interested party" to intervene in a registration proceeding, to request cancellation of a registration, or to object to the use of a mark when that mark is identical or similar to a well-known foreign mark and used for identical or similar goods, if the domestic use is "liable to create confusion."[8]

The TRIPS Agreement extends this obligation to include service marks as well as trademarks.[9] It also expands protection beyond classic source-confusion theory by mandating that a country prohibit uses or registrations that would indicate a connection with the foreign owner and would likely damage the interests of that owner. A post-TRIPS, nonbinding multilateral agreement, the Joint Recommendation Concerning Provisions on the Protection of Well-Known Marks ("Joint Recommendation"), provides many factors for assessing well-known status within a nation, including prohibiting conditioning well-known status on domestic use, but it stops short of an agreed standard for the level of domestic knowledge.[10] While the Joint Recommendation is simply an agreed but nonbinding recommendation for most signatories, the United States has bound itself to it through at least one bilateral agreement, a free trade agreement with Singapore.[11] And in light of the most-favored-nation

---

[6]   Agreement on Trade-Related Aspects of Intellectual Property Rights, art. 16(2)–(3), Apr. 15, 1994, Marrakesh Agreement Establishing the World Trade Organization, annex 1C, art. 22.1, 108 Stat. 4809, 869 U.N.T.S. 299 (1994) [hereinafter TRIPS Agreement].

[7]   *See* North American Free Trade Agreement, U.S.–Can.–Mex., art. 1708(6), Dec. 17, 1992, 32 I.L.M. 605 (1993); General Inter-American Convention for Trademark and Commercial Protection, art. 7, Feb. 20, 1929, 46 Stat. 2907, 2918; *see also* sources cited *infra* note 11.

[8]   *See* Paris Convention, *supra* note 5, art. 6*bis*. A minimalist interpretation of the Paris Convention would not require protection without domestic *use* of the mark and would only mandate protection of a well-known mark in the absence of domestic *registration*. *See, e.g.*, Dinwoodie, *supra* note 4, at 912–13. The Lanham Act's provisions providing rights to used, but unregistered marks would comply with that minimum requirement. *See* 15 U.S.C. § 1125(a)(1)(A) (2006); Two Pesos, Inc. v. Taco Cabana, Inc., 505 U.S. 763, 768–69 (1992).

[9]   *See* TRIPS Agreement, *supra* note 6, art. 16(2)–(3).

[10] *See* World Intellectual Property Organization, Joint Recommendation Concerning Provisions on the Protection of Well-Known Marks, WIPO Doc. 833(E), Sept. 29, 1999 [hereinafter Joint Recommendation] art. 2(3).

[11] *See* Free Trade Agreement, U.S.–Sing., arts. 16.1(2)(b)(i), 16.2(4), May 6, 2003, 42 I.L.M. 1026 (containing a commitment to "give effect" to articles 1–6 of the Joint Recommendation and a provision nearly identical to article 16(3) of

treatment provision in the TRIPS Agreement,[12] the United States has agreed to extend to the nationals of all WTO member nations the advantages provided to Singaporean nationals under the binding bilateral agreement.[13]

Continued international variation on the standard for finding a mark to be "well known," albeit using agreed factors, means that U.S. decision-makers may set a high standard of knowledge before protecting a domestically unused well-known foreign mark. And if there is no legal basis for federal protection, then of course courts should not provide it. But courts should not, however, refuse to recognize or apply the well-known foreign marks doctrine simply on the basis of an inadequate assessment of the significance and function of "territoriality."

III A BRIEF HISTORY OF WELL-KNOWN FOREIGN MARKS IN THE UNITED STATES

Until 2004, the direct recognition of rights in well-known foreign marks – meaning foreign marks not used in the United States but with an extensive reputation in the relevant sector of the consuming public – had been most clearly embodied in two New York state trial court decisions from 1936 and 1959. In *Maison Prunier v. Prunier's Restaurant & Café*,

---

the TRIPS Agreement); *see also* Free Trade Agreement, U.S.–Jordan, art. 4(1)(a), Oct. 24, 2000, 2000 U.S.T. LEXIS 160 (similar to provision in agreement with Singapore). The United States also incorporated the Joint Recommendation into a nonbinding free trade agreement with Chile. *See* Free Trade Agreement, U.S.–Chile, art. 17.2(9), June 6, 2003, 42 I.L.M. 1026 ("recogniz[ing] the importance of" the Joint Recommendation and agreeing to be "guided by [its] principles").

12 TRIPS Agreement, *supra* note 6, art. 4.

13 *Accord* Graeme B. Dinwoodie, *Some Remarks on the Limits of Harmonization*, 5 J. MARSHALL REV. INTELL. PROP. L. 596, 603–604 (2006). While binding as between the contracting nations, neither the binding bilateral free trade agreements nor the TRIPS Agreement is directly effective in U.S. law. *See, e.g.*, United States–Singapore Free Trade Agreement Implementation Act, Pub. L. No. 108-78, § 102(a), 117 Stat. 948, 950 (2003); Uruguay Round Agreements Act, Pub. L. No. 103-465, § 102(a), 108 Stat. 4809, 4815 (1994); S. Rep. No. 103-412, at 13 (1994). Nevertheless, courts should proceed with caution before construing U.S. domestic law in a manner inconsistent with our international obligations. *See* Murray v. Schooner Charming Betsy, 6 U.S. (2 Cranch) 64, 118 (1804).

Inc.,[14] and in *Vaudable v. Montmartre, Inc.*,[15] the trial courts granted relief to owners of foreign marks either alleged or determined to be internationally famous and well known – but not used – in New York City. In each case, a junior user[16] in the city had opened a restaurant using both the name of and certain other indicia connected to a long-established Parisian restaurant, and the courts found the evidence in each case to indicate intentional copying. Both cases applied state law without referring to the "well-known marks" doctrine as such, and the courts did not reference Paris Convention article 6*bis*.[17] *Vaudable*, decided after the Lanham Act became effective, did refer to the Lanham Act generally to support its statement that "[t]he trend of the law, both statutory and decisional, has been to extend the scope of the doctrine of unfair competition."[18]

The doctrine recognizing well-known foreign marks thereafter remained relatively dormant for over forty years. It earned only sporadic references in T.T.A.B. and judicial decisions where it was mentioned in passing without forming the sole basis of any ruling.[19]

In late 2004, the Ninth Circuit issued the first in a flurry of well-known foreign marks decisions. Its decision in *Grupo Gigante SA de CV v. Dallo & Co.* allowed a foreign senior user of a mark to assert priority over a domestic junior user of a mark by relying on the mark's well-known status within a United States market area, based on use of the mark outside the United States.[20] Grupo Gigante operated a grocery

---

[14] Maison Prunier v. Prunier's Rest. & Café, Inc., 288 N.Y.S. 529 (N.Y. Sup. Ct. 1936) (granting temporary injunction barring use of "Prunier de Paris" and related indicia).

[15] Vaudable v. Montmartre, Inc., 193 N.Y.S.2d 332 (N.Y. Sup. Ct. 1959) (granting permanent injunction restraining defendants from using the "Maxim's" name and providing for ascertainment of damages).

[16] In this chapter users of marks are characterized as "senior" or "junior" according to worldwide seniority, rather than according to domestic seniority.

[17] The first case did refer to Paris Convention article 10*bis*. *See Maison Prunier*, 288 N.Y.S. at 532.

[18] *See Vaudable*, 193 N.Y.S.2d at 335.

[19] *See, e.g.*, Buti v. Impressa Perosa, S.R.L., 139 F.3d 98, 102–107 (2d Cir. 1998); Person's Co. v. Christman, 900 F.2d 1565, 1570–72 (Fed. Cir. 1990); Mother's Rests. Inc. v. Mother's Other Kitchen, Inc., 218 U.S.P.Q. 1046, 1048 (T.T.A.B. 1983). In *All England Lawn Tennis Club, Ltd. v. Creations Aromatiques, Inc.*, 220 U.S.P.Q. 1069, 1072 (T.T.A.B. 1983), the T.T.A.B. approved a famous-mark argument as an alternate ground for successfully opposing an application for the WIMBLEDON mark.

[20] Grupo Gigante SA de CV v. Dallo & Co., 391 F.3d 1088 (9th Cir. 2004).

store chain in Mexico under the store name "Gigante." The chain expanded from one Mexico City store in 1962 to almost one hundred stores by 1991, with six stores in the Baja area of Mexico, two of which were in Tijuana, on the U.S.–Mexican border near San Diego. The Mexican company operated no stores in the United States before 1999.

Dallo opened a grocery store in San Diego called "Gigante Market" in 1991, adding a second area store in 1996. In 1998 and 1999, the Dallos and Grupo Gigante began their legal skirmish, and Grupo Gigante sued for trademark infringement. The Ninth Circuit, upon reviewing the district court's judgment recognizing potential rights in a well-known foreign mark, began by holding that the well-known marks doctrine did exist in the United States:

> We hold … that there is a famous mark exception [which the Ninth Circuit equated with a well-known mark "exception"] to the territoriality principle. While the territoriality principle is a long-standing and important doctrine within trademark law, it cannot be absolute. An absolute territoriality rule without a famous-mark exception would promote consumer confusion and fraud. Commerce crosses borders. In this nation of immigrants, so do people. Trademark is, at its core, about protecting against consumer confusion and "palming off." There can be no justification for using trademark law to fool immigrants into thinking that they are buying from the store they liked back home.[21]

The Ninth Circuit did not specify where in the rather large body of federal trademark law it located this protection.[22]

In applying an "exception" for a well-known mark, allowing the foreign senior user of the mark to assert priority over a domestic junior user, the Ninth Circuit set what might be termed a "secondary meaning plus" standard for granting protection to well-known foreign marks.[23] It held that "where the mark has not before been used in the American market, the court must be satisfied, by a preponderance of the evidence, that a *substantial* percentage of consumers in the relevant American

---

[21] *Ibid.* at 1094.

[22] It did rely, almost certainly, on federal law, since it expressly rejected the plaintiff's alternative arguments based on California state law and on the Paris Convention. It stated that a direct claim under article 6*bis* would be duplicative of the Lanham Act claim. *Ibid.* at 1099.

[23] "Secondary meaning" means that consumers in the relevant market see a word, name, or symbol used in connection with goods or services and think first of the brand or source significance of the mark rather than the primary, or "dictionary" or other common meaning, of the word, name, or symbol.

market is familiar with the foreign mark."[24] The court expressly limited the relevant American market to the geographic area of the defendant's allegedly infringing use. The concurring opinion in *Grupo Gigante* agreed with the legal standard announced, but it also explained in some detail why the evidence available in the case did not meet that standard.[25]

Also in 2004, in *Empresa Cubana del Tabaco v. Culbro Corp.*, the Southern District of New York held that section 43(a) of the Lanham Act[26] provided protection to the owner of a foreign mark that was well known in the United States at the time the defendant adopted the mark. A Cuban cigar manufacturer was the senior user of the mark "Cohiba," but a junior user had registered the mark in the United States and had used it in connection with cigars at various times over a 15-year period before the immediate legal dispute had begun in earnest.[27] The court referenced the common law "well-known" or "famous marks" doctrine as well as article 6*bis* of the Paris Convention, and it adopted the view that the common law doctrine protecting well-known foreign marks had been incorporated into federal law through section 43(a).[28] The court referred to *Vaudable* and T.T.A.B. decisions referencing *Vaudable* in determining that the plaintiff "need only show that the COHIBA mark had a 'known reputation' to premium cigar smokers" at the time the defendant adopted the mark.[29] The court then looked to the Joint Recommendation for guidance in applying a standard for well-known marks to the facts before it. Upon deciding that the "Cohiba" mark was well known within the meaning of the doctrine, it found that the plaintiff senior user had a protectable right in the mark at the relevant time. The court found the junior use likely to cause confusion under section 43(a) and cancelled the junior user's registration.

When the *Empresa Cubana* case reached the Second Circuit, however, the senior user's victory proved short-lived. Although the court recognized and left open the possibility that well-known foreign marks were protected in the United States, it applied Cuban embargo regulations to

---

[24]   *Grupo Gigante*, 391 F.3d at 1098.
[25]   *Ibid.* at 1107 (Graber J., concurring).
[26]   15 U.S.C. § 1125(a) (2006) (providing a confusion-based action for infringement of an unregistered mark).
[27]   *See* Empresa Cubana del Tabaco v. Culbro Corp., No. 97 Civ. 8399, 2004 WL 602295 (S.D.N.Y. Mar. 26, 2004).
[28]   *Ibid.* at *29–30.
[29]   *Ibid.* at *33–34.

bar the plaintiff from using the doctrine to acquire trademark rights in the United States.[30]

In two 2005 decisions by different judges, the Southern District of New York again addressed the question of protecting well-known marks in the United States. The court in *ITC Ltd. v. Punchgini, Inc.*[31] assumed without deciding that such protection was available. It then stated that the owner of an allegedly well-known foreign mark must, at a minimum, demonstrate that the mark had secondary meaning for the foreign owner in the United States market at the time the junior use began. The court determined that the senior user of the "Bukhara" mark for restaurant services had not demonstrated the existence of secondary meaning in the relevant market of New York City. And despite the senior user's U.S. registration for its mark and previous use of the mark in U.S. commerce, the court found that the senior user had abandoned its U.S. rights after closing the restaurants at which the mark was used.

Six months later, in *Almacenes Exito S.A. v. El Gallo Meat Market, Inc.*,[32] a court expressly held – for the first time – that federal trademark law does not protect foreign marks that are well known but not used within the United States:

> To the extent the doctrine is a creature of common law it may support state causes of action, but it has no place in federal law where Congress has enacted a statute, the Lanham Act, that carefully prescribes the bases for federal trademark claims. The Lanham Act nowhere specifies the well-known or famous marks doctrine.[33]

---

[30] Empresa Cubana del Tabaco v. Culbro Corp., 399 F.3d 462, 480–81 (2d Cir. 2005).

[31] ITC Ltd. v. Punchgini, Inc., 373 F. Supp. 2d 275 (S.D.N.Y. 2005), *aff'd*, 518 F.3d 159 (2d Cir. 2008).

[32] Almacenes Exito S.A. v. El Gallo Meat Mkt., Inc., 381 F. Supp. 2d 324 (S.D.N.Y. 2005).

[33] *Ibid.* at 327 (citations omitted). The *Almacenes Exito* court interpreted the *Empresa Cubana* Second Circuit opinion as rejecting the argument that section 44(b) of the Lanham Act incorporated article 6*bis* protection for domestically unused marks. *See ibid.* at 328. This was, quite simply, incorrect – although it ultimately accurately predicted the Second Circuit's later holding in *ITC*. In *Empresa Cubana*, the Second Circuit *expressly left open* the possibility that federal protection would be available for well-known foreign marks. *See* Empresa Cubana del Tabaco v. Culbro Corp., 399 F.3d 462, 480–81 (2d Cir. 2005).

Although the court rejected a federal claim, it allowed the foreign senior user to proceed with its New York state law claims, relying on *Maison Prunier*.[34]

In 2007, when the Second Circuit issued its opinion in the *ITC* appeal, it created the circuit split that still exists today.[35] The court affirmed the district court's abandonment finding and refused to allow ITC recourse to the well-known foreign mark doctrine, based not on the plaintiff's inability to demonstrate knowledge of its "Bukhara" mark in the relevant market, but instead on the court's absolute rejection of the doctrine itself under federal law.[36]

In refusing to follow the only appellate decision on point, the Second Circuit accurately observed, "[i]n *Grupo Gigante*, the Ninth Circuit did not reference either the language of the Lanham Act nor [*sic*] Article 6*bis* of the Paris Convention to support recognition of the famous marks doctrine."[37] The court concluded that the Ninth Circuit had rested its decision solely on "sound policy."[38] The Second Circuit then endorsed the approach of the *Almacenes Exito* court, which deemed the well-known foreign marks doctrine an unacceptably "radical change in basic federal trademark law" due to its conflict with "the territoriality principle [which is] 'a bedrock principle of federal trademark law.'"[39] The court's assessment of the "territoriality principle" proceeded as follows:

> The principle of territoriality is basic to American trademark law. ... [T]his principle recognizes that a trademark has a separate legal existence under each country's laws, and that its proper lawful function is ... to symbolize the domestic goodwill of the domestic markholder so that the consuming public may rely with an expectation of consistency on the domestic reputation earned for the mark by its owner. ...

---

[34] *See Almacenes Exito*, 381 F. Supp. 2d at 328. In *Almacenes Exito*, the junior user adopted a precise copy of the senior user's EXITO mark – including design features. *Ibid.* at 326. The senior user operated the largest retail superstore chain in Colombia, as well as stores in Venezuela. *Ibid.* The junior user applied the mark to local supermarkets – featuring Latin American produce – in upper Manhattan and the Bronx, in predominantly Hispanic neighborhoods. *Ibid.*

[35] For an intervening case positively addressing protection for well-known foreign marks but withholding it on the facts, see *DeBeers LV Trademark Ltd. v. DeBeers Diamond Syndicate, Inc.*, 440 F. Supp. 2d 249 (S.D.N.Y. 2006).

[36] *See ITC Ltd. v. Punchgini, Inc.*, 482 F.3d 135, 142, 154 (2d Cir. 2007).

[37] *Ibid.* at 160.

[38] *Ibid.*

[39] *Ibid.* at 161 (quoting *Almacenes Exito*, 381 F. Supp. 2d at 326, 328).

> Precisely because a trademark has a separate legal existence under each country's laws, ownership of a mark in one country does not automatically confer upon the owner the exclusive right to use that mark in another country. ...
>
> As we have already noted, United States trademark rights are acquired by, and dependent upon, priority of use. The territoriality principle requires the use to be in the United States for the owner to assert priority rights to the mark under the Lanham Act.[40]

According to the court, the territoriality principle doomed all of the senior user's federal claims because the senior user had abandoned its federally registered rights by discontinuing domestic use before the junior use began.[41]

These disparate decisions create significant practical enforcement challenges for foreign trademark owners and raise the question of compliance with the international obligations of the United States – an interesting question in its own right.[42] Viewed from another angle, these decisions also evidence conflicting visions of the function of territoriality in trademark law for both foreign and domestic marks. The Ninth Circuit decision overstates the need for an "exception" to territoriality rather than fully integrating domestic and international principles.[43] The Second Circuit *ITC* decision – in the course of just three brief paragraphs setting forth the "territoriality principle" – moves quickly from international territoriality to domestic territorial priority and back again. It ultimately merges the two and then misapplies an oversimplified domestic rule of

---

[40]   *Ibid.* at 155 (internal quotations and citations omitted).

[41]   *Ibid.* at 154–65. The Second Circuit certified to the New York Court of Appeals two questions regarding New York state law protection of well-known foreign marks. *See ibid.* at 172. The New York high court answered the questions by affirming the existence of state protection through a misappropriation theory under unfair competition law although denying that this constituted protection of "well-known" foreign marks. *See* ITC Ltd. v. Punchgini, Inc., 880 N.E.2d 852, 857–59 (N.Y. 2007). It provided a fairly generous standard to be met by the foreign mark in order for the protection to apply. *See ibid.* The Second Circuit found the facts before it insufficient to satisfy the clarified state law doctrine. *See* ITC Ltd. v. Punchgini, Inc., 518 F.3d 159, 164 (2d Cir. 2008).

[42]   *See supra* notes 8–13 and accompanying text; Lockridge, *supra* note 3, at 1357–65.

[43]   *See* Grupo Gigante SA de CV v. Dallo & Co., 391 F.3d 1088, 1098 (9th Cir. 2004) (stating that the Paris Convention's principle of independence of registrations from country to country "arguably requires ... [preservation of] the territoriality principle in some form"). But at least the Ninth Circuit separately considered international and domestic territoriality issues. *Ibid.* at 1097.

thumb to the complex issue presented in lieu of conducting a real analysis of the significance and function of territoriality. A deeper exploration of trademark territoriality is in order.

IV TERRITORIALITY IN TRADEMARK LAW

Would recognizing protection for a well-known foreign mark radically change federal trademark law by conflicting with a "bedrock" territoriality principle?[44]

Territorial limitations on trademark rights are, to be sure, supported by certain concepts and traditions within trademark law. Those concepts may be either intrinsic or extrinsic to the theory of trademark law.[45] Territorial limitations are intrinsic to common law trademark rights: an owner's right to prevent others from using a confusingly similar mark is limited to the area in which the owner possesses goodwill or reputation.[46] At the same time, territorial restrictions on trademark rights that are created through political bodies reliant upon the authority of a nation with territorially limited sovereign power, such as national trademark registrations, are extrinsic.[47]

---

[44] Universality of rights, rather than strict territoriality of rights, held sway within U.S. trademark law until the 1930s. *See, e.g.,* Walter J. Derenberg, *Territorial Scope and Situs of Trademarks and Good Will*, 47 VA. L. REV. 733, 734 (1961). With a long view of the development of the law in mind, it is historically unjustified to assert that territoriality is such a "bedrock" principle of trademark law that it cannot be reconsidered and contextualized in certain circumstances.

[45] *See* Dinwoodie, *supra* note 4, at 891–908. I credit Professor Dinwoodie with inspiring and supporting this portion of my analysis through his logical and thorough exegesis of the various territorial aspects of trademark law in his article.

[46] *See ibid.* at 888. Dinwoodie states:

For example, common law trademark rights are territorial because the intrinsic purpose of trademark law suggests extending (and limiting) rights to the geographic reach of goodwill. In contrast, registration systems designed to promote economic expansion derive their territorial character from their grounding in economic policymaking, effected by institutions that focus on the regulation or development of discrete economic regions. And rules regarding the enforcement of trademark rights assume their territorial quality because of their connection to political institutions with territorially defined sovereignty.

Ibid.

[47] *See ibid.*

No basis for the territoriality of trademark rights, however, supports the complete exclusion of well-known foreign marks from Lanham Act protection against infringement and unfair competition. Protecting senior well-known foreign marks with no domestic use but with a substantial domestic reputation promotes rather than diminishes the real root of the intrinsically territorial nature of a trademark. When trademark law recognizes and protects an owner's reputation and goodwill represented and implicated by a trademark, thereby protecting both consumer under-standings and producer interests, it protects and recognizes a trademark's intrinsic socio-cultural aspects that have territorial limitations. Political bases of territoriality, including concerns for comity often raised to fight any divergence from the strict territoriality of intellectual property rights, pose no problem. Both domestic, or intrinsic, territoriality and inter-national, or extrinsic, territoriality can be integrated without excluding well-known foreign marks from the protective reach of federal trademark law.

A   Intrinsic Territoriality

Trademark law aims to protect the reputation and goodwill of a mark, and thus the mark's owner, and to protect consumers from deception and confusion as to the source of goods and services.[48] Section 43(a) of the Lanham Act protects both registered and unregistered, or common law, marks.[49] It protects against false endorsement and false association or affiliation as well, even when the complaining party does not possess traditional trademark rights. It also provides a remedy against false and misleading advertising when such advertising causes injury to competi-tive interests. The primary difficulty courts and commentators seem to have with extending the protection of section 43(a) to owners of foreign marks that are well known in the United States is the rule of thumb, taken from domestic cases, that protectable trademark goodwill follows

---

[48]   There is some debate regarding whether U.S. trademark law protects both consumers and producers, or whether instead the historical focus has been on producer interests with consumer effects relevant only to a determination of the effect on the producer. *See* Mark P. McKenna, *The Normative Foundations of Trademark Law*, 82 NOTRE DAME L. REV. 1839, 1844–48, 1860–66 (2007). Nevertheless, both interests – or at least the effects of a junior use on both consumer understanding and producer investment – currently motivate and guide trademark decisions, as demonstrated by the factor analysis for likelihood of confusion and the rhetoric used by courts in deciding cases.

[49]   *See, e.g.*, Two Pesos, Inc. v. Taco Cabana, Inc., 505 U.S. 763, 784 (Stevens J., concurring).

the geographic extent of the trade in goods or actual provision of services bearing a trademark.[50]

The dominant animating context for the basic domestic territoriality rule was and continues to be priority disputes between users of similar marks in fully separate trading areas with no overlap of goodwill or consumers. Use of a mark in an area is simpler and easier to prove than the goodwill of a mark in the same area. Thus, courts allow evidence of use to serve as a proxy for evidence of goodwill. The Second Circuit went astray when it sidestepped the complexity of domestic territoriality, which allows for protection in areas of reputation as well as areas of use. While it is true that some use is required for goodwill to develop, domestic law does not hold that goodwill, and trademark rights protecting that goodwill, cannot extend beyond the area of use.

1   Territorial limits on unregistered trademark rights

In the early part of the twentieth century, the Supreme Court heard two cases that turned on the rules of priority governing trademark rights.[51] The resulting rule became known as the Tea Rose doctrine, named after the trademark at issue in the first of the two cases. According to the Court: "Into whatever markets the use of a trademark has extended, or its meaning has become known, there will the manufacturer or trader whose trade is pirated by an infringing use be entitled to protection and redress."[52]

Under the Tea Rose doctrine, courts presume that consumer associations have been made, and a reputation exists, anywhere the mark has been used.[53] The Supreme Court used this general statement of the limits of trademark rights to refine a general "first in time" rule:

> In the ordinary case of parties competing under the same mark in the same market, it is correct to say that prior appropriation settles the question. But where two parties independently are employing the same mark upon goods of the same class, but in separate markets wholly remote the one from the other, the question of prior appropriation is legally insignificant; unless, at least, it appear that the second adopter has selected the mark with some design

---

[50]   *See, e.g.*, ITC Ltd. v. Punchgini, Inc., 482 F.3d 135, 155 (2d Cir. 2007).

[51]   *See* Hanover Star Milling Co. v. Metcalf, 240 U.S. 403 (1916); United Drug Co. v. Theodore Rectanus Co., 248 U.S. 90 (1918).

[52]   *Hanover Star Milling*, 240 U.S. at 415–16.

[53]   *Ibid.* at 413–14 ("[T]he right grows out of use, not mere adoption. … In short, the trademark is treated as merely a protection for the good will, and not the subject of property except in connection with an existing business.").

inimical to the interests of the first user, such as to take the benefit of the reputation of his goods, to forestall the extension of his trade, or the like.[54]

Simple priority of use, however, is not the only issue: if a mark is not inherently distinctive, a measure of secondary meaning must be shown on the part of a senior user before that user can enjoin a junior use.[55] The creation of some consumer associations is thus arguably necessary in the case of non-inherently distinctive marks, but direct evidence on the specific geographic extent of those associations is not required. Circumstantial evidence of secondary meaning, moreover, such as proof of the length and manner of use and advertising expenditure, often suffices.[56]

In truth, then, proof of local use is a proxy for proof of protectable goodwill, which is the keystone of commercial and consumer interests protected by trademark law. The notion that trademark rights only extend to the area of use is a shortcut to approximate the geographic extent of a mark's goodwill. Use is, in a sense, a type of circumstantial evidence recognized as a valid substitute for direct evidence of goodwill. Proof of use allows a mark owner to prove the extent of the goodwill without having to resort to direct evidence, such as consumer surveys. It is the prior existence of goodwill within a certain consumer population that leads to a protectable interest, infringement upon which is identified by a likelihood of confusion if a second user begins use of the same or a similar mark in that area. The doctrine or "rule" that trademark rights are circumscribed by the territorial scope of use is only a rule of thumb.

Despite the long-standing nature of the Tea Rose doctrine linking goodwill and protection from confusion to the geographic area of use, U.S. law does not countenance an absolute rule that where direct sales or offerings of services do not exist, neither may a mark's reputation exist. U.S. law, in fact, recognizes the possibility that trademark reputation can

---

[54] *Ibid.* at 415.

[55] *See generally* 2 J. THOMAS MCCARTHY, MCCARTHY ON TRADEMARKS AND UNFAIR COMPETITION § 16:34 (4th ed. 2010) (explaining the priority rules that apply to secondary meaning).

[56] *See, e.g.*, Zatarain's, Inc. v. Oak Grove Smokehouse, Inc., 698 F.2d 786, 795 (5th Cir. 1983). When registering a non-inherently distinctive mark, neither direct evidence of consumer association nor circumstantial evidence will necessarily be required, even though the registration creates nationwide priority. Often, a claim of at least five years of "substantially exclusive and continuous use" suffices. 15 U.S.C. § 1052(f) (2006); U.S. PATENT & TRADEMARK OFF., TRADEMARK MANUAL OF EXAMINING PROCEDURE § 1212.06(d) (2010).

extend beyond use in some geographic areas.[57] And when reputation does so extend, the senior trademark user has a protectable interest there and is awarded rights superior to a junior user, even if the junior user was the first to actually use the mark in the particular geographic area.[58] In those circumstances, courts allow the senior user to enjoin the junior use, even when the senior user has not yet used the mark in commerce in that area and has no particular plans to begin use in that area.

An old and oft-cited example of reputation preceding actual use in a geographic location is the STORK CLUB case.[59] A New York club used the STORK CLUB mark in connection with a fairly upscale establishment. Despite lack of actual use outside New York City, the club obtained an injunction against a relatively lowbrow San Francisco club that attempted to use the same mark. The court based its decision on the fact that San Francisco residents would likely know of the New York establishment due to its widespread reputation. That reputation in San Francisco predated the junior use in San Francisco, meaning that the junior use could cause confusion. So the New York establishment prevailed, even though the junior user was the first to make actual use of the mark in San Francisco.

In the absence of direct proof of the extent of goodwill or reputation, a rule that goodwill, and thus an owner's protectable interest, cannot extend beyond the geographic range of use does operate efficiently. But in this age of easier, more affordable national and international travel and almost-zero-marginal-cost global communications networks, knowledge of a mark and its associated goods and services can certainly travel beyond the geographic reach of actual use. U.S. domestic law already recognizes this phenomenon, although most cases present facts spanning only domestic territory rather than crossing an international border.[60]

In creating the Tea Rose rule, the Supreme Court itself recognized the possibility that a mark might be known in a geographic area without actual use in that area when it stated: "Into whatever markets the use of a trademark has extended, *or its meaning has become known*, there will the manufacturer or trader whose trade is pirated by an infringing use be

---

[57]   *See, e.g.*, Fuddruckers, Inc. v. Doc's B.R. Others, Inc., 826 F.2d 837, 844 (9th Cir. 1987).

[58]   *See generally* 5 J. THOMAS MCCARTHY, MCCARTHY ON TRADEMARKS AND UNFAIR COMPETITION § § 26:16–19 (4th ed. 2010).

[59]   Stork Rest., Inc. v. Sahati, 166 F.2d 348 (9th Cir. 1948).

[60]   *See, e.g.*, cases cited *supra* notes 57 and 59 and *infra* notes 63 and 64.

entitled to protection and redress."[61] Some courts ignore the emphasized language.[62] Nevertheless, numerous cases have recognized the principle that reputation can precede use.[63] In those situations, courts have barred the junior user from establishing superior rights in a separate geographic area, even when that junior user did not himself know of the senior mark.[64] The remote, good-faith junior user defense only succeeds in domestic cases when the senior mark was not known either to customers or to the junior user at the time of the junior user's adoption.[65]

2 Territorial limits on trademark remedies

Current precedent in most of the federal circuit courts rejects injunctive relief for the owner of a federal trademark registration in certain circumstances, even if that owner clearly has registration-based priority in the defendant's geographic area of use. This is known as the *Dawn Donut* rule, after the Second Circuit's decision in *Dawn Donut Co. v. Hart's Food Stores, Inc.*[66] Although related to the Tea Rose doctrine, the *Dawn Donut* rule is distinct – rejecting a remedy despite priority, due to the extent of use and goodwill, rather than granting priority and a remedy, due to the extent of use and goodwill. The rule stems from an application of the requirement of likelihood of confusion, meaning a *present* likelihood of confusion, which must exist for a plaintiff trademark owner to obtain injunctive relief.

Neither a registrant's priority nor its lack of local use is determinative of the right to relief: an injunction will only issue if the owner is currently using the mark within the defendant's geographic area, has

---

[61] Hanover Star Milling Co. v. Metcalf, 240 U.S. 403, 415–16 (1916) (emphasis added).

[62] *See, e.g.*, ITC Ltd. v. Punchgini, Inc., 482 F.3d 135, 142 (2d Cir. 2007).

[63] *See, e.g.*, Peaches Entm't Corp. v. Entm't Repertoire Assocs., 62 F.3d 690, 693–95 (5th Cir. 1995) (using *Hanover Star Milling* to support its holding that the trade area for an unregistered mark extends to the "zone of reputation").

[64] *See, e.g.*, Champions Golf Club, Inc. v. Champions Golf Club, Inc., 78 F.3d 1111, 1120–24 (6th Cir. 1996); Golden Door, Inc. v. Odisho, 437 F. Supp. 956, 963, 968 (N.D. Cal. 1977), *aff'd*, 646 F.2d 347 (9th Cir. 1980); 5 McCarthy, *supra* note 58, §§ 26:16–17.

[65] *See, e.g.*, GTE Corp. v. Williams, 904 F.2d 536, 541–42 (10th Cir. 1990); *see also* Woman's World Shops, Inc. v. Lane Bryant, Inc., 5 U.S.P.Q.2d 1985, 1988 (T.T.A.B. 1988) (holding, in light of the *Hanover Star Milling* and *United Drug* cases, that adoption of a senior user's mark by a remote junior user had not created rights in the junior user because the mark had been adopted with knowledge of the senior use and thus was not a good faith or innocent adoption).

[66] Dawn Donut Co. v. Hart's Food Stores, Inc., 267 F.2d 358 (2d Cir. 1959).

plans to begin that use in the immediately foreseeable future, or has a reputation in that area in the mind of the relevant consuming public.[67] Emphasizing the final possibility, Thomas McCarthy, the author of a major trademark treatise, states: "Of course, if the federal registrant can prove that its mark *already* has established a *reputation* in the junior user's territory, then there is no need for proof of impending entry by an actual sales outlet, for a likelihood of confusion exists *now*."[68] The Sixth Circuit has gone even further, noting that the *Dawn Donut* focus on likelihood of actual local market entry may be inappropriate in certain circumstances. That court has plainly stated that a finding of infringement is based on a multi-factor test and cannot be defeated by a lack of likelihood of entry alone.[69]

In a sense, the *Dawn Donut* rule and the Tea Rose doctrine are both animated by the presence of a mark's goodwill in a market or an owner's immediately foreseeable market entry, with current presence of a mark's goodwill being identified *either* by actual use *or* by consumer understanding or reputation. If the senior user's reputation exists in the defendant's trade area at the time the defendant adopts the mark, then the senior user should be awarded an injunction against the junior use.[70]

---

[67] *See ibid.*

[68] *See* 5 MCCARTHY, *supra* note 58, § 26:34 (citing cases).

[69] *See* Circuit City Stores, Inc. v. CarMax, Inc., 165 F.3d 1047, 1056 (6th Cir. 1999).

> The law of this Circuit holds that no particular finding of likelihood of entry or irreparable harm is necessary for injunctive relief in trademark infringement or unfair competition cases. ... The Sixth Circuit has an eight point test for infringement liability under the Lanham Act. Likelihood of entry is just one of the eight factors under this test, and it is not dispositive of liability.

Ibid. (citations omitted).

A concurring opinion went even further, calling for re-examination of the *Dawn Donut* rule nationwide: "[O]ur society is far more mobile than it was four decades ago [now five decades ago]. For this reason, and given that recent technological innovations such as the Internet are increasingly deconstructing geographical barriers for marketing purposes, it appears to me that a re-examination ... would be timely." *Ibid.* at 1057 (Jones J., concurring).

[70] There are a number of cases applying this principle in the context of a federal registrant with senior rights to a junior user, when the registrant has a reputation in the junior trade area, although it has not yet actually begun to do business in that trade area. *See* Tisch Hotels, Inc. v. Americana Inn, Inc., 350 F.2d 609, 614 n. 6 (7th Cir. 1965); Supershuttle Int'l, Inc. v. Shafer-Schonewill & Assocs., 39 U.S.P.Q.2d 1762, 1764–65 (D. Colo. 1995); Gastown, Inc. of Del. v. Gastown, Inc., 331 F. Supp. 626, 632 (D. Conn. 1971); Travelodge Corp. v.

3 Applying domestic territoriality to well-known foreign marks

The basic territorial principles underlying domestic trademark law include both acknowledging that reputation can spread beyond the precise boundaries of a senior use and respecting any confusion likely to arise from a junior use. In the case of a well-known foreign mark, courts are reluctant – or even refuse – to recognize an analogue to the long-accepted domestic situation where reputation precedes local use. This resistance is due to the existence of an international territorial boundary between the area of actual use and an area where, despite lack of use, the foreign trademark owner enjoys a substantial reputation among consumers. The importance of a political boundary in law, and in trademark law in particular, however, demonstrates that international territorial boundaries should not pose an insurmountable barrier to the protection sought by an owner of a truly well-known foreign mark.

B Extrinsic Territoriality

In addition to being intrinsic to trademark law, as set forth above, concerns about the territorial reach of trademark rights are supported outside trademark law as part of a broader legal construct. The political concern of territoriality, the idea that a nation's laws only have prescriptive jurisdiction within that nation's territory, certainly finds traction in many areas of the law.[71] But providing protection to the foreign owners of well-known marks does not contravene the political basis for territorial limits on trademark rights.

The key concern with political territoriality is whether application of a nation's laws to govern conduct occurring outside the nation's territorial

---

Siragusa, 228 F. Supp. 238, 241 (N.D. Ala. 1964), *aff'd*, 352 F.2d 516 (5th Cir. 1965). A case including an international border is *Koffler Stores, Ltd. v. Shoppers Drug Mart, Inc.*, 434 F. Supp. 697, 704 (E.D. Mich. 1976), *aff'd*, 559 F.2d 1219 (6th Cir. 1977).

[71] *See, e.g.*, IAN BROWNLIE, PRINCIPLES OF PUBLIC INTERNATIONAL LAW 456–86 (8th ed. 2012) (explaining territoriality as the most common basis for prescriptive jurisdiction in civil matters and noting that the territoriality of prescriptive, or legislative, jurisdiction derives from the territorial sovereignty of each nation). If a nation's prescriptive power reaches only to the nation's territorial borders, then the force of its legislation or its common law rules will apply only within that nation's territory. In this way, each nation's trademark laws – and thus trademark rights granted or recognized under those laws – are said to be territorial.

boundaries will violate the principle of comity among nations.[72] Under the Paris Convention and TRIPS Agreement conceptions of protecting a well-known foreign mark, the conduct being governed by a nation's laws is only conduct occurring within that nation's territory. There is no comity concern; no nation's laws extend beyond its territory. The ownership rights recognized in a trademark may ultimately arise as a result of the owner's conduct – namely, extensive use – outside the territory, but the conduct being prescribed or restricted is only the defendant's conduct within the territory. And the rights recognized within the territory are based on effects – creation of a reputation, and subsequent confusion – felt within the territory.

Any injunction issued against a junior user's U.S. activity would restrain only activity in this country. Moreover, the protection of well-known foreign marks by U.S. courts and the U.S. trademark office within the United States is an obligation the United States willingly undertook close to a century ago. Enforcing that obligation does not negatively affect the territorial or political sovereignty of the United States. By including the obligation to protect well-known foreign marks within the relevant treaties, the member nations have agreed to recognize, under their own territorially limited prescriptive authority, the potential for the reputation of certain marks to extend beyond the territory of actual use or registration.

Advocating for the protection of well-known foreign marks creates a very slight divergence from intrinsic connotations of territoriality in that it requires examining the purpose and operation of certain shorthand rules of thumb or proxies that courts use in other, primarily domestic, contexts. But with respect to the political dimension of territoriality, there is no divergence whatsoever.

V LANHAM ACT IMPLEMENTATION OF WELL-KNOWN MARK PROTECTION

Sections 43(a), 44(b), and 44(h) of the Lanham Act can and should be construed to protect the owner of a well-known foreign mark – with both theoretical foundations and statutory text coalescing in support of the construction. Most of section 43(a), like the rest of the U.S. law of unfair competition, focuses on trademark protection in order to meet two

---

[72] *See, e.g.,* Hartford Fire Ins. Co. v. California, 509 U.S. 764, 797–98 (1993); *ibid.* at 813–15 (Scalia J., dissenting); *see also* McBee v. Delica Co., 417 F.3d 107, 116–21 (1st Cir. 2005).

underlying goals: (1) supporting a trademark owner's investment in a mark and reputation by giving a right of action to stop confusingly similar uses; and (2) avoiding consumer confusion in order to protect consumers.[73] But neither goal requires direct competition between two parties to an unfair competition dispute.[74] And neither goal requires a trademark-based unfair competition claim to rely on a senior use of a trademark in the same locality as the allegedly infringing junior use.

A   Implementation via Sections 43(a), 44(b), and 44(h)

It is well settled that a domestic senior user of a mark may obtain protection under section 43(a) of the Lanham Act for infringement of an unregistered mark if a junior user creates a likelihood of confusion.[75] As previously explained, that protection exists even if the confusion is likely to arise in a geographic area where the senior user has not yet used the mark, as long as the senior user has earned a reputation among the relevant consuming public in that area. A likelihood of confusion caused by a junior use of a mark leads to unfair competition actionable under section 43(a), even without direct competition between those users.[76]

In addition to including non-competitive claims, the text of section 43(a) also includes claims by persons without their own trademark rights or demonstrable uses of a mark in U.S. commerce.[77] It only requires that

---

[73]   *See, e.g.*, McKenna, *supra* note 48, at 1844–48, 1860–66 (surveying both older case law and more recent scholarship and finding support for the argument that both goals motivate the rules within and application of trademark law, although concluding that the producer interests outweighed the consumer interest in most historical cases). A third goal of trademark law, to promote free competition, is also cited to support certain features of trademark law, such as the prohibition on providing trademark rights in generic terms or descriptive terms that have not gained secondary meaning. *See ibid.* at 1845.

[74]   *See ibid.* at 1899–904.

[75]   *See* Wal-Mart Stores, Inc. v. Samara Bros. Inc., 529 U.S. 205, 210 (2000); *see also* 5 McCarthy, *supra* note 58, § 27:14 (including citations from all regional federal circuits).

[76]   *See* 15 U.S.C. § 1125(a) (2006) (containing no competition requirement).

[77]   *Compare ibid.* (containing no requirement of trademark ownership) *with* 15 U.S.C. § 1114(1) (2006) (containing a requirement that defendant use a mark similar to one owned by the plaintiff). *But see, e.g.*, DeBeers LV Trademark Ltd. v. DeBeers Diamond Syndicate Inc., 440 F. Supp. 2d 249, 269 (S.D.N.Y. 2006) ("Although the language of Section 43(a) imposes a requirement of 'use[ ] in commerce' only on the party who is alleged to have infringed an unregistered mark, courts impose the same requirement on plaintiffs who claim such infringement.").   It bears notice that in the cancellation context under Lanham

the complaining party prove that a "use[ ] in commerce [of] any word, term, name, symbol, or device, or any combination thereof" is "likely to cause confusion" within the United States "as to the affiliation, connection, or association of [the complained-of party] with [the complaining party], or as to the origin, sponsorship, or approval of [complained-of party's] goods, services, or commercial activities by [complaining party]."[78] The focus of the statute is not on the nature of the complain*ing* party's own prior use of any word, name, or other device. The focus is instead on whether the complained-*of* use is likely to create a confusing effect within the United States – and whether that effect relates to a relationship between the goods, services, or commercial activities of two unrelated parties. Section 43(a) as a general matter does not require trademark use in the same way that the rules governing trademark registration require use; section 43(a) is broad enough to encompass a wider range of unfair competition than mere trademark infringement or false advertising.[79] The statutory language includes and proscribes a range of activities that may result in a likelihood of confusion, mistake, or deception as to affiliation, connection, association, origin, sponsorship, or approval.

Another issue, beyond the wide range of actionable conduct by third parties, is the type of harm the statute addresses and redresses. The statute refers only to "any person who believes that he or she is or is likely to be damaged."[80] Courts have understandably restricted "any person who believes" to include only those persons who *reasonably believe* they are likely to be damaged, meaning those with a "reasonable

---

Act section 14, the T.T.A.B. also does not require domestic use in commerce of a mark – or trademark ownership – by the complaining party in order for it to possess standing to pursue certain theories for cancellation. *See* Lockridge, *supra* note 3, at 1377 n. 127 and sources cited therein.

[78]   15 U.S.C. § 1125(a).

[79]   For example, section 43(a) provides a claim for false endorsement. *See, e.g.*, Waits v. Frito Lay, Inc., 978 F.2d 1093, 1107–10 (9th Cir. 1992) (allowing a false endorsement claim under section 43(a) even when the complaining party has never commercialized his, her, or its name or image through a trademark or trademark-like use of that name or image). *See also* Trump Plaza of the Palm Beaches Condo. Ass'n v. Rosenthal, No. 08-80408-CIV, 2009 WL 1812743, at *11 (S.D. Fla. June 24, 2009) (dismissing dilution and cybersquatting claims for lack of standing because plaintiff was not the owner of the TRUMP PLAZA mark, but refusing to dismiss plaintiff's claim for false association or affiliation based on defendant's use of that mark).

[80]   15 U.S.C. § 1125(a).

interest to be protected" by the statute.[81] The statute protects commercial reputational interests, not personal or individual economic concerns.[82] As further argued below with respect to standing, this restriction to reasonable, but commercial, interests includes owners of well-known foreign marks when those marks have earned a reputation for the owner within a U.S. market, even when that reputation has been gained by means other than local use. The statute requires only that the reasonable belief of harm to the commercial interest arise from another person's "use[ ] in commerce [of a] word, term, name, symbol, or device … which is likely to cause confusion … as to [an] affiliation, connection, or association,"[83] which confusion could certainly arise between an owner of the well-known foreign mark and a domestic user of that mark. Section 43(a)'s text thus encompasses the commercial reputation underlying a well-known foreign mark.

Sections 44(b) and (h) ensure that foreign trademark owners may obtain relief under the same conditions as U.S. owners.[84] Compared with other portions of the Lanham Act, these provisions are relatively spare of specific substantive rights.[85] But in light of the design of section 44, that approach is entirely logical. Congress wished for foreign nationals to obtain the same rights and remedies as U.S. nationals, and it intended to

---

[81] *Waits*, 978 F.2d at 1108 (quoting Smith v. Montoro, 648 F.2d 602, 608 (9th Cir. 1981)) (internal quotation marks omitted).

[82] Courts presented with the question have almost universally held that a consumer does not have standing to sue under section 43(a), even though he or she might be "any person who believes that he or she is likely to be damaged" by the confusion engendered by the use of similar marks on similar goods or services. *See, e.g.*, Serbin v. Ziebart Int'l Corp., 11 F.3d 1163, 1166–76 (3d Cir. 1993) (surveying cases). Courts have excluded consumers from the group of plaintiffs with standing for false advertising claims by applying a rule requiring a commercial, or sometimes even competitive, injury. *See ibid.* at 1175 ("[T]he statute provides a private remedy to a commercial plaintiff who meets the burden of proving that its commercial interests have been harmed by a competitor's false advertising."). The commercial injury requirement applies to owners of well-known foreign marks as well.

[83] 15 U.S.C. § 1125(a).

[84] *See* S. REP. NO. 79-1333 (1946), *reprinted in* 1946 U.S. Code Cong. Serv. 1274, 1276 (indicating that Congress intended the Lanham Act "[t]o carry out by statute our international commitments to the end that American traders in foreign countries may secure the protection to their marks to which they are entitled" because "[i]ndustrialists in this country have been seriously handicapped in securing protection in foreign countries due to our failure to carry out, by statute, our international obligations").

[85] *See* 15 U.S.C. § 1126 (2006).

fully implement, or exceed, all minimum rights required by the international obligations of the United States.[86] By providing that foreign nationals may utilize Lanham Act provisions on the same terms as domestic nationals, rather than crafting separate provisions for foreign nationals, Congress ensured that both groups would enjoy consistent treatment regardless of statutory or jurisprudential developments.[87] The rights available to foreign nationals "piggyback," in a sense, on the text, the case law, and the theory of the remainder of federal trademark law.[88] The breadth of section 43(a) and the specific language of section 44(b) and (h)[89] – which together provide foreign owners access to section 43(a)'s breadth[90] – show that the Lanham Act provides an appropriate

---

[86]   *See, e.g.*, 15 U.S.C. § 1127 (2006) ("The intent of this chapter is … to provide rights and remedies stipulated by treaties and conventions respecting trademarks, trade names, and unfair competition entered into between the United States and foreign nations.").

[87]   Section 44(b) gives select foreign nationals the benefits of the remainder of section 44. *See* § 1126(b). Section 44(b)–(f) collectively provides access to the U.S. trademark registration system. *See* § 1126(b)–(f). The use of section 32 to obtain protection against infringement of a registered trademark depends on the ability of a foreign national to become the owner of a registered mark by way of section 44(b)–(f) and section 1. Section 44(h) provides foreign nationals with rights against unfair competition that go beyond ownership of registered rights. Within the scope of section 44(h)'s unfair competition protection is the ability to raise claims for unfair competition under section 43(a), as well as those actions provided in section 43(b)–(d) for import control, trademark dilution, and cybersquatting. *See* § 1126(h). The protection against unfair competition provided by section 43(a) includes the ability to bring a cause of action for false advertising, false endorsement, or false affiliation or association. *See* 15 U.S.C. § 1125(a) (2006).

[88]   Only section 44(c)–(e) creates separate mechanisms for use by foreign nationals – providing, for example, that foreign nationals who have obtained a registration for a mark in their country of origin may register that mark in the United States without proving use. *See* § 1126(c)–(e).

[89]   *See* 5 MCCARTHY, *supra* note 58, § 29:4 (arguing that protection for well-known foreign marks is incorporated into U.S. law through sections 43(a), 44(b), and 44(h) because 44(b) provides access to protection, 44(h) provides substantive rights coextensive with the protection owed to foreign nationals under relevant trademark treaties, and 43(a) gives the foreign national without a registration standing to sue); *see also* Andrew Cook, *Do as We Say, Not as We Do: A Study of the Well-Known Marks Doctrine in the United States*, 8 J. MARSHALL REV. INTELL. PROP. L. 412, 422–24, 426–28 (2009).

[90]   Unsettled is the question of whether section 44(h) provides foreign nationals a federal cause of action for unfair competition separate from and beyond the terms of section 43. *See* Lockridge, *supra* note 3, at 1385 n. 151.

and theoretically consistent statutory cause of action for the owners of well-known foreign marks.

B   Standing under Section 43(a)

Analysis of Lanham Act standing also supports well-known foreign mark protection. Lanham Act standing, like other standing matters under U.S. law, has three components: constitutional, prudential, and statutory, and owners of well-known foreign marks with a reputation within the relevant U.S. market satisfy them all.[91] The only issues brought into question by decisions such as the Second Circuit's *ITC* ruling are the Lanham Act's express standing and intended zone of interests.[92] The dispute, in terms of standing, is whether a foreign trademark owner who has not otherwise created U.S. trademark rights through registration or use falls within the zone of interests protected by the Lanham Act and its express standing for "any person who believes that he or she is or is likely to be damaged" by a third party's use in commerce of a confusingly similar mark.

Owners of well-known foreign marks easily fit within the zone of commercial and competitive reputational interests protected by the Lanham Act, even when the mark is not currently in domestic use.[93] In section 44(b), Congress even specifically included foreign nationals with relevant treaty connections within the Lanham Act's zone of interests.[94] When a junior user endangers the commercial or competitive interests of the owner of a well-known foreign mark, the owner must be protected

---

[91]   *See ibid.* at 1386–91.

[92]   *See, e.g.*, ITC Ltd. v. Punchgini, Inc., 482 F.3d 135, 155, 163 (2d Cir. 2007) (asserting that "[t]he territoriality principle requires the use to be in the United States for the owner to assert priority rights to the mark under the Lanham Act" and that "[t]he Lanham Act's unfair competition protections, as we have already explained, are cabined by the long-established principle of territoriality.").

[93]   The McCarthy treatise takes a slightly different, although ultimately harmonious approach. *See, e.g.*, 5 McCARTHY, *supra* note 58, § 29:4 (arguing for standing under section 43(a) for owners of well-known foreign marks using section 44(h) and its incorporation of treaty obligations rather than specifically using the zone of interests protected by section 43(a)); *ibid.* § 29:61 (similar). Other commentators have disagreed, finding no textual support for the construction I advocate. *See, e.g.*, Anne Gilson LaLonde, *Don't I Know You from Somewhere? Protection in the United States of Foreign Trademarks that Are Well Known But Not Used There*, 98 TRADEMARK REP. 1379, 1395–96 (2008). For additional citations to law review articles and comments on both sides of the issue, see Lockridge, *supra* note 3, at 1391 n. 175.

[94]   15 U.S.C. § 1126(b) (2006).

under section 43(a), whether the owner is a U.S. national or a foreign national. A junior user's use of the mark endangers these interests in areas in the United States where the senior foreign mark is well known, threatening the goodwill in that mark as well as the broader reputation, products, services, and commercial activities of the senior owner. The likely domestic confusion could damage the senior owner's ability to expand into the United States using the well-known mark or could so seriously affect the reputation of the senior owner that the owner would have difficulty operating successfully in the United States using any other mark.

Without exclusion by the statutory text, or failure to otherwise meet the requirements of standing, owners of well-known foreign marks face solely the argument that recognizing such marks would threaten or violate the "territoriality principle" underlying U.S. trademark law. As previously explained, however, those broad objections are unfounded. Careful statutory analysis, coupled with deep consideration of trademark policies and the real meaning of territoriality, maps a path to protecting well-known foreign marks.

VI CONCLUSION

The United States joined many other nations in agreeing that marks used only in foreign nations should be protected within domestic borders if they are sufficiently well known in the domestic market. U.S. decision-makers need to recognize the existing Lanham Act protection for well-known foreign marks. To do so they must fully come to grips with the significance and function of "territoriality" in trademark law.

Asking judicial decision-makers to confront the full meaning of territoriality may disturb some previously settled expectations and even case precedent. Graeme Dinwoodie is absolutely right to urge in his writing on this issue that before disturbing such expectations, we must be mindful of both the social and political values that inhere in the territoriality of trademarks.[95] In my view, this concern can best be addressed by requiring a strong showing of a well-known foreign mark's goodwill in the relevant market.[96] Courts ought not sideline our international obligations and interests or misapply the multifaceted concept of territoriality. Courts must seriously consider the complex nature of

---

[95] *See* Dinwoodie, *supra* note 4, at 932.
[96] *See* Lockridge, *supra* note 3, at 1406–12.

territoriality in order to correct current misunderstandings and make future enforcement more predictable and uniform in the United States.

12. The curious case of fake Beijing Olympics merchandise

Peter K. Yu[*]

I INTRODUCTION

Counterfeiting is a global challenge – a challenge that does not recognize territorial borders. Although the sale of counterfeit goods affects rights holders primarily in domestic markets, the export of these products can harm rights holders and third parties outside those markets. As the International AntiCounterfeiting Coalition and the International Chamber of Commerce estimated, the current global trade in illegitimate goods amounted to approximately $600 billion annually – based on an estimate of 5–7 percent of global trade.[1] Although the figures provided by the Organisation for Economic Co-operation and Development were more modest, they still amounted to $250 billion in 2007.[2]

Out of all the countries having substantial exports of counterfeit goods, China is the most notorious. Since reopening its market to foreign trade in the late 1970s, it has been repeatedly criticized for inadequate and ineffective protection and enforcement of intellectual property rights. Every year, the country finds itself in either the Watch List or the Priority Watch List in the Section 301 Report released by the United States Trade Representative (USTR).[3] As the U.S. International Trade Commission

* © 2014 Peter K. Yu. This chapter draws on research from the author's earlier articles in the *American University Law Review* and the *John Marshall Review of Intellectual Property Law*.

1 *About Counterfeiting*, INT'L ANTICOUNTERFEITING COALITION, http://www.iacc.org/about-counterfeiting/ (last visited Apr. 3, 2013).

2 ORG. FOR ECON. COOPERATION & DEV., MAGNITUDE OF COUNTERFEITING AND PIRACY OF TANGIBLE PRODUCTS: AN UPDATE 1 (2009).

3 The notable exception was during the honeymoon period following China's accession to the World Trade Organization in December 2001. In April 2005, the USTR elevated China back to the Priority Watch List. Peter K. Yu,

estimated in a recent report, "firms in the U.S. [intellectual property]-intensive economy that conducted business in China in 2009 reported losses of approximately $48.2 billion in sales, royalties, or license fees due to [intellectual property] infringement in China."[4]

For more than a decade, policymakers and commentators have heavily criticized the Chinese government for lacking the political will to clean up its massive counterfeiting problem. In their view, this problem would have immediately disappeared if it concerned an important issue such as censored products or the Beijing Olympics.[5] To many policymakers and commentators, the lack of fake merchandise during the Beijing Olympics provided an instructive example of how the Chinese government could muster up the political will needed to combat the country's massive counterfeiting problem.

The suddenly strengthened protection against counterfeit Olympic merchandise also provided a handy rebuttal to the Chinese government's oft-made claim of its lack of resources – a claim that was advanced in, for example, the recent U.S.–China dispute before the World Trade Organization (WTO) over the protection and enforcement of intellectual property rights.[6] To many rights holders, the Chinese government has repeatedly used this claim as an unconvincing excuse to delay the much overdue protection for foreign brands.

In a previous article, I exposed the flaws in this "political will" argument. As I pointed out, "it is not only the Chinese who lack political

---

From Pirates to Partners (Episode II): Protecting Intellectual Property in Post-WTO China, 55 AM. U. L. REV. 901, 925 (2006).

[4] U.S. INT'L TRADE COMM'N, PUB. NO. 4226, CHINA: EFFECTS OF INTELLECTUAL PROPERTY INFRINGEMENT AND INDIGENOUS INNOVATION POLICIES ON THE U.S. ECONOMY xiv (2011).

[5] On the Beijing Olympics, see SUSAN BROWNELL, BEIJING'S GAMES: WHAT THE OLYMPICS MEAN TO CHINA (2008); CHINA'S GREAT LEAP: THE BEIJING GAMES AND OLYMPIAN HUMAN RIGHTS (Minky Worden ed., 2008) [hereinafter CHINA'S GREAT LEAP]; PAUL CLOSE, DAVID ASKEW AND XU XIN, THE BEIJING OLYMPIAD: THE POLITICAL ECONOMY OF A SPORTING MEGA-EVENT (2007); OWNING THE OLYMPICS: NARRATIVES OF THE NEW CHINA (Monroe E. Price and Daniel Dayan eds., 2008) [hereinafter OWNING THE OLYMPICS]; XU GUOQI, OLYMPIC DREAMS: CHINA AND SPORTS, 1895–2008 (2008).

[6] On this dispute, see Panel Report, *China – Measures Affecting the Protection and Enforcement of Intellectual Property Rights*, WT/DS362/R (Jan. 26, 2009); Peter K. Yu, *The TRIPS Enforcement Dispute*, 89 NEB. L. REV. 1046 (2011); Peter K. Yu, *TRIPS Enforcement and Developing Countries*, 26 AM. U. INT'L L. REV. 727 (2011).

will, as many critics have claimed, but the Americans as well."[7] As far as U.S. priorities are concerned, the protection and enforcement of intellectual property rights simply does not compare favorably with other more important matters such as trade deficit, currency exchange, and nuclear proliferation.[8] As a former senior U.S. government official once told me candidly, intellectual property protection has always been "at the top of the second list."[9]

Instead of rehashing these arguments, this chapter will closely scrutinize the intellectual property developments before and during the Beijing Olympics to determine whether this world event has indeed provided the much-needed example to show that China could effectively address the counterfeiting problem when national interests were at stake. As this chapter will show, the case of fake Beijing Olympics merchandise is rather curious. Even though the sale of this merchandise was significantly reduced in Beijing and other major cities during the Olympic Games, such sale was widely present in other parts of the country. To a large extent, the presence of fake Olympic merchandise has shown that the challenge of confronting counterfeiting in China is more a reality than an excuse. It also provides an instructive example for understanding what the Chinese government can and cannot do in its effort to combat massive counterfeiting, the necessary complements for success, and the remaining challenges concerning efforts to protect trademarks in such a large, complex, and highly populous country.

This chapter begins by describing the measures that the Chinese government and the Beijing municipality took in the run-up to the Beijing Olympics. It then explains why the case of fake Beijing Olympics merchandise provides an instructive example of the challenges to combating massive counterfeiting in China. The chapter specifically focuses on the local protectionism problem, the need for both the government's will and the people's will, and the inevitable trade-offs concerning the use of enforcement resources. The chapter concludes with some lessons on the future protection of trademark rights in China.

---

[7] Peter K. Yu, *Three Questions that Will Make You Rethink the U.S.–China Intellectual Property Debate*, 7 J. MARSHALL REV. INTEL. PROP. L. 412, 413 (2008).

[8] *See ibid.* at 414–19.

[9] *Ibid.* at 414–15.

II THE BEIJING OLYMPICS AND ITS AFTERMATH

In July 2001, Beijing won the bid to host the 2008 Olympic Games, after failing to secure its bid to host the 2000 Games in Monte Carlo in 1993. Like Tokyo's successful bids in 1964 and Seoul's in 1988, Beijing's 2001 bid strongly suggested China's emerging world power status.[10] For many policymakers, the hosting of the Olympic Games not only would help position the country in the global economy, but might also trickle ripple effects to accelerate reforms in the country. These reforms included reforms of all sorts – political, social, economic, technological, and, of course, intellectual property.

Because the Olympics would generate significant international attention, Chinese leaders sought to use the widely anticipated sporting event to transform the country's world image. Indeed, in the run-up to the Beijing Games, policymakers, rights holders, and commentators wondered whether the Olympic flame would light up the dark spots in the Chinese intellectual property regime. As one commentator suggested, "winning the 2008 Olympics bid has not only given China a chance to demonstrate its cultural prowess, but it has also made intellectual property enforcement relevant to the Party agenda."[11] The Beijing Olympics therefore provided China with a perfect opportunity to strengthen intellectual property rights.

Since Beijing's successful bid in 2001, the Chinese government introduced a wide variety of measures to protect the marks related to the Olympic Games, including the Olympic symbol, rings, flag, anthem, motto, emblem, logos, mascots, names, and slogans. At the local level, the Beijing municipal government issued a decree laying down the Regulations on the Protection of Olympics-Related Intellectual Property.[12] Effective in November 2001, that decree protected all intellectual property rights associated with the Olympic Games. A month later, the

---

[10]   *See* Jean-Pierre Lehmann, *China and the East Asian Political-Economic Model, in* DOES CHINA MATTER? A REASSESSMENT: ESSAYS IN MEMORY OF GERALD SEGAL 87, 104 (Barry Buzan and Rosemary Foot eds., 2004); Nicholas Kristof, *A Lever for Change in China, in* CHINA'S GREAT LEAP, *supra* note 5, at 17, 18.

[11]   Stacey H. Wang, Note, *Great Olympics, New China: Intellectual Property Enforcement Steps Up to the Mark*, 27 LOY. L.A. INT'L & COMP. L. REV. 291, 310 (2005).

[12]   Regulations of Beijing Municipality on Protection of Olympic-related Intellectual Property (promulgated by Decree No. 85 of the Municipal People's Government of Beijing, Oct. 11, 2001, effective Nov. 11, 2001) (China), http://210.75.211.75:81/capinfo/html/info/1011011434539491.html.

Beijing Organizing Committee for the Games of the XXIX Olympiad (BOCOG) set up a legal affairs department to protect these rights. As a senior department official explained, "the establishment of the legal department is the first ever in the history of Chinese sports. ... During the bidding stage we have committed ourselves to the protection of the Olympic intellectual property rights. It is our indispensable responsibility."[13]

At the national level, China enacted the Regulations on the Protection of Olympic Insignia and the Measures for the Recordal and Administration of Olympic Insignia.[14] The authorities also actively cracked down on the sale of fake Olympic merchandise. As the *Weekend Australian* reported, BOCOG officials claimed that "60,000 bureaus and 440,000 personnel across China would be working round the clock between now and 2008 to protect the Olympic trademarks."[15] Likewise, the *South China Morning Post* reported that "Beijing [wa]s trying to burnish its image as an international city by cracking down on counterfeit brand-name goods and the ubiquitous hawkers of pirated CDs" as it prepared to host the Olympic Games.[16]

The heightened responses of the central and municipal governments were understandable. After all, China, in particular Beijing, obtained direct financial benefit from the sales of Olympic merchandise. As the *Los Angeles Times* observed:

> Beijing, the host city, stands to receive up to 15 percent of all revenue from Olympic merchandise, a figure expected to easily top the $62 million raised in Athens four years ago. Aside from the mascots, China is also reportedly collecting up to $120 million each from Coca-Cola, McDonald's, Adidas and other companies that have qualified as the highest-level Olympic sponsors.[17]

Indeed, in the candidature file, "the Chinese Government state[d] that it [would] take all necessary legal measures to strengthen the protection of Olympic marks, as represented by the formulation and promulgation of relevant legal regulations on the 2008 Olympic Games and Olympic

---

[13] *Beijing Sets up Department to Protect Olympics Logo*, XINHUA NEWS AGENCY, Dec. 27, 2001.

[14] Wang, *supra* note 11, at 302.

[15] Catherine Armitage, Editorial, *Run Rings Around Thieves*, WEEKEND AUSTRALIAN, Aug. 16, 2003, at T6.

[16] Nailene Chou Wiest, *Beijing Cracks Down on Fakes*, S. CHINA MORNING POST, Apr. 16, 2005, at A7.

[17] Maureen Fan, *China's Olympic Turnabout on Knockoffs*, WASH. POST, June 13, 2008, at A1.

Marks."[18] The BOCOG also "hired the New York-based legal firm Morrison & Foerster LLP to oversee its legal affairs."[19] Based on these developments, it is fair to infer that the International Olympic Committee (IOC) included specific stipulations in the publicly unavailable Host City Contract, calling for heightened efforts of intellectual property protection.

Since the 1996 Atlanta Olympics, the IOC has focused an increased amount of attention on the intellectual property aspects of the Games. Among its top priorities is the prevention of ambush marketing.[20] In the run-up to the London Olympics, for example, the growing and repeated problem in this area has led the IOC to adopt a rather controversial Rule 40. This new rule prohibited athletes from promoting unsponsored products during the Games. A case in point is the controversy surrounding Olympic swimmer Michael Phelps when two of his photos for a Louis Vuitton advertising campaign were virally circulated on the Internet at a time when athletes were prohibited from appearing in advertisements for non-Olympic sponsors.[21]

Notwithstanding the heightened protection of Beijing Olympics merchandise introduced by both the central and municipal governments, fake merchandise was widely available in China despite contrary reports in both China and abroad. For instance, there was wide discussion about the availability of fake Fuwa mascot dolls, t-shirts, caps, key chains, stuffed toys, and other souvenirs in China. As the *South China Morning Post* reported, "[a] week after the logo for the 2008 Beijing Olympics was unveiled, pirated T-shirts and other souvenirs bearing the emblem ... appeared on sale at several markets in the capital."[22] Likewise, an individual observer noted on *Huntington News* what she saw from Beijing less than a year before the Games:

> The last place you would expect to find fake and counterfeit Olympic merchandise would be in China. Yet everywhere you go in this country, street vendors rush you selling caps, T-shirts and other memorabilia with the logo of the Beijing Organizing Committee for the Olympic Games.

---

[18] 1 BOCOG, BEIJING CANDIDATURE FILE 41 (2000), *available at* http://images.beijing2008.cn/upload/lib/bidreport/zt2.pdf.

[19] BROWNELL, *supra* note 5, at 185–86.

[20] *See* Fraser Mendel and Chao Yijun, *Protecting Olympic Intellectual Property*, CHINA L. & PRAC., May 2003, at 33, 34.

[21] *See* Michelle Caruso-Cabrera, *Racy Photo May Get Michael Phelps in Hot Water*, NBC NEWS (Aug. 17, 2012), http://www.nbcnews.com/business/racy-photo-may-get-michael-phelps-hot-water-950265.

[22] Irene Wang, *Fake Olympic Shirts Make Quick Debut*, S. CHINA MORNING POST, Aug. 13, 2003, at 4.

...

> If you are a Westerner or on a tour bus stopping at any of the favorite tourist attractions in most of the major cities, you will be besieged by the vendors selling counterfeit 2008 Olympic merchandise. In downtown Beijing you can purchase memorabilia anywhere around your hotel or in Tiananmen Square, Forbidden City or the Summer Palace.[23]

In fact, as early as July 2006, two years before the Games, the *Sunday Telegraph* reported that European customs officials had seized fake Beijing Olympics merchandise.[24] If these examples are not enough, only two weeks before the Games' grand opening, Japanese television stations showed the display of mouse-shaped sports statues that were arguably similar to Disney's Mickey Mouse.[25] Shortly after the Games' commencement, pirated DVDs showing the opening ceremony also became widely available, competing directly against their official counterparts.[26]

In sum, the picture on the ground in China seemed to be rather different from the one painted by many policymakers, industry executives, and commentators. While those in search of conspiracy theories would be quick to question why the latter picture was so far away from the truth, it is more constructive to explore what lessons we can learn from this curious case of fake Beijing Olympics merchandise. Does it signify, as China critics have claimed, that the Chinese government could muster up enough political will to address massive counterfeiting when that problem concerned national interests? Or does it signify the contrary – that the government could not do so even if those interests were at stake?

The answers to these questions seem to be neither. On the one hand, in Beijing and other major cities, one could see a noticeable reduction in the sale of counterfeit merchandise, whether associated with the Olympics or other luxury brands. On the other hand, in the run-up to the Olympics, it was not difficult to purchase fake Olympic merchandise if one knew where to shop. The sale of such merchandise was widely available in Beijing, not to mention cities and towns in the inner part of the country

---

[23] Rene A. Henry, *Fake Olympic Merchandise Big Seller in China*, HUNTINGTON NEWS (Sept. 2, 2007), http://archives.huntingtonnews.net/columns/070902-henry-columnsbeijing.html.

[24] Robert Watts, *Fakes Are a Real Headache*, SUNDAY TELEGRAPH (London), July 16, 2006, at 8.

[25] *See Fake Mickey Mouse Statues at the Beijing Olympics*, JAPAN PROBE (July 24, 2008), http://www.japanprobe.com/2008/07/24/fake-mickey-mouse-statues-at-the-beijing-olympics/.

[26] *See China Gets DVD Jump on Pirates – OLYMPICS 2008*, THE AUSTRALIAN, Aug. 13, 2008, at 3.

that were further away from Olympic activities and that foreign tourists rarely visited.

III AN OLYMPIAN STORY OF MIXED SUCCESS

On August 8, 2008, at 8:08 p.m., the Olympic Games officially opened in Beijing, marking the third time this international sporting event was held in Asia. In the run-up to this event and in the few years after, policymakers, rights holders, and commentators have used this spectacle to illustrate how the Chinese government could combat its long-standing and massive counterfeiting problem if it had the needed political will. While the Games have indeed provided an excellent illustration of the massive counterfeiting problem in China, it does not show what these people have claimed. Instead, the Beijing Olympics show what the Chinese government can and cannot do, the necessary complements for success, and the remaining challenges concerning efforts to protect trademarks in such a large, complex, and highly populous country.

To highlight the "political will" argument advanced by China critics, consider the following article from the *South China Morning Post*:

> [P]rotecting intellectual property is ... a matter of national will. Nothing offers a better example than the job Chinese officials have so far done to protect the Olympic symbols. Since China won the right to host the 2008 Games three years ago, they have passed a series of national laws protecting copyright of the Olympic images and more than 100 phrases like "Green Olympics", "Hi-tech Olympics" and "People's Olympics" that the city will use to promote the Games. They have conducted a national public education campaign encouraging citizens to turn in offenders, and have ordered commerce ministry officials to seize pirated Olympic merchandise.[27]

While the claim that intellectual property protection was "a matter of national will" seemed well reasoned and logical, it ignored that counterfeit Olympic merchandise had already appeared in China at that time, especially in markets further away from Beijing. The only difference between the protection of Olympic symbols and that of foreign trademarks seems to be the difference between the protection of movies produced by famous Chinese film directors such as Chen Kaige, Feng Xiaogang, and Zhang Yimou and those produced by Disney, Paramount, Warner Brothers, and

---

[27] Craig Simons, *Faking It*, S. CHINA MORNING POST, Jan. 10, 2005, at 18.

other major foreign movie studios.[28] Although stronger protection exists for local works when they are first released, piracy occurs shortly afterwards; in the long run, the difference is somewhat minimal.[29]

Thus, if one could draw any lesson from the protection of Olympic symbols in China, it is how serious and entrenched the counterfeiting problem has been. This is what I have described as "the flip side of the Beijing Olympics." Due to the country's rapid decentralization, the central government did not have the ability to fully protect the Olympic symbols throughout the country, not to mention a large and rich variety of luxury brands and foreign trademarks. It would therefore take more than a few WTO complaints, several rounds of intellectual property lawmaking and international treaty negotiations, many public awareness and education campaigns, and a considerable amount of active cooperation between the Chinese and Western stakeholders to solve the massive counterfeiting problem.

To understand why China has great difficulty in enforcing intellectual property rights, one has to appreciate the country's size and heterogeneity. China is large, complex, diverse, and "sometimes internally contradictory."[30] The Chinese speak different languages, enjoy different cuisines, grow up with different cultures, and subscribe to different historical and philosophical traditions. Conditions in Beijing are often very different from those in Guangzhou, intellectual property strategies that are effective in Shanghai are likely to fail in a village in Guizhou, and the trade patterns found near the coasts are very different from those found inland.

To complicate matters, local protectionism has been a dominant problem in China throughout its millennial dynastic history. As Oded Shenkar noted, one of the imprints of China's imperial past is "the persistence of local interests that compete for power with each other and especially with the center."[31] During the late Qing dynasty, for example, provincial leaders were more eager to strengthen the foundation of their

---

[28]   Coincidentally, Zhang Yimou was also the artistic director of the opening ceremony of the Beijing Olympics.

[29]   *See* Joseph Kahn, *The Pinch of Piracy Wakes China Up on Copyright Issue*, N.Y. TIMES, Nov. 1, 2002, at C1; Mark Magnier, *A Tiger Still Crouching*, L.A. TIMES, Aug. 22, 2004, at E4.

[30]   John J. Hamre and C. Fred. Bergsten, *Preface* to C. FRED BERGSTEN, BATES GILL, NICHOLAS R. LARDY AND DEREK MITCHELL, CHINA: THE BALANCE SHEET: WHAT THE WORLD NEEDS TO KNOW NOW ABOUT THE EMERGING SUPERPOWER ix (2006).

[31]   ODED SHENKAR, THE CHINESE CENTURY: THE RISING CHINESE ECONOMY AND ITS IMPACT ON THE GLOBAL ECONOMY, THE BALANCE OF POWER, AND YOUR JOB 30 (2005).

personal power than to cooperate with each other to modernize their country.[32] Despite foreign attacks, "[t]heir sense of regionalism and their eagerness for self-preservation persisted so strongly" that the Peiyang and Nanyang fleets refused to rescue the Fukien fleet during the Sino-French war of 1884–85.[33] For similar reasons, the Nanyang fleet and two provincial squadrons maintained their "neutrality" during the Sino-Japanese war of 1894–95, leaving the Peiyang fleet behind to fight the Japanese navy alone.[34] A few years later, during the Boxer Uprising in 1900, "the provincial authorities in Southeast China refused to follow the court order of supporting the Boxers, and out of 'self-preservation' independently entered into agreements with foreign powers."[35] When Sun Yat-sen's revolutionary forces took Wuchang (now part of Wuhan) after launching the 1911 Revolution, "the provincial authorities declared their support of the revolution and by so defying the court hastened the downfall of the [Qing] dynasty."[36]

In the Republican era, regionalism gave way to warlordism, creating one of the most chaotic periods in modern Chinese history.[37] Although the subsequent founding of the People's Republic of China in 1949 helped centralize the country to a certain extent, strategic planning in the country's formative years and the rapid economic development in China within the past two decades have led to greater economic development in certain parts of China at the expense of others. As Deng Xiaoping reasoned, "some people have to get rich first."[38] As a result of the national economic policies, there are now enormous disparities across the country in the levels of wealth and income, the purchasing power of local consumers, and the stages of economic and technological development.[39]

As far as intellectual property enforcement goes, the proverb "the mountains are high, and the Emperor is far away" (*shān gāo huángdì yuǎn*) remains fairly accurate. That proverb is illustrated well by the experience of a senior USTR official who visited the Guangdong

---

[32]   *See* IMMANUEL C.Y. HSU, THE RISE OF MODERN CHINA 287–88 (6th ed. 2000).

[33]   *Ibid.* at 288.

[34]   *Ibid.* at 340.

[35]   *Ibid.* at 252.

[36]   *Ibid.*

[37]   *See ibid.* at 482–86.

[38]   BERGSTEN ET AL., *supra* note 30, at 31.

[39]   *See* Peter K. Yu, *Intellectual Property, Economic Development, and the China Puzzle*, *in* INTELLECTUAL PROPERTY, TRADE AND DEVELOPMENT: STRATEGIES TO OPTIMIZE ECONOMIC DEVELOPMENT IN A TRIPS PLUS ERA 173, 203 (Daniel J. Gervais ed., 2007).

province shortly after the signing of the 1992 memorandum of understanding between China and the United States.[40] As Joseph Massey, the former Assistant USTR for Japan and China, recounted, that official "was [literally] told by a senior provincial government leader that 'Beijing's agreement' with the US was 'mei you guanxi' (irrelevant) in that southern province."[41]

Moreover, as Andrew Mertha pointed out, the complex bureaucracies related to intellectual property protection and enforcement have resulted in considerable differences among protections at the national, provincial, and local levels.[42] The less developed parts of the country are also likely to present considerable structural problems for intellectual property enforcement, including inefficient administration, low penalties, shortage of funds, local protectionism, and severe conflicts of interests.[43] Sadly, despite all of these regional differences and the country's heavily decentralized state, intellectual property developments in China are often analyzed as if the country were homogeneous.[44] Such an analysis, no doubt, was easier to conduct; however, its end result also presented a misleading, if not inaccurate, picture.

In the near future, China is likely to remain what I have described as "a country of countries."[45] Under this scenario, stronger intellectual property protection will appear in Beijing, Shanghai, Guangzhou, and other major cities and coastal regions.[46] Meanwhile, the massive piracy and counterfeiting problems will stay in China, migrating from the

---

[40] Memorandum of Understanding on the Protection of Intellectual Property, P.R.C.–U.S., Jan. 17, 1992, 34 I.L.M. 677.

[41] Joseph A. Massey, *The Emperor Is Far Away: China's Enforcement of Intellectual Property Rights Protection, 1986–2006*, 7 CHI. J. INT'L L. 231, 235 (2006).

[42] *See* ANDREW C. MERTHA, THE POLITICS OF PIRACY: INTELLECTUAL PROPERTY IN CONTEMPORARY CHINA 90–100 (2005).

[43] *See* Keith E. Maskus, Sean M. Dougherty and Andrew Mertha, *Intellectual Property Rights and Economic Development in China*, *in* INTELLECTUAL PROPERTY AND DEVELOPMENT: LESSONS FROM RECENT ECONOMIC RESEARCH 295, 309 (Carsten Fink and Keith E. Maskus eds., 2005).

[44] The rare exception is when the USTR undertook a special provincial review of intellectual property protection in China. *See* Office of the U.S. Trade Representative, *Special Provincial Review of Intellectual Property Rights Protection in China: Request for Public Comment*, 71 FED. REG. 34,969 (June 16, 2006); Yu, *supra* note 39, at 204.

[45] Yu, *supra* note 3, at 963.

[46] *See* Peter K. Yu, *International Enclosure, the Regime Complex, and Intellectual Property Schizophrenia*, 2007 MICH. ST. L. REV. 1, 25.

country's developed parts to its less developed parts. To strike a compromise between the different regional needs, interests, and development goals, Chinese leaders may take some rather "schizophrenic," or pragmatic, positions in designing their intellectual property policies. The resulting regional conflicts and rivalries may also become major factors affecting the future development of intellectual property protection in China.

In sum, the Beijing Olympics have vividly shown not only what the Chinese government *can* do in Beijing and other major cities, but also what it *cannot do.* Although commentators knowledgeable about China's counterfeiting problem have repeatedly identified local protectionism as a key challenge to protecting intellectual property rights in China,[47] foreign policymakers and rights holders tend to focus on the shortcut of introducing stronger rights on the books. While trademark protection would be strengthened on paper, such protection would be meaningless to rights holders if the strengthened rights could not be effectively enforced throughout the country. It is therefore no surprise that commentators have become increasingly frustrated with the flawed strategies advanced by both the USTR and multinational corporations.[48]

IV LESSONS FOR BRAND OWNERS

While fake Beijing Olympics merchandise could be easily found in China, even in Beijing, there was no denying that the counterfeiting problem had greatly dissipated during the Olympic Games. The sale of luxury goods in the Silk Market and other areas had also been more

---

[47] *See* Daniel C.K. Chow, *Counterfeiting in the People's Republic of China*, 78 WASH. U. L.Q. 1, 26 (2000); Li Yiqiang, *Evaluation of the Sino-American Intellectual Property Agreements: A Judicial Approach to Solving the Local Protectionism Problem*, 10 COLUM. J. ASIAN L. 391, 395–401 (1996); Tao Jingzhou, *Problems and New Developments in the Enforcement of Intellectual Property Rights in China*, in INTELLECTUAL PROPERTY AND TRIPS COMPLIANCE IN CHINA: CHINESE AND EUROPEAN PERSPECTIVES 107, 109 (Paul Torremans, Hailing Shan and Johan Erauw eds., 2007).

[48] *See, e.g.*, Peter K. Yu, *From Pirates to Partners: Protecting Intellectual Property in China in the Twenty-First Century*, 50 AM. U. L. REV. 131 (2000); Daniel Chow, *Anti-Counterfeiting Strategies of Multi-National Companies in China: How a Flawed Approach Is Making Counterfeiting Worse*, 41 GEO. J. INT'L L. 749 (2010).

subdued. So, the Beijing Olympics had clearly generated some interesting dynamics that were not present in situations involving foreign luxury brands.

In addition, due to the wide variety of temporary regulations the central and municipal governments had introduced and the stepped-up market raids they had undertaken, the protection and enforcement of trademark rights had indeed strengthened in Beijing and other major cities. As the *Los Angeles Times* recounted:

> In the last few years [before the Olympic Games], Beijing has seized hundreds of thousands of fake Olympic items and toys, according to government and state media reports. Dozens of people have been prosecuted and fined well over $1 million. The Chinese government set up a hotline – and is offering rewards of up to $14,700 – for people to report counterfeiting of Olympic merchandise.[49]

In an interview with the newspaper, Tao Xinliang, the dean of Shanghai University's Intellectual Property School, also acknowledged that "the crackdown effort this time [was] stronger and the scale larger."[50] Although the sale of counterfeit Olympic merchandise existed, the operations had become more covert, involving backrooms, side alleys, and hidden suitcases.[51] Such operations had also become increasingly rare as the Games approached.

Nevertheless, while policymakers, industry executives, and commentators were quick to point out that protecting the intellectual property rights in Olympic merchandise was "a matter of national will," they tended to ignore the fact that protecting those rights was also a matter of the *people's* will. It was not sheer propaganda that the 2008 Games were referred to as the "People's Olympics" (*rénwén àoyùn*). To a large extent, the mixed success in protecting Beijing Olympics merchandise has shown the effectiveness of the government's effort when such effort was aligned with the will of individual citizens. As a Beijing resident declared disapprovingly over the sale of counterfeit Olympic merchandise: "The Olympics are a grand event involving a lot of countries in the world.

---

[49] Don Lee, *Countdown to Beijing; Let the Piracy Begin*, L.A. TIMES, July 27, 2008, at P3.

[50] *Ibid.*

[51] *See* The Vancouver Province, *Fake "Olympic" Goods Easily Had … You Just Have to Ask*, CANADA.COM (Aug. 11, 2008), http://www.canada.com/theprovince/news/story.html?id=af071385-0b58-4d7a-997a-bb103676f850.

Fake products are not good for the image of Beijing during the Olympics."[52]

The pride Chinese nationals derived from Beijing's successful bid to host the Olympics was understandable, especially against a background of China's painful struggle with the "century of humiliation" and the ongoing and repeated criticisms the country has received from the United States and other foreign powers.[53] As with citizens of any host country of major international sporting events, these proud individuals wanted to showcase the country's ability to meet international standards in the face of heavy media scrutiny. Even more important, "face" runs deep in Chinese culture.[54] The ability to put the best face forward for the world to see was important to not only the central and municipal governments, but also individual citizens. Indeed, many commentators held the view that the Beijing Olympics served as "China's long awaited 'coming out party' [that] would present the world with a relatively clear picture of how Beijing *want[ed]* to be seen."[55]

Moreover, the sponsors of Olympic events had carefully co-branded their merchandise. For example, NBC Universal included on its DVDs not only its trademarks, but also the Olympic logo – a symbol that had special socio-cultural significance.[56] To a large extent, the NBC Universal merchandise indicated not only that the merchandise was protected by trademark law, but also that the merchandise was associated with an event that was of great pride to every Chinese citizen. The co-branding efforts therefore directly appealed to individual citizens, thereby helping China to muster up its people's will. As Doris Long rightly noted:

> The heightened public perception of the importance of protecting the Olympic Symbols from unauthorized uses, and the active role that the public has taken in helping to protect Olympic Symbols may not be readily transferable to other commercial marks. From the point of view of trademark law, there is no significant difference between an Olympic logo and any other trademark when it comes to the need for protection against counterfeit and other infringing uses. Yet culturally, the Olympic Symbols may not be perceived as

---

[52] Sergey Bushtruk, *Beijing Olympics: Pirated Goods on Sale* (Aug. 6, 2007), http://myolympicgames.blogspot.com/2007/08/beijing-olympics-pirated-goods-on-sale.html.

[53] *See* BROWNELL, *supra* note 5, at 152.

[54] *See* Yu, *supra* note 3, at 951–55.

[55] Emily Parker, *Dragons Win: The Beijing Games and Chinese Nationalism*, *in* CHINA'S GREAT LEAP, *supra* note 5, at 273, 274.

[56] *See* Doris Estelle Long, *Trademarks and the Beijing Olympics: Gold Medal Challenges*, 7 J. MARSHALL REV. INTELL. PROP. L. 433, 451.

the functional equivalent of a Louis Vuitton logo or the Prada trademark, two popular luxury brands in China.[57]

Finally, the Chinese government has shown time and again its ability to successfully target specific piracy and counterfeiting problems in the country. When the U.S. government threatened to impose 100 percent tariffs on over $1 billion worth of Chinese imports in response to China's continued failure to protect American intellectual property assets, the central government quickly agreed to close 29 CD factories, including the notorious Shenfei Factory in Shenzhen.[58] The 1995 Agreement that the Chinese and U.S. governments ultimately reached also included a detailed action plan providing for a special enforcement period of six months. As stated in section I.C of that Agreement, China would make intensive efforts to crack down on major infringers of intellectual property rights and to target regions in which infringing activity was particularly rampant at the time of the Agreement.[59]

Although local protectionism remained, especially in such an early stage of China's development of the intellectual property system, the central government successfully mustered up both the resources and political capital needed to undertake such "special" enforcement. Following these special enforcement actions, most rights holders, including those in the U.S. entertainment industries, had been largely satisfied with the government's ability to close down the specified factories. For example, many commentators at that time considered the 1995 Agreement "the single most comprehensive and detailed [intellectual property] enforcement agreement the United States had ever concluded."[60] American government officials also found the early implementation of the Agreement "very promising."[61]

The drawback of the "special enforcement" approach, however, is that such enforcement is costly and unsustainable. While the central government has the ability to undertake such special enforcement or, more

---

[57]   *Ibid.* at 450.

[58]   Martha M. Hamilton and Steven Mufson, *Clinton Hails Accord with China on Trade*, WASH. POST, Feb. 27, 1995, at A1; Steven Mufson, *Trade War Averted by U.S. China*, WASH. POST, Feb. 26, 1995, at A1.

[59]   Action Plan for Effective Protection and Enforcement of Intellectual Property Rights pmbl., § I.C, *in* Agreement Regarding Intellectual Property Rights, Feb. 26, 1995, P.R.C.–U.S., 34 I.L.M. 881, 892–93 (1995).

[60]   Helen Cooper and Kathy Chen, *China Averts Trade War with the U.S., Promising a Campaign Against Piracy*, WALL ST. J., Feb. 27, 1995, at A3.

[61]   *See Implementation of U.S.–China Accord "Very Promising," USTR Official Says*, 12 INT'L TRADE REP. (BNA) D-9 (May 31, 1995).

recently, campaigns to combat massive counterfeiting, few of these special actions have provided long-lasting effects. When these actions expire, counterfeits tend to return very quickly, to the frustration of local policymakers and foreign rights holders.

Finally, we cannot ignore the significant costs incurred in addressing the counterfeiting problem associated with Olympic merchandise. While China has considerable aggregate resources for the enforcement of intellectual property rights, it does not have sufficient resources to address the counterfeiting problem on a per capita or per sector basis. The difference between enforcement resources at the aggregate level and the per capita level is strikingly similar to the difference between China's aggregate GDP and its GDP per capita. Although China has recently overtaken Japan to become the world's second largest economy on an aggregate basis, behind only the United States, Japan still dominates China dramatically on a per capita basis. While Japan has a GDP per capita of 45 903 in 2011, China has a GDP per capita of only 5445.[62]

Moreover, as some rights holders have acknowledged, during the Beijing Olympics, they had a difficult time getting the Chinese government to respond to requests to crack down on counterfeit merchandise *unrelated* to the Olympics. In light of these complaints, one therefore has to wonder about the amount of resources and political capital the central government actually has to combat massive counterfeiting in the country. To a large extent, efforts to address this problem constitute a zero-sum game. While the country may have enough resources to deal with short-term enforcement on a *specific* type of good – in this case, Olympic merchandise before and during the Beijing Games – it may not have adequate resources to facilitate long-term enforcement concerning *all* types of trademarked goods and services.

Even in a major U.S. city like New York, it is not uncommon to find street vendors selling counterfeit goods in Canal Street, the Counterfeit Alley in the Garment District, and the Harlem district. As Tim Philips, a strong advocate of tough enforcement, readily admitted, it is "simply impossible [for the New York Police Department] to raid all the warehouses all of the time without swallowing the entire NYPD anticounterfeiting budget and taking officers off other duties."[63] Likewise, Tim Trainer, the former president of the International AntiCounterfeiting

---

[62] *GDP per Capita (Current US$)*, WORLD BANK, http://data.worldbank.org/indicator/NY.GDP.PCAP.CD (last visited Mar. 31, 2013).

[63] TIM PHILLIPS, KNOCKOFF: THE DEADLY TRADE IN COUNTERFEIT GOODS 36 (2005).

Coalition, lamented: "[T]he staff dedicated solely to [intellectual property] enforcement [in the U.S. Government] could be counted on two hands."[64]

In sum, the Beijing Olympics have vividly shown the immense challenge of protecting trademarks in China. Even when the Chinese government was determined to crack down on counterfeiting in view of national interests, it had only mixed success in addressing that problem. Although policymakers, rights holders, and commentators have attributed the counterfeiting problem to the lack of political will on the part of the Chinese government, we cannot ignore the many structural challenges that are inherent in the country's massive counterfeiting problem, such as local protectionism, the lack of willingness for the public at large to cooperate with the government on intellectual property enforcement, and the government's limited enforcement resources on a per capita, per sector basis.

V THE FUTURE OF TRADEMARK PROTECTION IN CHINA

Given the Chinese government's mixed success in addressing the counterfeiting of Olympic merchandise, one has to wonder what the future will hold for the protection and enforcement of trademark rights in China. One could also question the lasting effect of the Beijing Games on the future development of the Chinese trademark system.

To get a glimpse of the future of the Chinese trademark system, it may be useful to juxtapose the promising developments surrounding the Beijing Olympics with the growing awareness and understanding of trademark law among the Chinese leaders and local businesses. Although the Beijing Olympics did not provide a dramatic change in the trademark landscape in China, it has signaled many attractive prospects for greater protection of trademarks in China. These prospects become even more important in light of the recent adoption of the Third Amendment to the 1982 Chinese Trademark Law.

When Legend, China's leading manufacturer of personal computers, expanded overseas many years ago, it painfully learned that its name had already been registered and used for similar products in many other

---

[64] Timothy P. Trainer, *Intellectual Property Enforcement: A Reality Gap (Insufficient Assistance, Ineffective Implementation)?*, 8 J. MARSHALL REV. INTELL. PROP. L. 47, 58 (2008).

countries.[65] To avoid potential infringement, and to ensure that it could become an official sponsor of the 2008 Beijing Olympics,[66] it had no choice but to develop the new LENOVO mark, which combined the first two letters in the LEGEND mark with the word "novo."[67] Such a name has since become famous around the world following the extensive Western media coverage of Lenovo's purchase of IBM's personal computers division.

Today, however, a number of local firms have already achieved prominence in the international market, with their trademarks being recognized as well known outside China. Examples of these famous local brands include BAIDU (for technology), GALANZ (for microwave ovens), GEELY (for cars), HAIER (for household appliances), HUAWEI TECHNOLOGIES (for telecommunications equipment), KONKA (for household appliances), LENOVO (for personal computers), LI-NING (for sportswear), TCL (for mobile phones and other electronic products), and ZTE (for mobile phones and other electronic products). Even the monks of the Shaolin Temple reportedly registered the name of their temple as a trademark.[68]

From the standpoint of China's internal development, strengthening the country's trademark protection makes a lot of sense. As commentators have noted, there are two primary reasons why countries are reluctant to offer stronger trademark protection.[69] First, the country wants to encourage its export businesses to free ride on the investment of foreign trademark holders by earning profits as if they were selling genuine goods that bear the infringing trademarks. Second, the country does not want its consumers to pay a higher premium just because a foreign trademark has an established reputation with consumers in the country.

---

[65] *See* Bruce Einhorn and Dexter Roberts, *A New Twist in Legend's Tale*, BUS. WK., June 23, 2003, at 50; Mark Hall, *Welcome, China*, COMPUTERWORLD, Dec. 13, 2004, at 18.

[66] Lenovo is one of the 12 Olympic Partners during 2005–2008, along with Atos Origin, Coca-Cola, GE, Johnson & Johnson, Kodak, Manulife, McDonald's, Omega, Panasonic, Samsung, and Visa. Alan Tomlinson, *Olympic Values, Beijing's Olympic Games, and the Universal Market*, in OWNING THE OLYMPICS, *supra* note 5, at 67, 75.

[67] *See* LING ZHIJUN, THE LENOVO AFFAIR: THE GROWTH OF CHINA'S COMPUTER GIANT AND ITS TAKEOVER OF IBM-PC 334–35 (Martha Avery trans., 2006).

[68] *See* Zhao Jiemin, *Chinese Companies Learn to Protect their IPR*, XINHUA NEWS AGENCY, Apr. 26, 2005.

[69] *See* Edmund W. Kitch, *The Patent Policy of Developing Countries*, 13 UCLA PAC. BASIN L.J. 166, 168 (1994).

By not protecting famous trademarks, the country therefore will save the much-needed foreign exchange while making consumer products more affordable for its people.

As the Chinese economy continues to change and as its market continues to grow, however, neither reason will provide a satisfactory justification for a nationwide policy offering limited protection to foreign trademarks. A strategy based on the first reason is misguided, because it "will result in a parasitical business that will always be dependent on the willingness of the targeted countries to tolerate the infringing imports ... [and that] will never have an established market position that can lay a foundation for the development of an internationally competitive business."[70] In fact, it does not require much investment to create a famous trademark; even developing countries have succeeded in doing so, with CORONA (for Mexican beer) and TSINGTAO (for Chinese beer) being very good examples.[71]

A strategy based on the second reason is equally harmful, because it will ultimately backfire on local consumers, who will be unable to use trademarks to identify the source of origin of goods and services due to widespread counterfeiting. As a result of a lack of trademark protection, local consumers not only will have to spend more time searching for products, but will have no guarantee that they will get the products they want. Consumer confidence will suffer, and producers will have little incentive to control the quality of their products. In the end, consumers may be charged inflated prices for poor-quality goods, some of which will expose them to health and safety risks.[72]

In addition, greater trademark protection could result from four additional developments that are unique to China but that commentators seldom mention. First, trademark protection will create fewer obstacles to China's modernization efforts than copyright or patent protection. While

---

[70]   *Ibid.*

[71]   *See* Janet H. MacLaughlin, Timothy J. Richards and Leigh A. Kenny, *The Economic Significance of Piracy*, *in* INTELLECTUAL PROPERTY RIGHTS: GLOBAL CONSENSUS, GLOBAL CONFLICT? 89, 104 (R. Michael Gadbaw and Timothy J. Richards eds., 1988).

[72]   It is important to note that consumers do not necessarily get inferior products due to a lack of trademark protection. For example, many counterfeit products in China are made using the same raw materials and design patterns. The products are counterfeits because the manufacturers did not have the rights holders' authorization at the time of production, rather than because they used inferior raw materials or production processes. Indeed, the counterfeiters could be former contractors who had prior authorization to use the related design patterns.

copyright protection affects the country's ability to maintain cultural and media control and may have a negative impact on its extensive propaganda efforts,[73] patent protection slows down the country's efforts by draining foreign exchange reserves in the form of royalty and license fee payments. By contrast, trademark protection promotes economic development and commercial activities. As Peter Feng reminded us, trademarks "were a state planning tool before they became a marketing device and private property."[74] It is therefore no surprise that trademark registrations continued even during the Cultural Revolution,[75] when trademarks were politicized to the point that manufacturers only dared to use such "politically correct" pseudonyms and non-identifying labels as "Red Flag" (*hóngqí*), "East Wind" (*dōngfēng*), "Liberation" (*jiěfàng*), "The East Is Red" (*dōngfāng hóng*), and "Worker-Peasant-Soldier" (*gōng nóng bīng*).[76]

Because trademarks did not affect China's modernization efforts as much as copyrights and patents, it is understandable why the 1982 Trademark Law has become the first intellectual property statute to be enacted after China reopened its market to foreign trade in the late 1970s. For comparison purposes, the Patent Law was not introduced until two years later, and the Copyright Law was not adopted until 1990 following significant pressure from the U.S. government.[77]

Today, policymakers continue to find trademark protection more attractive than other forms of intellectual property protection, perhaps because of its association with economic and commercial activities. In fact, had the State Council and the State Intellectual Property Office not actively pushed for the development of the patent system through the National Intellectual Property Strategy and the National Patent Development Strategy,[78] trademarks might have a brighter future in China than copyrights and patents. Now that these agencies have introduced these

---

[73] *See* MERTHA, *supra* note 42, at 133–34, 140; Peter K. Yu, *Piracy, Prejudice, and Perspectives: An Attempt to Use Shakespeare to Reconfigure the U.S.–China Intellectual Property Debate*, 19 B.U. INT'L. L.J. 1, 28–32 (2001).

[74] PETER FENG, INTELLECTUAL PROPERTY IN CHINA 344 (2nd ed. 2003).

[75] *See ibid.* at 293; MERTHA, *supra* note 42, at 197.

[76] *See* TAN LOKE-KHOON, PIRATES IN THE MIDDLE KINGDOM: THE ENSUING TRADEMARK BATTLE 10 (2nd ed. 2007); Mark Sidel, *Copyright, Trademark and Patent Law in the People's Republic of China*, 21 TEX. INT'L L.J. 259, 272 (1986).

[77] *See* Zhang Naigen, *Intellectual Property Law in China: Basic Policy and New Developments*, 4 ANN. SURV. INT'L & COMP. L. 1, 8 (1997).

[78] *See* Peter K. Yu, *Five Oft-Repeated Questions About China's Recent Rise as a Patent Power*, 2013 CARDOZO L. REV. DE NOVO 78; Peter K. Yu, *The Rise*

strategies, it is likely that the future of both trademarks and patents will be brighter than that of copyrights.

Second, although trademark protection requires local consumers to pay a premium for products with well-known foreign brands, it encourages local firms to catch up and compete with these brands by developing more attractive products and focusing on brand positioning. That the Chinese commercial market is still at an early, immature stage will only serve to benefit Chinese firms. As one commentator noted, "China's market is ... dynamic, with consumer loyalty still developing: consumers are still experimenting, and brands come and go with great speed."[79] Under such rapidly changing conditions, local firms have the opportunity to attain market position and develop the next promising brands.

Indeed, the ability to develop local brands has been greatly enhanced by the failure of foreign businesses to understand local Chinese market conditions. Studies in the early 2000s have "estimated that less than 10 percent of Chinese consumers have the level of disposable income that can afford to buy Western products."[80] Notwithstanding this financial reality, many foreign businesses only focus on the high-end market, ignoring the mid-to-low-end customers. A case in point is the microwave market, which Galanz overtook in the early 2000s: "[I]n 1993 only 1 percent of Chinese consumers had microwaves. Consumption grew – but not in the way predicted. By 2006, nearly 90 percent of the market was in cheaper models, with the Chinese company Galanz dominating."[81]

Unlike foreign firms, Chinese firms usually "produce their own brands at low cost first, then gradually develop very strong brand positioning."[82] For example, instead of competing directly against such famous Japanese household brands as Panasonic and Fujitsu, Haier "aimed for the middle ground, positioning itself between the leading overseas innovators and lower cost, lower quality domestic rivals."[83] Once Chinese firms have built up their market share, they will focus on developing their brand

---

and Decline of the Intellectual Property Powers, 34 CAMPBELL L. REV. 525, 530–31 (2012).

[79] HAROLD CHEE WITH CHRIS WEST, MYTHS ABOUT DOING BUSINESS IN CHINA 30 (2nd ed. 2007); *see also* JOHN L. CHAN, CHINA STREETSMART: WHAT YOU MUST KNOW TO BE EFFECTIVE AND PROFITABLE IN CHINA 54–55 (2003); Rick Yan, *Short-Term Results: The Litmus Test for Success in China*, in DOING BUSINESS IN CHINA 79, 95 (Harvard Business Review ed., 2004).

[80] CHEE WITH WEST, *supra* note 79, at 31.

[81] *Ibid.*

[82] *Ibid.* at 32.

[83] *How China's Most Valuable Brand Found Its Niche*, MANAGING INTELL. PROP., Apr. 1, 2005, at 38.

positioning. Indeed, many of these firms have been spending a substantial amount of money on brand building. According to Nielsen Media Research, "only two foreign brands were ranked among the top ten most advertised products in China (Procter and Gamble's 'Crest' and 'Safeguard')."[84]

Third, trademark protection creates the least friction with Chinese culture, and the justification for trademark protection, in particular its emphasis on goodwill, is easy for the Chinese to understand. Given the importance of "face" in Chinese culture, it is not hard to explain why trademark protection is important. Just as "face" is about an individual's self-respect, prestige, and social standing, trademarks, especially well-known ones, provide information about the quality, reputation, and commercial standing of the products. In the wake of the WTO accession, China strengthened its protection of well-known marks. Such protection is both important and urgently needed, as licensed foreign products are increasingly sold in different parts of the country.

Fourth, "the Chinese themselves are ... very brand conscious, a legacy of Confucian hierarchy and of their imperial past where rank was prominently displayed on bureaucrats' clothing."[85] The fact that the Chinese language consists of pictorial characters and "is strongly visual and semiotically promiscuous" also makes trademarks and other related symbols more important in Chinese culture.[86] Moreover, active brand building "fits with the government's strategy of consolidating strategic industries ... to create national champions that can hold their own in global markets and ... to restore its imperial glory."[87] As Professor Shenkar noted:

> From building the world's tallest building to hosting the Olympics, which is a traditional coming-of-age for Asian nations, symbols are important to the Chinese regime, whose legitimacy increasingly rests on delivering economic performance and growth on the one hand and on nationalist sentiments on the other. Showcase projects are there to impress citizens and outsiders with the regime's capabilities and signal that the aspiration to be counted among the world's leading nations is attainable.[88]

---

[84] CHEE WITH WEST, *supra* note 79, at 32.

[85] SHENKAR, *supra* note 31, at 157.

[86] BOB HODGE AND KAM LOUIE, THE POLITICS OF CHINESE LANGUAGE AND CULTURE: THE ART OF READING DRAGONS 8 (1998).

[87] SHENKAR, *supra* note 31, at 158.

[88] *Ibid.* at 36.

Finally, as the Chinese economy grows and the middle class becomes larger, the Chinese will have more disposable income and purchasing power. When people are poor, they are more willing to settle for fake Gucci belts, Louis Vuitton handbags, or Rolex watches. When they become richer, however, they may start looking for higher-priced luxury goods. Indeed, some commentators have suggested that China's WTO accession might improve local living standards to the point that Chinese consumers will be more interested in buying genuine products.[89]

As early as 2005, Ernst & Young made the following forecast:

> The Chinese luxury market ... is expected to grow 20%, annually until 2008 and then 10% annually until 2015, when sales are expected to exceed US$11.5 billion. By 2010, China is expected to have a quarter-billion consumers who can afford luxury products, nearly 17 times the present number. By 2015, Chinese consumers could be as influential as the Japanese and account for 29% of all global luxury goods purchases.[90]

Although this forecast was already quite impressive a few years ago, a new forecast showed that the Chinese middle class and luxury goods market grew more rapidly than many had anticipated. As Bain & Company estimated in December 2011:

> Luxury goods purchases in China and by Chinese consumers reached a total of 212 B RMB [over US$30 billion] in 2010. Luxury purchases grew by 27 percent in Mainland China in 2010 and by 45 percent in Hong Kong and Macau, while Chinese luxury purchases abroad grew by 38 percent. When including Hong Kong and Macau spending, Greater China becomes the world's third largest luxury market, bypassing Italy and amounting to nearly 40 percent of the US luxury market.[91]

In sum, the trademark landscape in China is now undergoing a very significant and promising change. Although the Beijing Olympics provided China with an opportunity to improve trademark protection, it was not the only major opportunity. Only two short years after the Beijing Games, China held the World Expo in Shanghai. Since then, the country has also served as an active host of a wide variety of trade fairs and international exhibitions. As the Chinese market continues to mature and

---

[89]   *See* DANIEL C.K. CHOW, A PRIMER ON FOREIGN INVESTMENT ENTERPRISES AND PROTECTION OF INTELLECTUAL PROPERTY IN CHINA 254 (2002).

[90]   ERNST & YOUNG, CHINA: THE NEW LAP OF LUXURY 1 (2005).

[91]   *2011 China Luxury Market Study*, BAIN & CO. (Dec. 15, 2011), http://www.bain.com/publications/articles/2011-china-luxury-market-study.aspx.

as its middle class continues to grow, the country's trademark landscape can only become more attractive to brand owners – from both inside and abroad.

The Beijing Olympics were held at a time when the trademark landscape in China was undergoing a rapid and dramatic change. Through the establishment of licensing arrangements with the BOCOG, Chinese firms gained important expertise regarding the mechanics of the intellectual property system. Looking back, it is no surprise that trademark protection in China has improved after the Olympics. Nevertheless, as this chapter has shown, many additional factors have also contributed to this gradual but significant improvement in the Chinese trademark system.

VI CONCLUSION

Policymakers, industries, and commentators have widely used the Beijing Olympics to illustrate how the Chinese government could successfully combat massive counterfeiting if such a problem concerned national interests. While the 2008 Games have provided an excellent illustration of the counterfeiting problem in China, as China critics have claimed, they do not support the claim that China could effectively address the counterfeiting problem when national interests were at stake. Instead, the Beijing Olympics have vividly illustrated the ongoing challenges of combating the massive counterfeiting problem in China. It shows what the Chinese government can and cannot do, the necessary complements for success, and the remaining challenges concerning efforts to protect trademarks in such a large, complex, and highly populous country.

If anything, the curious case of fake Beijing Olympics merchandise has confirmed the claim made repeatedly by Chinese policymakers as well as commentators knowledgeable about the intellectual property problems in China – namely, the counterfeiting problem is harder to solve than foreign government officials, industry executives, and rights holders are ready to admit. Nevertheless, this curious case also reminds us that the Chinese government has the ability to successfully target specific counterfeiting problems for a short period of time. Whether the Chinese government could also provide sustainable, long-term, and meaningful protection remains to be seen.

13. Trademark enforcement in developing countries: counterfeiting as an externality imposed by multinational companies

Daniel C.K. Chow[*]

I INTRODUCTION

In recent years, multinational companies (MNCs) have repeatedly warned the public about the unprecedented and staggering financial losses that they claim to be suffering due to a surge in the global trade in counterfeit goods. Recent industry estimates place annual worldwide losses due to counterfeiting and other forms of commercial piracy in the hundreds of billions of dollars per year. MNCs – owners of the world's most commercially valuable intellectual property – claim that they suffer the vast bulk of these losses. MNCs claim that counterfeiters located in developing countries are the main culprits of this surge in counterfeit goods. According to MNCs, corrupt governments in many of these countries – in particular, China – protect or support counterfeiters that harm their businesses and the global economy.

Despite their claims, however, MNCs are not really harmed by counterfeiting. Upon closer examination, the financial losses that MNCs claim to suffer from lost sales caused by counterfeiting are based on methods that grossly exaggerate both the levels of counterfeit goods sold and the losses suffered. These claims of severe financial losses are unsubstantiated and based upon dubious assumptions that do not withstand scrutiny. The actual losses suffered are most likely only a tiny fraction of the amounts claimed; in dollar terms, lost sales of genuine

* Joseph S. Platt-Porter Wright Morris & Arthur Professor of Law, the Ohio State University Moritz College of Law. This chapter is adapted from my article, Daniel Chow, *Counterfeiting as an Externality Imposed by Multinational Companies on Developing Countries*, 51 VA. J. INT'L L. 785 (2011).

products due to counterfeits are likely insignificant and cause little or no financial damage to a majority of MNCs. Suppressing counterfeiting is not a major business priority of MNCs – it is part of the larger effort of MNCs to control every facet of how their brands are presented to the consuming public. Counterfeiting undermines the ability of MNCs to control their brand image, but these types of harms do not translate into lost sales of genuine products. Harm to goodwill is difficult to measure in economic terms, and MNCs have made no attempts to do so, but the economic impact of these harms as measured in lost sales, when and if a scientific study is done, will most likely be revealed to be trivial in comparison with the tens and hundreds of billions of dollars that MNCs claim that they lose to global counterfeiting.

Although MNCs may not be harmed by counterfeiting, substantial harms do occur because of counterfeiting. Most of these harms are social and political costs that fall on the developing countries in which the bulk of counterfeiting occurs. Once the opportunity for counterfeiting is presented (which typically occurs when MNCs introduce commercially valuable intellectual property into developing countries), organized crime, working in conjunction with corrupt governments, quickly seizes the opportunity to earn huge profits from this lucrative but illegal trade in counterfeit goods.[1] Some counterfeit goods, such as foods and drugs, contain substandard and dangerous ingredients that lead to health and safety hazards. Illness and death from counterfeit foods and medicines occur disproportionately in developing countries and least developed countries,[2] and rarely occur in advanced developed countries, such as the United States. In developing countries where counterfeiting occurs, there is an increase in organized crime, government corruption, and health and safety issues. All of these harms have serious social, political, and human costs. No doubt these harms also result in substantial economic losses, although no comprehensive attempts have been made to quantify them.

---

[1] *See* Daniel C.K. Chow, *Organized Crime, Local Protectionism, and the Trade in Counterfeit Goods in China*, 14 CHINA ECON. REV. 473, 473–84 (2003).

[2] There is no official definition of a developing country or a least developed country. The classifications used by the World Bank, although not mandatory, are widely followed. The World Bank divides all countries into four income groups:

Low Income: $975 or less; Lower Middle Income: $976–$3855; Upper Middle Income: $3856–$11 905; and High Income: $11 906 and above. Of these categories, countries that fall within the first three – low income, lower middle income, and upper middle income – are all considered developing countries. *See How We Classify Countries*, WORLD BANK, http://data. worldbank.org/about/country-classifications (last visited Apr. 28, 2013).

Because the bulk of harms from counterfeiting do not fall on MNCs but on the developing countries in which the counterfeiting occurs, counterfeiting is a corporate externality for MNCs.[3] An externality is a cost (or benefit) that is not directly borne by the actor whose conduct causes the externality.[4] Rather, the costs fall on others. Externalities can lead to inefficiencies because the actor does not take into account all of the costs (or benefits) of its conduct. In making their decisions to locate their manufacturing operations overseas in low-cost countries, MNCs do not consider the costs of counterfeiting imposed on developing countries. Like other rational economic actors, MNCs do not consider the social harms created by counterfeiting in their decision-making since MNCs do not bear these costs. But these costs, while external to MNCs, fall upon others. Primarily, they fall on developing countries, their national governments, and their constituencies, including those in advanced industrialized countries, which are being asked to fund the costs of enforcement against the global trade in counterfeit goods. Of course, all conduct creates some externalities and different externalities may attach to the same conduct. The externalities that are the focus of this chapter are the social harms imposed on developing countries by counterfeiting.

The analysis above suggests that the real attribution of responsibility for the global counterfeiting problem may be the reverse of what is popularly portrayed in the media. Developing countries are usually portrayed as the perpetrators or supporters of counterfeiting and commercial piracy, but these countries, not MNCs, in fact suffer the bulk of the harms created by counterfeiting. By contrast, MNCs are often portrayed as the victims of counterfeiting, but they actually contribute significantly to creating the problem that harms developing countries. MNCs are responsible because counterfeiting is a predictable result of moving manufacturing and production to developing countries in order to take advantage of low labor and manufacturing costs. As part of establishing manufacturing facilities in developing countries, MNCs transfer commercially valuable intellectual property rights to developing countries with weak legal systems and corrupt governments. By introducing commercially valuable intellectual property rights that are easily copied in countries where corruption and crime are rampant and enforcement is

---

[3] Simon Mackenzie first elaborated the economic thesis that counterfeiting is an externality for MNCs in Simon Mackenzie, *Counterfeiting as Corporate Externality: Intellectual Property Crime and Global Insecurity*, 54 CRIME L. & SOC. CHANGE 21 (2010).

[4] The classic discussion of externalities is set forth in Harold Demsetz, *Toward a Theory of Property Rights*, 57 AM. ECON. REV. 347 (1967).

weak, MNCs are providing an opportunity for lucrative economic crimes that prove impossible to resist for many segments of the poor population in developing countries. As long as MNCs benefit from low-cost manufacturing in developing countries that involve the transfer of technology to those countries, global trade in counterfeit goods will continue to grow because the bulk of the harms of counterfeiting are corporate externalities for MNCs.

II MNCS' CLAIMS OF FINANCIAL LOSSES FROM COUNTERFEITING

In the past several decades, the global trade in counterfeit goods has surged at an unprecedented pace. In 1982, the U.S. International Trade Commission (USITC) estimated that commercial piracy caused annual worldwide losses of $5.5 billion.[5] Just six years later, in 1988, the USITC revised its estimate to over $60 billion in annual losses.[6] In 2009, the Organisation for Economic Co-operation and Development (OECD) estimated that the global trade in counterfeit goods was over $250 billion (almost 2 percent of world trade) and caused losses of $150 billion to the G20 countries, the leading industrialized nations of the world, led by the United States.[7] Estimates that are circulated directly by industry groups are significantly higher. Some industry groups estimate that counterfeit goods comprise 7 percent of total world trade, and that the total annual losses on a global basis to counterfeiting are $650 billion per year;[8] of

---

[5]   *See* S. REP. NO. 104-177, at 3 (1995); *see also* USITC, PUBL.'N NO. 1479, THE EFFECTS OF FOREIGN PRODUCT COUNTERFEITING ON U.S. INDUSTRY xiv, 24 (1984).

[6]   *See* USITC, PUBL'N NO. 2065, FOREIGN PROTECTION OF INTELLECTUAL PROPERTY RIGHTS AND THE EFFECT ON U.S. INDUSTRY AND TRADE app. H (1988).

[7]   *See* Press Release, World Intellectual Property Organization, Counterfeiting and Piracy Endangers Global Economic Recovery Say Global Congress Leaders, WIPO Press Release PR/2009/621 (Dec. 3, 2009), *available at* http://tinyurl.com/yd9edmq.

[8]   The Coalition for Intellectual Property Rights credits the World Customs Organization (WCO) and Interpol with this estimate. *See First Global Congress on Combating Counterfeiting*, COALITION FOR INTELLECTUAL PROPERTY RIGHTS (CIPR), http://tinyurl.com/4nckel6 (last visited Mar. 26, 2011); *Putin Assures ICC that Global Business Concerns Will Be on G8 Agenda*, INT'L CHAMBER OF COMMERCE [ICC] (July 5, 2006), http://tinyurl.com/4fu5xug.

this figure, the United States suffers between $200 billion and $250 billion in annual losses.[9]

These statistics are impressive and present a daunting picture, but on what are these figures based? All of these statistics, including the ones provided by the USITC and OECD, rely on information provided by MNCs and their industry groups. What methods do MNCs use to arrive at these figures?

MNCs estimate the size of the counterfeiting trade and the losses suffered using the following methods or a variant thereof. First, MNCs will determine the size of the counterfeit trade in any given location by conducting an on-the-ground market survey to determine the total amount of product in that location. The MNC then determines how many units of genuine product are shipped through the MNC's own distribution channels to the particular location. The difference between the amount of total product and the amount of product shipped by an MNC is treated as counterfeits. For example, suppose that a market survey indicates that there are 1000 units of total product in a given location, and the MNC's own records indicate that 800 units were shipped by the MNC's own factories and warehouse to the location. The MNC will conclude that the additional 200 units are counterfeits and that counterfeits comprise 20 percent of the market. The same approach, with some variations, is used for business or entertainment software. The MNC will conduct a survey to determine the number of applications in a given location and then review its records to determine how many applications were supplied to the location by the MNC. The difference between the number of total applications and the number supplied by the MNC equals the number of pirated applications in that location.

Once the amount of counterfeit product is determined, MNCs will determine the losses sustained from counterfeiting. Some MNCs seem to take the position that the existence of a counterfeit product on the market is the equivalent of a lost sale of the genuine product at the retail price. In our example above, if the size of the counterfeit trade is 20 percent of total trade, or 200 units in the location in question, MNCs will estimate

---

[9] INT'L ANTI-COUNTERFEITING COALITION, THE NEGATIVE CONSEQUENCES OF INTERNATIONAL INTELLECTUAL PROPERTY THEFT: ECONOMIC HARM, THREATS TO THE PUBLIC HEALTH AND SAFETY, AND LINKS TO ORGANIZED CRIME AND TERRORIST ORGANIZATIONS 3–4 (2005), *available at* http://tinyurl.com/4p95qcj; Press Release, Fed. Bureau of Investigation, The Federal Bureau of Investigation and the U.S. Customs Service Today Announced the National Intellectual Property Rights Coordination Center's First Conference for Members of Congress and Industry in Washington (July 16, 2002), http://tinyurl.com/4rugjza.

the losses due to counterfeiting to be 20 percent of total trade or the revenue that would have been earned on sales of 20 percent, or 200 genuine products, at the retail price. The gist of this approach is that the mere existence of a counterfeit – regardless of whether there is any evidence that the counterfeit was sold to a consumer – equals a loss of a sale of the genuine product at the retail price. There appears to be no defensible justification for this approach; one of the reasons given by MNCs for the use of this approach is the difficulty in tracking sales of counterfeits, which often occur out of plain sight and under clandestine circumstances. Other MNCs seem to take the approach that every sale of a counterfeit product blocks a sale of the genuine product; thus, each counterfeit that is sold results in a loss of a sale of the genuine product at the retail price.

A   Assumptions Used by MNCs in Determining Volume and Losses from Counterfeiting

These methods for determining the size of the counterfeit trade and the resulting losses suffered are based upon several questionable assumptions. First, in determining the size of the counterfeit trade for a given location, the method described above makes the assumption that the only genuine goods in a particular location are those that were directly shipped by the MNC. This assumption ignores the possibility of the horizontal movement of goods, that is, genuine goods sold by the MNC in one location that are then resold or reshipped to another. For instance, in our example above, the market survey indicated that MNC supplied only 800 units, or 80 percent, of the genuine product to a particular location, so the other 200 units, or 20 percent, were deemed to be counterfeits. But suppose that the MNC had previously supplied a large number of genuine products to a different location, and a wholesale distributor purchased those products and then resold them to retailers in the location in question. It would also be possible for a retail chain that purchased goods for a store in one location to ship some of the goods to stores in other locations to meet increased demand in the other locations. In this instance, because of the horizontal movement of genuine goods from one location to another, it is quite possible that genuine goods were supplied to the location in question for legitimate business reasons by a business entity other than the MNC. In this case, the number of genuine products is higher than that supplied by the MNC, and the number of counterfeits is correspondingly lower. The same result would hold true if parallel imports or gray market goods were involved. Gray market goods are genuine goods originally intended for sale in a location abroad that are then imported into the home market, such as the United States, often without the permission of the U.S. trademark owner. If some of the MNC's products were manufactured in foreign factories for sale abroad but then purchased abroad by an unrelated distributor, who then exported them back to the United States (or another home market), genuine goods would also be available in markets that are unaccounted for by the MNC. These parallel imports or gray market goods would be treated as counterfeits.

The assumptions on which economic losses are calculated are also questionable. As noted earlier, some MNCs adopt the approach that every sale of a counterfeit results in the loss of the sale of a genuine product at the retail price. This approach seems to be based on the assumption that consumers who purchase counterfeits intended to purchase a genuine product but have mistakenly purchased a counterfeit instead. The mistake is caused by fraud or deception on the consumer; the counterfeiter has fooled the consumer into believing that the knock-off is a genuine product. However, several factors indicate that, today, many if not most consumers who purchase counterfeits make a knowing and rational choice to do so and are not deceived. Most counterfeits sell at prices that are significantly lower than prices for genuine products, sometimes many multiples lower. In some cases, counterfeits sell for a fraction of the price of the original. For example, certain types of high end luxury goods with prestigious brand names (such as handbags, purses, luggage, and carrying cases) might sell for one-tenth, or less, of the price of the original. An original brand name luxury handbag might sell for $700 whereas a counterfeit might sell for $50. It would be typical for a high-end basketball sneaker to sell at $100 and for a counterfeit of the same shoe to sell at $20. Even in the case of hygienic consumer products, such as shampoos, there is a significant price difference: high-quality counterfeits sell for about 30–50 percent less than the price of the original. Given the significant price difference between counterfeits and genuine products, it is likely that consumers who pay significantly lower prices for branded goods know that they are purchasing a fake item, a smuggled product, or other contraband. A consumer who purchases a handbag for $50 – knowing that the retail price of the genuine article is $700 – knows that the item is a counterfeit.

Not only is the price difference a clear indication that the product is a counterfeit, but the place and circumstances of purchase provide another clear indication of the origin of the goods. MNCs have developed strong distribution networks consisting of qualified distributors who are contractually required to deal only in genuine goods upon the pain of penalties and loss of distribution rights. Counterfeiters find it difficult to penetrate an established high-quality distribution network system to mix fakes with real products. As a result, counterfeits are rarely, if ever, found in certain types of retail establishments that use qualified distributors. In the United States, counterfeits are almost never found in large department stores or well-known national chains or discount stores, such as Walmart, Target, or Costco. These companies have strong distribution networks that cannot usually be penetrated by counterfeits, smuggled goods, or other contraband. Counterfeiters must look to find soft spots, such as corrupt sub-distributors in less reputable distribution chains that deliver to smaller retail stores and individually owned discount stores, as well as individual proprietorships ("mom and pop" stores) or transient street vendors. These distributors are more likely to be willing to accept goods of a dubious origin to mix in with genuine goods, and their retail customers are usually more willing to accept such goods in exchange for lower prices.

In China and other developing countries flooded with counterfeits, many or most consumers are well aware of locations where counterfeit goods are sold and where they are not. As with the case of the United States, in China, counterfeit goods are not found in large state-run or privately owned department stores; rather, they are found in small retail shops, street stalls, and open-air kiosks. In some cases, there are well-known markets and parts of cities that are notorious for their dealing in counterfeit goods; in other parts of the city, such as central business district areas, counterfeits are rarely, if ever, available in large retail department stores.

In the United States, consumers who purchase counterfeit goods do so from street vendors, private sellers who arrange to come to the homes of consumers, or small retail stores in immigrant neighborhoods where the counterfeit products are hidden from plain sight but are available for the asking consumer. Some individual consumers can also purchase goods from the Internet from sellers in foreign locations, such as China, Thailand, and Vietnam, at steep discount prices. In other words, consumers who wish to purchase counterfeit goods make an active effort to find and locate vendors of such products. Conversely, consumers who shop in mainstream commerce, such as shopping malls and large department stores, rarely, if ever, encounter counterfeit goods.

In fact, due to the differences in price, location, and circumstances of sale between real and counterfeit products, it appears that different groups of consumers are involved in purchasing real and counterfeit products. Consumers who purchase genuine products are willing to pay a premium for the goodwill and prestige associated with the genuine brand. By contrast, consumers who purchase counterfeit goods may, in general, be less affluent and may be willing to engage in riskier behavior by dealing with vendors of unknown reputations in less secure locations. Consumers who purchase counterfeit goods may not be a target market for the genuine product at all because of their different habits, tastes, and economic status. When counterfeits are not available, consumers who actively seek to purchase counterfeits either forgo purchasing any products or buy an alternative at a price point that is similar to the price of the counterfeit.

B Consumers and the Knowing Purchase of Counterfeits

If many consumers do not mistakenly purchase counterfeit goods when they are really seeking to purchase a genuine product, then the removal of a counterfeit from the market will not necessarily result in the recovery of a sale of a genuine product. This point would seem to be especially applicable in all cases where there is a significant price difference of many multiples between the genuine product and the counterfeit. In the area of luxury goods, the claim that a consumer who purchases a counterfeit handbag for $50 would pay $700 for an original if the counterfeit is removed from the marketplace seems preposterous. Even in the case of computer business software, the major differences in price would indicate that there is no one-to-one correspondence between the sale of a counterfeit and the loss of the sale of a genuine application at the retail price. The assumption that every sale of a counterfeit blocks the sale of a genuine product at the full retail price appears to be fictitious.

This analysis indicates that the methods used by MNCs to calculate the volume of the global counterfeit trade and the resulting economic losses are not supported by reliable evidence. MNCs claim to be losing tens, even hundreds, of billions of dollars per year to counterfeiting and commercial piracy based on data that is derived from methods of simplistic and spurious assumptions. Until MNCs can provide reliable evidence of those losses, claims of billions of dollars of annual losses due to counterfeiting should be viewed by the public with skepticism and as unsubstantiated and fanciful claims.

III HARMS FROM COUNTERFEITING

If MNCs have not demonstrated that they suffer serious financial losses from counterfeiting and commercial piracy, what are the harms, if any, caused by the rising global trade in counterfeit goods, and who suffers from them?

A MNCs' Loss of Control of How Brands Are Presented to the Public

Many MNCs now view their brands as their most valuable business assets. These MNCs have generally invested significant resources in creating brands that appeal to the public. In order to protect their investment, MNCs wish to exercise complete control over every facet of how that brand is presented to the public. MNCs wish to control advertising in print and visual media, as well as the use of the Internet to display their brands to protect the goodwill of the brand. MNCs view any attempt by unauthorized parties to present the brand in any light as a threat to one of the MNC's most valuable and core business assets.

Although MNCs have not demonstrated that counterfeit goods directly preclude sales of genuine products, the use by counterfeiters of famous trademarks may diminish the image of the brand. Even though most consumers are not confused into thinking that inexpensive counterfeits are the famous branded product, the availability of knock-offs at a low price may impair the exclusivity of the brand. MNCs have invested considerable financial resources to create, in some cases, an image of exclusivity, glamour, and prestige, and for those reasons, they are able to charge consumers a considerable premium to obtain the brand. MNCs might consider the widespread availability of cheap knock-offs as a way of diminishing the value of the genuine product to the consumer who has paid a premium for the genuine product. A consumer who has paid a hefty premium (well above the cost of the materials of the product) might balk at seeing cheap knock-offs widely available on the street. The sale of counterfeits and smuggled products in discount stores, open street stalls, and small retail stores may also harm the image of the brand. Some brand owners might view the availability of knock-offs in dis-reputable locations as a tarnishment of the brand. Some counterfeiters also use a famous brand on a product that is not sold by the brand owner. For example, some counterfeiters might use a trademark for a famous shampoo to sell skin cream or toothpaste, or a famous brand name of an automobile to sell furniture. These uses may also create some blurring of the distinctiveness of the mark and cause consumer confusion, thereby damaging the goodwill of the brand.

Even the harm to goodwill by counterfeits, however, might not be as damaging as it must first appear to the brand owner. The most serious harms caused to goodwill exist in cases where there is a passing-off – that is, where fakes are presented as the genuine product and consumers are then fooled into purchasing counterfeits. However, as discussed earlier, this is unlikely to be true in most cases today. Most consumers are savvy enough to understand that branded goods that are sold at a fraction of their original cost in disreputable locations are not likely to be genuine and are not authorized for sale by the brand owner. The sale of knock-offs might even have commercial benefits for the brand owner since these sales help to increase the recognition by consumers of the brand name. However, for most brand owners, whether the counterfeits do any serious and actual harm to the goodwill of the brand is really beside the point. The harm is the presentation of the brand to the public that has not been authorized by the brand owner, and that is not under the control of the brand owner. This undermines the core business principle in many MNCs that they must have absolute and complete control over every facet of the presentation of their brands in any form and by any means to the public.

This type of harm is vastly different from the claims of brand owners that counterfeits preclude the sale of genuine products at full retail price, at least measured in terms of directly lost sales. So while counterfeiters do limit the ability of brand owners to exercise exclusive control over their brands, this type of harm might not be very significant in terms of monetary losses. MNCs have never attempted to place a monetary figure on the amount of loss from this type of harm, but it is likely to be trivial in comparison with the hundreds of billions of dollars that MNCs claim to lose from lost sales due to counterfeiting.

For MNCs, counterfeit goods today are viewed as an illegal and unauthorized, but often highly desirable, line of goods that are traded on the brand's prestige, and that are intended to appeal to a certain sizeable group of consumers in both developing and developed countries who seek to purchase such goods with knowledge that they are counterfeits. This second line of goods takes a free ride on the goodwill established by the original brand and threatens the control by MNCs of their brands. But these are different types of harm from the lost sales of the genuine product that has traditionally been viewed as the harm caused by counterfeiting. Consumer confusion – once the crux of counterfeiting – is no longer present in most cases in the modern age of globalization and wide availability of information. Most consumers who purchase counterfeit goods are not deceived into thinking that they are purchasing a genuine product; rather, they are seeking the prestige of the trademark or brand name at a lower price. Many consumers view counterfeits as goods that are less expensive (and of a lesser quality) than the original genuine product but still carry a similar level of prestige associated with the brand. Depending on the type of goods involved, many consumers are not concerned about the lower quality of the counterfeit since quality is of secondary or minor importance.

B Harm to Developing Countries

Contrary to popular belief, developing countries, not MNCs, suffer the most harm from the global counterfeiting trade.

1 Organized crime

The introduction of famous brands into developing countries has provided an irresistible lure to criminal organizations to branch out into this lucrative area of crime. In East Asia – the hotbed of counterfeiting – criminal organizations involved in gambling, prostitution, smuggling, narcotics, and human trafficking have now migrated to counterfeiting because of its highly lucrative rewards and the low-risk nature of the crime. Penalties for trafficking in narcotics are notoriously severe in Asia; long prison sentences and capital punishment are common for narcotics violations, but penalties for trading in counterfeit goods that do not result in injury or death are almost trivial by comparison.[10]

A comparison between the trade in illegal narcotics and the trade in counterfeit cigarettes illustrates why counterfeiting has become so attractive to organized crime in Asia. Criminal organizations in Asia are now largely responsible for the trade in counterfeit cigarettes. Every day, large metal shipping containers of counterfeit cigarettes manufactured in China pass undetected through the port of Los Angeles in the United States. The counterfeit cigarettes in these containers cost about $80 000 to produce but have a street value of about $1 million. These profit margins rival those of the trade in illegal narcotics. Counterfeit cigarettes, unlike illegal drugs, can be shipped in daylight in plain sight using ordinary means of transport (such as trucks and rails) and can be stored in commercial warehouses. By contrast, illegal drugs must use clandestine means of transport and storage, thereby adding to the risk and the costs of the trade. Considerable organization is involved in this global trade in

---

[10] In China, trafficking in narcotics is ruthlessly suppressed, but criminal punishment for counterfeiting is rare. *See, e.g.*, Chen Hong, *Nigerian Sentenced to Death for Drug Dealing*, CHINA DAILY, Mar. 11, 2010, http://tinyurl.com/4dxpju9; *World Day Against Drugs, China Carries out Eight Death Sentences*, ASIA NEWS, June 24, 2010, http://tinyurl.com/4p276bd; *see also* Daniel Chow, *Anti-Counterfeiting Strategies of Multi-National Companies in China: How a Flawed Approach Is Making the Problem Worse*, 41 GEO. J. INT'L L. 749, 754–60 (2010).

counterfeit cigarettes: tobacco must be grown and procured, cigarettes must be produced and packaged in counterfeit packaging, export arrangements for shipment in containers must be arranged, import documents using false and stolen information must be produced in order for the products to pass through U.S. customs, and the counterfeits must then be distributed through weak links in distribution networks in the United States where they can finally reach the end-use consumer. All of these steps require large-scale organization and resources, as well as many participants located in China and in the United States (sometimes referred to as "foot soldiers"). Only a highly efficient criminal organization has the resources to conduct this kind of trade, and reports indicate that these criminal organizations are as violent and ruthless as any of the organizations involved in drug trafficking.

Given that several containers of counterfeit cigarettes worth $1 million pass through the port of Los Angeles each day, the trade in such cigarettes is highly lucrative and can rival the profit that can be earned in narcotics. The penalties for trafficking in counterfeit goods, however, are very low compared with the penalties for dealing in illegal drugs.[11] Because cigarettes are not viewed sympathetically by large segments of the consumer public in the United States, counterfeiters also have the advantage of working in an out-of-favor industrial sector that attracts little media attention or public sympathy.

Although the example discussed above concerns counterfeit cigarettes, the same type of organized operations occur with clothing, shoes, handbags, auto parts, and electronics. Generally, though, profit margins in these other industries are not as high as those for the trade in counterfeit cigarettes. However, many of the same organizations involved in smuggling counterfeit cigarettes also deal in counterfeit consumer

---

[11] The Trademark Counterfeiting Act of 1984 criminalizes "trafficking" in counterfeit goods. Pub. L. No. 98-473, 98 Stat. 2178 (1984). The maximum term of imprisonment is ten years and the maximum fine is $5 million. *See* 18 U.S.C. § 2320(a) (2006). Criminal penalties for trafficking in narcotics include imprisonment for not more than ten years, fines in the amount provided in Title 18, or, in the case of an entity, fines of not more than $10 million, or both. 21 U.S.C. § 1906(a) (2006). However, criminal penalties under other federal statutes may often double and triple sanctions for drug trafficking. For example, under the Racketeer Influenced and Corrupt Organizations Act (RICO), the term "racketeering activity" includes a broad assortment of state and federal crimes, including federal offenses that involve controlled drugs; defendants may receive prison sentences separate from, but in addition to, sentences for the individual acts that constitute a pattern of racketeering. 18 U.S.C. § 1961(1)(D) (2006).

goods for similar reasons: high profit margins and low risk of capture and punishment.

Organized crime is a serious global problem: it has existed long before counterfeiting at its current levels emerged. But the emergence of the global trade in counterfeit goods has provided organized crime in developing countries a new and highly lucrative means to earn profits. An additional, lucrative source of profits strengthens these organizations, thereby allowing them to recruit new members, expand their reach, finance other dangerous criminal activities, and increasingly harm those societies in which they operate.

2 Government corruption and local protectionism

Organized crime often works hand in hand with corrupt government officials in developing countries. For example, in China (considered by most experts to be the source of most of the world's counterfeits), corrupt government officials work actively to protect and support the trade in counterfeit goods. In fact, the role of local governments in supporting the trade in counterfeit goods often blurs the distinction between the criminal organizations involved in the trade and the government officials who support the trade. In other words, corrupt local government officials themselves might be considered to be part of the criminal organization behind the trade in counterfeit goods.

Local governments in China protect the trade in counterfeit goods in various ways. In many instances, local government administrative units invest in wholesale markets that distribute counterfeit goods, both within China and for sale in countries abroad. The local Administration of Industry and Commerce, a bureau charged with developing trade and commerce, invests millions of dollars in establishing these markets, and then rents out the stalls (each stall representing a wholesale distribution outlet for counterfeit goods) and charges a fee for business licenses. These wholesale markets sell several tons of counterfeit and infringing goods to retail stores all over China for resale to consumers. Many of these counterfeit goods will also be purchased by overseas buyers for export to countries around the world. Some local governments have established management companies to operate these wholesale markets, and some have even privatized these companies so that they are free to keep their profits.

These wholesale markets that deal in counterfeit and infringing goods can earn millions of dollars in sales revenue and can be vital to the local economy. Not only do these markets generate substantial sales revenues, but the illegal trade in counterfeit goods also supports a host of businesses that are dependent on counterfeiting. For example, trucking and rail, warehouse and storage, restaurants, hotels, and nightclubs all depend on the trade in counterfeit goods to bring in business. Moreover, despite the claims of MNCs to the contrary, counterfeiters also pay taxes to local governments. Clever counterfeiters often negotiate a flat tax rate in order to satisfy local tax authorities. Because counterfeiting brings substantial benefits to the local economy, local governments are reluctant to shut down counterfeiting. In a country such as China, local government enforcement authorities, including judges and the police, are appointed by local mayors and other political officials. These officials put pressure on enforcement authorities to refrain from shutting down the counterfeiting trade. In China and in many other parts of the developing world, enforcement against counterfeiting does not result in serious civil or criminal sanctions, but instead results in penalties that are so minor they may be considered part of the cost of doing business. Counterfeiters often pay a minor fine and are back in business in a few weeks. Few criminal prosecutions are brought, and imprisonment is rare.

Developing countries have many systemic weaknesses, including organized crime and weak, corrupt governments. Counterfeiting has significantly exacerbated these problems by providing a highly lucrative and high-volume business that provides a significant source of revenue. To the extent that criminal organizations are financially strengthened through counterfeiting and that government corruption becomes even more serious and embedded, it is the country where counterfeiting occurs that suffers real social costs. Countries with corrupt governments and high levels of organized crime are not likely to make progress in important social institutions such as the rule of law, human rights, clean and transparent government, and control of crime. These are the real costs of counterfeiting that are imposed on developing countries by the MNCs.

3 Health and safety risks
Another type of externality suffered by developing countries is health and safety hazards caused by the proliferation of substandard counterfeit medicines. According to some recent media accounts, 10 percent of the world's drugs are counterfeit; fake baby infant formula, cough syrup, and other medicines have led to serious illness or death. However, almost all of these harms to human health and safety occur in developing and least developed countries, which have weak border control systems that allow counterfeits that are mostly manufactured in China to pass through undetected. Almost no serious health or safety incidents have occurred in advanced industrialized countries, such as the United States and many European countries. Consumers in these countries are too savvy, and

distribution networks are too professional to allow low-quality medicines to penetrate distribution channels to reach consumers. As with the other harms associated with counterfeiting, developing countries, least developed countries, and, in particular, the poorest countries in the world, tend to suffer the most harm.

IV HOW MNCs CONTRIBUTE TO COUNTERFEITING

This part now turns to a closer examination of how MNCs have contributed to the rise of the global trade in counterfeiting, and why they may bear both ethical and financial responsibility for alleviating the problem.

A Branding

In the past several decades, MNCs and many other business entities have invested enormous financial resources in trademarks or brands and have created intellectual property rights in brands themselves. Traditionally, trademarks served an origin function – that is, trademarks indicated the source of goods. Historically, the law of trademarks developed when several businesses started using the same mark to sell goods, creating consumer confusion. A trademark gives the owner of the mark a right to use the mark on certain types of goods to the exclusion of competing vendors, but it does not create any intellectual property rights in the trademark itself. The trademark is to be used in commerce to avoid consumer confusion. A consumer who views a trademark will know that the product is from a particular manufacturer and will have the assurance that the product will be of the same quality as goods previously purchased from the same manufacturer.

In recent decades, however, this view of trademarks has changed. MNCs are increasingly viewing trademarks or brands as property rights and their most valuable business assets. According to one recent report:

> [b]randing used to be practiced by companies that sold packaged goods to consumers – and almost no one else. Developing a brand included advertising, package design, and maybe a few promotions and was seen as far less central to the corporate mission than serious stuff such as floating debentures, quickening inventory turns, or boosting capacity utilization.

> That was in a different millennium. As the new one unfolds, brands have been taking center stage in a sweeping shift that some compare to the wave of mass marketing that occurred in the years following World War II. Pharmaceutical companies, which have been liberated to promote their products directly to

consumers, have been spending hundreds of millions to create entirely new brands such as Viagra and Claritin. Professional services companies such as Andersen Consulting, rebranded as Accenture, have realized that conveying a sense of trust and shared mission is as important as technical competence in winning multimillion-dollar contracts. Universities, government agencies, entertainment properties, and even individuals – Michael Jordan, Martha Stewart, Madonna – have come to be regarded as brands: Their names stand for an implicit promise of quality, innovation, or reliability.[12]

The report goes on to explain that:

> [a] strong brand acts as an ambassador when companies enter new markets or offer new products. It also shapes corporate strategy, helping to define which initiatives fit within the brand concept and which do not.
>
> That's why companies that once measured their worth strictly in terms of tangibles such as factories, inventory, and cash have realized that a vibrant brand, with its implicit promise of quality, is an equally important asset. A brand has the power to command a premium price among customers and a premium stock price among investors. It can boost earnings and cushion cyclical downturns …[13]

The world's most valuable brands, measured by the value of the brand alone as a revenue-producing business asset, are listed in Table 13.1. The enormous value of these brands is the result of the significant resources that MNCs have invested in creating property rights that result in a goodwill that in many cases is far beyond the cost of the materials of the product. The role of the brand is no longer just to indicate the origin of the goods but to create goodwill: an image of prestige, glamour, innovation, a certain lifestyle, a youthful and energetic attitude, and exclusivity. Branding creates a premium that allows brand owners to recoup their advertising costs and earn even higher profits because it allows brand owners to charge much higher prices for some types of goods than would be justified by the cost of the materials alone. This premium is created by a significant investment in advertising, promotion, and media, thereby creating a brand image that now has taken on a business asset value apart from its traditional origin function. The premium created by the goodwill of the brand through significant investments has created a valuable asset that also creates an incentive to copy. In most cases, consumers, fueled by advertising and promotion,

---

[12]   Gerry Khermouch et al., *The Best Global Brands*, BLOOMBERG BUSINESS-WEEK, Aug. 6, 2001, at 53–54.

[13]   *Ibid.* at 50–52.

want the prestige of the brand even more than they want the product itself. The branding phenomenon has created vast new financial incentives to produce counterfeited and pirated goods.

Table 13.1   The World's Ten Most Valuable Brands in 2012[14]

Rank	Brand	2012 Brand Value ($ billions)
1	Coca-Cola	77.8
2	Apple	76.8
3	IBM	75.5
4	Google	69.7
5	Microsoft	57.8
6	GE	43.6
7	McDonald's	40.0
8	Intel	39.3
9	Samsung	32.8
10	Toyota	30.2

B   Globalization and Foreign Direct Investment

In the past several decades, MNCs have begun an unprecedented wave of foreign direct investment (FDI) as part of the globalization movement that has revolutionized the way business (and many other aspects of life) is now conducted in the modern world. FDI occurs when MNCs acquire a permanent ownership interest in a business entity located in a foreign country. The clearest example of FDI is when a hypothetical MNC, with its headquarters in the United States, establishes a wholly owned subsidiary in France, India, Brazil, or China. When the MNC establishes the wholly owned subsidiary in France, the subsidiary is a French business entity under French law. The MNC, a United States corporation, is the foreign owner of all of the stock or assets of the domestic French company.

---

[14]   Interbrand, *Best Global Brands 2012*, INTERBRAND, http://www. interbrand.com/en/best-global-brands/2012/Best-Global-Brands-2012-Brand-View. aspx (last visited April 10, 2013).

During the wave of globalization that occurred in the past several decades, the amount of new FDI exceeded all of the other channels of trade in the modern world. Many MNCs have established foreign subsidiaries or joint ventures in developing countries, such as China, Vietnam, and India, in order to take advantage of low manufacturing and labor costs and lenient regulatory regimes. In FDI, a crucial component is the transfer of technology from the parent MNC to the foreign business entity. For example, if an MNC engaged in the manufacture of pharmaceuticals were to establish a foreign subsidiary to manufacture drugs in a foreign country, the MNC must transfer technology – that is, knowledge and know-how often protected by forms of intellectual property such as patents, copyrights, trademarks, and trade secrets – to the foreign subsidiary. Without access to such technology, the foreign subsidiary will be unable to manufacture the products for sale. Indeed, the technology or intellectual property component of the foreign investment is usually the most critical element of the foreign subsidiary's eventual success or failure. In the modern global marketplace, competitiveness of products and services is directly linked to the level of technology involved, and, in general, the higher and more advanced the level of technology, the more competitive the product will be. MNCs, in order to take advantage of low manufacturing costs, set up foreign subsidiaries and then transfer technology to those subsidiaries so that they can effectively produce goods for sale in the foreign markets or import them back to the United States.

The globalization of manufacturing operations by MNCs has been a hallmark of the modern age and has allowed MNCs to greatly increase their power and influence. MNCs play a central role in the movement of capital and technology from developed countries to developing countries and thus have become major players in determining the economic, political, and social welfare of nations, particularly in developing nations that have a strong hunger for foreign capital and technology.

When MNCs take advantage of lower manufacturing costs in developing countries, they introduce technology in environments that often have weak legal systems and inept and corrupt governments. The rudimentary nature of legal systems in developing countries is one of the main reasons why costs are lower than in developed countries, which have more sophisticated legal systems with more stringent legal standards imposing higher costs of compliance. A sophisticated legal system, however, is not likely to be found in developing countries because such systems require a significant investment of resources that these countries usually lack. A legal system similar to that in the United States is supported by significant resources such as law schools, a system of courts, government lawyers, and private attorneys, as well as enforcement officials such as federal prosecutors, federal marshals, customs officials, the FBI, and the police. The costs of such a legal system are significant and are far beyond the capability of many developing countries, which often have, by comparison, a rudimentary system that cannot be compared with those in advanced industrialized countries such as the United States, Japan, and many European countries. In addition, many developing countries have governments that are inept and seriously corrupt, who tolerate or work hand in hand with criminal organizations.

In such an environment, it is predictable that the transfer of technology by an MNC to a foreign subsidiary in a developing country will lead to counterfeiting and piracy on a scale that would not occur if the FDI did not take place. Because MNCs are not really harmed by counterfeiting and piracy and because MNCs enjoy many advantages when investing in developing countries, MNCs make these decisions to invest without considering the external harms and costs of counterfeiting, which fall primarily on the host country.

C Why MNCs Exaggerate Losses

If MNCs cannot substantiate their claims of severe financial losses and if the losses appear to be only a tiny fraction of the amounts claimed, why do MNCs vehemently assert these claims? First, many MNCs have a corporate culture in which it is necessary to frame a business problem in terms of hard financial numbers in order for the problem to be viewed seriously within the company. Even though brand managers may not consider counterfeiting to really cause losses, brand managers have incentives to characterize the sale of counterfeits as "lost sales" because these lost sales are ostensibly reducing what would be even higher revenue numbers for the brand managers that would merit a higher performance rating and annual evaluation for the brand manager. Brand managers have an incentive to argue that, but for counterfeits, their revenue numbers would be even higher and that they should not be penalized by way of a reduction in salary increases or promotions for a problem that they did not cause. Many brand managers will therefore argue that counterfeits are lost sales and report seizures of counterfeit products as "recovered sales," thereby adding to the bottom line of the company and enhancing their individual performance. Sales and brand managers within MNCs have long been accustomed to a corporate culture in which serious business problems must be framed in terms of losses to the bottom line and, of course, also have incentives to portray their own performance in as positive a light as possible. A second reason is that decrying huge losses engenders public sympathy and portrays

MNCs as the victim of a global crime wave that is causing serious financial losses to MNCs, their host countries, consumers, and taxpayers. Portraying themselves as incurring massive financial losses to counterfeiting might help bolster claims by MNCs that they need to charge premium prices in order to recoup research, development, and promotional costs. Claiming huge losses also helps to divert public attention from the role that MNCs have played in creating the global trade in counterfeit goods and inflicting serious harms upon developing countries that suffer the brunt of the costs of counterfeiting. A third reason for portraying counterfeiting as a massive and costly global crime wave is that it helps MNCs argue that national governments must share the costs of combating counterfeiting. By depicting themselves as the victims of counterfeiting, MNCs can shift some, or even the bulk, of the costs of enforcement to the public, rather than bearing the entire costs themselves. Some MNCs have even suggested that revenues earned from counterfeiting support terrorism, but this connection appears to be tenuous and unsubstantiated.

When counterfeiting is seen as a corporate externality for MNCs, and it is understood that the harms of counterfeiting fall disproportionately on developing countries, then the proper responsibility for creating those harms and bearing the financial costs of addressing those harms changes significantly. MNCs – once cast as the victims of counterfeiting – now may bear an ethical and financial responsibility to compensate for the harms caused by counterfeiting. Developing countries, which were once viewed as the major perpetrators of counterfeiting, may now have legitimate claims against MNCs for introducing and spreading the counterfeit system (a serious economic crime with many social costs) into their economies. National governments and taxpayers, once viewed as having to bear the costs of enforcement against global counterfeiting, may have a claim against MNCs for contributions to the costs of enforcement. To some extent, similar issues arose in connection with industrial pollution several decades ago. Pollution to the environment – a byproduct of industrialization – was an externality to MNCs since the harms to the environment were cast upon others. Only when these costs were internalized and imposed on MNCs through government requirements did real progress in pollution reduction occur. A similar process of imposing some of the costs of spreading and creating counterfeiting may need to occur in order to internalize some of the costs associated with counterfeiting. Internalizing some of these costs will force MNCs to consider these costs as they make decisions to expand low-cost manufacturing operations into countries where counterfeiting is a predictable consequence of FDI. Undoubtedly, developing countries will need to develop a strategy to make these demands known in an international forum such as the World Trade Organization (WTO) because they are the ones who suffer the brunt of the harms from counterfeiting.

V CONCLUSION

Within the past decade, counterfeiting and other forms of commercial piracy have been portrayed in the media as an illegal global trade that is reaching crisis levels leading to financial losses of unprecedented proportions. MNCs often portray themselves as the victims of these economic crimes and claim that they are losing billions, or even hundreds of billions, of dollars on an annual basis with many of these losses passed on to their governments and their consumers. A closer examination, however, indicates that these claims of severe financial losses are unsubstantiated and are based on spurious and dubious assumptions, resulting in reports of losses that are grossly exaggerated. Rather than suffering massive financial losses due to counterfeiting, many MNCs view counterfeiting and piracy as undermining the fundamental principle that MNCs must exercise complete control over every facet of how their brands are presented to the public. This appears to be the core harm caused by counterfeiting, and not the alleged billions of dollars in lost sales.

Not only are the claims of MNCs of severe financial losses unsubstantiated, but MNCs themselves have contributed in crucial ways to the rise of counterfeiting, such as making deliberate business decisions to transfer their technology and intellectual property to their manufacturing facilities in developing countries in order to take advantage of low production costs and lax regulations. Many of these countries have notoriously weak, ineffective, and corrupt governments that often tolerate or work cooperatively with criminal elements in their countries. In such an environment, it is predictable that the introduction of intellectual property that is easily copied will create inducements for counterfeiting on a vast scale, and such inducements will prove impossible for criminal entities in these countries to resist. MNCs ignore the harms that such counterfeiting imposes on developing countries because these costs are externalities. Until the costs of counterfeiting are internalized and brought to bear on their business decisions, MNCs will not have pressing incentives to change their conduct that feeds the steady rise of the global trade in counterfeit goods, thereby resulting in harms that fall primarily on developing countries.

PART V

Trademark territoriality and the regulation of cyberspace

14. Trademarks, free speech, and ICANN's new gTLD process

Jacqueline Lipton* and Mary Wong**

I INTRODUCTION

When the domain name system was first introduced in the 1990s, it rapidly became apparent that the new form of Internet addressing would cause issues for trademark holders. Cybersquatters hit the scene early, attempting to extort money from trademark holders for transfer of their valuable online property. Later, more nuanced disputes arose in the domain name space involving contests between competing legitimate trademark holders for the same domain name, as well as contests between trademark holders and gripe site operators – those who wanted to utilize intuitive domain names to complain about or otherwise criticize a trademark holder. Issues also arose as to what would qualify as a protected trademark in the domain name space for purposes of legal protection. Domain name arbitrators and courts have accepted trademarks in personal names, some place names, and culturally significant terms, despite their questionable trademark status: this is most obvious in cases where secondary meaning is not apparent.

While these issues remain challenging for courts and arbitrators alike, the new generic top level domain (gTLD) process implemented by

---

* Baker Botts Professor of Law and Co-Director, Institute for Intellectual Property and Information Law, University of Houston Law Center.

** Senior Policy Director, ICANN. When this chapter was submitted for publication, Mary Wong was the Faculty Chair for Global Intellectual Property Partnerships; Chair, Graduate Intellectual Property Programs and Founding Director, Franklin Pierce Center for Intellectual Property, University of New Hampshire School of Law. The developments discussed in this chapter deal with issues that were ongoing and current as of March 2013. For updates to the status of GAC Advice and various applications affected thereby, see http://www.icann.org and http://newgtlds.icann.org.

ICANN[1] in 2012 is likely to raise the stakes for all players. Under this new process, it is possible to apply for a new gTLD, in other words, the right to run a registry relating to a string of characters "to the right of the dot." This system will allow any number of new gTLDs to be introduced alongside the 22 existing gTLDs such as ".com," ".org," ".net" and ".biz." The first round of applications for new gTLD registries has been closed, and terms applied for include ".sucks," ".gripe," ".wtf" and ".fail." The applicants for these strings likely have in mind the possibility of attracting registrants who want to run gripe sites under these gTLDs. Other new gTLDs applied for include a number of trademarks, including major brands and geographic terms such as ".patagonia" for the sporting goods company, as well as a number of cultural and religious terms such as ".church" and ".islam."

This new gTLD process is the most ambitious extension of the domain name system since its inception. It has attracted both support and criticism from trademark holders, government entities, and others. It will likely expand the number of conflicts in the domain name space from those identified above to various new permutations and combinations involving both strings of characters to the left of the dot and to the right of the dot. Domain name disputes have always posed serious challenges to the legal and regulatory system because of their extra-territorial nature. The existing Uniform Domain Name Dispute Resolution Policy (UDRP) has been very successful in practice precisely because it was developed to effectively address the cross-border nature of many domain name disputes. This was achieved by using private contractual arrangements mandating online arbitration between domain name disputants. The new gTLD process will raise the same challenges as the pre-existing system in terms of formulating approaches to dispute resolution that will be effective and efficient across international borders.

This discussion briefly explains the inception of the new system and the process for its implementation. It then summarizes the kinds of legal issues and conflicts we might expect to see arising in the new domain name spaces. These legal issues are unique in that no one body has the constitutional power to regulate policy such as the balance of trademark interests and free speech within what is effectively a privately managed global system. ICANN is only entitled under its bylaws to make policy with respect to the technical aspects of the system, yet many of these

---

[1]   The Internet Corporation for Assigned Names and Numbers that administers the technical aspects of the gTLD system. *See Internet Corporation for Assigned Names and Numbers*, ICANN, http://www.icann.org (last viewed on Jan. 1, 2013).

policies and their implementation have a broader impact on the global public interest. Thus, legal regulation of these new domain spaces, like regulation of existing spaces, is likely to be achieved through norms and market forces along with judge-made and arbitral precedents. In other words, regulation is likely to be bottom-up rather than top-down and will be made on a case-by-case basis by those empowered to resolve trademark-focused disputes in the new gTLD spaces. While this may be a preferable alternative to top-down rule-making by a private corporation (that is, ICANN), it may also lead to uncertainty and lack of predictability for trademark owners as well as consumers and users.

II THE NEW gTLD PROGRAM

ICANN's Board of Directors formally approved the latest expansion of the domain name system in 2008. Previously, such expansions had been extremely limited, with approvals going largely to only a handful of so-called "sponsored" new gTLDs, meaning specialized gTLDs that have a sponsor that takes on the responsibility of much of the policy development in the use of the gTLD on behalf of the group of stakeholders most likely to be impacted by that gTLD; for example, the General Services Administration, a United States government agency, is the sponsor for the .gov gTLD, while the Universal Postal Union is the sponsor for the .post gTLD. Until this latest expansion round, there have been only 22 gTLDs in the domain name system, with only a few – such as .com, .org, and .net – being unrestricted in terms of their operation and registration, and with only four unsponsored gTLDs (.biz, .info, .name and .pro). When this new expansion round was launched in January 2012, an unprecedented 1930 applications for new gTLDs flooded into ICANN. These applications included what is now commonly known as "dotbrand" gTLDs, meaning trademarks and brand names that, instead of having to be registered as second-level domains within an existing gTLD (such as .com), could for the first time be their own registry. There were also applications for geographically based gTLDs (such as .africa), internationalized domain names (meaning TLDs in non-Latin scripts such as Chinese and Arabic), and generic words (such as .app, .book, .cloud, .green and .search).

The applications, procedures, and evaluation processes were developed over several years, culminating in the final and ninth version of the new gTLD Applicant Guidebook being released in June 2012. Coming in at over 300 pages, the Applicant Guidebook covered a slew of issues ranging from the technical and financial requirements to operate a gTLD registry to dispute resolution processes that would govern a number of pre-launch and post-launch phases, from initial challenges to an application to resolving trademark-related disputes.[2] A few of the features of the Guidebook most salient to the current discussion include:

- the ability for individuals and entities to lodge formal objections against an application, even (in some cases) where the complainant did not herself apply for a new gTLD;
- the creation of new and untested rights-protection mechanisms for trademarks, to be applied in addition to the existing Uniform Dispute Resolution Policy (UDRP) dating from 1999;
- the recommendation that so-called "contention sets," that is, two or more applications for strings that are either identical to one another or so similar as to be likely to create user confusion if allowed to co-exist in the domain name system, be resolved primarily (and preferably) through negotiation and agreement amongst the contending applicants, or, as a mechanism of last resort, by way of an auction that will effectively function as a tie-breaker.[3]

Certain features of the Applicant Guidebook call for further elaboration and analysis, as their operations and outcomes will affect the often conflicting balance of interests that is inherent in a global system which does not permit concurrent uses of the same name or word at the top level, that is, as a gTLD.

First, in relation to the possibility of objecting to a new gTLD application, ICANN has formulated four bases for such objections, namely, objections grounded in either: (a) string similarity as between two applied-for new gTLDs, in the sense that they are so similar that it is probable that user confusion will result; (b) existing legal rights such as trademarks; (c) limited public interest grounds, in that the applied-for gTLD will contravene accepted principles or norms of public international law; or (d) community-based objections, where a significant portion of the community targeted by the applied-for gTLD objects to the application. For each of these four grounds of objection, different dispute resolution service providers have been appointed by ICANN. These are the International Center for Dispute Resolution, which will handle string

---

[2]   The final Applicant Guidebook, in the form used for the formal launch of the new gTLD program, can be found at *Applicant Guidebook | ICANN New gTLDs*, ICANN, http://newgtlds.icann.org/en/applicants/agb (last visited Feb. 26, 2013).

[3]   *See ibid.* at Applicant Guidebook, Module 4: String Contention.

similarity and community-based objections; the World Intellectual Property Organization (WIPO) Arbitration and Mediation Center, which will administer objections based on existing legal rights; and the International Chamber of Commerce, which will take charge of objections filed on limited public interest grounds. Each ground of objection also has different standing requirements, and each dispute resolution service provider has set its own procedural rules and fee schedules.[4]

Where legal rights objections are concerned, the basis upon which a successful objection will be upheld will be familiar to trademark lawyers and litigators, namely, that the applied-for gTLD string "takes unfair advantage of the distinctive character or the reputation of the objector's registered or unregistered trademark or service mark ... or unjustifiably impairs the distinctive character or the reputation of the objector's mark ... or otherwise creates an impermissible likelihood of confusion between the applied-for gTLD and the objector's mark."[5] This could signal a new frontier in online trademark disputes in that, for the first time, the outcome of a new gTLD application could, if a formal objection is lodged by an affected rights-holder, depend on the application of legal standards and precedents found in traditional trademark law, especially United States trademark law. This concern leads inevitably to the possibility of further overlaps between trademark law doctrines and the policies and procedures developed specifically for the new gTLD program. In particular, the introduction of new and additional rights-protection mechanisms for trademarks merits further analysis. Of these mechanisms, what is possibly going to be the single most impactful process is the new Uniform Rapid Suspension mechanism that will apply to second-level domain name registrations, further described below.

At the top level, a potential new gTLD registry operator has to run the gamut of a number of detailed and complicated application and evaluation procedures and timelines. It has to undergo background checks on its officers, provide sufficient information as to its planned technical operations and financial capacity, and, as initial experience with the new gTLD program showed, endure several delays caused either by technical

---

[4] *See generally ibid.* at Applicant Guidebook, Module 3: Dispute Resolution Procedures.

[5] *Ibid.* at § 3.2.2.2 and § 3.5.2 (which sets out a list of non-exhaustive factors, greatly resembling the so-called Polaroid factors utilized in United States trademark law, which will be considered in determining the outcome of the objection and dispute); *see* Polaroid Corp. v. Polaroid Elec. Corp., 287 F 2d 492, 495 (2d Cir. 1961), *cert. denied*, 368 US 820 (1961).

glitches in ICANN's TLD Applicant System software or other operational problems.[6] Where ICANN had initially hoped to announce contention sets by July 2012 (which date was then changed to October) and start to release the results of its initial evaluations by November 2012, the timeline as of January 2013 had been pushed back to February and March 2013 respectively. The formal objection period was also extended by two months, to conclude in March 2013. Despite these delays and timeline changes, however, ICANN has announced that it is on track to recommend for delegation into the domain name system certain new gTLDs that will have passed initial evaluation and which have not been subject to any formal objections or contention sets as early as April 2013. As of February 2013, however, it is still not clear when these new gTLDs will actually launch, as they will first have to sign a finalized registry agreement with ICANN and complete pre-delegation testing. ICANN had previously hoped that these would be completed by the second quarter of 2013; its most recent announcement was for pre-delegation testing to commence in late April.[7]

Assuming a potential registry operator clears all evaluation processes and survives any formal objection or other roadblocks, upon its launch it will have to comply with certain rights-protection mechanisms geared toward ensuring that trademark owners and other legal rights-holders are adequately protected in this vast expansion of the domain name space. With the delegation and launch of new gTLDs, attention – and legal disputes – will shift toward second-level registrations within these new gTLDs. As mentioned above, the new Uniform Rapid Suspension (URS) system will likely be the process most heavily relied upon by rights-holders. Modeled after the current UDRP, the URS differs from it in two major respects: (a) the standard of proof is higher, requiring clear and convincing proof rather than a mere preponderance of the evidence; and (b) its remedies, which lie only in suspension of the offending second-level domain name rather than in cancellation or transfer to the prevailing rights-holder. As an additional and alternative avenue for trademark protection on top of the UDRP, the URS is designed to be faster and cheaper than the UDRP while utilizing the same substantive grounds as the latter, namely, that the respondent has no legitimate rights to the disputed domain and has registered it in bad faith. Its contours are

---

[6] For a full description of the application process and evaluation procedures, *see supra* note 2, at Applicant Guidebook, Modules 1–2.

[7] For the most up-to-date timelines and other updates about the new gTLD program, *see ICANN New gTLDs*, ICANN, http://newgtlds.icann.org (last visited Feb. 26, 2013).

therefore familiar to trademark lawyers, brand owners, and WIPO panelists; its speed and lower cost are likely to mean that these stakeholders will certainly utilize it when the time comes, possibly heavily.[8]

III THE RIGHT OF THE DOT

One of the most obvious new challenges for legal regulation under the new gTLD process will be resolving questions over who has the better right to run registries for particular new gTLDs. As noted above, ICANN has implemented several procedures for dealing with disputes involving this question. In fact, the question probably breaks down into two constituent elements:

1. Are there some character strings that should never be approved as new gTLDs?
2. How should ICANN determine who has the right to run a gTLD that is otherwise unobjectionable, if more than one body seeks to apply for a particular TLD?

Both of these issues are difficult, and neither has been fully resolved at the time of writing. With respect to the first question, certain organizations have lobbied to have their trademarks and names exempted from the new gTLD process, possibly via the creation of special protections for such marks and names. Internationally protected, well-known names, such as those owned by the International Olympic Committee and the International Federation of the Red Cross, are examples of this. These organizations object to having to either spend resources defensively registering domain names in, or even potentially running registries for, new gTLDs that match or closely resemble their marks, or in the alternative having to fight to oppose others from registering them. Similarly, some international governmental and non-governmental organizations have argued that their names, acronyms, and designations ought

---

[8] For an in-depth analysis of the various rights-protection mechanisms and the potential consequences of reliance on ICANN-mandated private dispute resolution processes, *see* Jacqueline Lipton and Mary Wong, *Trademarks and Freedom of Expression in ICANN's New gTLD Process*, 38 MONASH U. L. REV. 188 (2013) *and* Jacqueline Lipton and Mary Wong, *Imperatives of Private Arbitration in International Intellectual Property Disputes*, 24 SING. AC. L.J. 978 (2012).

to be protected from third-party registrations, especially (but not solely) at the second level.[9] There are likely a large number of other public interest organizations, in particular smaller non-profit organizations, who could make similar arguments but who may not have the financial wherewithal to take action to protect their intellectual property within the new gTLD process.

One complication that has been highlighted by the process of dealing with these international organizations' demands is the fact that many of their names, acronyms, and designations are not necessarily protected by strict trademark rights either in national jurisdictions or via international treaty. Rather, some of these "marks" are protected on a completely different basis altogether, such as the recognition of the names and symbols of the International Federation of the Red Cross as protected by international humanitarian law under the Geneva Conventions. In relation to intellectual property, the prohibition against unauthorized commercial registration under the 1981 Nairobi Treaty on the Protection of the Olympic Symbol in relation to the five interlocking rings constituting the visual symbol of the International Olympic Committee probably comes closest to trademark law, and possibly also the protection afforded by Article 6*ter* of the Paris Convention for the Protection of Industrial Property to "armorial bearings, flags, other emblems, abbreviations and names" of international intergovernmental organizations which have as members states that signed on to the convention. Even where the Olympic symbol and related names, or the names and abbreviations applicable to other organizations, are additionally protected under various national trademark laws, it can be said that the basic rationale for their protection lies not in the need – well recognized in trademark law – to guard against the likelihood of user confusion, but rather in the acknowledgment that such names and symbols by their nature belong to a

---

9   At the time of the launch of the new gTLD program, the ICANN Board imposed a moratorium on certain International Olympic Committee and Red Cross/Red Crescent names. Subsequently, a formal working group was established to determine if and how second-level registrations (i.e. registrations to the left of the dot) in new gTLD registries for these names, and possibly also the names, acronyms, and designations of certain international governmental and non-governmental organizations, would be handled. This policy development process occurred concurrently with ICANN's technical and operational evaluations of the new gTLD applications. As of this writing, it remains to be seen what recommendations, if any, the working group will come up with for adoption by ICANN that may result in some of these names and marks being withheld from registration by non-affiliated entities and individuals after the approval and launch of the new gTLDs.

specialized category of marks that deserve special trademark-like protections. Regardless of the justification for legal protection, however, the treaties and national laws that go to protect these names, acronyms, symbols, and designations have an obvious impact on free speech rights in that they can be seen to be incursions into the right of an individual to use these terms freely and fairly but for these treaties and laws. Nonetheless, the different basis for such protections, and in particular the fact that these organizations are not all protected by the same treaties or laws, or to the same extent, make the exercise of treating them as equivalent to commercial trademarks a potentially risky approach that could result in an unjustifiable and ill-considered expansion of trademark rights by ICANN.

Apart from the valuable intellectual property (or related rights) of public-interest-based organizations, there may be other words and phrases that should arguably not be part of the new gTLD process. However, it will be difficult to formulate clear and objective rules as to where to draw lines exempting certain words and phrases from the system, and, to date, no clear rules are in effect. Categories of character strings that arguably should not be granted as new gTLDs might include offensive terms such as curse words and racial slurs, governmentally significant terms such as city and country names, or names of significant political figures. Interestingly, the current application for ".wtf" includes a connotation of a curse word in the letter "f" which obviously stands for a well-known four-letter word in the English language. However, ".wtf" also has a colloquial connotation which is perhaps not as offensive as the f-word standing alone.

The current process does allow for individuals and governments to raise formal objections to the approval of an application for a new gTLD, and governments may also raise pre-objection concerns about particular applications in the form of so-called Early Warnings.[10] For example, the Australian government has expressed concern at the ".wtf" application along with a number of other gTLDs. Applicants could also find their applications addressed through formal advice to be provided to the

---

[10] 242 Early Warnings were issued by various governments against a total number of 145 new gTLD applications, across a range of industries and concerns. They ranged from worries that certain applications raised problems with actual geographic names designated on the internationally recognized ISO-3166 country and territory list to questions about whether certain other applications would raise either cultural sensitivities or otherwise have overly negative connotations. The last include, unsurprisingly, applications for .fail, .gripe, .sucks and .wtf.

ICANN Board by way of the Government Advisory Committee,[11] which operates by member consensus and consists of over a hundred individual countries and a number of international organizations as observers. Since formal objections have to be filed via voluntary act and upon the payment of a not insignificant filing fee, however, it is possible that formal objections may not be filed at all to the registration of certain objectionable or offensive gTLDs. In such cases, and notwithstanding the fact that those terms may be politically, culturally, racially, or otherwise offensive to some, ICANN may simply grant the authority to run the registry to the applicant provided that the applicant satisfies the criteria that have been laid down by ICANN for new registries – including technical capacity and the financial wherewithal to maintain the registry.

With respect to the second question highlighted above – that of who has the better right to a given gTLD when there are multiple applicants to run the same gTLD registry – there are some limited rules in place under the new process, including the auction possibility as described above. For instance, a formal objection may be filed against a new gTLD application by those who have an interest or concern about the relevant character string being granted approval by ICANN. This would include objectors whose trademarks or other legal rights may be infringed by the use of the new gTLD by someone other than the relevant rights-holder. Formal objections could also be filed on the basis of community concern with the application in question, or on the basis that the proposed new gTLD would cause confusion with a rival application. Beyond the formal objection process, there are also further and subsequent processes – described briefly above – for resolving any remaining disputes between multiple applicants for the same name, culminating in an auction process if all else fails.

The question arises whether these procedures are the most effective for regulating commercial and expressive speech interests in the domain name space. The auction process in particular may raise concerns because it effectively puts a price on valuable expressive online real estate. It effectively allows those with the resources to place the highest bid to control an online asset that has significant expressive components.

---

[11] Such advice is provided only on the basis of consensus in the Committee, which requires that no member object to the substance of the recommended advice. The ICANN Bylaws specify that, while the ICANN Board is not obligated to follow such advice, it has to provide a rationale in the form of an explanation as to why it chose not to accept the advice in any one instance; *see* ICANN Bylaws, art. XI, § 2.(j)–(k), *available at* https://gacweb.icann.org/display/gacweb/ICANN+Bylaws (last visited Apr. 21, 2013).

The process also prioritizes the interests of those who have the ability to object to particular gTLDs, such as governments who likely have more resources to object to what they consider to be impermissibly offensive or culturally sensitive applications than private individuals who may be generally concerned about the launch of a new gTLD that might harm them in some way.

The resolution of issues about which character strings *should* be available as new gTLDs and who should have the right to run registries for appropriate new strings will be an important step in global dispute resolution of a private communications medium that comprises both speech and commercial interests. Because of the conglomeration of interests across national borders and across expressive/commercial boundaries, resolution of these challenges will not be easy. These challenges are also made more complex by the fact that no one body has legal or constitutional authority to legislate for the commercial/speech balance in the global context. Thus, players in new domain spaces will be dealing with issues on a case-by-case basis through whatever means are available. In the case of new gTLD applications, the means will basically be the processes set out in the Applicant Guidebook for the new gTLD program by ICANN, with some possible amendments or tweaks developed subsequently through ICANN's internal policy processes as appropriate. While these processes may not be foolproof or optimal, they at least outline the scope and boundaries of the possible types of actions and consequences that attach to applications that find themselves at the wrong end of an objection or which necessitate specific ICANN Board action through formal Government Advisory Committee consensus advice. However, issues to the left of the dot in new domain spaces will be even more challenging because they will involve the possibility of arbitration through private means or domestic courts.

IV THE LEFT OF THE DOT

As with the 22 existing domain name spaces, the new gTLD system will raise the specter of a significant number of disputes arising with respect to character strings to the left of the dot in new gTLD spaces. While some legal presumptions have developed with respect to existing gTLDs, the new process may throw many of the current presumptions out of alignment. For example, domain name arbitrators and courts have generally erred on the side of protecting the ".com" space for legitimate trademark holders over and above all others, including gripe site operators and operators of unauthorized fan sites. While some gripe site and unauthorized fan site operators have managed to retain ".com" domain names that invoke their target's trademark to the left of the dot,[12] most have failed to do so.[13] Judges and arbitrators have been prepared to accept what is effectively a quasi-presumption that the ".com" space should be reserved to the rightful trademark holder, even occasionally in cases where the domain name registrant has included a pejorative term to the left of the dot, such as "airfrancesucks.com."[14]

Judges and arbitrators have also been prepared to err on the side of protecting personal names in the ".com" space as trademarks, even where secondary meaning is questionable[15] and even though there is a ".name" space under the existing system which is available for personal names. In the case of competing legitimate interests in personal names or trademarks, the legal rule has been "first come, first served." This is more than a presumption. This is in fact how the system works. A domain name registration will only be cancelled or transferred under relevant legal principles if the registrant has no legitimate interest in the name, and this usually requires a trademark interest.

An important question under the new gTLD process will be to determine the extent to which the exponential increase in available gTLDs might impact the way judges and arbitrators will apply existing

---

[12] *See, e.g.*, Bosley Med. Inst., Inc. v. Kremer, 403 F.3d 672 (9th Cir. 2005); Lamparello v. Falwell, 420 F.3d 309 (4th Cir. 2005).
[13] *See, e.g.*, People for the Ethical Treatment of Animals v. Doughney, 263 F.3d 359 (4th Cir. 2001); *Julia Fiona Roberts v. Russell Boyd*, WIPO Arbitration and Mediation Center, Case No. D2000-0210 (2000).
[14] *Societé Air France v. Virtual Dates, Inc.*, WIPO Arbitration and Mediation Center, Case No. D2005-0168 (2005).
[15] This issue was addressed by a WIPO Dispute Resolution Panel in *Bruce Springsteen v. Jeff Burgar and Bruce Springsteen Club*, WIPO Arbitration and Mediation Center, Case No. D2000-1532 (2000):

> It appears to be an established principle from cases such as Jeanette Winterson, Julia Roberts, and Sade that in the case of very well known celebrities, their names can acquire a distinctive secondary meaning giving rise to rights equating to unregistered trade marks, notwithstanding the non-registrability of the name itself. It should be noted that no evidence has been given of the name "Bruce Springsteen" having acquired a secondary meaning; in other words a recognition that the name should be associated with activities beyond the primary activities of Mr. Springsteen as a composer, recorder, and performer of popular music. In the view of this Panel, it is by no means clear from the UDRP that it was intended to protect proper names of this nature.

presumptions and principles to new disputes. For example, if the applications for "gripe site" registries are successful, will judges and arbitrators refuse to allow any gripe sites in existing ".com" (and perhaps also ".net", ".org" and ".biz" spaces)? If a person seeking to criticize, say, the Nike Corporation can register "nike.sucks" or "nike.gripe," will judges be less prepared to tolerate the registration of "nikesucks.com" by a gripe site operator?

Under the new gTLD system, would a case like *Bosley v. Kremer*[16] be decided differently? In that case, a gripe site operator was permitted to maintain registration of "bosleymedical.com" in the face of trademark infringement, dilution, and Anti-Cybersquatting Consumer Protection Act proceedings because he was not making a commercial use of Bosley's trademark as required by at least the infringement and dilution actions. If he could have registered "bosleymedical.sucks," would the judges have regarded the case differently? Under legal principles, one would think not as his use was non-commercial. However, judges may have been swayed in their reasoning by the lack of availability of a more obvious "gripe" zone in cyberspace for Kremer's efforts.

The new process will also raise a number of additional headaches for legitimate trademark holders who may have to defensively register their marks in myriad new domain name spaces to pre-empt cybersquatting and curtail cybergriping. This will be a costly and time-consuming process, given that well over a thousand new gTLDs are pending ICANN approval. Additionally, problems will arise in cases where a trademark holder applies to run a registry for a generic term that is in some way connected with both its own products and those of competitors. For example, if Corporation X registers ".shop," ".jewelry" or ".travel" and Corporation Y happens to be in the retail, jewelry, or travel business, Corporation X can effectively corner the market in the relevant domain space by running the registry privately and denying Corporation Y any second-level domain presence within the new gTLD. In fact, this type of "closed" generic TLD is permitted in the new gTLD program, and a number of applicants, including some major brand owners, have applied for generic names germane to their business interests but for which they likely do not have – and may not qualify under traditional trademark law to have – any trademark rights. To some this may seem like a "land grab" to secure a competitive advantage by controlling a generic word that may not even qualify for trademark protection; to others, the potential business innovations – and consequent consumer benefits – that may

---

[16]   Bosley Med. Inst., Inc. v. Kremer, 403 F.3d 672 (9th Cir. 2005).

come from permitting brand owners and others to create new uses and markets for new gTLDs are exactly what the new gTLD program was meant to induce in the first place. As with the issue of whether to create specific protections for certain international governmental and non-governmental organizations, ICANN may find itself treading in risky waters beyond pure trademark laws and related protections, should it venture to add additional mechanisms or rules that regulate whether and how generic TLDs can be operated and used.[17]

In terms of administration of new gTLD registries, with such a large number of new gTLDs likely to be registered and much autonomy[18] granted to the registries after the initial application process, there is a clear opportunity for the implementation of rules within the new registries that are unfair to entities who want to register within a new gTLD. As noted above, a private registry operator can deny second-level domain name registration to competitors. Such a registry operator could presumably also deny registration to those with a political viewpoint that differs from their own. For example, if the ".islam" gTLD is registered to a pro-Islamic group, the registry operator may deny registration in the second level to anyone who seeks to promulgate an anti-Islamic message. Similar issues may arise where, say, a trademark holder registers a domain name that corresponds with a geographically or culturally significant term. For example, if the Patagonia Sporting Goods company is successful in its application to run the registry for ".patagonia," it is unlikely to grant a second-level domain presence to the Patagonian

---

17   Just as it created a working group for the international governmental and non-governmental protections issue, ICANN decided to take another look at the issue of permitting generic words as TLDs when such words will be operated exclusively by a registry to the possible exclusion of its competitors. Again, this happened after the formal launch of the new gTLD program and concurrently with the ongoing evaluation of all new gTLD applications. To the extent that ICANN ultimately adopts new rules or guidelines for such "closed" TLDs, for example, by including new and additional provisions in its binding registry agreement with all new gTLD registries, that could change the landscape of and for new domain name usages after the formal launch of those new "closed" generic gTLDs that end up being approved by ICANN.

18   Subject, of course, to any new policies developed by ICANN and that are binding on all its registries (known as "Consensus Policies" – the long-standing Uniform Dispute Resolution Policy being perhaps the best known of these) and to any new provisions that may end up being added – either by way of negotiation on a case-by-case basis between ICANN and the new gTLD registry in question or by adoption of new rules for these agreements across the board.

government. It would certainly be under no obligation under the current draft new gTLD registry agreement with ICANN[19] to do so.

V REGULATORY CHALLENGES

Clearly, the new gTLD process raises many new issues involving the balance of free expression and commercial certainty online. Balancing speech and commerce has always been a difficult issue even within domestic legal systems. When the issues rise to the global stage, the problems of finding an appropriate balance become more fraught. Jurisdictions differ in the way they determine these questions domestically. Even countries with similar legal systems may vary greatly in their free speech protections. For example, Australia – despite being a Western-style democracy with much of its federal constitution based on United States constitutional principles – has no express constitutional guarantee of free speech. This may be one reason why the Australian government has been particularly vocal in its opposition of a number of new gTLD applications. There are no constitutional constraints against the government taking a strong speech-regulating stance.

When speech versus commerce issues are played out on a global scale, the resolution of conflict and the identification of appropriate legal principles is an extremely tall order. Add to this the difficulties of regulation in a global system which boasts no obvious body with constitutional competence to resolve such matters. While ICANN will maintain technical control of the domain name system, it is reliant for policy development (including for the new gTLD program) on governments, corporate entities, and public interest groups advising it through lobbying and other political mechanisms, as it was established expressly to govern through a multi-stakeholder model that relies on these various, and sometimes divergent, inputs which then require much negotiation and compromise among the affected parties. As a private not-for-profit corporation, it is also not clear whether ICANN should have the power or authority to craft definitive rules for behavior and issues that go beyond its technical mandate, even though the origin of such behavior and issues may be activity in the domain name system because they implicate the security and stability of the system. The new gTLD program in many ways is a perfect example of such a problem, originating in ICANN's

---

[19] *See New gTLD Agreement (Draft)*, ICANN, *available at* http://new gtlds.icann.org/en/applicants/agb/base-agreement-specs-04jun12-en.pdf (last visited Feb. 26, 2012).

consideration of whether such an unprecedented expansion to the domain name system will cause any instability or security issues, and evolving into policies being developed that do not just address that fundamental concern but that have potential consequences for national laws and public interests beyond technical Internet coordination issues. There is no one entity – private, government, or internationally mandated – which can simply legislate clear policy rules to assure adequate protections for speech and commercial certainty in the domain name system. It is not clear, however, that there should be or that ICANN should have such broad authority.

Because of this regulatory vacuum, regulation within the new system will by default be achieved case by case in a bottom–up process. This will be fascinating to watch. However, it does pose certain problems. Notably, the entities with the most power to initiate complaints and disputes about domain name issues to the right and to the left of the dot will likely be corporate interests which have stakes in the continued expansion of the domain name industry, trademark holders who need to control unauthorized uses and abuses of their trademarks and brands, and government entities which believe they need to act to protect an articulated global public interest or national sovereignty. These actors in the ICANN ecosystem do not embody the whole range of interests that potentially could be protected in new domain name spaces, including the speech interests of private individuals who seek to comment, criticize, or politically agitate for government reform, among other legitimate and fair uses especially of generic words and names. This result is arguably no different from the situation with a domestic regime where private individuals often do not have the wherewithal to protect their interests in the face of powerful corporate and government interests. However, the resolution of disputes in favor of governments and trademark holders on a global scale potentially has a more significant impact on international freedom of expression than a purely domestic resolution.

VI CONCLUSIONS

The new gTLD process is extremely ambitious and is likely to have a major impact on speech and commerce worldwide. It is also the first time a private system has arisen which allows the effective purchase of commercially valuable online expressive assets to those with the resources and ability to acquire and maintain them.[20] The system is also unique because of the dearth of obvious bodies with overriding regulatory competence. This is largely due to the truly international and extra-territorial nature of the domain space. No one national government can exercise sovereignty over the domain name system as a whole, and ICANN is limited under its by-laws in its policy-making capacity. The development of the new gTLD process is, therefore, a fertile ground for the study of alternative methods of international rule-making outside treaty negotiation and implementation, which is the typical focus of international intellectual property law. At best, approaches taken to domain name disputes under the new gTLD system will become models for new ways of cooperative bottom-up rule-making through norms, market forces, and private arbitration. At worst, they will emphasize the risks of this form of international rule-making. When the first set of applications goes into effect probably sometime in 2013, and the URS and UDRP are reviewed in light of recent developments, commentators and regulators will have a better idea of the directions the system is heading in. Hopefully, the above thoughts can serve as a starting point for examination of the kinds of issues that will need to be taken into account as the system is refined and revised in coming years, and as ICANN begins to prepare for the second round of introduction of even more new gTLDs into the domain name system.

---

[20]   *See* Jacqueline Lipton, *Speech for Sale: Commerce and Free Speech in ICANN's new gTLD Process*, 87 Australian L.J. 24 (2013).

Index